Religion and Nationa

Religion and nationalism are two of the most potent and enduring forces that have shaped the modern world. Yet there has been little systematic study of how these two forces have interacted to provide powerful impetus for mobilization in Southeast Asia, a region where religious identities are as strong as nationalist impulses. At the heart of many religious conflicts in Southeast Asia lie competing conceptions of nation and nationhood, identity and belonging, loyalty and legitimacy. In this accessible and timely study, Joseph Chinyong Liow examines the ways in which religious identity nourishes collective consciousness of a people who see themselves as a nation, perhaps even as a constituent part of a nation, but anchored in shared faith. Drawing on case studies from across the region, Liow argues that this serves as both a vital element of identity and a means through which issues of rights and legitimacy are understood.

JOSEPH CHINYONG LIOW is Dean and Professor of Comparative and International Politics at the S. Rajaratnam School of International Studies, Nanyang Technological University. He is also the inaugural holder of the Lee Kuan Yew Chair in Southeast Asia Studies and Senior Fellow in the Foreign Policy Program at the Brookings Institution in Washington, D.C. Liow's research focuses on comparative politics, Islamic studies, international relations, and political sociology. He has a particular interest in Muslim politics and social movements in Southeast Asia and has published books on the topics of Muslim politics in Malaysia and Islamic education in Thailand.

Religion and Nationalism in Southeast Asia

Joseph Chinyong Liow

CAMBRIDGE UNIVERSITY PRESS

CAMBRIDGE
UNIVERSITY PRESS

University Printing House, Cambridge CB2 8BS, United Kingdom

Cambridge University Press is part of the University of Cambridge.

It furthers the University's mission by disseminating knowledge in the pursuit of education, learning and research at the highest international levels of excellence.

www.cambridge.org
Information on this title: www.cambridge.org/9781107167728

© Joseph Chinyong Liow 2016

This publication is in copyright. Subject to statutory exception and to the provisions of relevant collective licensing agreements, no reproduction of any part may take place without the written permission of Cambridge University Press.

First published 2016

Printed in the United States of America by Sheridan Books, Inc.

A catalog record for this publication is available from the British Library

ISBN 978-1-107-16772-8 Hardback
ISBN 978-1-316-61809-7 Paperback

Cambridge University Press has no responsibility for the persistence or accuracy of URLs for external or third-party internet websites referred to in this publication, and does not guarantee that any content on such websites is, or will remain, accurate or appropriate.

For Keng Teck and Dorothy,
otherwise known to me as Dad and Mum

Contents

Preface	page ix
Acknowledgments	xii
Glossary	xv

	Introduction	1
	Why Religion and Nationalism?	2
	The Argument at a Glance	9
	Why "Framing"?	12
	Organization of the Book	14
1	Faith and Flag	18
	Religion	18
	Nationalism	32
	What is Religious Nationalism?	42
	Religious Nationalism and Mobilization: The Use of Frames	51
	Conclusion	60
2	Southern Philippines: Reframing Moro Nationalism from (Bangsa) Moro to Bangsamoro	62
	Contours of the Bangsamoro Struggle	63
	Identity: Who is a Bangsamoro?	70
	History, Sovereignty, Landlessness	75
	Prognostic Frames: From Rebellion to Reconciliation	78
	The Motivational Frame of Islam	83
	Unpacking the Narrative of Bangsamoro "Unity"	90
	Conclusion	97
3	Thailand's Southern Border Provinces: Constructing Narratives and Imagining Patani Darussalam	99
	Patani History as "Anti-Thai" History	101
	"Anak Patani" as Subject or Citizen?	105
	Prognostic Frames	116
	Religious Narratives in the Southern Thailand Struggle	120
	Conclusion	133

4 Malaysia: Religion, Ethno-Nationalism, and Turf-Guarding — 135
A Brief Note on the Religious Imperative in Malay(sian) Nationalism — 137
Christianity in Malaysia: History and Social Context — 139
Ethnicity as Presumed Destiny — 141
Prognostic Frames: Christian Mobilization and Legal Recourse? — 152
East Malaysia — 164
The Hindu Community — 166
Islamization and *Ketuanan* in Context and Retrospect — 168
Conclusion — 174

5 Indonesia: Contesting Principles of Nationhood — 175
Religion, Nationalism, and Indonesia — 177
Christianity in Indonesia — 181
Negotiating the Bases of Nationhood and Statehood — 184
"Religious Conflict" in Eastern Indonesia — 194
Unpacking the Religious Master Frame — 200
What Lies Beneath the (Religious) Master Frames — 207
Subversive Narratives within the Indonesia *Ummah*:
The *Ahmadiyah* Question — 210
Nationhood and Narratives — 213
Conclusion — 216

Conclusion — 218
Religion, Nationalism, Modernity — 220
Competing Conceptions of Nationhood and Legitimacy — 222
Narratives, Contexts, and Contingencies — 225
So What Does It All Mean? — 228

Bibliography — 232
Index — 254

Preface

Religion has always been an important theme in Southeast Asian history and culture. It has also been a crucial feature of the region's politics and specifically, as I hope to demonstrate in this book, in the conception of nationhood and the political contestations that have defined the history of the nation in Southeast Asia. Indeed, since the emergence of anti-colonial movements in the region, religion has animated and colored nationalism in Southeast Asia. Romantic nationalists from Myanmar (Burma) to Indonesia and the Philippines, in possession of great capacities for invention and myth-making, frequently capitalized on the "immutable" religious identity of "their people" in order to construct narratives that frame conceptions of nationhood beyond the imperative of material self-interest.

Such is the currency of these narratives, it harkens to Hugh Trevor-Roper's observation, made in his illuminating tome, *The Invention of Scotland*, that "for what people believe is true is a force, even if it is not true." This conceptualization of nationhood using religious metaphors, vocabularies, and referents, I should add, was not merely confined to those anti-colonial movements that agitated successfully to liberate their nations from Western imperialism. Religion has been an equally robust, if at times overlooked, phenomenon on at least two further counts: first, as a feature in the process of post-independence nation and state building and consolidation and, second, in the articulation of resistance by groups within the territorial state but who do not share in its conception of nationhood. It is in the hope of untangling this dynamic thematic combination of religious identity, nationalism, and political contestation that *Religion and Nationalism in Southeast Asia* has been written.

The topic of religion and conflict has fascinated many a scholar of the region. The result has been the production of several excellent studies that explore the role of religion in political conflict from a wide array of perspectives ranging from economic inequality to minority identity, political legitimacy, and integration. Of particular note are Thomas McKenna's illuminating study of local politics in Cotabato, Edward Aspinall's study

x   Preface

of how religious identity blended with nationalism in Aceh, Duncan McCargo's work on southern Thailand that focuses on the legitimacy-deficit of the Thai state in the Malay south, and John Sidel's masterly analysis of the kaleidoscopic violence perpetrated by religiously inspired groups in Indonesia.[1] This book hopes to add to this literature in at least two ways.

First, notwithstanding their high quality, much of the best scholarship in this field remains single-country studies. There is a dearth of comparative work undertaken in this area. In this regard, the aim of this book is to complement the existing corpus by locating single-country cases in a historically and culturally grounded, comparative interrogation of what religious identity entails for the politics of conflict, taking into account the remarkable depth and diversity of religious conceptions of identity and politics across Southeast Asia.

Second, although religion and nationalism are two of the most potent and enduring socio-political forces that have shaped the modern world, commanding much loyalty and for which men and women have willingly spilt blood and sacrificed lives, there has been little systematic study of how these two forces have interacted and combined to provide powerful impetus for mobilization and political contestation. This is particularly striking in the study of Southeast Asia, a region where the salience of religious identity is matched only by the strength of nationalist impulses. To that effect, the purpose of *Religion and Nationalism in Southeast Asia* is also to foster a better understanding of the role and place of religion in a range of intrastate conflicts across Southeast Asia where religious identity has been invoked. It aims to do so by unpacking the religious metaphors and narratives associated with these conflicts and interrogating them against the cultural and historical backdrops within which they are embedded. In addressing these issues, this book hopes not only to cast light on the themes of religion, conflict, and nationalism in the region, but also to bring Southeast Asian studies to bear on current debates over the role of religion in the study of nationalism and conflict in contemporary society and politics.

This book is a result of my interest in and research on issues of identity, religion, and conflict in the southern Thailand, Mindanao, and Malaysia

---

[1] Thomas M. McKenna, *Muslim Rulers and Rebels: Everyday Politics and Armed Separatism in the Southern Philippines*. Berkeley, CA.: University of California Press, 1998; John T. Sidel, *Riots, Pogroms, Jihad: Religious Violence in Indonesia*. Ithaca, N.Y.: Cornell University Press, 2006; Duncan McCargo, *Tearing Apart the Land: Islam and Legitimacy in Southern Thailand*. Ithaca, N.Y.: Cornell University Press, 2008; Edward Aspinall, *Islam and Nation: Separatist Rebellion in Aceh, Indonesia*. Palo Alto, CA.: Stanford University Press, 2009.

which I have cultivated over the last two decades. Having written on each individual case on numerous separate occasions earlier in my career, I decided to challenge myself to undertake a comparative investigation that would draw together all that I have observed and studied over this period of time, especially during periods of fieldwork in Pattani, Yala, Narathiwat, Mindanao, and almost every state in Malaysia. The one regret I have, however, even as the process of writing drew to a conclusion, is that I was never able to spend a substantial period of time undertaking fieldwork in Indonesia. This was in large part because by the time I decided to embark on this project, I was already in the dean's office and could no longer afford the luxury of long periods away in the field. Indeed, this is my biggest regret, and if it has resulted in a poorer book, *tolong ma'afkan saya*. Nevertheless, I still hope that the ideas contained in this book can provide some impetus for reconceptualizing and rethinking of the social and political undercurrents presently playing out in the region, purportedly in the name of religion. So long as this book is able to prompt further discussion, generate new scholarship, or even elicit criticism, its goals would have been achieved.

Acknowledgments

I have incurred many debts in the course of writing this book. In particular, I would like to acknowledge the career debt I owe to four individuals: Barry Desker, former dean of RSIS, has always been unstinting in his support throughout my entire career after my Ph.D.; S.R. Nathan first employed me as a research assistant at the Institute of Defence and Strategic Studies, precursor of RSIS, and remains very generous with his time and advice; Yuenfoong Khong has been an academic mentor *par excellence*, whose continued keen interest in my work remains a great source of encouragement; and Eddie Teo, chairman of the Board of Governors of the School, entrusted me with the duties of the deanship of the School but was always encouraging of my efforts to continue researching and writing despite those responsibilities. Without the backing of these four people, I would never have made it as a scholar. For that, I am forever grateful.

If this book has any merit, it is only because of the kind support I have received from many people and institutions, even if I myself am responsible for any deficiencies in this book. Over the years, I have benefitted greatly from numerous conversations, discussions, and debates with Greg Fealy, Ed Aspinall, Sidney Jones, Kirsten Schulze, Julie Chernov-Hwang, Bob Hefner, Greg Barton, Don Pathan, Farish Noor, Chaiwat Satha-anand, Duncan McCargo, Rungrawee Chalermsripinyorat, Michael Vatikiotis, Don Horowitz, Don Emmerson, Meredith Weiss, Mohamed Nawab, Tom McKenna, Paul Hutchcroft, Renato Cruz de Castro, and Julkipli Wadi, all established scholars in their own right and who have had formative influence on my own work. Ed Aspinall and Paul Hutchcroft kindly provided valuable advice on an earlier outline of this project, while Greg Fealy, Alex Arifianto, and Duncan McCargo read and provided much-appreciated feedback for various chapters.

Research for this book would have proven a far more arduous endeavor if not for the enthusiasm, resourcefulness, and professionalism of a number of people who provided various forms of assistance, including fieldwork assistance ranging from driving to scheduling of meetings to

Acknowledgments

sourcing for documents to translation. These friends include Yusup Abdullah, Mike Abdullah, Danial, Mustaffa Harun, Fadli Ghani, Pui Yee, Afif Pasuni, Vinay Pathak, Redzuan Salleh, Hanisah Sani, Rajni Gamage, and Mahfuh Halimi. Hunter Marston must be acknowledged for his assistance in preparing the manuscript for publication. I would also specifically like to thank Al-Haj Murad Ibrahim for sparing time to answer questions about the MILF and Tito Karnavian for generously sharing his insights on Maluku and Sulawesi from a practitioner's perspective.

Over the course of writing, I had the opportunity to present parts of this book at various seminars and conferences. Special thanks to IDEAS at the London School of Economics and the Islamic Studies Program at the University of Michigan – Ann Arbor for providing opportunities to present my chapters on the Philippines in October and December 2013, respectively. The chapter on Thailand was built on earlier work done that received support from the Lowy Institute, and that was presented in Canberra in April 2010. An earlier version of the chapter on Malaysia was also presented in Bangkok in May 2011 courtesy of a kind invitation from an old friend, Ajarn Chaiwat Satha-anand, and the support of the Toda Institute.

The first stage of writing of this book benefited from a Fulbright Fellowship which allowed me to spend three months at the Asia-Pacific Research Center at Stanford University between October and December 2011, where Don Emmerson kindly hosted me at his Southeast Asia Forum and provided his usual probing comments and suggestions. The presentation I made at the Forum's "brown bag" set me on the path to crystallizing many of the ideas that eventually found their way into this book. Between October and November 2013, I embarked on a second stage of writing which was kindly arranged for me at Exeter University by its vice chancellor and an old friend of mine, Sir Steve Smith, and Sir Paul Newton, who hosted me at Exeter's Strategy and Security Institute. The final stage of writing and revisions was undertaken while I served as the inaugural Lee Kuan Yew Chair in Southeast Asia Studies at the Brookings Institution between August 2014 and July 2016. I am indebted to Ong Keng Yong, executive deputy chairman of RSIS since November 2014, who kindly agreed to my absence from RSIS in order to accept the chair at Brookings. In Washington, D.C., Strobe Talbott, Martin Indyk, and especially Richard Bush welcomed me to "bring along" this project to Brookings in order to complete it, even though it was well within their right to insist that I prioritized other projects they may require of me as the chair. Amidst my growing administrative and managerial responsibilities, my trusty assistant, Caroline Chin, made sure to jealously protect whatever pockets of free time I had to devote to reading and writing. I am grateful also to Lucy Rhymer and Cambridge University Press for not only seeing something worthwhile in the manuscript, but also ever so efficiently shepherding it through the publication process. Thank you also to the two anonymous reviewers for their encouraging remarks and suggestions for further improvements. And to Danial, thanks for the fascinating front cover photo.

Writing a book can be an exacting, protracted, and lonely endeavor. For me, the process was made much more tolerable with the blessing from fellowship and intellectual and moral encouragement extended by fellow academic travelers from RSIS, especially Bhubhindar Singh, Ralf Emmers, Tan See Seng, Ang Cheng Guan, Kumar Ramakrishna, and Farish Noor. Most importantly, to my wife, Ai Vee, and two beautiful children, Euan and Megan, thank you for your steadfast encouragement, love, and support which puts things in perspective for me and keeps me grounded. In a sense, writing something of religion also forces me to examine my own confession, my own faith: *"The certainty which rests on God's Word exceeds all knowledge" – John Calvin* (Colossians 3:17).

Glossary

abangan	Nominal Muslims or less observant Muslims
ABIM	*Angkatan Belia Islam Malaysia* or Islamic Youth Movement of Malaysia
adat	Customary practices or laws
ad-din	Comprehensive way of life
aliran	Streams. A term used in Indonesia to differentiate between the various currents of Islam and their representative political parties or organizations
al-Kitab	Malay bible
Amirul Mujahidin	Commander of Muslims who take part in jihad
Anak Patani	Children of Patani, usually used to refer to the Malay-Muslims of southern Thailand
ARMM	Autonomous Region of Muslim Mindanao
ASG	Abu Sayyaf Group
baatil	Falsehood
Babo	Traditional Islamic teacher in southern Thailand
Baitullah	House of God
Bhinneka Tunggal Ika	Unity in Diversity
BIFF	Bangsamoro Islamic Freedom Fighters
BIFM	Bangsamoro Islamic Freedom Movement
BNPP	*Barisan Nasional Pembebasan Patani* or National Liberation Front of Patani
BPUPKI	*Badan Penyelidik Usaha-Usaha Persiapan Kemerdekaan Indonesia* or Committee for the Preparatory Work for Indonesian Independence
BRN	*Barisan Revolusi Nasional* or National Revolutionary Front
BUF	Bishops-Ulama Forum
Bumi Patani	Land of Patani

Bumiputera	Sons of the soil, indigenous groups
Bunga Emas	Flowers of Gold
CAB	Comprehensive Agreement on the Bangsamoro
CBCS	Consortium of Bangsamoro Civil Society
CCM	Council of Churches in Malaysia
CFM	Churches of Federation of Malaysia
Chat	Nation
Dakwah	Proselytization; inviting or calling people to Islam
Dar-al-Harb	The abode of conflict; domain of the unbelievers
Dar-al-Islam	Territory of Islam
Darul Islam	See *Dar-al-Islam*
datu	Clan chief
da'awah	See *dakwah*
Dewan Bahasa dan Pustaka	Institute for Language and Literature
FAB	Framework Agreement on the Bangsamoro
fard'ayn	Individual obligation
fatwa	Legal opinion issued by Islamic religious scholars
FES	Fellowship of Evangelical Students
FKM	*Fron Kedaulatan Maluku* or Front for Moluccan Sovereignty
FPI	*Fron Pembela Islam* or Islamic Defenders' Front
GCF	Graduate Christian Fellowship
GMIP	*Gerakan Mujahidin Islam Patani* or Mujahidin Movement of Patani
Golkar	*Partai Golongan Karya* or Party of Functional Groups
GPM	*Gereja Protestan Maluku* or Maluku Protestant Church
GRP	Government of the Republic of the Philippines
haj	The annual Islamic pilgrimage to Mecca, which is one of the five pillars of Islam
halqah	Islamic study circle
haqq	Truth
HINDRAF	Hindu Rights Action Force

Glossary

ibadah	Act of worship
ICMI	*Ikatan Cendekiawan Muslim Se-Indonesia* or Indonesian Association of Muslim Intellectuals
Ikatan Muslimin Malaysia	Muslim Community Union of Malaysia
imaan	Faith
Islamisasi	Islamization
jahiliyyah	The time of ignorance before the coming of Islam
JAKIM	*Jabatan Agama Kemajuan Islam Malaysia* or Malaysian Department of Religious Development
Jawi	Traditional Malay script
jihad	Holy struggle
jihad qital	Armed struggle
Ka'abah	The cube-shaped building at the centre of the great mosque in Mecca, believed to be built by the Prophet Ibrahim. Also known as *Baitullah* or House of Allah. It is toward the Ka'abah that Muslims turn when praying.
kafir	Unbeliever, infidel
Kalimah Allah	The word "Allah"
Kamus Dewan	Institutional dictionary
Kaum Muda	New generation/Reformists/Modernists
Kaum Tua	Old generation/Traditionalists
kecematan	Subdistrict
Kesatuan Melayu Muda	Young Malays Union
Ketuanan Agama	Dominance of religion
Ketuanan Melayu	Malay lordship, Malay dominance
Ketuanan Rakyat	Dominance of the people
Khaek	Guests, foreigners (sometimes with racial connotations)
kibr	Pride
Kristenisasi	Christianization
kufr	See *kafir*
Lumad	Non-Muslim indigenous communities of the southern Philippines
Majlis Shura	Consultative Council
Masuk Melayu	Literally means to enter into "Malayness," to become a Malay. In Malaysia, it is used to denote the embrace of Islam by a non-Muslim.

MILF	Moro Islamic Liberation Front
MIM	Mindanao Independence Movement, Moro Independence Movement
MKI	*Majlis Kebangsaan Hal Ehwal Ugama Islam Malaysia* or the Malaysian National Association of Islamic Affairs
MMI	*Majelis Mujahidin Indonesia* or Indonesia Mujahidin Council
MNLF	Moro National Liberation Front
MOU-AD	Memorandum of Understanding on the Ancestral Domain
MPR	*Majelis Permusyawaratan Rakyat* or Peoples' Consultative Assembly
MPW	Mindanao Peace weavers
MUI	*Majelis Ulama Indonesia* or Indonesian Ulama Association
Mujahid/Mujahidin or *Mujahideen* (plural)	One who engages in holy struggle
munafiq	Hypocrite, someone who pretends to be Muslim
murtad	Apostate
Nayu	*Melayu* or Malay
NECF	National Evangelical Christian Federation
PAS	*Parti Islam Se-Malaysia* or Pan-Malaysian Islamic Party
pattanakarn	Socioeconomic development
pela-gondong	Traditional Malukan oath of allegiance
pemuda	Youth
perjuang	Fighters
Permesta	*Piagam Perjuangan Semesta* or Charter of Universal Struggle
Phramahakasat	King, monarchy
Piagam Jakarta	Jakarta Charter
Pondok	Traditional Islamic boarding school
Ponoh	See *Pondok*
PPKI	*Panitia Persiapan Kemerdekaan Indonesia* or Preparatory Committee for Indonesian Independence
PPP	*Partai Persatuan Pembangunan* or United Development Party
PSII	*Partai Sarekat Islam Indonesia* or Sarekat Islam Party

Glossary

PULO	Patani United Liberation Organization
rido	Blood feuds, clan wars
RMS	*Republik Maluku Selatan* or Republic of South Moluccas
RSM	Raja Solaiman Movement
santri	Observant, practicing Muslims
Sasana	Religion
shari'a	Path, Islamic legal system
Solat	Prayers
surau	Prayer facilities, prayer room
Tadika	Kindergarten
tanah	Land
Tanah Melayu	Malay lands
taqwaa	Piety
tarbiyyah	Education and upbringing
Tiga Wilayah	Three provinces, referring to the Malay-Muslim provinces of southern Thailand
Tok Guru	Traditional Islamic teacher in a *Pondok*
ulama	Religious scholar
ummah	Universal brotherhood of believers in Islam
UMNO	United Malays National Organization
VOC	*Vereenigde Oost- Indische Compagnie* or Netherlands United East India Company
Wadah	Gathering or congregation, referring to a Malay-Muslim faction within the Thai Rak Thai Party in Thailand
Yang di-Pertuan Agong	Reigning King of Malaysia

Introduction

Southeast Asia is doubtless one of the most dynamic economic regions in the world. It is, at the same time, also home to some of the most enduring post-colonial intrastate conflicts. A brief look at the headlines of major broadsheets over the last decade and a half is a good indicator of how this has cast a shadow over the region. In Myanmar (Burma), violence has broken out between Buddhists and Muslims even as the country creeps down the path of democratization. In Thailand and the Philippines, Muslim minority groups in their respective southern provinces are purportedly waging *jihad* or "holy war" against what we are told are majoritarian prejudices of predominantly Buddhist and Catholic states and societies, respectively. While Malaysia has thus far avoided the outbreak of violence, the country nevertheless has witnessed an alarming escalation of tension as a Muslim-dominated government has allowed the expression of acutely exclusivist majoritarian views on religion in the name of "defending" the Islamic faith to go unchecked, the deleterious effect of which has been the constriction of the religio-cultural space afforded to non-Muslims by the Constitution. In Indonesia, post-Suharto political transformation appeared in its early years to have given rise to sectarianism and religious intolerance, which in many cases have also boiled over to violence not only between Muslims and non-Muslims, but within Indonesia's kaleidoscopic Muslim community as well.

On close inspection, a common thematic thread appears to weave through many of these conflicts – the role of religion. Because of how religious language and symbolism are evoked in some form or other, many of the aforementioned conflicts have been the subject of a great deal of media and academic attention that have chosen intuitively to cast them as religious conflicts.[1] Given the popularity and appeal of such views,

---

[1] For a sample of this writing in media and academia, see Carlos H. Conde, "On Mindanao, Jihad Looms if Peace Talks Fail," *New York Times*, October 12, 2004; Greg Sheridan, "Jihad Archipelago," *The National Interest*, No. 78, Winter 2004; Simon Elegant, Andrew Perrin, Robert Horn, Mageswary Ramakrishnan, "The Road to Jihad," *Time*

particularly those emanating from media circles, both local and international, a proper understanding of the role of religion in these conflicts is necessary and urgent. It is for this purpose that this book is written.

The book poses the following questions: how and why did religion come to assume such a prominent role in intrastate conflicts in Southeast Asia, and how should we endeavor to understand this role? In order to address these questions, this book aims to unpack the religious metaphors and narratives associated with these conflicts and interrogate them against the cultural and historical backdrops within which they are embedded. The arguments and line of inquiry that follow depart significantly from much of the conventional wisdom on the linkage between religion and political life in the context of conflict. To be sure, the fact that religion plays a prominent role in politics is hardly novel. The current literature is attended by rich coverage on debates that meander across themes such as the global resurgence of religion, jihadi violence and "new" (that is to say, religiously motivated) terrorism, clash of civilizations, and inter-religious conflict (not necessarily limited to, but certainly dominated by, Muslim-Christian relations), all of which explore one facet or other of the nexus among religion, conflict, and politics. For this book, the point of departure is over whether religious belief lies at the core of the problem of political conflict and many presumed acts of religious mobilization and violence; to wit, the book will demonstrate that many of the "religious conflicts" in Southeast Asia are better understood as extensions and outcomes of how collective identities of communities and nations are framed and contested rather than expressions of faith and acts of piety *per se*.

Why Religion and Nationalism?

Religion and nationalism are two of the most potent and enduring sociopolitical forces that have shaped the modern world. Few ideas have commanded as much loyalty over history. For faith and flag, countless men and women have willingly spilt blood and sacrificed lives. Yet there has been little systematic study of how these two forces have interacted and combined to provide powerful impetus for mobilization and action in

International, October 5, 2004; Wattana Sugunnasil, "Islam, Radicalism and Violence in Southern Thailand: *Berjihad di Patani* and the April 28, 2004 Attacks," *Critical Asian Studies* Vol. 38, No. 1, 2006; Michael Jerryson, *Buddhist Fury: Religion and Violence in Southern Thailand*. New York and Oxford: Oxford University Press, 2011; Joel Brinkley, "Islamic Terror," *World Affairs*, Vol. 176, No. 2, July/August 2013; Virginie Andre, "From Colonialist to Infidel: Framing the Enemy in Southern Thailand's 'Cosmic War'" in Joseph Camilleri and Sven Schottmann (eds.), *Culture, Religion and Conflict in Muslim Southeast Asia: Negotiating Tense Pluralisms*. London: Routledge, 2013.

Southeast Asia, a region where religious identities are as strong as nationalist impulses. To begin answering the questions posed above, we need to also consider how the two concepts hew together analytically. In addition to that, we must also give some thought to how religion and nationalism co-exist, not only in abstract terms but also as practical means through which mobilization can take place.

While modernization and secularization theory predicted an erosion of religion in the civil sphere, a cursory glance at the world today readily proves such predictions misguided. Yet, on the other hand, there is the other, equally misguided, extreme, which is occupied by perspectives that tend to promulgate religion as the definitive causal variable to explain intrastate conflicts that express a communal or sectarian nature.[2] This view has been particularly prevalent in Southeast Asia, where we seem to be witnessing conflicts that involve groups arrayed along religious lines taking place with increasing frequency.[3] This tendency to interpret conflict as being essentially religious in nature has undoubtedly been reinforced by the zeal with which the international press has portrayed, in headlines of broadsheets and weblogs, a vast number of "religious" conflicts, "cosmic wars," *jihad*, and "clash of civilizations" spanning Europe and the Middle East to Africa and South Asia. Thanks in no small measure to a parallel cottage industry (including but not confined to the study of terrorism) that has privileged "religious extremism" or "religious radicalism" as explanatory factors, this view has gained considerable currency in both academic and wider popular discourse.[4]

---

[2] See, for example, Mong Palatino, "Don't Let the Flames of Nationalism Engulf Southeast Asia," *The Diplomat*, April 6, 2013. A *New York Times* article describes the outbreak of violence in Myanmar in the following manner: "the violence that swept through this village took with it the final vestiges of what had until very recently been a peaceful place, where Muslims and Buddhists had coexisted amicably for generations before the loosening of the hard hand of the old junta freed some of Myanmar's demons." See Thomas Fuller, "Elderly Woman's Killing Lays Bare Myanmar's Religious Divisions," *New York Times*, November 9, 2013.

[3] Peter Berger asserts instead that "the assumption we live in a secularized world is false.... The world today is as furiously religious as it ever was." He points out that religious movements have not adapted to secular culture in order to survive but have successfully developed their own identities and retained a focus on the supernatural in their beliefs and practices. See Peter Berger (ed.), *The Desecularization of the World: Resurgent Religion and World Politics*. Washington, D.C.: Wm. B. Eerdmans Publishing, 1999. In fact, some such as S.N. Eisenstadt have argued that the resurgence of religion and ethnicity is not necessarily an anti-modern backlash, but rather are part of what he terms "multiple modernities" that have emerged in the era of globalization in the form of new social movements and novel visions and identities to erode the monopoly of nation-states. See S.N. Eisenstadt, "Multiple Modernities," *Daedalus*, Vol. 129, No. 1, Winter 2000, pp. 1–29.

[4] At the other end of the spectrum is an equally voluminous literature on "moderation" in religion.

The analytical template that characterizes this genre of scholarship is the recurrent theme that inveighs against religion by arguing it possesses inherent features that predispose it to conflict, and at its extreme, violence. According to this school of thought, this propensity to conflict is rooted in Manichean conceptions of the sacred (good) and the profane (evil) that are purportedly found in religion, in contradiction to "progressive" modernist assumptions that extol the virtues of rational secularism (as opposed to the "irrational ills" of religion). While such suppositions certainly give pause for thought, they tend to gloss over very complex forces of modulation and adaptation of religion as a marker of identity according to the vicissitudes of context and circumstance, and as a consequence strike a discordant note in how they tend to promote the reification of religion as ahistorical and transcendent.

If the reification of religion lies at one end of the explanatory spectrum, the instrumentalization of faith and piety arguably lies at the other. By this logic, religion serves merely as a tool that can be instrumentalized for purposes of mobilization toward social and political change, assertion and/or reconfiguration of power, or even the pursuit of myopic self-interests. Opportunistic politicians are the chief culprits in this enterprise, deftly capitalizing on fears, preconceptions, and, at times, blatant stereotypes by adroitly playing the religious card in order to win political points. This Benthamite utilitarian logic is captured in Edward Gibbon's famous quote: "the various modes of worship which prevailed in the Roman world were all considered by the people as equally true; by the philosophers as equally false; and by the magistrate as equally useful." There may some truth to this, but only up to a point. While it explains why political leaders might want to play up religious issues (and many are certainly culpable), it does little to illuminate the source of the fears and preconceptions that a religious discourse triggers – why, to turn Gibbon's logic on its head, do "the people" consider the veracity of religion to be "equally true" such that they can be influenced so easily by the magistrate? This surely speaks to the salience of the content of the message itself, and not just the creative and opportunistic use of it for other more self-serving ends.

The point to stress is that the successful instrumentalization of religion hinges precisely on its currency for the people whom political opportunists seek to mobilize; and this currency is determined by dint of how religious creed and confessions provide meaning and intelligibility for them in terms of the frames and narratives, as well as the invention of tradition, they are individually and collectively exposed to and familiar with. Indeed, the power of ideational frames and narratives cannot be underestimated for one simple reason: they provide a more convincing explanation than purely materialist arguments as to why some would take up arms for a cause despite the high cost of their sacrifice and uncertainty of success.[5] Bearing this in mind, this book seeks to advance the debate beyond the familiar discussion about the utilitarian relationship between ideas and interests. It contends that such an approach is far too simplistic and reductionist in its disregard for the intangible but no less important role that religion can play as a source of meaning ascribed for the purposes of identity construction and the implications that flow from this.

The fact of the matter is that be it the reification or instrumentalization of confessional faith, either extreme obscures as much as it reveals. This is because they effectively deny the agency of religion, fail to recognize the salience of non-material factors such as ideas, and reduce the role of religious creed to mere political epiphenomena when the reality portrays a far more complex picture. Concomitantly, while both the above approaches can potentially shed some light, they can also potentially lend themselves to caricature.

This book begins with the basic premise that teleological and terminal arguments about the decline of religion in the wake of modernity are unsustainable. Indeed, as the next chapter will argue in detail, religion is not an archaic cultural artefact that exists as an anachronism in modern society but is very much part of a community's negotiation of its identity in the context of modernity, a feature of which would be the conception of nationhood. Neither did the emergence of "secular" and "modern" nationalism come about as a result of the decline of religion, but rather the renegotiation and refashioning of the relationship between religion, nationalism, and the state, for which the secularization of society was not a cause of the rise of nationalist movements, but a consequence.[6]

The most obvious evidence of this can be found in Europe, where nationalism arguably first emerged, and where a case can be made that the church paved the way for the emergence of "modern" and "secular" nationalism by providing the (national) symbols and delineating the (national) identity. Simon Walker's observation, that the desire of successive kings to promote national and dynastic unity through the medium of a revitalized public religion, is hence instructive in that regard.[7] But one

---

[5] This point has been persuasively demonstrated by Elisabeth Wood's path-breaking work on El Salvador. See Elisabeth Jean Wood, *Insurgent Collective Action and Civil War in El Salvador*. Cambridge: Cambridge University Press, 2003. While Wood does not focus on religion *per se*, her argument is similarly premised on the considerable influence of non-material factors, similar to the kind of role that religion would play.
[6] Geneviève Zubrzycki, "Religion and Nationalism: A Critical Re-examination," in Bryan Turner (ed.), *Sociology of Religion*. Sussex: Blackwell Publishing, 2010, pp. 611–619.
[7] Simon Walker, "Between Church and Crown: Master Richard Andrew, King's Clerk," *Speculum*, Vol. 74, No. 4, October 1999, p. 957.

can also immediately discern the resonance with Myanmar and Thailand, where the Buddhist Sangha underpinned the foundations of the modern state, or with Malaysia, where constitutional tension between religious (Islamic) authority and the non-Muslim right to freedom of worship has colored to a considerable extent the narrative of Malay nationalism. Indeed, as Sudipta Kaviraj explained: "When faced with the challenges of modernity, traditional forms do not drop their weapons and die. Some of these groups ignore their historical duty to decline and find unreasonable ways of adapting and even flourishing in the new cultural ecology."[8]

Turning to nationalism, there are three constituent elements to the idea that need to be considered as we approach the task of unpacking it conceptually alongside religion: first, the idea of the state as a politico-legal entity; second, the nation which is or is taken to be a community of people sharing in some important way a common culture; and, third, the nation-state which is a nation, or possibly a collection of nations, organized as a (territorial) state.[9] Another way of putting it is that these three constituent elements of nationalism speak to, and correspond with, legitimacy, collective identity, and statehood.

Legitimacy is a critical component of nationalism, because it essentially poses a central question: by whom should one be ruled and on what terms? In answering this question, it can be hypothesized that one reason why some states struggle to create a sense of "we-ness" by obtaining agreement and acceptance of the view that their "official" identities should supersede other identity signifiers that their populations possess can be attributed to a deficit in legitimacy, or an absence of legitimacy altogether. Furthermore, even if a collective is prepared to accept the need for integration and assimilation in order to make the idea of a nation-state work in practice, it also matters to them on whose terms these processes "legitimately" take place.

Equally pertinent to nationalism is the matter of the existence of a resilient and resonant collective identity. By drawing attention to nationalism, and more specifically the terms and process through which national identities are conceived and constructed – a process which we can term the "conception of nationhood" – the book aims to explore competing conceptions of nationhood as they relate to not only physical space in several Southeast Asian cases, but ideational and ideological space as well, in order to bring into sharper focus the role of religion and how it relates to contestations that occur within the contours of national identity

---

[8] Sudipta Kaviraj, "On Thick and Thin Religion," in Ira Katzelson and Gareth Stedman Jones (eds.), *Religion and the Political Imagination*. Cambridge: Cambridge University Press, 2010, p. 340.
[9] P.W. Preston, *Political/Cultural Identity: Citizens and Nations in a Global Era*. London: Sage Publications, 1997, p. 33.

and state building. By "nation," the book refers not to "an objectively abstract society of strangers, usually connected by a state" but to "a subjectively embodied community whose members experience themselves as an integrated group of compatriots" tied together, as it were, by notions of myths of origin, language, culture, and a common territorial association which may or may not be congruent to the physical borders of an existing modern nation-state, or the ideational borders of its "official" narrative of nationhood.[10] Apropos to this, it needs to be clarified that notwithstanding the common usage of the term "nation-state" in popular parlance, this book abides by the more analytically precise academic view that "the nation" is not *ipso facto* synonymous with "the state."

The previous discussion suggests that in most cases the politico-cultural entity called "the nation" is not, and has never been, consonant with the politico-juridical entity of "the state." Even the most homogeneous nation-states today have significant minorities who may not share in the majority's all-encompassing conception of nationhood. Indeed, it is this fact that requires us to give heed to alternative conceptions of nationhood in our analysis, in addition to the "official" nationalisms and their underlying narratives through which independent Southeast Asian states came into being.[11] In other words, while the book is interested in nationalist narratives, in relation to the unfolding of history this interest should not be confined to the narratives that won the day (i.e., that secured official independence). Rather, it is the matter of how "official" nationalisms have been contested and resisted, what are the contents of the narratives that have been used to frame this resistance to the official meaning of nationhood as it relates to the matter of who is included or excluded, and what the terms of this inclusion into or exclusion from nationhood are, that need to be grasped. The need to fathom this complex raft of issues is important in view of William Petersen's cautionary statement that: "the principle of the self-determination of nations has been applied rather too openhandedly. In fact, most of the new nations, however tiny, include two or more ethnic subpopulations that compete vigorously and sometimes violently for dominance in the unprecedented setting. As in Central Europe so in the rest of the world, it proved to be impossible to bestow its own nationhood on every ethnic grouping of a jumbled population."[12]

---

[10] Paul James, *Nation Formation: Towards a Theory of Abstract Community*. London: Sage Publications, 1996, p. 34.
[11] That said, this interest does not necessarily lead the book down the path of subaltern studies in the disciplinary sense as it is not so much interested in popular resistance per se but rather how resistance narratives are conceived and framed.
[12] William Petersen, *Ethnicity Counts*. New Brunswick, N.J.: Transaction Publishers, 2012, p. 245.

The third element we need to pay attention to when discussing nationalism is the matter of statehood. To that end, the book's treatment of nationalism will also consider the relationship between nationhood and statehood, in terms of how distinct religious values as an expression of the religious identity of a collective are or are not enshrined in the state and its institutions, which are then expected to defend, if not perpetuate, this identity and the values that underpin them. This is in essence implied in John Breuilly's observation that nationalism is "a form of politics, principally oppositional politics," which is "based on the relationship between the nationalist movement and the existing state. Very broadly, a nationalist movement can stand in one of three relationships to the existing state. It can seek to break away from it, to take it over and reform it, or to unite it with other states."[13]

This link between nationhood and statehood consequently returns the discussion back again to the pivotal question of legitimacy and how it relates to identity. The importance of this point can be seen in how, for example, nationalist narratives often purvey the view that some people are unequal not for economic or political reasons (which are merely symptoms) but because of their ascriptive identity. In other words, they are victims of discrimination. By this account, concerns for legitimacy relate conceptually to efforts of the state to fulfil the aspirations of a people divided by group identities by focusing attention on particular needs of particular groups – for example, "sons of the soil" – rather than (or at the expense of) more universal (or "national") causes.[14] Hence, it is in this manner that conflict and contestations expressing a religious hue are also the outcome of how the validity and legitimacy of the exercise of conceiving the nation and constructing nationhood are questioned, challenged, negotiated, undermined, and rejected by certain collectives within the territorial nation-state.

Religion and nationalism come together as an analytical framework in the form of religious nationalism. A detailed discussion on religious nationalism as a means to understand intrastate political conflicts in Southeast Asia that have been colored by confessional faith and religious identities will be undertaken in the next chapter. Suffice to say at this juncture that the fundamental premise of religious nationalism begins with the observations that the ascriptive quality of any nationalism is, first and foremost, premised on a discourse of identity difference and differentiation from an "other." At the same time, the currency of a confessional nationalism lies not only in its ability to frame narratives of

---

[13] John Breuilly, *Nationalism and the State*. Chicago, IL.: University of Chicago Press, 1994, p. 9.
[14] A similar argument is developed against a different context in Amy Gutmann, *Identity in Democracy*. Princeton, N.J.: Princeton University Press, 2003, pp. 126–127.

identity in order to mobilize social forces to overturn a legacy of cultural or political subordination, but also in its utility to reinforce legitimacy.[15] Certainly, because of its strong appeal, religion can provide an effective vocabulary to legitimize and frame political mobilization when combined with nationalism.[16] Building on Genevieve Zubrzycki's intimation that "Instead of thinking of the relationship between religion and nation as a dyad, scholars should look at it as part of a triad where statehood plays a key role to develop an analysis of the triadic relationship between state (re)formation, the (re)construction of national identity, and the (re)definition of religion's role in society," one can surmise that religious frames are also used to legitimize opposition, conflict, and, in extreme cases, violence in the name of (religious) nationalism against the state on the premise that the national identity that undergirds "official" nationalism in fact confers an inferior status to some members of the nation-state.[17]

If the foregoing assumptions about religion and nationalism hold true, then it follows that religious nationalism can be construed as a means by which, first, identity differentiation is constructed on the premise that religion is important for the ascription of identity for a community that sets it apart; and, second, by providing the source of legitimacy for the leaders of the nation to mobilize toward some form or other of self-determination with the intent to represent the aspirations and defend, or press, perceived denizen rights of neglected nations – all defined in reference to religion and religious identity – within the territorial state. Expressed in this manner, the phenomenon of religious nationalism underpins many religious conflicts in Southeast Asia and continues to play a definitive role in conflict and contestations over conceptions of nationhood in the region.

The Argument at a Glance

When scholars try to deduce what causes conflict, there is often a tendency to confuse the matter with the cognate question: why groups and

---

[15] See Muthiah Alagappa, "The Bases of Legitimacy," in Muthiah Alagappa (ed.), *Political Legitimacy in Southeast Asia: The Quest for Moral Authority*. Stanford, CA.: Stanford University Press, 1995, pp. 39–41.

[16] However, as established earlier, its value cannot and should not be reduced to mere flippant instrumentality. This is because even if religious metaphors and vocabulary are successfully deployed toward instrumentalist ends by political entrepreneurs and opportunists, this very success still relies on the appeal and currency that religion holds for the population in the first place. The key difference being argued here is that religion is more than just mere rhetorical device conjured to cloak utilitarian or materialist goals; it is a matter of ascriptive identity that invests meaning in conceptions of nationhood.

[17] Zubrzycki, "Religion and Nationalism," p. 613.

movements engage in conflict. These are, in essence, two different things, and the danger is to confuse which is the conclusion and which is the presupposition of an argument. Religion may cause contestations, and conflicts may be waged in defense of confessional faith, but more often than not that may not necessarily be what the fight is about, and to cast them as merely cases of religious or sectarian strife threatens to miss the proverbial forest for the trees. Put differently, it is erroneous to assume that conflicts are religious in nature simply because they appear religious in manifestation.

Bearing this epistemological conundrum in mind, this book, as suggested above, offers a perspective on religious conflict that departs from approaches that either ahistorically reifies religion or caricatures its pertinence in Southeast Asia. It argues that while conflicts and contestations in the Southeast Asian cases to be investigated in the following chapters may appear, *prima facie*, to be about religion and hence lend credence to arguments that hypothesize a causal relationship between (confessional) creed and conflicts, a closer examination will uncover more complex contours that speak to competing modes as to the conceptualization of nationhood and nation formation, to wit, it is within these (competing) modes of conceptualization (of nationhood) that religious identities are embedded. Concomitantly, this book contends that at the heart of many seemingly religious conflicts in Southeast Asia lies a clash of competing conceptions of nation and nationhood, identity and belonging, as well as loyalty and legitimacy.

Religion enters the equation on grounds that religious identity nourishes collective consciousness of a people who see themselves as a nation, or perhaps even as a constituent part of a nation ("nations without states"), but anchored in shared faith, and this serves as a vital element of identity and a means through which issues of rights (especially denizen rights) and legitimacy (i.e., the notion of citizenship and protection of denizen rights) are understood, especially when it becomes immediately tied to political, cultural, and historical reproduction of a community's identity and its invention (and reinvention) of tradition. In other words, many conflicts attributed to religion are arguably not about religion *per se*, but: (1) how it fosters and animates national consciousness and the collective "national" will toward aspirations for self-determination, (2) in defense of a community's identity and cultural values, or (3) how questions of legitimacy are understood and resolved. If one re-frames the discussion in this manner, the case can be made that the factor of religion – through its institutions and narratives – resonates as what Rogers Brubaker has termed an "idiom of nationhood" and serves as an effective means of mobilization for conflict and collective action predicated on the grounds that religion is an effective frame for the nationalist imagination.[18]

Insofar as the element of conflict is concerned – which is defined in this book as virulent and vehement disagreements that are expressed either discursively or physically – religious contestations in Southeast Asia have occurred when nations are conceptualized along religious lines on the basis of ascribed identity, and these conceptualizations have clashed over issues of rights and belonging as a nation and the legitimacy of the political interests who either claim to represent or defend these rights, or who are perceived to be undermining them.

It should be evident then, that as relevant points of inquiry, identity and legitimacy get to the heart of what a nation is, and what a nation – or the state that represents it – does. Both generate mutually reinforcing logics that easily enhance perceptions of differences, and because of that, foment conflict. In order to fully appreciate these logics, it is imperative to study broader historical, structural, and sociological dynamics, and the narratives that frame them, in order to have a sense of how they provide the conditions and context for conflict. Because of the imperative of context, it follows that the role of religion in the formation of the nation is not static but is shaped and colored by changing political, economic, and social circumstances. Conceptions of the nation change over time and are often contingent on shifting circumstance and multiple overlapping factors and hence are inseparable from social and political developments.

While the conceptual framework outlined above will be discussed in greater depth in the next chapter, a few further prefatory points may be appropriate here. First, it should be apparent from the discussion thus far that in order to attain explanatory traction, religion as an analytical concept needs to be understood and studied here not as doctrine and theology, but as a phenomenon embedded in a broader set of historical, social, and political contexts. This is because religion, like nationalism, provides the myths, symbols, belief systems, and languages that underpin conceptions of nationhood, and it is this aspect of religion that we are interested in. It is also by this token that religion has currency in terms of the formation of the nation in Southeast Asia through how it is employed to inform narratives that, in turn, provide persuasive nationalist frames through which identity can be differentiated, and resistance articulated and mobilized. Consequently, the role of religion as an ethical order, a social order, a political order, an intellectual system, and a means through which power is asserted or resisted, all in the process of the

---

[18] See Rogers Brubaker, *Citizenship and Nationhood in France and Germany*. Cambridge, MA.: Harvard University Press, 1992.

conceptualization of nationhood, should be appreciated in the tradition of the nationalist enterprise of meaning production and the discursive formation of the nation.

Second, rather than pigeonhole nationalism as a product of either a primordialist or modernist paradigm, the conceptual framework here aims to bridge, if not transcend, this exercised debate between these two dominant but ultimately dichotomous schools of thought in the field of nationalism studies, which in any case represent more the abstract polar extremes than the reality of any given brand of nationalism. The framework does so by accepting to some extent the validity of the exclusivist logic implied in primordialist accounts of religious identity, but also maintaining that this identity is itself constructed by its advocates and adherents toward the "modern" end of nation building, thereby accounting for its ascriptive quality. The important point to bear in mind here is that religion is a marker of ascriptive identity and not the assumed immutable, but ultimately fictitious, identity that primordialist scholars (and not a few nationalist leaders themselves) often present.

The conceptual framework and argument presented here lie at the intersection of theories of the nation, sociology of religion, and social movement theory. To that effect, this book brings together the three subdisciplines in the following manner: the emergence of religion as a key identity marker to the task of conceptualizing nationhood in Southeast Asia is located against the backdrop of theoretical debates on nationalism, while conflict that follows from conceptions of nationhood is taken beyond the narrow confines of the literature on religion and violence, and considered through the lens of social movement theory, in particular its emphasis on the framing of collective action.

Why "Framing"?

Social movement theorists have argued persuasively that the ability to engage in collective action is paramount for social and political transformations to occur. They advance these claims on the grounds that coordinated group activism is more politically influential and effective than individual activism. It follows that for sustainable and effective collective mobilization and sacrifice to take place, especially against opponents who have greater wherewithal at their disposal, resonance with a cause is critical. As Sidney Tarrow avers: "Leaders can only create a social movement when they tap more deep-rooted feelings of solidarity or identity. This is almost certainly why nationalism and ethnicity or religion have been more reliable bases of movement organization than the categorical

Why "Framing"?

imperative of social class."[19] Tangible inducements may prompt initial effort, but it takes more than that to sustain it, especially against heavy odds. Further to that, competing conceptions of nationhood generate contentious politics, a term in social movement theory lexicon that has commanded much attention of late.[20] Finally, to better appreciate how religion has animated nationalism and invested it with greater meaning and intelligibility such that it facilitates mobilization of collective action, this book employs the qualitative notion of framing, drawn from a body of social movement theory.

Framing refers to the use of narratives to lend credibility and facilitate mobilization for a particular social or political cause. Narratives are understood to be "a collection of stories... that relate to one another with coherent themes, forming a whole that is greater than the sum of its parts" that are constructed, nourished, and perpetuated for purposes of framing.[21] The power and appeal of narratives as a framing device to inspire collective action have been described by Gilam, Grosack, and Harms in the following manner:

Regardless of its possible historical inaccuracies or misrepresentations, however, the narrative remains both instantly recognizable to, and deeply resonant with, many audiences. Even where an audience may know full well that the narrative does not correspond precisely to historical truth, it can nonetheless remain emotionally compelling as an expression of ideals, aspirations and guidance. The optimism inherent within it can boost morale, too. Conversely, challenging the narrative carries risks.[22]

Needless to say, this book will show that religious narratives can be especially powerful and potent when used to frame self-determination as an expression of contentious politics.

A framing approach throws light on the contextual dimensions of religious conflicts, because it speaks to key aspects of the wider order of meaning within which such conflicts take place: ergo, need to be properly and contextually understood. The precise application of framing borrowed from social movement theory will be discussed at a later point. For now, it is instructive to consider that as an analytical framework, framing

---

[19] Sidney Tarrow, *Power in Movement: Social Movements and Contentious Politics*. Cambridge: Cambridge University Press, 1998, p. 6.
[20] For the definitive statement of contentious politics as a research paradigm, see Charles Tilly and Sidney Tarrow, *Contentious Politics*. New York: Oxford University Press, 2006.
[21] Jeffry R. Halverson, H.L. Goodall, Jr., and Steven R. Corman, *Master Narratives of Islamic Extremism*. New York: Palgrave McMillan, 2011, p. 1.
[22] See Nils Gilman, Michael Grosack, and Aaron Harms, "Everyone is Special," *The American Interest*, Vol. VIII, No. 4, Winter 2012/2013, pp. 18–19.

is useful on at least two grounds. First, it takes non-material factors seriously. This is important given that intrastate conflicts are more often than not driven by multiple causes, including those of a non-material nature, and hence do not lend themselves to monolithic explanations. Framing takes into account cultural and ideational constructs that inform a communities' understanding of conflict, which may not necessarily be rooted in tangibility and materialist logics.[23]

Second, framing allows us to account for change through "reframing," which means: "to change the conceptual and/or emotional setting or viewpoint in relation to which a situation is experienced and to place it in another frame which fits the 'facts' of the same concrete situation equally well or even better, and thereby changing its entire meaning."[24] Accounting for change is necessary when the process of the conceptualization of nationhood with religious referents is a context-specific one that is defined by negotiation and contestation.

Organization of the Book

Since Fred von der Mehden's seminal study published in 1963, there has not been another major scholarly book that has undertaken a comparative study of religion and nationalism in the context of political contestations in Southeast Asia.[25] While there are several volumes that investigate nationalism from a regional perspective, they have mostly provided descriptive accounts of conflicts. Among scholars of Southeast Asia, explicit conceptual and analytical focus on the linkage between religion and nationalism has been, at best, oblique.[26] Hence, it is the view of this book that revisiting this theme after five decades is timely, especially given that von der Mehden's book was published in the 1960s, when religion was analytically crowded out by seemingly more urgent themes

---

[23] A path-breaking study of this genre in the field of international relations is Robert Jervis, *Perception and Misperception in International Politics*. Princeton, N.J.: Princeton University Press, 1976.

[24] Paul Watzlawick, John Weakland, and Richard Fisch, *Change: Principles of Problem Formation and Problem Resolution*. New York: Norton, 1974, pp. 175–176.

[25] Fred R. von der Mehden, *Religion and Nationalism in Southeast Asia: Burma, Indonesia, the Philippines*. Madison, WI.: University of Wisconsin Press, 1963.

[26] Among the more prominent are David Brown, *The State and Ethnic Politics in Southeast Asia*. London: Routledge, 1997; Sri Kuhnt-Saptodewo, Volker Grabowsky, and Martin Grossheim (eds.), *Nationalism and Cultural Revival in Southeast Asia: Perspectives from the Centre and the Region*. Wiesbaden: Harrassowitz Verlag, 1997. An otherwise fine collection, the factor of religion was significantly absent in Jacques Bertrand and André Laliberté (eds.), *Multination States in Asia: Accommodation or Resistance*. Cambridge: Cambridge University Press, 2010.

of the day: colonialism, decolonization, and the Cold War ideological conflict, all of which dominated the field of political science.

Extrapolating from its conceptual framework, this book will make its case by discussing religious conflicts in Indonesia, Malaysia, Thailand, and the Philippines. Individually, each of these countries offers a rich trove of data on conflict, religion, and nationalism that can be mined. However, constraints of length and the imperative of analytical rigor necessitate that the case studies themselves avoid broad sketches and lengthy background details in order to "drill deep" into the questions of where religious and nationalist narratives have fused into a conception of nationhood, how they have been contested, and why.

To that end, the following chapters will provide in-depth discussions of specific conflicts (including political violence) and/or sources of social-political tension in the respective countries. The conflicts are chosen for some or all of the following reasons: they have been widely reported and described as religious conflicts, and as conflicts they have been framed by participants in religious language, using religious metaphors. Drawn from the four Southeast Asian countries mentioned earlier, the specific conflicts under scrutiny here are the struggle of the Moro Islamic Liberation Front (MILF) in the southern Philippine island of Mindanao, an ongoing armed insurgency being waged by "Muslim militants" in Thailand's southern border provinces, increased tension and conflict between Muslims and non-Muslims (particularly Christians) in Malaysia, and the sectarian violence that took place in Sulawesi and Maluku in Indonesia between 1999 and 2002 against the backdrop that has come to be known as "*Kristenisasi*" (the perceived "Christianization" of Indonesia). Each chapter will proceed by unpacking key contestations and points of tension in the respective countries, locating them in the context of discourses and debates over conceptions of nationhood in each instance. The focus will fall on, among other things: (1) the use of resonant religious narratives by political agents to construct and articulate national identity and challenge/reinforce legitimacy of the state; (2) the religious content of these nationalist narratives, in particular, religious inflection of nationalist discourses and the religious identity of key agents; and (3) how religion provides an arena for contests of identity and legitimacy, and as vehicle of mobilization.

Needless to say, because this book is interested in competing conceptions of nationhood in terms of the conflicts and contentious politics they have generated, analytical attention cannot be limited to the genesis and content of "official" nationalisms, that is to say, the narratives of nationalism that informed the independence of the states concerned, and that subsequently formed the basis for the post-independence nation-state. Equal, if not more, attention needs to be devoted to the challengers that emerged to negotiate, contest, and, at its extreme, reject the meaning, currency, and legitimacy of the dominant narrative.

Following this Introduction that has set out the broad conceptual parameters and established the main arguments for the book, Chapter 1 will focus on elaborating further the themes of religious violence and conflict, formation and negotiation (and re-negotiation) of conceptions of nationhood, religious nationalism, and framing for collective action. It should be pointed out that the primary purpose of this book is to cast light on how conceptions of nationhood have been constructed and conceived in religious terms in Southeast Asia and the conflicts that have arisen from this process. It does not purport to present a general theory of religious nationalism, although observations gleaned are likely to resonate with other regions.

From here, the rest of the chapters are mainly concerned with exploring specific cases of religious conflict from the conceptual lens already outlined. Chapter 2 discusses the case of the Philippines, focusing specifically on the struggle for self-determination among the Muslim minority population in the southern island of Mindanao, and to a lesser extent the outer islands of Sulu and Palawan. The chapter sheds light on the framing and reframing of Bangsamoro national identity undertaken by the MILF as the dominant Bangsamoro actor and how it has shifted from an exclusivist to an inclusivist register, how the narratives that framed the struggle of that Muslim minority saw Islam reconstructed from a vocabulary of armed resistance to one of reconciliation, and the tensions that these process of conceptualization and reconceptualization of Bangsamoro nationhood generated.

Chapter 3 takes the discussion to Thailand, and specifically, the Malay-Muslim provinces in the southern border region. The chapter unpacks the competing narratives underlying fraying center–periphery relations in terms of the legacy of the Thai state's inability (or reluctance) to accommodate Malay-Muslim conceptions of nationhood and belonging and how religion has surfaced to frame the local narratives, goals, and motivations of the latter.

Chapter 4 will spell out how hope for civic and pluralist underpinnings of national identity have undergone a forceful and difficult process of reconceptualization and reinterpretation triggered by the growth of an exclusivist Malay-Muslim religious discourse rooted in the mutually constitutive relationship rendered visible in the concept of *Ketuanan Melayu* (Malay lordship or supremacy) that speaks of, on one hand, a sense of entitlement evidenced in a discourse of muscular Malay-Muslim supremacy, and on the other, an acute sense of vulnerability that calls for mobilization in defense of the Islamic faith against Christian "incursion." The dynamics that result from the interaction of these two divergent phenomena has had severe repercussions for the status, identity, and rights of non-Muslims, particularly the Christian communities in Malaysia who discursively resist the gradual imposition of this new confessional conception of Malay and Malaysian nationhood on non-Muslims.

Similar exclusionary tendencies can be discerned from a close study of shifts in Indonesian nationalist ideas and discourses since independence. Focusing primarily (though not exclusively) on the egregious violence between Christians and Muslims in the Indonesian islands of Maluku, North Maluku, and Sulawesi at the turn of the century, Chapter 5 will demonstrate how attempts to rearticulate and renegotiate nationhood by religious actors at the national level came to animate local clashes among confessional communities that had hitherto co-existed in relative peace, if not harmony. In addition to this, the chapter also looks at the tensions that have arisen within the Muslim community in Indonesia, in terms of how fringe Islamic groups have sought to assert both their identity as part of the Indonesian nation and their rights as citizens of the country in the face of attempts by mainstream majoritarian Islamic discourses on nationhood to marginalize them precisely because of their claims.

To avoid any misplaced expectations, it needs to be highlighted again that given the magnitude of the task it would be impossible to cover every aspect of political life in each case where religion has exerted influence. Hence, the primary purpose of each of the empirical chapters is not to sketch out grand historical trajectories or to provide a blow-by-blow descriptive account of controversies of the moment, but rather to facilitate an integrated analysis of broader, enduring trends of competing conceptions of nationhood within Southeast Asian nation-states, and how religion is, in unique and different ways, a factor in this process. As such, the book will not engage in a detailed examination of the modalities of conflict and will instead focus on underlying trends and tensions as they relate to the framework presented above.

1   Faith and Flag

Religion has a powerful hold on the nationalist imagination. Many a nationalist struggle has come to be inflected, even appropriated, by religious discourses and authority figures. At the same time, the rise of nationalism and the emergence of nation-states have also produced nationalizing effects on religious communities. Either way, it is clear religious identity and conceptions of nationhood cannot be understood divorced from the social, cultural, and historical contexts of societies and their interactions with power. This contention is premised on the view that "nationalism is a field of debates about the symbol of the nation, and national identity is a relational process enacted in social dramas and 'events' as well as in everyday practices."[1] It is bearing this in mind that the following proposition is made: in Southeast Asia, the role of religion in political conflicts and contestations is best understood in the context of national identity formation and contestation that continues to define much of post-independence politics in the region.

Before proceeding to see how this plays out in the study of religious conflicts in several cases drawn from Southeast Asia, it is necessary to first consider the theoretical literature in terms of the political aspects of religion and the religious impulses of nationalism. Towards that end, this chapter will introduce and discuss the current literature and debates that define the fields of religious conflict and nationalism studies, and how they intersect and speak to each other, before making its case for a view of religious nationalism that accounts for the dynamic and intimate relationship between the notions of religious faith, identity, rights, and belonging.

Religion

Until recently, scholarly study of religion – whether in its monotheistic or polytheistic forms – as a sociological phenomenon had been for the most

---

[1] Genevieve Zubrzycki, "National Culture, National Identity, and the Culture(s) of the Nation" in Laura Grindstaff, John R. Hall, and Ming-cheng Lo (eds.), *Sociology of Culture: A Handbook*. London: Routledge, 2010, p. 514.

part relegated to the backwaters of social sciences. With the emergence of modernization and rationalist theory as dominant paradigms in the field after the Second World War, interest in religion as a phenomenon that impacted on social, political, and economic developments diminished considerably.[2] Consequently, its study was largely confined to the disciplines of theology and religious studies. Yet today, it is readily and ironically apparent that religion continues to shape social and political affairs in many parts of the world. The most evident example of this, of course, can be found in the field of terrorism studies, which experienced something of a resurgence after the September 11 terrorist attacks. This has in turn triggered widespread interest in the role of confessional faith as a cause of political contestations in societies that have witnessed conflict.[3]

The intent here is not to examine the whole tangle of issues associated with religion in society. Rather, it is to find a path through which observations on religious violence and conflict can be made and interrogated against the social and historical contexts in which they have emerged. To that end, any attempt to explain the salience of the factor of religion in contemporary politics will have to come to terms with that most provocative school of thought, which resonates as strongly as ever today, that posits a causal relation between religion and violence.

Religion as a Source of Conflict and Violence?

A vast literature on the relationship between religion and political violence emerged immediately after the terrorist attacks of September 11, although there was some scholarly interest in the topic prior to the tragic events of that day. A major school of thought that emerged from this literature proceeds from the premise that religion is in essence predisposed to conflict and, in extreme cases, violence. While arguments hypothesizing a correlation between religion and conflict are varied, they essentially turn on one main point: religion causes violence because it inherently promotes identity politics of the most conflictual kind by way of establishing truth claims that its adherents maintain are infallible and

---

[2] Jeffrey K. Hadden, "Towards Desacralizing Secularization Theory," *Social Forces*, Vol. 65, No. 3, 1987, pp. 587–611; Daniel Philpott, "The Religious Roots of Modern International Relations," *World Politics*, Vol. 52, No. 2, 2000, pp. 206–245.

[3] To that end, it is worth noting that a rudimentary survey on conflicts driven by religious nationalism since the 1980s has identified that such conflicts are on the rise. See Jonathan Fox, "The Rise of Religious Nationalism and Conflict: Ethnic Conflict and Revolutionary Wars, 1945–2001," *Journal of Peace Research*, Vol. 41, No. 6, November 2004, pp. 715–731.

transcendent. This implies an epistemological rigidity that is given to rejection of nuance or alternatives.

To scholars such as Mark Juergensmeyer, the debate over religious violence is polarized between two camps. On one side, non-religionists argue that religion is "the problem" due to its propensity for a militant brand of politics. Proponents of this view point specifically to Islam's complex relationship to politics, for instance, as the central causal factor for violence that has plagued the Middle East.[4] On the other side stand those who argue that in cases where violence was perpetrated in the name of religion, what actually transpired was that confessional faith had been hijacked by militant groups to justify other objectives. Religion, then, was but a veil that concealed insidious yet mundane intentions. With respect to how religion might be instrumentalized in this fashion, the point is made that such groups are more often than not driven by secular motivations, and religion is only tangentially implicated by way of being used as tropes to legitimize their cause. This latter interpretation has been particularly prevalent in discussions of extremism in Southeast Asia, where scholars and policy-makers have dismissed the actions of militants as being those of "misguided" Muslims who had been "led astray" by rogue clerics. For Juergensmeyer, the susceptibility of religion to instrumentalization by such political actors is a result of "the involvement of religion in public life" where "a strain of violence... may be found in the deepest levels of the religious imagination."[5]

Juergensmeyer further suggests that acts of religious violence take the form and logic of symbolic performance and are often conceived of as cosmic wars where the struggle is perceived as a defense of basic identity and dignity, hence losing the struggle would be unthinkable even though the struggle ultimately cannot be won in any real sense. Central to this conception of religious violence as cosmic conflagrations is the fact that they are often fought on a symbolic plane and are not given to immediate resolution because their timeline extends far into the distant future (i.e., the return of Christ or the Mahdi, the attainment of Nirvana, God's eternal judgment), unlike secular political violence which tends toward a utilitarian and strategic endgame.

Another fact about the emphasis on the symbolic is that it also effectively delineates boundaries, thereby lending itself to conflictual depictions of identity and difference defined in religious terms. This idea is developed by Wellman and Tokuno, who opine that "the symbolic

---

[4] See, for instance, Bernard Lewis, *The Crisis of Islam: Holy War and Unholy Terror*. New York: Random House, 2004.

[5] Mark Juergensmeyer, "Is Religion the Problem?" *Hedgehog Review*, Vol. 6, No. 1, Spring 2004, pp. 4–5.

boundaries of religion provide a powerful engine for individual and group identity formation."[6] These boundaries shape individual and social identities and inspire group formation and mobilization, in the process engendering and entrenching communal identities and establishing in- and out-groups. As the two authors explain, the symbolic and social building blocks of religion allow "religious communities to gain their identity through conflict and tension with out-group cultures."[7] In this regard, conflict is not merely a function of social interaction; rather, it forms the basic sustenance of religious identities. It is this divisive quality to religion – particularly in the monotheistic Abrahamic faiths one is often reminded – that lends it to conflict. As Talal Asad cautions, religion is "the source of uncontrollable passions within the individual and dangerous strife within the commonwealth. It could not, for this reason, provide an institutional basis for common morality – still less a public language for rational criticism.... Religion is what actually or potentially divides us, and if followed with passionate conviction, may set us intolerantly against one another."[8]

The work of religious conflict scholars bears striking similarities with each other. The point about religion fomenting discord and being prone to violence because of its propensity to establish truth claims that are infallible and transcendent – namely, the absolutist and non-rational nature of religion – is reinforced to varying degrees in the scholarship of Hector Avalos, Charles Kimball, R. Scott Appleby, and Charles Selengut. According to this train of thought, religion is prone to violence because its claims are unverifiable (Avalos), rely on blind obedience (Kimball), premised on the defense of the sacred (Appleby), and beyond scientific understanding (Selengut).[9] To interrogate the details of every assumption underlying these works would take this study too far afield. Rather, the pertinent point here is that the "religion is prone to violence" argument casts a harsh light on religion by depicting it as a transhistorical and transcultural phenomenon on the basis of any combination of the aforementioned points. Yet such over-simplification tends however to obscure more than illuminate, for, as the rest of this chapter intends to

---

[6] James K. Wellman, Jr. and Kyoko Tokuno, "Is Religious Violence Inevitable?" *Journal for the Scientific Study of Religion*, Vol. 43, No. 3, September 2004, p. 292.
[7] Ibid., p. 292.
[8] Talal Asad, *Genealogies of Religion: Discipline and Reasons of Power in Christianity and Islam*. Baltimore, MD.: Johns Hopkins University Press, 1993, pp. 205–207.
[9] See Hector Avalos, *Fighting Words: The Origins of Religious Violence*. Amherst, N.Y.: Prometheus Books, 2005; Charles Kimball, *When Religion Becomes Evil*. New York: HarperCollins, 2008; Scott Appleby, *The Ambivalence of the Sacred: Religion, Violence, and Reconciliation*. New York: Rowman & Littlefield, 2000; Charles Selengut, *Sacred Fury: Understanding Religious Violence*. New York: Rowman & Littlefield, 2008.

illustrate, religious conflicts have to be properly contextualized according to culture and historical circumstances that give rise to it.

There are two crucial points that stand out from this discussion thus far on how religious violence has been theorized in the field. First, as suggested earlier and as scholars like William Cavanaugh have persuasively argued elsewhere, far from being transhistorical and transcultural, the role of religion has to be contextualized, particularly in relation to conceptions of identity since the element of "othering" plays such an important part in conceptualizing religious conflict.[10] Second, it is the matter of intent behind violence and not merely the act itself – the "why" rather than "how" question – that should be subjected to closer scrutiny. While it is reasonably clear from this literature how communities read and understand their faith in a way that may provoke violence in the name of religion, why they chose to do so is arguably less apparent.

In terms of our interest in conflictual interactions over the nature of national identity that might lead to contentious politics, the point needs to be made that violence in the name of religion is not merely an expression of "othering" as noted above but, more to the point, the politics of exclusion that defines the process of the conceptualization and building of the nation. This is a particularly salient point in many instances because religion is often inextricably linked to other facets of identity and by virtue of that plays an important role in the construction and collective mobilization of these identities, where the symbolic and social building blocks of religion allow religious communities to reinforce their identity through conflict with the out-group.[11] It is for this reason that, as Amy Gutmann explains, "the enduring power of religion over people's sense of identity can scarcely be doubted."[12]

In the main, explanations of conflicts based on arguments about religion's inherent propensity toward violence thence do not take us far in explaining why groups and communities chose religion through which to frame their collective action, let alone the many instances when confessional piety has not triggered conflict. In order to obtain a clearer picture of the identity construction, exclusion, and "othering" effect of religiously defined conflicts and contestations, it is apropos to first have a sense of religion as a social phenomenon and ascriptive identity, and

---

[10] See William T. Cavanaugh, *The Myth of Religious Violence: Secular Ideology and the Roots of Modern Conflict*. New York: Oxford University Press, 2009.

[11] Consider, for instance, the burning of churches in Malaysia in the wake of the controversy over the rights of non-Muslims to use the word "Allah" in reference to their own God, which can be interpreted as an act to reinforce and defend the boundaries of the Malay nation, defined in religious terms, against encroachment by the non-Malay, non-Muslim "others."

[12] Gutmann, *Identity in Democracy*, p. 153.

the social, political, and cultural dynamics that both generate, and are informed by, it. For those who study the non-Western world, it can be argued that colonialism has played a pivotal role in constructing these ascriptive elements to religious identity. Hence, it is to this that we now turn.

Religion and Colonialism

In terms of the importance of context to understanding religious conflicts, a major epistemological problem with the scholarship on religious violence cited above is the tendency to overlook how religion is often imbricated with the configurations of power and authority of the day. In response, a poignant note of caution has been sounded by William Cavanaugh, who in his study of the etymology and history behind the term "*religio*" concludes that the concept in fact developed different meanings and understandings over time so as to encompass, among other things, civic oaths, family rituals, and even habituated disciplines of body and soul. Of particular relevance for current purposes is his point that even in Western societies, religion was traditionally never separated from politics, culture, family obligations, devotion to God or gods, and civic duties. In other words, rather than an abstract transhistorical and transcultural concept that is devoid of any sort of context, religion was, and remains, highly contextualized in how it relates to and reflects culture, history, and society of the circumstances around which it emerged.[13]

On this matter of religion as an ontological reality, a further note of caution should be sounded. At a more fundamental level of etymology, as a concept religion is a decidedly Western concept, born of Western civilization and superimposed onto Asian societies. The tendency to view religion as separate from secular politics is indeed a facile demarcation that can be traced to two monumental developments in Western civilization from the early 16th through to the late 17th centuries – the Reformation and the Renaissance.[14] Briefly, the period of the Reformation in Christendom sought to reform the doctrines and ecclesiastical structure of the Roman Catholic Church. This precipitated a break from the Roman Catholic Church's dominance and sole authority, and the forceful challenge against corruption in Rome subsequently undermined the link between religion and the political structure in a way that eventually

---

[13] Cavanaugh, *The Myth of Religious Violence*, p. 61.
[14] Consider the essays in Ira Katznelson and Gareth Stedman Jones (eds.), *Religion and the Political Imagination*. Cambridge: Cambridge University Press, 2010.

gave rise to many "new (Christian) religions" in the form of Lutheranism, Calvinism, Anabaptists, Gnosticism, and so on. The age of the Renaissance, on the other hand, set great store by the advance of scientific rationality and the birth of a new political economy across Western civilization. This development in the late 17th century triggered something of a retreat of religion as it was cast in contradistinction to the secular. By this token, the Renaissance proved a midwife to a secular order premised on the purportedly neutral, factual, and quantifiable, where natural laws could be derived through scientific rationality. In this novel conception of the world, scientific knowledge was construed as a product of natural human processes distinct from "revealed" religious knowledge. Consequently, religion was relegated to the realm of personal piety and the private domain of belief and practice. With this, the separation of church and state came into being. Not only that, this materialist prism through which religion came to be viewed would also influence social scientific study of the phenomenon in time to come.

What transpired in Europe was soon transplanted elsewhere. The imperialist expansion of the Western worldview through the vehicle of the European colonial enterprise into Africa, the Middle East, and Asia transformed this ideological division of religion from the secular into a tool of domination in these societies. Specifically, the attribution of religion to backward traits of indigenous people, as compared to European rationality, served as a way to depoliticize their cultures, whereby the demarcation of native practices as "religious" allowed the colonizer to relegate them to the realm of superstition and irrationality, after which they (both the religions and those who practiced them) could be dismissed as inconsequential artefacts of the past. Even when indigenous religions were engaged, they were interrogated through the lens of Christian religiosity via the discipline of comparative religion, which predictably resulted in local religious beliefs registering at the lower end of the evolutionary scale of Enlightenment logic.[15]

In this manner, colonialism provided both the mechanism and vehicle through which the Western conceptualization of religion was imposed onto non-Western cultures, which they then labeled and reified. This scientific process combined with the military power of imperialism

---

[15] Typifying this scholarship is E. B. Tylor, Max Muller, James G. Frazer, etc. See Joan Leopold, *Culture in Comparative and Evolutionary Perspective: E. B. Tylor and the Making of Primitive Culture*. Berlin: Dietrich Reimer Verlag, 1980; Jon R. Stone (ed.), *The Essential Max Muller: On Language, Mythology, and Religion*. New York: Palgrave, 2002; Timothy Fitzgerald (ed.), *Religion and the Secular: Historical and Colonial Formations*. London: Equinox Publishing Ltd, 2007.

ensured that there was no closely equivalent concept that approximates religion in any culture that has not been influenced by Western intellectual tradition.[16] What the colonial enterprise refused to acknowledge or accept was the fact that while forms of "religious systems" did exist in the colonized worlds, each community's religious system was neither identified as, nor were they conceived as, something that was distinct from other facets of society: "it (religion) was not a distinct entity in the lives, or in the minds, of the people."[17] For the non-Western world, religion was – and remains – very much a part of their identity, their society, and their modernity.

A central premise behind colonial conceptions of identity was the primordialist view of how claims of collective exclusivity and inherent tendencies tend toward xenophobia and intolerance, which, primordialists would in turn argue by extension, are predictable outcomes of the uncivilized (or natural) human condition and their pathologies. Indeed, one example of such gratuitous racialized thinking is the English word "amok" – which has become a recognized scientific term today for an apparently diagnosable psychological condition in the field of clinical psychology – which was derived from the observed and recorded (by the British) tendency of Malays to be given to unpredictable and violent frenzied behaviour.[18] On the other hand, this primordialist focus on inherency tends to overlook peaceful relations between communities which otherwise have significant cultural differences.[19]

More to the point, these primordial explanations are flawed since "they fail to make the distinction between cultural identity and politically relevant cultural identity" and merely assume that all cultural markers lend themselves to exclusionary claims that may incite extremism and violence.[20] In contrast to this view, it is contended here that it is not

---

[16] Wilfred Cantwell Smith, *The Meaning and End of Religion*. Minneapolis, MN.: Fortress Press, 1991.

[17] Cavanaugh, *The Myth of Religious Violence*, p. 54.

[18] See John E. Carr, "Ethno-Behaviorism and the Culture-Bound Syndromes: The Case of Amok," in Ronald C. Simons and Charles C. Hughes (eds.), *The Culture-Bound Syndromes: Folk Illnesses of Psychiatric and Anthropological Interest*. Dordrecht: D. Reidel Publishing Company, 1985, pp. 199–223; S. Mohamed Hatta, "A Malay Crosscultural Worldview and Forensic Review of Amok," *Australian and New Zealand Journal of Psychiatry*, Vol. 30, No. 4, 1996, pp. 505–510.

[19] See Beverly Crawford, "The Causes of Cultural Conflict: An Institutional Approach" in Beverly Crawford and Ronnie D. Lipschutz (eds.), *The Myth of "Ethnic" Conflict: Politics, Economics, and "Cultural" Violence*. Berkeley, CA.: University of California-Berkeley, 1998. She elaborates on this using the example of Bulgarian Muslims and Christians, and Germans and French in Alsace-Lorraine.

[20] Ibid., p. 16.

the identity marker itself that triggers conflict and violence, but the fact that these identities can become politically charged through processes of ascription, as when cultural identity interacts with context and becomes a criterion, for example, for discrimination and privilege in the distribution of resources. In addition to that, primordialists tend to "ignore the role that the institutions of the state play in easing, perpetuating, or triggering cultural conflict by structuring incentives in ways that either exacerbate or attenuate the political relevance of cultural identity," meaning to say that institutions and incentives – oftentimes associated with the modern state – are just as culpable for religious conflicts.[21]

Over time, the colonial enterprise and politics of (colonial) state building laid the foundations upon which new polities were to be structured as political leadership changed hands from colonial administrators to an indigenous elite. This had two effects. First, this transition bequeathed not only institutions of modern statehood, but social and cultural constructions of identity as well, the ubiquitous *national census* being a foremost example. Coupled with the emergence of a global political economy, this ensured that colonial structures of governance, in particular the dissociation of religion from politics, remained, at least in theory, entrenched within newly independent nation-states. Second, the process of colonization had arbitrarily demarcated territorial boundaries within which a novel form of "modern" identity – civic brands of nationalism as Ernest Gellner termed them – was meant to trump indigenous loyalties based on ethnicity and religion.

The efficacy of the colonial enterprise, however, barely masks a critical conceptual tension. At the heart of this conceptual tension is the fact that when concepts such as "politics," "nationalism," and "religion" are analyzed, the tendency is to objectivize by presupposing the meanings they carry to be self-evident and clearly compartmentalized. Hence, extending this logic, what constitutes the "political" is supposedly distinct from what constitutes the "religious." As Ralph Nicholas points out, the Western notion of the "political" relies on the dichotomy between the sacred and secular, spiritual and temporal, and this explains why religion is often not taken seriously in the study of political phenomenon, or if it is, it tends to be reified as a destabilizing and anti-modern phenomenon, a tendency the preceding discussion on the themes of religion and political violence has already identified.[22] By this token, the political as a secular and instrumentalist pursuit is somehow different from, or even contrary

---

[21] Ibid., p. 12.
[22] Ralph W. Nicholas, "Social and Political Movements," *Annual Review of Anthropology*, Vol. 2, 1973, pp. 63–84.

to, religion, which lies deep in the realm of the sacred;[23] furthermore, the obsession with the secular state as "the epitome of political modernity, where religion is seen as anti-modern and off the political map" has tended to "deny or play down, even in the face of contrary evidence, the importance of religion in the daily lives of citizens and the state."[24]

The crux of the matter is that when modernity as defined by the West is confronted with very different notions of the political, they have difficulties explaining them. It is in the attempt to resolve this tension that Nicholas suggests concepts such as "culture" and "religion" are invoked to explain many aberrations from the expected patterns and conventions of political development rather than treated as fundamental to an understanding of what politics is conceived to be in different social and political contexts.[25]

The Intersection of Religion and Politics

All this is to say that, contrary to popular belief rooted in Western conceptions of the separation of church and state, religion can be a highly charged political phenomenon, and one that exists in a mutually constitutive relationship with modernity. This occurs when political entrepreneurs and actors define politics as a religious obligation, and legitimacy claims are articulated using religious vocabulary. In the event, not only does religion provide a sense of community and ascriptive identity, as well as moral and ethical direction, for many in the world, but also it can potentially translate to an alternative political order. This is perhaps most profoundly, though not exclusively, demonstrated today in Islam, or more specifically Islamism, where, contrary to the claims of some scholars, the ideological belief that in Islam lies the panacea to the social, economic, and political problems confronting the Muslim world today appears to be on the rise.[26] Indeed, Peter van der Veer acknowledges this when he criticizes secularization theory for transplanting presuppositions

---

[23] In this regard, consider Ernest Gellner's claim that the agrarian world was "far too well provided with religions" for them all to survive "even in transmogrified form, as ethnic units." See Ernest Gellner, *Nations and Nationalism*. Ithaca, N.Y.: Cornell University Press, 1983, p. 72.

[24] Judith Nagata, "Open Societies and Closed Minds: The Limits of Fundamentalism in Islam," *ICIP Journal*, Vol. 2, No. 2, March 2005, p. 3.

[25] Nicholas, "Social and Political Movements," p. 67.

[26] The French scholars of Islam, Olivier Roy and Gilles Keppel, have both offered arguments in favor of the decline of Islamism. See Olivier Roy, *The Failure of Political Islam*. Cambridge, MA.: Harvard University Press, 1994; Gilles Keppel, *Jihad: The Trail of Political Islam*. Cambridge, MA.: The Belknap Press of Harvard University Press, 2002; Olivier Roy, *Globalized Islam: The Search for a New Ummah*. London: C. Hurst & Co., 2004.

about religion that were in fact limited to Christianity and its interactions with the social and political forces that surrounded it onto other religions and their own encounters with society.[27]

Obviously, not all manifestations of identity are politically charged. Yet there is more than ample evidence that points to how culturally defined markers of identity, such as ethnicity or religion, tend to be more inflammatory than others, ergo, of potentially greater political utility. This has little to do with inherent traits, but much to do with policies of colonial divide-and-rule that separated subjugated populations along ethnic and sectarian lines in ways that not only amplified differences but also give them political content and expression. A classic example of this dynamic would be policies of transmigration and the classification of the population that colonial administrations, as well as those to whom the state was subsequently bequeathed, often enacted in their colonies for both economic as well as social reasons, that resulted in marginalization and dislocation of local communities. The impact of such policies on local demographics and, eventually, identity formation is evident in a range of cases as diverse as Fiji, Sri Lanka, Bangladesh, and Kenya.[28] A more contemporary example of the devastating consequences of such policies can be witnessed in Iraq today, where the ethnicized, sectarian divide-and-rule measures undertaken by the Bush administration after the Second Gulf War have spawned the Islamic State of Iraq and al-Sham and brought Iraq to the brink of collapse as a governable territorial nation-state.[29]

In the post-colonial milieu, divisive narratives of cultural identity are reiterated and manipulated by new political entrepreneurs who "draw on cultural identities to mobilize resistance to imperial control, gain access to political power and territory, and exercise power in the construction of new national institutions when colonial power collapsed."[30] According to this view, the cultural features of the nation are harnessed to organize

---

[27] See Peter van der Veer, "The Secular Production of Religion," *ETNOFOOR*, Vol. VIII, No. 2, 1995, p. 5.
[28] For instance, in Sri Lanka the influx of Tamil plantation labor under British colonial policy created a situation of ferment that eventually erupted in inter-ethnic violence. The influx of indentured laborers from India into Fiji during the colonial era sowed the seeds for inter-communal discontent and rivalry that often spilled over into conflict. In Nigeria, deep divisions were sown during the colonial era which spilled over to civil war after independence. In Kenya, colonial policy creating "native reserves" was met with disapproval and rejection by local communities. These cases are elaborated in several essays in Jeffrey Herbst, Terence McNamee, and Greg Mills (eds.), *On the Fault Line: Managing Tensions and Divisions within Societies*. London: Profile Books, 2012.
[29] Juan Cole, "How the United States Helped Create the Islamic State," *Washington Post*, November 23, 2015.
[30] van der Veer, "The Secular Production of Religion," p. 19.

a constituency for acquiring cultural and political resources. In other words, cultural identity or religious identity is transformed to political identity when political entrepreneurs capitalize on such cleavages so as to derive a local narrative that suits their advantage in instrumentalist fashion, which can in turn be modulated and adapted to changing circumstances and exigencies in order to justify and interpret discrimination, oppression, and privilege in post-independence nation-states. This means that not only antecedent external colonial domination but ongoing internal political domination and discrimination as well, oftentimes codified in political institutions, contrive to bring about the politicization of culturally identified categories (religion being one of the most popular).[31] The measure of how national identity and conceptions of nationhood are constructed by political entrepreneurs to take on religious form through inflection or appropriation is all too evident in narratives that talk about the defense of religious rights and praxis of a given community, or even the rights of a denizen religious community to land and the resources in it.[32] In sum, the main claim amongst the proponents of the instrumentalization of religion is that to mobilize partisan support, political entrepreneurs have been seen to "define groups with a mythical and heroic past, a sense of mission and messianism, or a belief that the group had intrinsic and unique rights to territory by virtue of its ethnic or religious identity."[33]

Yet at issue is the fact that though identity markers like ethnicity and religion can obviously be given to manipulation, in order for them to be instrumentalized in this fashion and to have sufficient appeal so as to mobilize a group toward collective action, they need first to resonate with an intended audience.[34] It is all too easy and indolent to dismiss the mobilizational potential of constructed narratives, but the uncomfortable reality is that more often than not, these narratives have had their desired effect. To understand this, we should appreciate that what is subjective to the scholar is oftentimes "real" to the common people, and "it is not what is, but what people believe" that has behavioural consequences.[35] The cautionary thoughts of John Langan are worth registering in this

---

[31] A case in point is Lebanon, where, as Roschanack Shaery-Eisenlohr tells us, multiple "distinct nationalisms" emerged and competed. See Roschanack Shaery-Eisenlohr, *Shi'ite Lebanon: Transnational Religion and the Making of National Identities*. New York: Columbia University Press, 2008.
[32] For instance, Gutmann, *Identity in Democracy*, pp. 151–191.   [33] Ibid., p. 20.
[34] For instance, Elliott D. Green, "Understanding the Limits to Ethnic Change: Lessons from Uganda's 'Lost Counties,'" *Perspectives on Politics*, Vol. 6, No. 3, September 2008, pp. 473–485.
[35] Walker Connor, *Ethnonationalism: The Quest for Understanding*. Princeton, N.J.: Princeton University Press, 1994, p. 75.

regard: "we cannot dismiss this aspect of a people's life or fail to take it seriously, even though it may itself stand in need of moral criticism and revision. Until these peoples feel that their experience has been recognized and evaluated, it is probably beside the point to preach to them on the economies of scale provided by larger national markets and on the advantages of belonging to larger political units."[36] The currency (and contradiction) of communal identity boundaries such as religion lies in the fact that it is both constructed and yet real. Because religion can be invested with ascriptive meaning that resonates with a community, it can be instrumentalized with a measure of certitude for purposes of legitimation and mobilization.

So, what does this discussion regarding how religion might be instrumentalized have to say about the separation of the religious and secular spheres? Even if one can defend the claim that church and state are clearly demarcated in Western cultures and societies such that religion has little currency in everyday politics, beyond the Western world these epistemological waters are, arguably, considerably more murky. As Donald Horowitz presciently explains: "Outside the West, religion remained an *ascriptive affiliation*. For many groups, religion is not a matter of faith but a given, an integral part of their identity, and for some an inextricable component of their sense of peoplehood" (emphasis in original).[37]

The point about religion being very much a facet of everyday life in contemporary non-Western societies has been argued by a number of scholars who have championed cultural dimensions to power, legitimacy, and authority in different contexts.[38] Numerous examples bear this out. From Bosnia to Egypt to India, or even evangelical Christians in the United States, religion has served as a force for mobilization toward social and political change, the assertion and reconfiguration of power, some measure of self-determination, or even outright secession.[39] Southeast Asia has not been immune to these trends. In fact, there is

---

[36] John Langan, "Nationalism, Ethnic Conflict, and Religion," *Theological Studies*, Vol. 56, No. 1, March 1995, p. 122.

[37] Donald L. Horowitz, *Ethnic Groups in Conflict*. Berkeley, CA.: University of California Press, 2000, p. 50.

[38] See, for instance, Paul R. Brass, *Language, Religion and Politics in North India*. New York: Cambridge University Press, 1974; Lucian Pye and Mary W. Pye, *Asian Power and Politics: The Cultural Dimensions of Authority*. Cambridge, MA.: Harvard University Press, 1985; Donald Swearer, *The Buddhist World of Southeast Asia*. New York: State University of New York Press, 2010. An entire academic journal, *Politics and Religion*, has been created to explore this theme.

[39] Likewise, nationalism cast in religious terms is a common theme in many non-Western countries, as their modern national identities and nationalist movements were suffused with religious myth and narrative, symbolism and ritual. This has been the case in Iran, Israel, Pakistan, Palestine, and India, to name a few.

substantial evidence indicating that religion plays a considerable role in Southeast Asian society and politics today.[40] These trends are also evident in a number of quantitative surveys undertaken in recent times. As but one example, according to the Pew Survey titled "The World's Muslims: Religion, Politics and Society," 86 percent of Muslims in Malaysia, 77 percent in Thailand, and 72 percent in Indonesia favor some degree of *shari'a* as the law of the land.[41] While no equivalent survey on Buddhist political engagement in Southeast Asia is available, it would be of interest to note that in Thailand, pressure has increased from certain quarters for the secular state to declare Buddhism the official state religion, while in Myanmar (Burma), activist Buddhist social movements have coalesced to form the National Development Party to contest in recent elections amidst a newfound climate of political freedom.[42] In the Philippines, Roman Catholic lobby groups almost succeeded in blocking the passage of a reproductive health bill designed to encourage responsible parenting and reduce poverty through the sanctioning of abortion, an act condemned by the Roman Catholic Church.[43] Even in Indonesia, where the post-independence state has to some extent overcome the fragmented character of Indonesian society through its manufacturing of a common unifying ideology known as Pancasila, residual faultlines remain that have been animated by religious identity even as conservative Islamic groups dominate public discussion in ways incommensurate to their actual numbers.[44]

The ontological and epistemological problems associated with much of received wisdom on the topic of religion and its relation to politics that arise from Western intellectual traditions such as those discussed earlier allow our discussion to segue into the concept of religious nationalism. To that end, the next section addresses two specific questions: with regards to conceptions of nationhood, how do religion and nationalism constitute

[40] See Andrew C. Willford and Kenneth M. George (eds.), *Spirited Politics: Religion and Public Life in Contemporary Southeast Asia*. Ithaca, N.Y.: Cornell University Press, 2005.

[41] The results of the survey can be obtained from: www.pewforum.org/2013/04/30/the-worlds-muslims-religion-politics-society-overview/ (accessed November 7, 2013). It should be noted that Malaysia is ranked below only Afghanistan (99 percent), Iraq (91 percent), and the Palestinian territories (89 percent). It is also ranked above Pakistan (84 percent). Indonesia is ranked higher than Jordan (71 percent) and Tunisia (56 percent), and only slightly below Egypt (74 percent).

[42] Seth Mydans, "Thailand Set to Make Buddhism the State Religion," *New York Times*, May 24, 2007; Phyo Thiha Cho, "Burma's New Nationalist Party Surges into Election Race," *The Irrawaddy*, October 29, 2015. Available www.irrawaddy.org/election/feature/burmas-new-nationalist-party-surges-into-election-race.

[43] Liz Ford, "Philippines: Where Catholics, Condoms and Conservatism Collide over Health," *The Guardian*, May 30, 2013.

[44] As Chapter 5 will argue, even the "secular" nature ascribed to Pancasila is itself questionable.

each other, and how should we understand this phenomenon of religious nationalism?

Nationalism

This book maintains that nationalism is an ideology based on principles of unity and identity that are constructed, or as Benedict Anderson describes it, "imagined," in the course of the formation of the nation.[45] The nation, furthermore, is taken to mean a collective people who share a sense of solidarity based on either all or some of the following: a common culture, history, religious faith, and language, and that usually (though not always), inhabit a defined territory. On the basis of this identity, nations are further defined at least in part by their belief in a right to express themselves in institutional form as a state within this territory, although, as we shall discuss later, there are also many instances where nations exist in the sense that a collective identity has been formed, but do not find institutional expression in the form of the creation of a coterminous state.

Most students of nationalism will agree that there are essentially three main schools of thought on how the nation comes into being – primordialist, perennialist, and modern. Primordialists suggest that nations are an extension of intrinsic and natural configurations of communities. Proponents of this school of thought often point to cultural attachments such as kinship, custom, and language as elemental categories that override civil and political ties. Primordialist theorists such as Anthony Smith and Adrian Hastings see these as immutable markers of identity from which a nation is formed. For primordialists, these markers are a given. Much in the same vein, perennialists argue that the nation is not exclusively modern but has existed since antiquity as either recurrent or continuous manifestations, of which the nation-state is but a modern iteration.[46]

In sharp contrast to either the primordialist or perennialist schools, modernist theories of the nation suggest that it is an entirely modern construct whose emergence can be placed within a specific historical context, namely, the cultural, political, and social development of the Western (European) world of the 18th and 19th centuries. According to modernists, nations and nationalism are recent and novel products of modernization and the conditions that define it. Aside from locating the

---

[45] An extensive and easily accessible discussion of the range of definitions of nationalism can be found on www.nationalismproject.org.
[46] Perennialists, however, distinguish themselves from their primordialist cousins by giving greater credence to history, while in the process critiquing their counterparts for being reductive and ahistorical in their analysis.

rise of nationalism on the timeline of European history, modernists also take into account cultural and technological revolutions brought about by industrialization, mass education, and progressive ideals of equality, secularism, and individualism. Hence, modernists do not merely place the emergence of nationalism against a linear timeline; they also locate it within the sociological context of unprecedented social, economic, and ideological change. It is by this token that Ernest Gellner, one of the chief advocates of modernist conceptions of the nation, distinguishes agrarian from modern societies, and argues that agrarian societies are not nations because of the existence of a less literate low culture given to the draw of kinship.[47] For Gellner, a nation can only develop when a society is levelled through cultural equity, and this is brought about by education. Gellner's conception of the nation is therefore deeply wedded to modernist assumptions of equality and mobility, which he suggests can only be observed in modern societies with the attendant ideological and social reformations such as mass education, something inconceivable in the past.

In much the same way, Benedict Anderson, the architect of the idea that the nation is an "imagined" community and a cultural artefact, focuses on the technological revolutions of the modern era – the rise of print media, production of modern maps, creation of the census, and so on – to press home the point that modern technology was instrumental for the process of imagination to take root. These vehicles of mobilization bind groups of people together within the parameters of territorial sovereignty and legal-political configurations of statehood such that they can indulge in a specific yet diffused nationalist ideology.

Compared to Gellner's treatment of nationalism, however, Anderson's cultural constructivist approach is relatively better equipped to reconcile primordialist factors such as religion and ethnicity with its modernist assumptions, although Anderson presciently stresses that these qualities are constructed rather than immutable.[48] Nevertheless, Anderson also maintained that the existence of such factors alone do not account for the conceptualization of a nation or the rise of nationalism. What is required is the means through which a nation can be constructed or imagined by a

---

[47] For a thorough and insightful treatment of Gellner's contribution to the study of nationalism, see Brendan O'Leary, "On the Nature of Nationalism: An Appraisal of Ernest Gellner's Writings on Nationalism," *British Journal of Political Science*, Vol. 27, No. 2, 1997, pp. 191–222.

[48] However, Anderson's explicit engagement with religion is still remarkably thin despite recognizing its role in the inception of the modern state. See Mark Hamilton, "New Imaginings: The Legacy of Benedict Anderson and Alternative Engagements of Nationalism," *Studies in Ethnicity and Nationalism*, Vol. 6, No. 3, December 2006, pp. 73–89.

collective that would otherwise have little in common: ergo, the catalytic effect of print capitalism.[49]

Obviously, modernist theories of nationalism challenge the primordial and perennial conceptions of nationhood with their suggestion that a nation, unlike any other social configuration that came before it, arose out of specific circumstances associated with modern political life and the conditions of modernity. Not dissimilar to the modernist notions of religion discussed earlier, nationalism spread across the globe through the vehicle of Western (European) colonialism and imperialism. Yet the modernist conception of the nation is not without its detractors either, including ripostes from scholars of primordialist and perennialist persuasion. Among the more prominent is Anthony Smith, who criticized the notion of a modern nation as yet another "myth" borne out of a partial and occluded vantage point, which he argues highlights an instrumentalism which regards cultural attributes as malleable and subject to the manipulation of vested interests.[50] Though Smith also distances himself from an extreme primordialist or perennialist account of the nation insofar as their ahistoricalism is concerned, he nonetheless shares most of their underlying assumptions, namely the elemental categories of cultural attachments such as race, religion, and language which are presumed to be enduring.[51]

Smith counters constructivist accounts of the nation by arguing that though modern, nations ultimately rest on a pre-modern, shared cultural past. These pre-modern traits form the basis of what he terms *ethnies* – communities who possess shared traits that go on to form the nation. In so doing, he sidesteps to some extent allegations of ahistoricity and proposes to provide an "evolutionary" modernist explanation in contradistinction to Anderson or Gellner's "revolutionary" modernist explanations for the nation.[52] The difference, according to Smith, lies in the fact that while

---

[49] As a Southeast Asianist, Anderson's theory has elicited much interest among scholars working on the region. To that effect, there are echoes of these processes of construction and negotiation, for instance, in how the "Islamic state" conceptualized by Malaysian and Indonesian Islamists is imagined, constructed, and (re)negotiated to account for non-Muslims that would come under its jurisdiction should such an entity come into being in their respective countries, or how predominantly Christian Karen nationalism in Myanmar had to be reconsidered in light of increasingly assertive demonstrations of religious identity among Karen Buddhists.

[50] See Anthony D. Smith, "The Myth of the 'Modern Nation' and the Myths of Nations," *Ethnic and Racial Studies*, Vol. 11, No. 1, 1988, p. 126.

[51] See Anthony D. Smith, *The Antiquity of Nations*. Cambridge: Polity Press, 2004.

[52] In contrast, Samah Sabra suggests that Gellner and Anderson posit a "social evolutionary" conception of the emergence of nations given their view that nations are produced by necessary social-cultural changes. See Samah Sabra, "Imagining Nations: An Anthropological Perspective," *Nexus*, Vol. 20, 2007, p. 78.

the nation may be a modern phenomenon, it is dependent on "the much longer time-spans of pre-modern *ethnies*, and the survival of ethnic ties and ethnic mosaics from these periods into the modern world."[53] In short, the nation is not a wholly modern construct as it requires pre-modern ethnic elements and is almost always founded on older *ethnies*.[54]

Notwithstanding their glaring disagreements, there are aspects of both modernist and primordialist accounts of nationalism that are in fact compatible. Needless to say, one such area is the place accorded to religion in their explanatory framework. Religion, whether in its abstract or institutional form, is clearly muted in the key modernist literature, and to some extent in their primordialist foils as well. This reflects the dominance of modernist influences among scholars of nationalism, even among some who are of the primordialist persuasion. One of the reasons for this must stem from the tendency, discussed earlier, to bracket out religion in contrast to "modern" features of contemporary society. This being the case, to further our discussion on the role that religion plays in the formation of the nation, it is important to re-examine the notion of modernity and its ontological assumptions. It is to this that we now turn.

Beyond the Primordialist–Modernist Divide: Religion as Ascriptive Identity and Alternative Modernity

The epistemological tension that exists between revolutionary modernist and evolutionary primordialist theories of the nation centers on the conception of modernity, specifically a singular and biased Eurocentric (or Western-centric) model of modernity. Revolutionary modernist theorists place great purchase on functionalist conditions of modernity such as print media or mass education, which are assumed to unite a diverse populace through the creation and perpetuation of a civic identity while paying scant regard to pre-existing (as opposed to pre-modern) identities based on ethnicity, religion, or language. However, this process, or what Smith refers to as the "revolutionary" break from which modern civic nationalism develops, cannot account for and renders much difficulty in explaining the presence of competing communities within modern

---

[53] Anthony D. Smith, *The Ethnic Origins of Nations*. Oxford: Blackwell, 1988, p. 10.
[54] At this juncture, it should be noted that much of the debate in nationalism studies focuses on the place of ethnic identity, and not religion per se. Indeed, the factor of religion has been conspicuous in its absence in contemporary studies on nationalism and nation building, despite the fact that even modernist theorists would concede that the European tradition of state building owed much to the influence of religion. Nevertheless, some of the assumptions do apply quite easily to attempts to conceptualize the place of religion in conceptions of the nation.

nation-states today, including competing religiously defined communities that attempt to renegotiate, resist, and/or reject the dominant parameters of nationhood.

Yet on the other hand, Smith's theory of the nation, which sets great store by the notion of *ethnies* as an ontological, unchanging reality, and which favors certain types of societal configurations above others, is equally limited in its explanatory power, particularly given its inability to account for functionalist and ascriptive aspects of national identity building, or, for that matter in regards specifically to religion, how confessional faith complicates the identity and status of *ethnies* through the vehicles of proselytization and conversion.[55] In the main, to the extent that they deal with religion at all, primordialist sociological accounts tend simplistically to cast it as a sacred foundational pillar upon which ethnic identity is established, rather than an outcome of the process of identity construction from which religious identity is ascribed as a form of nationalism.[56]

The intent here is not to wade too far into meandering debates on which theory of nationalism is right. The purpose of this survey of the dominant schools of thought on nationalism is to make the case that when one conceptualizes religious nationalism, as the following section will do, it is imperative to consider how both visions of the nation – whether primordialist or modern, ethnic or civic – are constructed, conceptualized, and, oftentimes, conflicted. This is because ethnic and civic definitions of the nation are in their abstract form polar extremes, and more often than not nations would fall in between them on the definitional spectrum with respect to how they (the "nation") came into being. To that end, a key point of departure here is that the role of religion in the conception of nationhood should not be presumed to be something that is pre-existing or immutable, as the primordialist might claim, or whose mobilising efficacy is readily self-evident. Nor, at the same time, should it be willy-nilly inferred that features of collective identity around which notions of nationhood are constructed have declined in the wake of modernity's onslaught, as the modernist would have it.

Indeed, the tendency among many scholars to assume religious nationalism to be inherently hostile to the secular nation-state and to modernity in general is erroneous. Religious nationalism, as the later part of this chapter will argue, can exist in patently "modernist" form in how they accept and acknowledge the legitimacy of the modern nation-state and

---

[55] For further discussion on the problems of both perspectives, see Paul Lawrence, *Nationalism: History and Theory*. Harlow: Pearson Education Limited, 2005.
[56] Adrian Hastings, *The Construction of Nationhood: Ethnicity, Religion, and Nationalism*. Cambridge: Cambridge University Press, 1997.

are sympathetic to the development of modern statehood. The key to understanding this aspect of religious nationalism is, first of all, to see religion as a matter of ascriptive meaning, "perpetuated through narratives about difference from, conflict with, and resistance to the oppression of some specific Other, (and) not only the theologies of nationhood, that help us to understand how communities that belong to the same religious tradition have come to view each other as Other."[57]

By way of the above observations, it stands to reason that in order for religion to be examined as a social and constructed category whose manifestations change over time and context, and whose continuous engagement with conceptions of nationhood and national consciousness manifests through the different types and adaptations of (and at times, competing) nationalisms, we need first to transcend the skewed representations of Eurocentric theory that conceive of nationalisms elsewhere in the world as little more than distorted extensions of their European counterparts. Instead, it behooves to explore the possibility that other societies might have their own identity and national forms and processes that incorporate social categories of religion as *complicit configurations, rather than an outright rejection, of the modern nation.*[58] Further, we should also examine how this identity, which underpins the concept of the nation, changes over time, is contingent on how the nation understands itself throughout history, and the process through which separate identities which exclude others developed and congealed.

To unpack the heavily skewed assumptions of modernity that inform much of received wisdom on nationalism and national identity building, the work of S.N. Eisenstadt provides valuable insights and reference points. In contrast to classical theories of modernization which predicted that the convergence of industrial societies in the mid-20th century would usher in a cultural program of modernity as developed in modern Europe and later spread throughout the world, Eisenstadt proposed on the contrary that since the Second World War, structural differentiations across nations have in fact varied to great enough extents so as to "(give) rise to multiple institutional and ideological patterns."[59] In the main,

---

[57] Ibid., pp. 30–31. Ironically, while Hastings would stand in the primordialist camp, by according salience to narratives – stories as opposed to some presumed "reality," he seems to entertain some measure of a constructivist understanding of nationhood.

[58] For instance, Bruce Robertson writes of how Hindu nationalists chose to adapt their religious beliefs to new cognitive procedures and intellectual styles rather than be "swept aside" by the tide of modernity in the form of European colonialism. See Bruce Carlisle Robertson (ed.), *The Essential Writings of Raja Rammohan Ray*. Delhi: Oxford University Press, 1999.

[59] Shmuel N. Eisenstadt, "Introduction" in S.N. Eisenstadt (ed.), *Multiple Modernities*. New Brunswick, N.J.: Transaction Publishers, 2002, p. 2.

Eisenstadt points to the ambivalence of many post-colonial nations toward Western models as exemplary world systems on one hand, and the violent memory of colonial rule on the other. As a consequence, competing cultural and social systems adapted to the modern framework and generated different programs of modernity based on unique social, ontological, and political dynamics. Herein lies a crucial point: modernity and Westernization are not necessarily synonymous, and Western patterns of modernity are not the only "authentic" modernities, notwithstanding their historical precedence. For Eisenstadt, it is out of this interaction that the core characteristics of modern political institutions arise, such as the restructuring of centre–periphery relations as the principal focus of political dynamics in modern societies; a strong tendency toward politicizing the demands of various sectors of society and the conflicts between them; and a continuing struggle over the definition of "the realm of the political."[60]

Eisenstadt's recasting of modernity poses an epistemological challenge to modernist theories of nationalism. This is arguably evident in the small but growing literature on "Asian" nationalism.[61] By arguing that modernity is not an inevitable outcome of historical evolution (as proposed by the "end of history and the last man" thesis in the book carrying the same title) but rather of a process of negotiation and contestations in which stakeholders of a society engage in, he challenges linear renditions of Eurocentric modernist theory that underpin much of the modernist theorizing on nationalism.[62]

This paradigmatic shift proposed by Eisenstadt allows us to consider how religious groups and identities have arisen to contest, negotiate, and challenge the prevailing conception of the nation-state by opening the way to alternative conceptions of nationhood, not as resistance to modernity, but, on the contrary, as an integral part of a distinctly "modern" project of conceptualizing the nation. This logic resonates with what Gert Pickel considers "contextual secularisation," which he suggests transcends secularization or religion in terms of their relevance or irrelevance for our understanding of modern society, and instead talks about the "different constellations (that) lead to multiple religious vitalities and variations

---

[60] S.N. Eisenstadt, "Multiple Modernities," *Daedalus*, Vol. 129, No. 1, Winter 2000, p. 6.
[61] Albeit, much of this literature also confines the discussion to nationalism defined as the anti-colonial forces that ultimately won over or inherited the colonial state. See Partha Chaatterjee, *The Nation and Its Fragments: Colonial and Postcolonial Histories*. Princeton, N.J.: Princeton University Press, 1993; Stein Tonnesson and Hans Antlov (eds.), *Asian Forms of the Nation*. London: Curzon, 1996; Michael Leifer (ed.), *Asian Nationalism*. London: Routledge, 2000.
[62] Francis Fukuyama, *The End of History and the Last Man*. New York: Free Press, 1992.

in the timing of secularization."[63] Contextualization brings into greater relief the histories, politics, and identities of the societies being studied, and points not to the irrelevance of secularization or religion, but the "different constellations that lead to multiple religious vitalities and variations in the timing of secularization."[64]

According to the above logic, religion was not merely replaced by secular nationalism in a linear sequence as modernists argue, nor was it an immutable, atavistic feature of the *ethnies* which eventually formed nations as primordialists would maintain. Rather, it frames and shapes the collective identities and boundaries of a community, much in the way that alternative modernities are identified by Eisenstadt, and hence is mutually imbricated with nationalism. In fact, it is this interaction that has prompted Bryan Turner to point out the irony behind "secular" nationalism, in how it was originally suffused with the religious:

Nationalism became the underlying cultural principle of nation states, and religious identity became the core of national culture, because religion often provided the powerful symbols and rituals required by national sentiment. Language is obviously crucial to the creation of an 'imagined community' but often the national language of a community is preserved by its religious institutions.[65]

Others have gone further, contending that the rise of national identity and nationalism can in and of themselves be considered forms of sacralization, thereby testifying to the endurance of religious consciousness.[66]

Here, then, is where we find conflict and contestation purportedly waged in the name of timeless religion but in actual fact rooted in historically contingent narratives of difference, conflict, and resistance that result when faith meets, and animates, faultlines created via the process of the conceptualization of nationhood.

---

[63] Gert Pickel, "Contextual Secularization – Theoretical Thoughts and Empirical Implications," *Religion and Society in Central and Eastern Europe*, Vol. 4, No. 1, 2011.

[64] Ibid., p. 3.

[65] Bryan Turner, "Religious Nationalism, Globalisation and Empire" keynote address at the Conference on Transnational Religions: Intersections of the 'Global' and 'Local', Cambridge, July 19–20, 2004. Others who have argued for the religious origins of Western secular states include Reinhard Bendix, *Kings or People: Power and the Mandate to Rule*. Berkeley: University of California Press, 1978; W. G. McLoughlin, *Revivals, Awakenings, and Reform: An Essay on Religion and Social Change in America, 1607–1977*. Chicago: University of Chicago Press, 1978; Peter Harrison, *The Bible, Protestantism, and the Rise of Natural Science*. Cambridge: Cambridge University Press, 1998.

[66] See Timothy Crippen, "Old and New Gods in the Modern World: Toward a Theory of Religious Transformation," *Social Forces*, Vol. 67, No. 2, 1988, pp. 316–336. This view has been advanced by Josep Llobera, who points out that modern nationalism not only has all the trappings and rituals of a religion, but also, like religion, has tapped into the emotional reservoir of human beings and operates at the level of deep elemental emotional attachments. See Josep Llobera, *The God of Modernity*. Providence, R.I.: Berg, 1994.

The Legitimacy Question: Nations without States

Beyond the need to interrogate assumptions about modernity in the dominant paradigms of nationalism studies, there is another conundrum that confronts the current literature which warrants further scrutiny for our analytical purposes. This regards how the study of nationalism has for the most part privileged the sovereign nation-state, and the logic underlying its creation, as its main point of inquiry.

A prevailing, if implicit, assumption in the conventional study of nationalism, whether in its primordial or modern form, is that its ultimate objective is to create a sovereign territorial state. While this may be the intention or outcome of many a nationalist movement, the assumption itself obscures the fact that nationalism can also find expression via other outcomes short of the actual agitation for the creation of a sovereign state. One illustration of this dynamic is what M. Montserrat Guibernau terms "nations without states."[67] Through a detailed study of Quebec, Scotland, Catalonia, and Basque, Guibernau identified how nations once expressed as separate political units are today renegotiating and asserting their status as "independent" nations but within the context of the territorial state.[68] That is to say, while these nations develop strong regional identities, they do not represent a challenge to the official conception of national identity, or even to the territorial integrity of the nation-state. Concomitantly, two important observations flow from this: first, nationhood represents something deeper than mere membership in a territorial state, and second, nationhood and statehood may not necessarily be correlated or synonymous. Indeed, it is often the absence of congruence between nationhood and statehood which prompts nationalists to seek a legitimation of the political nation's distinctive identity by emphasizing specific religious and/or ethnic referents.[69] All this implies that aside from being a source of political identity, nationalism also plays a role in the maintaining and negotiating of legitimacy.

What distinguishes nationalism emanating from "nations without states" with that which is more commonly identified with the creation of a sovereign territorial state is the fact that the former is more concerned for the legitimacy of the state in terms of access (or lack thereof) to and equitable distribution of power and resources commanded by it

---

[67] M. Montserrat Guibernau, *Nations without States*. Cambridge: Polity Press, 1999.

[68] There certainly is no shortage of Asian examples either, as the histories of Myanmar and India will attest. In Myanmar especially, the central state has to contend with up to thirty different ethnic communities who are seeking to have their interests accommodated within the emergent democratic state.

[69] F.M. Barnard, "National Culture and Political Legitimacy: Herder and Rousseau," *Journal of the History of Ideas*, Vol. 44, No. 2, April–June 1983, p. 231.

(the state) rather than the creation of a sovereign state itself, through separatism or irredentism. After all, being a passport-carrying member of a state should ipso facto accord one constitutional rights and privileges. Ergo, nationalism can be expressed in relation to those rights, as interpreted from the vantage of a "nation" within a state that consciously identifies itself along ethnic, cultural, religious, or linguistic lines as distinct from other nations within the state. Oftentimes, such "sub-state" nationalisms contest not the territorial integrity of the state, but rather issues of public policies, representation, and distributive equality, all of which are issues of concern for "nations without states."[70] In this manner, nationalism can also be conceived of as a form of agitation for any variation of political rights that is referenced to collective identity and conceived as the right of the said collective (the "nation"), yet short of separate statehood.[71]

In juxtaposition with the above perspective, nationalism can also find expression as a desire for institutions of the state to reflect, defend, and perpetuate identity signifiers such as religion, language, and ethnicity. This arises from the fact that not infrequently, nationalists have sought to enshrine distinct cultural values in the state, in the process deliberately discriminating in favor of those with which they share cultural affinity, for example, co-ethnics or co-religionists, and against others.[72] In this sense, nationalism can take the form of expressions of loyalty to the state by claiming to defend its institutions, particularly those institutions that serve to perpetuate the identity of the (dominant or majoritarian) nation. At its extreme, nationalism in this form transforms the affirmation of collective dignity into a proclamation of cultural superiority, and is correspondingly accompanied by majoritarian demands that minorities acknowledge particular religious or ethnic identities as such (i.e., "superior") prior to acceptance as part of a political community.

Scholars of comparative politics often talk of legitimacy as the right to rule. But, the point of the above discussion is to highlight the fact that issues of legitimacy also bear on the question of collective identity and belonging, and vice-versa. This implies that conceptions of nationhood have something to say about legitimacy. In its most rudimentary form, legitimacy can be understood as the acceptance on the part of a collective

---

[70] See, for instance, Daniel Béland and André Lecours, "Sub-state Nationalism and the Welfare State: Québec and Canadian Federalism," *Nations and Nationalism*, Vol. 12, No. 1, 2006.
[71] Alternatively, the objective of sovereign statehood – separatism – could be a last resort after all other attempts at carving out political space have faltered.
[72] See Jack L. Snyder, *From Voting to Violence: Democratization and Nationalist Conflict*. New York: W.W. Norton & Company, 2000, pp. 22–23.

that their will and concerns can be represented by a political body, even in the event that the final decisions of this body may not always accord with the desires of the said collective.[73] However, in order for this notion of legitimacy to hold, it presupposes the existence of a more fundamental premise of identity, which then translates to loyalty. In the words of Rousseau, it has to be predicated on some "union of origin, interest, or convention" in order to work.[74] At the core of whether something is deemed legitimate or not is the matter of the identification of the collective with the state, and this can be rooted in a common culture or identity. Concomitantly, it stands to reason that the "nation," in this sense, is at least in part constituted by the existence not just of shared identity, but shared concerns, and by extension, nationalism speaks to the relationship that the collective shares with the state which is supposed to represent its will.

This leads to several obvious questions: what happens when people cannot identify with the political institutions of a state because of perceived discrimination on grounds of identity, culture, or for the purpose of our discussion, religion? What if these institutions are not neutral, in the sense that they are designed to privilege one intemperate group over another who define their core collective identity in reference to language, ethnicity, or religion, thereby abetting majoritarianism pursued at the expense of those who do not fit an ethnic or religious profile? The outcome of such tension, as Jack Snyder warns in his evaluation of the process of democratization as a source of political violence, is the risk of conflict: "nationalist conflicts arise as a by-product of elites' efforts to persuade the people to accept divisive nationalist ideas."[75]

What is Religious Nationalism?

From Ireland to Sri Lanka to the former Yugoslavia, numerous conflicts have had – and continue to have – elements of the religious and the nationalist play out in them. In many of these cases, conflict groups can be quite easily differentiated by their confessional faiths and identities because of how they have mobilized, but at the same time their ultimate ends can be avowedly nationalist in terms of agitating for recognition and

---

[73] In the sense that it is highly unlikely a government will be able to please its population each and every time they formulate and implement a policy, even segments of the population that are staunchly supportive of it.
[74] Jean Jacques Rousseau, "On the Social Contract," in Donald A. Cress (ed.), *Basic Political Writings*. Indianapolis, IN.: Hackett, 1987, p. 169.
[75] Snyder, *From Voting to Violence*, p. 32.

legitimacy as a nation within a state, or even seeking to be ruled under a different flag altogether.

This tension between faith and flag has been at the heart of many of the most intractable internal conflicts, some of exceedingly violent nature, for a long time. Yet, as the earlier discussion surveying the current literature on nationalism foregrounded, for all the contemporary interest it elicits, religion remains little more than an oblique reference in the larger discussions on nationalism.[76] How does one de-mystify religion while bringing into sharper focus the ascriptive nature of national identity defined with reference to religion? To consider this, we turn to the works of Clifford Geertz and Peter van der Veer, while at the same time recalling aspects of the tension between primordial permanence on one hand and modernist malleability on the other in the earlier discussions on the concept of nationalism.

Clifford Geertz defined culture as "a historically transmitted pattern of meanings embodied in symbols, a system of inherited conceptions expressed in symbolic forms by means of which men communicate, perpetuate, and develop their knowledge about and attitudes toward life."[77] Extrapolating from this, it should not be a surprise to find proponents of religiously characterized nationalist movements, such as advocates of modern-day Zionism or the Hindutva movement in India for instance, or, for our purposes, Malay nationalism in Thailand and Bangsamoro nationalism in the Philippines, embracing this while laboring both the "natural" contiguity of their religiously constituted nation as a territorial state, and the immutability of their narratives of identity, by espousing a radical particularism derived from religion.[78] Peter van der Veer,

---

[76] There are possible exceptions, though, if one interrogates some assumptions made in the literature. For example, in terms of belief systems, Smith alludes to its role in the formation of nations, specifically in how both imbue a sacred purpose in the people. See Anthony D. Smith, *Chosen Peoples: Sacred Sources of National Identity*. Oxford: Oxford University Press, 2003. Indeed, he makes a convincing case that in constructing a group identity, religious ideologies "homogenize (the community) and differentiate it" from all others. This happens on account of his emphasis on sacred beliefs and rituals, and "the very core of traditional religions, their conception of the sacred and their rites of salvation" (p. 15). Even then, it can be argued that, Smith's interest lies more in religion's functional contents – in its body of ideas, beliefs, and theologies of belonging – than its mobilizational possibilities and, critically for us, its potential as ascribed identity. See Sinisa Malesevic, *Identity as Ideology: Understanding Ethnicity and Nationalism*. New York: Palgrave MacMillan, 2006, p. 125. See also David Little, "Belief, Ethnicity, and Nationalism," *Nationalism and Ethnic Politics*, Vol. 1, No. 2, Summer 1995. Smith notwithstanding, the pertinent point is that for the most part, religion remains silenced in the study of nationalism.

[77] Clifford Geertz, *The Interpretation of Cultures*. New York: Basic Books, 1973, p. 89.

[78] See Peter van der Veer, *Religious Nationalism: Hindus and Muslims in India*. Berkeley, CA.: University of California Press, 1994, pp. 194–198.

however, has criticized conceptions of religious nationalism that rest on "primordial attachments" perpetuated by the colonial sociological enterprise. Instead, he holds to the idea that religious nationalism, as with most other sociological and political phenomenon, is a function of time and space, of changing contexts and identities.[79]

One arena where religion can feature prominently is in debates over the nature and basis of national community, especially when "religiosity and patriotism become intertwined when individuals come to associate religious expression with the character of their country."[80] Because it is commonly accepted that nations are characterized by boundaries that define a group and differentiate it from others since "groups tend to define themselves not by reference to their own characteristics but by exclusion, that is by comparison to strangers," it stands to reason that religion is an important component of such differentiation in how it can provide a reference point for an in-group and an out-group in the conception of nationhood.[81] Indeed, this would lie at the heart of any rudimentary definition of religious nationalism.

Building on this characterization, religion offers an institutionally and culturally specific way to organize this modern form of collective representation (granted its viability is understandably dependent on whether the collective share a common religious referent). In this manner, religious nationalism does not change the form of collective representation; it inhabits existent forms, filling them with new cultural content and new sources of authority.[82] Put another way, if nationalism expresses that a nation is conceived on the basis of culturally and historically constituted characteristics, and the state exists as a political expression of this conception, then religious nationalism locates such collective solidarity in religious faith (as opposed to a social contract enacted by abstract individual citizens) and describes the aspiration of people heavily imbued with a sense of, specifically, a common religious identity for political self-determination or rights backed up with the assertion that a nation is, or should be, premised on and articulated with primarily religious

---

[79] Ibid.
[80] Matthew Wright and Tim Reeskens, "The Pious Patriot: Establishing and Explaining the Link Between Religiosity and National Pride Among European Mass Publics." Paper presented at the 19th International Conference of the Council for European Studies, Boston, MA., March 22–24, 2012, p. 5.
[81] Cited in John A. Armstrong, *Nations Before Nationalism*. Chapel Hill, N.C.: University of North Carolina Press, 1982, p. 5.
[82] Religious nationalism, however, should not be mistaken for religious fundamentalism; while the latter seeks to conform the government to religious dictates, the former is targeted at some religious minority and has a communitarian and territorial logic at its core. See Roger Friedland, "Religious Nationalism and the Problem of Collective Representation," *Annual Review of Sociology*, Vol. 27, 2001, pp. 139–140.

referents. Hence, one can surmise that religious nationalism rests on the claims that: (i) religion can be a vital feature of the identity of a collective that seeks to conceive of themselves as a nation, (ii) religion can form the basis for the creation of a state, and (iii) religion provides an important source of legitimacy for that state.[83] With regard to these three claims, Barbara-Ann Reiffer elaborates with insight:

> It is a community of religious people or the political movement of a group of people heavily influenced by religious beliefs who aspire to be politically self-determining. In many cases, they desire some type of self-government for the national group and that their own independent political unit (state, region, and so on) be influenced or governed according to religious beliefs. In religious national movements, the influence of religious beliefs, ideas, symbols and leaders is essential to the development and success of the national movement in a particular territory. In these cases, religion is so important to the nationalist movement that it adopts religious language and modes of religious communication, builds on the religious identity of a community, cloaks itself in the religion and relies on the assistance of religious leaders and institutions to promote its cause. Furthermore, when a religious national movement is successful in obtaining some form of political autonomy, often the religious beliefs will be institutionalized in laws or procedures governing the region.[84]

In sum, religious nationalism is a condition where religious identity and nationalism are blended together, resulting in a situation where religious groups are bent on asserting their presence toward the ends of establishing or defending their own conception of nationhood in religious terms. Correspondingly, religious conflicts arise when such assertions are met with resistance or opposition by other groups within the territorial state or, indeed, by the state itself.

What accounts for the relative ease with which religious and national identity hew together conceptually? According to Franz Hoppenbrouwers, this can be attributed to the fact that both share a number of characteristics in common in terms of structures, functions, and content: they foster social homogenization, peace, order, and unity, and claim to follow the example of venerated predecessors (saints or national heroes).[85] Both religious and nationalist organizations alike advocate an egalitarian society (at least in theory), but at the same time, their view of the world is paternalistic and hierarchical. What results is a condition whereby both religious and nationalist movements ascribe to themselves the role of

---

[83] See Friedland, "Religious Nationalism and the Problem of Collective Representation," pp. 125–152.
[84] Barbara-Ann J. Rieffer, "Religion and Nationalism: Understanding the Consequences of a Complex Relationship," *Ethnicities*, Vol. 3, No. 2, 2003, p. 225.
[85] See Frans Hoppenbrouwers, "Winds of Change: Religious Nationalism in a Transformation Context," *Religion, State and Society*, Vol. 30, No. 4, 2002.

interpreter or teacher of an "ultimate truth" for all.[86] Religion and nationalism also resemble one another in structure. Both construct an "inner force" to define the essence of faith or nation, which then encounters resistance from enemies in the outside world, thereby further facilitating the construction of identity on the basis of difference from a presumed "other."[87] This "inner force" has an authoritative, tradition-oriented interpretation, derived from religious clerics or indigenous culture, and therefore both religion and nationalism provide social and psychological guidelines and ideological motivation.

Religious Nationalism as National Identity

Roger Friedland contends that religious nationalism can be understood as "a culture's autonomy manifested in the formation of politicized religious groups and a source of identity," albeit a limited one.[88] It is limited because institutionalized religion often concurs with the nation as being territorially defined, for it is itself expressed in terms of bounded entities such as religious groups and political parties, transnational concepts such as the "*ummah*" or "universal brotherhood of believers" in Islam or the universal Catholic church (in both its Roman Catholic and ecumenical sense) notwithstanding. This, in turn, rests upon the identification of a particular religious group with a specific culture combined with a claim on national history and heritage.[89] In this manner, "(r)eligion (becomes) a powerful reservoir, as religious revelations are turned into national shrines, religious miracles become national feasts, and holy scriptures are reinterpreted as national epics."[90] Hence, religious motifs and symbols are deep cultural resources that can be mined to provide the basic cultural and ideological building blocks for nationalists.[91]

The construction of such themes to nurture a belief that the nation is inextricably tied to territory and culture is particularly pertinent for current purposes. For instance, Jack Fong finds in his study of Thailand that such social and cultural constructions are useful because they effectively grant for "significant sectors" of the population a chronology based on relations of descent that reinforce a common ancestry, a repository of shared memories, differentiating elements of a

---

[86] Ibid., p. 311. [87] Ibid., p. 312.
[88] Friedland, "Religious Nationalism and the Problem of Collective Representation," p. 130.
[89] Hoppenbrouwers, "Winds of Change," p. 310.
[90] Catarina Kinnvall, "Globalization and Religious Nationalism: Self, Identity, and the Search for Ontological Security," *Political Psychology*, Vol. 25, No. 5, 2004, p. 756.
[91] Rogers Brubaker, "Religion and Nationalism: Four Approaches," *Nations and Nationalism*, Vol. 18, No. 1, 2012, p. 7.

common culture, an association with a homeland and a sense of solidarity, albeit much of this being constructed rather than immutable.[92] Furthermore, since both nationalism and religion are intimately linked to chosen traumas and glories, this link makes for powerful identity signifiers that are more likely to become persuasive rallying points, by virtue of their superior ability to convey unity, security, and inclusiveness in times of crisis, thereby providing meaning and intelligibility which can then facilitate mobilization.[93] Both religion and nationalism appeal to the human urge for identification with movements that transcend the individual, thereby protecting the individual against the most terrifying breakdown of identity by relating the individual to a "memory" shared by a collective.[94]

While the above discussion considers religious nationalism in relation to statehood, it needs to also be emphasized that, as with "nations without states," this is not necessarily the desired endgame of all religious nationalist movements. Religious nationalism can just as well be manifested as an aspiration for some form of recognition for religious identities or traditions within the parameters of an existing state, and it relies on the influence of religious beliefs, ideas, symbols, and leaders for the sustenance and success of such a national movement.

Equally resonant with previous discussions on nationalism is the fact that the logic of religious nationalism also reflects primordialist proclivities, though not necessarily primordialism in its crude sense.[95] Religious nationalists often construct confessional faith and homeland as "immutable" features of identity that lie at the heart of conceptions of nationhood in which the territorialization or institutionalization of this identity is vested. In the process of realizing aspirations for their own regional and local socio-political formations, religious nationalist movements also employ religion to mobilize regional or subregional reactions and resistance to what is seen as an over centralized and hegemonic state (including a colonial state) in order to achieve those ends.[96] This leads Stanley Thambiah to explain that: "(R)eligion is not purely a matter of belief and worship; it also has social-political resonances and communitarian associations.... Similarly, territory has multiple implications,

---

[92] Jack Fong, "Sacred Nationalism: The Thai Monarchy and Primordial Nation Construction," *Journal of Contemporary Asia*, Vol. 39, No. 4, November 2009, pp. 677–679.
[93] Ibid., p. 763.
[94] John A. Armstrong, "Religious Nationalism and Collective Violence," *Nations and Nationalism*, Vol. 3, No. 3, 1997, p. 597.
[95] See Sabina Mihelj, "Faith in Nation Comes in Different Guises: Modernist Versions of Religious Nationalism," *Nations and Nationalism*, Vol. 13, No. 2, 2007.
[96] Stanley J. Tambiah, *Leveling Crowds: Ethnonationalist Conflicts and Collective Violence in South Asia*. Berkeley: University of California Press, 1996, p. 16.

which go beyond spatial location to include charged claims about 'homelands' and 'sons of the soil.'"[97]

At its extreme, religious nationalism often employs the rhetoric that it is the responsibility of the nation to defend its religion. In Judaism, this is legitimated by the claim that each Jewish kingdom had a divine mission to resist organized Christianity, while organized Islamist militancy in the medieval era was a result of intense ethno-religious identification in response to the Crusades.[98] More recent examples include the efforts by the extremist Muslim Sudanese government to suppress the Christian Nilotic group of its southern provinces; and the 1960s Nigerian civil war between the Hausa Muslims and Christian Ibos.[99] In Asia, the Muslim–Christian cleavage, marked by insurgent violence on the part of minorities (Muslims in the southern Philippines, Christians in East Timor) and severe repression by the establishment, remains, as we shall soon see in the following chapters, as sharp as ever; and in India violence took place between the Sikh religious community and the Hindu majority, the latter who claimed that the Hinduvata, as they call Hindu national culture, is the defining characteristic of Indian nationalism.

Religious nationalists therefore employ narratives that speak of the resurgence, perpetuation, or defense of religious identity as vital for the preservation of the nation. Through such narratives, they attempt to either appropriate or reinforce control of the state, or, conversely, seek autonomy or defend (constitutional) rights in cases where the state is ruled by those professing a different faith and, more pertinently, who employ this faith as a basis to govern through religiously defined discriminatory policies.

Religious Nationalism as a Source of Legitimacy

The point has been established previously that aside from providing a basis for ascriptive identity toward the end of creating a nation-state, religious nationalism also provides an important source of legitimacy.

If we accept the view, as Ernest Renan put forward, that the creation of a nation state requires "the actual consent, the desire to live together, the will to preserve worthily the undivided inheritance which has been handed down," then what is of interest here is the absence of such a desire and will (or, at least, the presence of desire and will that is nevertheless equivocal) on the part of certain communities within a territorial

---

[97] Ibid., p. 22.
[98] Armstrong, "Religious Nationalism and Collective Violence," p. 599.
[99] Ibid., p. 603.

nation-state.[100] In the words of Genevieve Zubrzycki, who elaborates the point quite cogently: "Indeed, the creation of national identity through the production of a homogeneous national culture and a master narrative of the nation necessarily implied the repression of alternative memories, discourses, identities, and loyalties."[101] Concomitantly, the contentious process of how nationhood is conceived is defined by how the state uses its power to subdue contending and alternative visions in the process of legitimizing its rule, and how this is being resisted and subverted even after independence.

Bearing this in mind, it can be argued that religion, in this regard, can be used to mobilize popular sentiment behind an existing pattern of social order, or be invoked to challenge and transform it. Either way, it illuminates how religion can frame identities, shape actions, and be used to mobilize masses toward the ends of either reinforcing or undermining the legitimacy of an existing state.[102] At issue is the question of state coercion and favoritism along religious lines, as well as the viability of a religiously based justification for a discriminatory state, as when a regime includes religious law, religious practice, or the religious establishment within a framework of governance that actively sidelines or discriminates against other faith communities. It is in this context that it can be argued nationalism is also an arena of legitimacy contestation between various claimants to religious elements of national identity over what the content of that identity should be, and who gets to define it.[103]

It can be hypothesized that one area where such intrastate contentious politics surfaces is over the issue of whether the national identity of the people within a territorial state, along with their conception of belonging, can legitimately be defined by allegiance to the nation's political creed, for example the constitution, or by other features of identity such as religion – and how this tension is manifested in the process of national identity construction. Presaging later discussions, Indonesia comes immediately to mind, as does Myanmar (Burma), where the more pluralist and, presumably, accommodating civic national ideology of

---

[100] Ernest Renan, "What is a Nation?" in Homi Bhabha (ed.), *Nation and Narration*. London: Routledge, 1990, p. 8.

[101] Zubrzycki, "National Culture," p. 517. See also Prasenjit Duara, *Rescuing History from the Nation: Questioning Narratives of Modern China*. Chicago, IL.: University of Chicago Press, 1995.

[102] Zubrzycki, "Religion and Nationalism," p. 610. Here, it is imperative to bear in mind that groups that mobilize religion to press their goals of self-determination are contesting against territorial states that in many instances were themselves formed in much the same way as a result of earlier nationalist struggles against colonialism.

[103] As Chapter 4 will show, the way non-Muslims are silenced in national discussions over the implementation of Islamic law in Malaysia serves as an obvious case in point.

Pancasila and as encapsulated in the Panglong Agreement, respectively, have periodically (in Myanmar's case, since independence) been contested by religious nationalists with their alternative visions of national identity.[104] This dynamic is evident too in Malaysia, albeit expressed in different forms. Unlike in Indonesia and Myanmar, where the central state is premised supposedly on civic conceptions of the nation at least in theory, in Malaysia the state is very much inclined toward the assertive primacy of one ethnicity and religion, much to the consternation of its minority populations who contest state encroachment on their constitutional rights on those terms.

One of the bases upon which the legitimacy claims of religious nationalists rest are the resources that confessional institutions bring to bear to the conceptualization of nationhood. Using the cases of elites and communication channels, John Coakley highlights on how religion in fact provides an organizational base to project national identity.[105] He points out that, first, in terms of the social contribution of religion, it breaks down communication barriers among communities that adhere to the same belief system, thereby providing the impetus for solidarity and a common reference point. Second, religion provides essential organizational resources, such as its ability to act as an effective medium of communication with the masses through religious institutions and leaders. In other words, these organizations possess penetrative power that is essential in the formation of a national identity.[106] Finally, religion further contributes to the development of nationalism by generating new modes of imagining and constructing social and political relationships,

---

[104] Held in February 1947, in the lead-up to Burma's independence, the second Panglong Conference essentially established the basis for the formation of the Union of Burma. During the meeting, Aung San did much to ally lingering fears among ethnic leaders about the possible unequal treatment of minorities in a future Union. Representatives of the Shan States, the Kachin hills, and the Chin hills signaled their willingness to cooperate with the interim Burmese government by signing the final Panglong Agreement on February 12, 1947, and to join a future Union of Burma. The agreement accepted in principle "full autonomy" in internal administration for the Frontier Areas, the colonial term for most of the areas where the country's ethnic minorities lived. The Agreement provided for a representative of the Supreme Council of the United Hill Peoples, an ethnic minority organization representing several groups to be appointed to the Governor's Executive Council and the Frontier Areas brought within the purview of the Executive Council. The Agreement meant that ethnicity had become part of the independence process as the Union of Burma came into being in January 1948.

[105] John Coakley, "Religion and Nationalism in the First World," *Ethnonationalism in the Contemporary World: Walker Connor and the Study of Nationalism*, 2002, p. 213. http://easyweb.easynet.co.uk/conversi/Coakley.pdf.

[106] Ibid., p. 215.

promoting literacy in and standardization of vernacular languages, and bringing polity and culture into a tighter alignment.[107] In addition to the above, religious nationalism also legitimizes by playing an ideological function for the conceptualization of nationhood.[108] During the 18th to 20th centuries, churches played a decisive role in raising both national awareness and through the denominationally colored teaching of religion, history, reading, and writing, churches prepared their members for life in a modernizing society.[109] Consider, too, how outside of Europe, the importance of a religious narrative of nationalism has been evident in the role of Hinduism in the development of Indian nationalism, the role of Judaism in contemporary Israeli nationalism, or, as we shall soon see, the role of Islam in Indonesian and Malay nationalism. This is due in no small part to sacred religious texts also being revered national texts, and religious tradition and ethno-national myth being inextricably intermingled.[110]

Religious Nationalism and Mobilization: The Use of Frames

Having established the conceptual basis for religious nationalism, the discussion moves on now to how it mobilizes. To better understand this process of how religion frames conceptions of nationhood, and the mobilizing outcomes that flow from that, the literature on social movement theory offers important conceptual insights.

Broadly defined, social movements refer to "collective challenges, based on common purposes and social solidarities, in sustained interaction with elites, opponents, and authorities."[111] By this token, nationalist

---

[107] Rogers Brubaker, "Religion and Nationalism: Four Approaches." Available www.ssc net.ucla.edu/soc/faculty/brubaker/Publications/religion_and_nationalism_forthcoming .pdf, pp. 8–9. The promotion of literacy in vernacular languages lays the groundwork for imagining nationhood through the medium of language, while the proliferation of printed material laid the bases for national consciousness by creating unified fields of exchange and communication. It is no surprise, then, that in Southeast Asia, it was religious organizations that stood at the forefront of nationalism in the heyday of anti-colonial struggle. Indeed, while many nationalist struggles in the region were subsequently won by secular nationalists, the movements themselves were often first instigated by religious organizations such as Sarekat Islam in Indonesia and the Young Man's Buddhist Association in Burma, and Islamic journals and printing presses in Malaya.
[108] Hoppenbrouwers, "Winds of Change," p. 313.
[109] For instance, Roman Catholic priests were instrumental in the survival and emancipation of indigenous languages from Belgium to Lithuania. Ibid., p. 314.
[110] Coakley, "Religion and Nationalism in the First World," 2002, pp. 215–216.
[111] Tarrow, *Power in Movement*, p. 4.

groups and movements can be considered social movements because of the collective action they mount, and religious identity can provide the common purpose and social solidarity that mobilizes, legitimizes, and sustains them. Scholars working on social movements have maintained that the interactive process of meaning construction, articulation, and dissemination is central to movement mobilization, and framing provides useful conceptual tools to study these processes. Extrapolating from this, the case can be made that agents of nationalism – nationalists – can, and often do, employ resonant cultural concepts for such meaning construction. Religion is one such concept.

While a copious literature has emerged that attempts to investigate the phenomenon of framing, the broad consensus is that frames are interpretive frameworks or schemata that function to allow agents (or recipients) to determine how the words and actions of others should be understood, in a way that "enable(s) participants to locate, perceive, and label occurrences."[112] In this connection, frames can be understood as the condensing of symbols of meaning through a process that fosters shared understandings of events, experiences, and histories.[113] In short, frames help individuals make sense of events taking place around them. As regards religion, the process through which frames mobilize is aptly described by William Vendley and David Little:

Each religion is constituted by a set of stories that make up its central identity. In effect, these narratives constitute the seedbed of a religious tradition that can be transmitted and developed across time. Religious traditions can be passed on orally or by means of sacred texts, learned commentaries, and a variety of other carriers of meaning... In turn, each tradition's collection of stories, narratives, religious customs, and artistic expressions can be usefully understood as the religion's primary language. Religious primary language establishes and defines a religious community. It constitutes the community's living memory, provides for the possibility of shared experience and interpretation of reality, and offers a fertile foundation for that community's passage through time – orienting it to the

---

[112] David Snow, E. Burke Rochford Jr., Steven Worden, and Robert Benford, "Frame Alignment Processes, Micromobilization, and Movement Participation," *American Sociological Review*, Vol. 51, No. 4, 1986, p. 464.

[113] For extensive discussions on framing, see Deborah Tannen (ed.), *Framing in Discourse*. New York: Oxford University Press, 1993; Enrique Larana, Hank Johnston, and Joseph Gusfield (eds.), *New Social Movements: From Ideology to Identity*. Philadelphia: Temple University Press, 1994; Hank Johnston and Bert Klandermans (eds.), *Social Movements and Culture*. Minneapolis: University of Minnesota Press, 1995; Marc Steinberg, "Tilting the Frame: Considerations of Collective Action Framing from a Discursive Turn," *Theory and Society*, Vol. 27, 1999, pp. 845–872; Pamela Oliver and Hank Johnston, "What a Good Idea! Ideologies and Frames in Social Movement Research," *Mobilization*, Vol. 5, 2000, pp. 37–54.

past, the present, and the future. The strength and fecundity of primary language can be seen in its ability to secure the religious identities of believers and orient them in the constantly changing vicissitudes of history.[114]

In the study of social movements, shared understandings are foremost designed toward one end – to justify, inspire, and legitimize collective action on the part of the audience or recipient by facilitating their excogitation of their current situation. This process of meaning construction is known in sociological parlance as framing. Simply put, framing entails the identification of a problem and its contexts and causes, and the offering up of solutions to it. Hence, while many sociologists describe framing colloquially as depicting "the world out there," on closer inspection it is perhaps more accurate to say that framing depicts, from the perspective of the agent, the world both "as it is out there" as well as "as it should be." The salience of frames to the creation of meaning for an individual or a collective has been described in the following manner: "in one's scope of experience, frames indicate what to look at and what is important, and thereby indicate what is going on. A frame may also indicate, by directing attention away from other things, what is not important."[115]

At one level, for collective action to take place, framing requires the successful production and articulation of meaning that resonate with potential movement participants. This is what is termed "frame alignment" or "frame resonance." What this means is that, first, agents, be they religious personalities, political leaders, teachers, village elders, or leaders of armed rebel groups, must be in possession of social and cultural capital and legitimacy in the eyes of their audience for their frames to resonate and have appeal; and, second, networks or structural pathways must also exist in order to facilitate the transmission of frames and their narrative and ideational content.

The Framing Process

According to David Snow and Robert Benford, there are three steps to the framing process that reveal how individuals and collectives relate to

---

[114] William Vendley and David Little, "Implications for Religious Communities: Buddhism, Islam, Hinduism, and Christianity," in Douglas Johnston and Cynthia Sampson (eds.), *Religion, The Missing Dimension of Statecraft*. Oxford: Oxford University Press, 1994, p. 307.

[115] Hank Johnston, "Verification and Proof in Frame and Discourse Analysis," in Bert Klandermans and Suzanne Staggenborg (eds.), *Methods of Social Movement Research*. Minneapolis, MN.: University of Minnesota Press, 2002, p. 64.

social and political activism.[116] The first is diagnostic framing, whereby a problem or condition is identified, culprits are identified, and blame is assigned. Over and above this, diagnostic framing also identifies the causes (whether an individual or a group, or a state, for that matter) of the problem or condition. Among the most frequent diagnostic frames employed by social movements are injustice frames. These provide interpretations that point to violation of rights and principles. For religious nationalists, the diagnostic frame is likely to be the marginalization of a people of different religion on the basis of their creed, the need to defend the religion against external forces which threaten the faith (and the faithful), or even the imposition of one's faith and creed onto a minority in the name of "nation building." Prognostic framing often follows on from diagnostic framing. This is the stage where solutions are suggested to solve the problem. These solutions can exist at the strategic, tactical, or individual levels. Finally, motivational framing takes place as a means through which to mobilize for collective action by calling on the audience to take part in a particular (nationalist) movement. Motivational frames are crucial because while potential participants may share their understanding of the causes and solutions, it is the motivational frame that prepares them to engage in collective action.

While frames can be very emotive, enduring, and undeviating, depending on circumstances they can also vary and change. Several examples serve to illustrate this. Consider, as a case in point, the transformation of the frames that drove Muslim activism in the 1960s and 1970s. If Arab Muslim activism in the 1960s was marked by its embrace of Gamal Abdel Nasser's anti-imperialist and socialist-leaning clarion call for social and political change throughout the Muslim world, the erosion of Marxist ideology and demise of Nasserite pan-Arab nationalism after the 1967 Arab-Israeli war, the oil boom of 1973, and the 1979 Soviet Union invasion of Afghanistan all contrived to shift in the collective action frames among Arab Islamic movements toward a religious, or more accurately, Islamist, register. Something of how frames shift is also evident when we consider how the recent emergence of a transnational Jihadi discourse may arguably have created a new frame of resistance as Muslim communities involved in localized struggles are inspired to view their cause as emblematic of the larger conflict between Islam and the Western world.[117]

---

[116] See David A. Snow and Robert D. Benford, "Ideology, Frame Resonance, and Participant Mobilization," *International Social Movement Research*, Vol. 1, 1988, pp. 197–217.

[117] David Leheny, "Terrorism, Social Movements, and International Security: How Al Qaeda Affects Southeast Asia," *Japanese Journal of Political Science*, Vol. 6, No. 1, 2005, pp. 98–99.

Other examples closer to Southeast Asia can be found in Eastern Indonesia, where, as Jacques Bertrand argues, Papuans and Cordillerans used different frames to articulate their grievances as they gravitated strategically between putting forward their claims as "nations" or as "indigenous peoples."[118] He adds that the Cordillerans moved toward the indigenous peoples frame when their attempts to identify themselves as a nation were largely unsuccessful.[119] Meanwhile, Papuans framed their struggle by emphasizing brutality on the part of the Indonesian armed forces, repression of Papuan culture, and land seizures.[120] Unlike the Cordillerans, they continued to frame their struggle in terms of both nationhood and their claimed status as indigenous peoples.[121] Likewise, in the case of Malaysia, the dominant frame of "*Ketuanan Melayu*" (the Lordship of the Malays) soon took the form of "*Ketuanan Agama*" (the supremacy of religion, in this case, Islam) in the context of the acceleration of the Islamization of Malaysia evident from the mid-1980s onwards, while in the southern Philippines, the more exclusivist (Bangsa) Moro nationalism soon gave way to the egalitarian Bangsamoro nationalism. The point to stress here is that frames, and framing processes, are dynamic, contingent, and constantly revised and negotiated in a process of reframing.

Frame Articulation and Amplification: Narratives

In the case of self-determination movements, it is important to stress that the struggle against central authorities is not merely limited to political violence and armed clashes; it also involves deeper struggles over meaning, identity, and legitimacy, which are often captured in the construction of history, folklore, and even mythology that arouse deep attachments. Concomitantly, a significant ingredient in the cultural and ideational framing process of nationalism is the role of narratives that nourish frames by stirring emotions and evoking symbolisms that

---

[118] Jacques Bertrand, "Indigenous Peoples' Rights as a Strategy of Ethnic Accommodation: Contrasting Experiences of Cordillerans and Papuans in the Philippines and Indonesia," *Ethnic and Racial Studies*, Vol. 34, No. 5, 2011, p. 853.

[119] Ibid., p. 855. The Cordillerans were initially part of the New People's Army (NPA) but broke away from the Communist movement in the early 1980s, forming the Cordilleran People's Liberation Army (CPLA).

[120] Ibid., p. 857.

[121] For further empirical evidence of shifting frames, see Mona Harb and Reinoud Leenders, "Know Thy Enemy: Hizbullah, 'Terrorism' and the Politics of Perception," *Third World Quarterly*, Vol. 26, No. 1, 2005, pp. 173–197; Joas Wagemakers, "Legitimizing Pragmatism: Hamas' Framing Efforts From Militancy to Moderation and Back?" *Terrorism and Political Violence*, Vol. 22, No. 3, 2010, pp. 357–377.

resonate with a collective, particularly in times of crisis.[122] Anderson notes, to that end: "Awareness of being embedded in secular, serial time, with all its implications of continuity, yet of 'forgetting' the experience of this continuity... engenders the need for a narrative of 'identity.'"[123] This hews closely to Tarrow's elaboration on the role of emotions and symbols in collective action:

> The culture of collective action is built on frames and emotions oriented toward mobilizing people out of their compliance and into action in conflictual settings. Symbols are taken selectively by movement leaders from a cultural reservoir and combined with action-oriented beliefs in order to navigate strategically among a parallelogram of actors, ranging from states and social opponents to militants and target populations. Most important, they are given an emotional valence aimed at converting passivity into action.[124]

Turning to the oft-discussed factor of grievance that is commonly evoked to explain the resilience of resistance movements, if resentment is the potent rocket fuel that is so crucial to the success of any nationalist movement, and narratives need not necessarily be based on "fact," then indeed, the power of narratives lies precisely in the mythical quality of folklore, for it is the stuff of legend that best captures the imagination. Through narratives, events and experiences are aligned and connected in a way that makes them unified and compelling (though not necessarily accurate or novel) for an audience, and, where necessary, amplified through the accenting of particular events and beliefs seared into collective memory so as to render them more salient.

For the present purposes, narratives can be understood as "analytic constructs... that unify a number of past or contemporaneous actions or happenings, which might otherwise have been viewed as discrete or disparate, into a coherent relational whole that gives meaning to and explains each of its elements and is, at the same time, constituted by them."[125] Rooted in literary theory, the salience of narratives as drivers and animators of political phenomenon has been described by the leading strategic studies thinker Lawrence Freedman as such:

> Here was a concept (narratives) that could explain how meaning was given to lives and relationship and how the world was understood. It fit in with theories of cognition and accounts of culture. The narrative turn therefore captured

---

[122] For a compelling case of how historical narratives gain currency in times of crises, see Paul A. Cohen, *History and Popular Memory: The Power of Story in Moments of Crisis*. New York: Columbia University Press, 2014.
[123] Benedict Anderson, *Imagined Communities*, 3rd edition. London: Verso, 2006, p. 205.
[124] Tarrow, *Power in Movement*, p. 112.
[125] Larry J. Griffin, "Narrative, Event-Structure Analysis, and Causal Interpretation in Historical Sociology," *The American Journal of Sociology*, Vol. 98, 1993, p. 1097.

the uncertain confidence about what was actually known, the fascination with the variety of interpretations that could be attached to the same event, and the awareness of the choices made when constructing identity. It highlighted the importance of human imagination and empathy while challenging the idea of a perfect knowledge of an external reality.[126]

To this, Freedman hastens to add: "Narratives could have a number of functions: means by which support could be mobilized and directed, solidarity sustained and dissidents kept in line, strategies formulated and disseminated."[127]

Yet not only do narratives create experiences for its audience; it also elicits responses from them. It does so by drawing the audience into the narrative itself. Scott Atran has suggested with reference to religion: "Religious doctrine and liturgy lack any thoroughgoing logical and empirical constancy. Nevertheless, their quasi-propositional elements are well-tuned for human memory.... (M)yths optimize storage and retrieval of information that is culturally general and personally idiosyncratic. The myth-teller adapts a theme inherited from his or her audience in such a way that the specific time and space of the telling and participation become instantiations of universal themes."[128]

For nationalist movements, including religious nationalists, it is often the case that narratives not only map out the history of resistance by relaying the struggles of previous generations, but also ask the present generation: "What are you going to do about it?" When narratives gestate in this manner, they configure experience through a process of infusing a pattern of events with significance and exploiting them for specific ends, and elicit responses by way of drawing the audience into the narrative.

Narratives of resistance promoted by nationalist movements, including those of religious persuasion, are often predicated on familiar themes such as repression, depredations of colonization including "internal colonization," loss of power, victimization, marginalization, and injustice. To generate narratives of resistance, nationalist movements construct meanings that provide intelligibility, and articulate and disseminate these meanings through narrative frameworks that resonate with potential participants in order to motivate and catalyze collective action. Given that framing speaks of conscious strategic efforts by groups of people to fashion shared understandings of the world and of themselves that legitimate and motivate collective action, then it stands to reason that it is resistance

---

[126] Lawrence Freedman, *Strategy: A History*. New York: Oxford University Press, 2013, p. 429.
[127] Ibid., p. 430.
[128] See Scott Atran, *In Gods We Trust: The Evolutionary Landscape of Religion*. New York: Oxford University Press, 2002, p. 150.

narratives that produce and reproduce precisely such ideas, discourses, and meanings that constitute them.[129]

Apropos the prevailing arguments identified in the previous chapter that dominate conventional wisdom on the topic of intrastate conflicts, it is imperative to highlight the point that narratives speak to issues of agency, context, and language, and these, in turn, serve as an important check to structural and interest-based explanations. Social movement theorists have often pointed out that, based solely on structural and interest-based explanations alone, there would be little incentive for individuals to resist the status quo.[130] By virtue of their control over the state, central authorities possess vast resources to bring to bear against any organization or movement that attempts to challenge its authority. On the other hand, resistance movements often have considerably less material resources at their disposal that can be used to entice participation, not to mention dim prospects of success and high costs of participation.

What resistance movements (potentially) possess is the capacity to weave narratives that are central to the negotiation of meaning and identity for local communities, and that resonate with their experiences and those of their community or "people" in a way that can trigger a challenge to the "official" narrative of national identity.[131] It is in this manner that nationalist movements share much in common with social movements, especially where the latter "are not viewed merely as carriers of extant ideas and meanings that grow automatically out of structural arrangements, unanticipated events, or existing ideologies. Rather, movement actors are viewed as signifying agents engaged in the production and maintenance of meaning for constituents, antagonists, and bystanders or observers."[132] Clearly then, for insurgents a resilient nationalist

---

[129] Doug McAdam, John D. McCarthy, and Mayer N. Zald, "Introduction: Opportunities, Mobilizing Structures, and Framing Processes – Toward a Synthetic, Comparative Perspective on Social Movements," in McAdam, McCarthy, and Zald (eds.), *Comparative Perspectives on Social Movements: Political Opportunities, Mobilizing Structures, and Cultural Framings*. Cambridge: Cambridge University Press, 1996, p. 6.

[130] See Elisabeth Wood's seminal study in Wood, *Insurgent Collective Action and Civil War*.

[131] See Lewis Hinchman and Sandra Hinchman, *Memory, Identity, Community: The Idea of Narrative in the Human Sciences*. New York: SUNY Press, 1997.

[132] Robert D. Benford and David A. Snow, "Framing Processes and Social Movements: An Overview and Assessment," *Annual Review of Sociology*, Vol. 26, 2000, p. 613. While some have preferred to treat frames as a psychological phenomenon consistent with the cognitive concepts of "schema" and "schemata," this neglects the processes of construction and negotiation that, as this discussion has described, are integral to the framing process. For a discussion of framing and schema, see Bert Klandermans, *The Social Psychology of Protest*. Oxford: Blackwell, 1997.

narrative is a central component of the framing exercise.[133] When constructed in ways and language that appeal to an intended audience through references to everyday experience and encounters, narratives of resistance can bring out the identity that will dispose individuals to support the movement.[134] The case here is that it is a religious narrative that provides this ascriptive sense of identity, and a language that resonates.

A final note on the malleability of frames is in order. As crucial as frames are to the motivational aspect of collective action, we must recognize that they are not only pliable and selective in nature, but often given to inherent contradictions as well. This accords with earlier vignettes regarding the constructed character of conceptions of nationhood. Because frames are not an aggregate of individual attitudes and perceptions but a result of a negotiated shared meaning, they are not static, reified structures but continuously being constructed, challenged, reproduced, modified, and replaced during the course of social movement activity, *including within the claimant community itself.*

Nationalists are cognizant of the need to reinvent and modify frames to take advantage of strategic opportunities and possibilities created by other actors or by changing circumstances. This makes framing a dynamic, ongoing process, and one that is affected by various elements of the sociocultural context in which the movement is embedded. This is certainly so when one considers how in efforts to construct or revive markers of identity, movement progenitors engage in what Eric Hobsbawm termed the "invention" of traditions, which involve "those establishing or symbolizing social cohesion or the membership of groups, real or artificial communities (and) those establishing or legitimizing institutions, status or relations of authority."[135]

The reinvention of nationalism was evident across Eastern Europe, and especially among those states which sought and obtained European Union membership, when the nation became a fulcrum for inter-party contestation as nationalist parties reinvigorated their age-old struggle for

---

[133] The centrality of narratives to the framing process has been argued by Francesca Polletta, *It Was Like a Fever: Storytelling in Protest and Politics*. Chicago, IL.: University of Chicago Press, 2006. Polletta draws attention to the not only need to consider the narratives themselves but also how the story developed, who tells the story, the language through which the story is transmitted, the audience, and the audience's relationship to the storyteller.

[134] Roberta Garner, *Contemporary Movements and Ideologies*. New York: McGraw-Hill, 1996, p. 58.

[135] Eric Hobsbawm, "Introduction" in Eric Hobsbawm and Terence Ranger (eds.), *The Invention of Tradition*. Cambridge: Cambridge University Press, 1983, p. 9.

kin-state solidarity across borders by harnessing the transborder character of the Union.[136] A similar shift was evident in nationalist discourse in Mexico in the 1980s, when revolutionary nationalism gave way to a functionalist narrative used by the elite of the Salinas administration to undermine the social state in the transformation of the Mexican political economy.[137]

Conclusion

This chapter has defined the parameters and production of religious conceptions of nationhood, and established the conceptual basis upon which to consider religious nationalism an important framework through which intrastate conflicts in Southeast Asia that take on a religious hue can and should be viewed. The basic premise is that inasmuch as collectives will seek to preserve their identities and cultural values, religion very often animates these very values, hence the turn to religion as an identity marker.

Of course, it would be erroneous to suggest that all ethnically or religiously defined groups or nations aspire to have their own state, or to change the political status quo in the territorial states they find themselves in. There are countless examples of distinct ethnic and religious groups that have not agitated for their own state, or sought to challenge the status quo in the name of self-determination. That being said, there are also many instances where communities do indeed confront conditions that compel them to pursue self-determination, which can be defined as anything from self-rule to the assertion of some measure of cultural and/or political autonomy depending on the group in question, and whether it deems it possible to achieve its goals within the existing framework of the state or whether it should seek a state of its own. This is the case in the Southeast Asian nation-states that will be studied in the chapters to follow, where some groups do seek to agitate for their own state or challenge the status quo using religious referents. This accords with the fundamental underlying logic of nationalism and self-determination – that security is best ensured by communities either through seeking their own institutions, renegotiating (using force, if necessary) existing institutions in

---

[136] See Peter Vermeersch, "Backdoor Nationalism: EU Accession and the Reinvention of Nationalism in Hungary and Poland." Paper presented at the Association for the Study of Ethnicity and Nationalism, London, April 1–3, 2009. For a discussion on the concept of kin states, see Joseph Chinyong Liow, *The Politics of Indonesia-Malaysia Relations: One Kin, Two Nations*. London: Routledge, 2006.

[137] Gavin O'Toole, *The Reinvention of Mexico: National Ideology in a Neoliberal Era*. Liverpool: Liverpool University Press, 2010.

order to accommodate their aspirations, or defending their institutions from the encroachment of others. Given these considerations, it should be no surprise that religious nationalism is such a combustible force that can catalyze a whole range of political responses from civil mobilization to intractable armed separatist insurgency.

2 Southern Philippines
Reframing Moro Nationalism from (Bangsa) Moro to Bangsamoro

On October 15, 2012, Philippine president Benigno Aquino III and Al-Haj Murad Ibrahim, chairman of the Moro Islamic Liberation Front or MILF signed the Framework Agreement on the Bangsamoro at the Malacañang Palace in Manila. On January 25, 2014, representatives of the Philippine government and the MILF signed the last of the annexes to the Framework Agreement. With the annexes complete, the landmark Comprehensive Agreement on the Bangsamoro (CAB) was signed on March 27, 2014. The signing of the Comprehensive Agreement was a remarkable achievement given how both parties have been locked in armed conflict for the better part of the last three decades, including the Philippines state's waging of an "All-Out-War" in 2000 under the presidency of Joseph Estrada. With this set of agreements, a Bangsamoro autonomous state, encapsulating parts of what had come to be known as the Moro lands in the southern Philippines, will finally be formed within the territory of the Philippines.

The Moro areas of southern Philippines have widely been defined as the territories of Mindanao as well as the surrounding islands in the Sulu Archipelago. It includes the five provinces where Muslims remain a majority of the population: Maguindanao, Basilan, Tawi-Tawi, Lanao Del Sur, and Sulu. Within the geopolitical body of the Philippines, these areas stand out on at least three counts. First, they are where the vast majority of Filipino Muslims, which according to most census figures number around four to five million, are concentrated, even though Muslims in actual fact form numerical majorities only in the five aforementioned provinces. Second, these are areas identified as among the poorest in the Philippines, if not the entire Southeast Asian region. Indeed, numerous studies have been produced that draw attention to how these areas lack basic infrastructural and institutional pillars necessary for the proper functioning of society, such as education, transport, healthcare, and sanitation services.[1] Third, until relatively recently, large segments of the

---

[1] Eric Gutierrez and Saturnino Borras Jr., "The Moro Conflict: Landlessness and Misdirected State Policies." Policy Studies Series No. 8. Washington, D.C.: East-West Center Washington, 2004.

local population, known in the lexicon today collectively as Bangsamoro – a term that has come to be used synonymously with Moro despite significant definitional differences between them that speak to competing conceptions of national identity (not to mention the fact that in truth, Moro identity is itself a fragmented community), have been waging protracted armed rebellion against central authority since the time of Spanish attempts to colonize the region. In fact, some have pointed out that the Bangsamoro struggle had antecedents traceable almost five centuries earlier when the Spanish arrived in the Philippine Archipelago and waged what has become popularly known as the "Moro Wars" on the Muslim sultanates in the southern islands of Mindanao and Sulu that met them on their arrival.[2]

Because of the persistence of conflict in contemporary times and the region's current state of abject poverty, there has been a tendency to assume a causal relationship between these two factors. About the severity of economic problems there can be no question, and some of it broaches primary issues of the politics of corruption; but while there is no extenuating the economic inequalities, conflicts such as that which has unfolded in the southern Philippines, are seldom mono-causal. Hence, due consideration should also be given to other factors, such as issues of identity and conceptions of belonging, and how these are perceived to have been undermined.[3] Indeed, despite the fact years of transmigration from elsewhere across the Philippine Archipelago have diluted the Muslim population of Mindanao reducing it to a minority, their sense of identity and purpose as Muslims remain sufficiently strong such that religious identity has underpinned narratives of self-determination, but later also narratives of reconciliation as Bangsamoro nationalists conceptualized their identity and belonging within the territorial and ideational context of the Philippine nation-state.

Contours of the Bangsamoro Struggle

Most observers agree that rebellion waged by the Moro – Muslim inhabitants of the southern islands of the Philippines – peaked in the 1970s when the MNLF (Moro National Liberation Front, formed in 1968)

---

[2] See Cesar Adib Majul, *Muslims in the Philippines*. Quezon City: University of Philippines Press, 1973, pp. 107–316.
[3] See www.ploughshares.ca/content/philippines-mindanao-1971-first-combat-deaths. Others have placed the number of deaths much higher, between 140,000 and 200,000. See Paul Oquist and Alma Evangelista, *Peace-Building in Times of Institutional Crisis: Ten Years of the GRP-MNLF Peace Agreement*. Makati City: United Nations Development Programme, 2006, p. 26.

managed to mount and sustain armed struggle in the wake of the Marcos administration's policy of martial law instituted in 1972. There is, of course, a long and painful precedence to this conflict. Historians have traced the genesis of conflict to the 16th century and the arrival of the Spanish in the Philippines, even though the region itself was, in truth, hardly tranquil and devoid of violence prior to this (this is a point to which we will return).[4] Driven by objectives of establishing and expanding their trading empire in the Philippine Archipelago on one hand and the Christian missionary zeal to "save souls" on the other, the Spanish moved to gradually subdue pockets of the Muslim populations of southern Philippines. According to conventional wisdom, what followed was 350 years of warfare between the Spanish and the inhabitants of the southern Philippines, and Spain's ultimate failure to subdue the entire region and place it under its formal colonial control despite numerous attempts.

For the Moros, the struggle against Spanish colonization eventually segued into one against American colonization. This fin-de-siècle shift took place in 1898 when Spain ceded control over its Philippine territory to the United States with the Treaty of Paris. Moros vehemently resisted the inclusion of the southern territories in the treaty on the grounds that the Spanish never exercised control over them in the first place. A series of skirmishes beginning in 1902 marked this new phase of Moro rebellion, and culminated in the Battle of Bud Bagsak on the island of Jolo in 1913 when severely outnumbered Moro militia were decisively defeated by American forces in a flagship act of resistance that quickly entered local folklore and mythology as a moral victory for Moro sacrifice against imperialism.

At this point, it is important to register the fact that this historical narrative of Moro encounters with the Spanish and later the Americans, perpetuated by Moro nationalists and echoed by some (usually Moro) scholars, choruses a distorted discourse of centuries of uninterrupted Moro struggle against Spanish and American, and later, Philippine, colonialism. This conventional wisdom precludes the possibility that local forms of authority emerged at various times during these periods that either enjoyed autonomy from or worked closely with colonial powers. Indeed, relations between these local power centers and Spanish or American imperial power were not always defined by conflict and resistance. At these local quotidian levels, as several scholars have convincingly

---

[4] It is generally recognized that Islam had arrived about three centuries prior to the Spanish. By the time the Spanish set foot in the Philippine Archipelago, there were already well-established Muslim sultanates in Mindanao and beyond (further north).

documented, the relationship was equally predicated on engagement, cooperation, and where convenient and necessary, *entente cordiale*.[5]

American colonization of southern Philippines took the form of various attempts to integrate the region and peoples of "Moro Province," as the region became administratively known, into the wider Philippine colony. One of the primary instruments of integration were policies of transmigration, which saw people from more heavily populated islands such as Luzon relocated to Mindanao, partly a consequence of colonial policy but also in search for economic opportunity given the region's vast untapped resources.[6] This led to not only a dilution of the indigenous populations – scholars point to this as the genesis of demographic transformation that witnessed the Muslim majority in the southern Philippines eventually dwindle into a mere 20 percent of the population today – but also a tussle between locals and migrants for land and resources. This was particularly pronounced in new settlement areas where conflicts between Christian settlers and Moro landowners proliferated.[7] Be that as it may, alongside integration there was a further legacy of American colonialism for the southern Philippines that needs to be made – the creation of a Moro identity. This last point bears repeating, for it was colonial encounters that provided disparate local identities, which knew nothing of the political and social structures that stitched European empires together, a sense of affinity and coherence based on the construction of a transcendent Moro identity.[8] On this, Tom McKenna offers the following analysis: "American colonial polities had the effect of ethnicizing Muslim identity in the Philippines. By 'ethnicizing' Islam, it meant that American colonial rulers encouraged the development of a self-conscious Philippine Muslim identity among a generation of educated Muslim elites

---

[5] Consider, for instance, the following studies: James Francis Warren, *The Sulu Zone, 1768–1898: The Dynamics of External Trade, Slavery, and Ethnicity in the Transformation of a Southeast Asian Maritime State*. Honolulu, HI: University of Hawaii Press, 1981; Reynaldo C. Ileto, *Magindanao, 1860–1888: The Career of Datu Utto of Buayan*. Pasig City: Anvil Publishing Inc, 2004.

[6] We should note though, that there were at the time also opinions in American quarters that the heavily populated Moro areas in the south of Mindanao should be made autonomous or even independent of the rest of the Philippines and governed as a new territory to be known as the "Mindanao Plantations." See Patricio Abinales, *Making Mindanao: Cotabato and Davao in the Formation of the Philippine Nation-State*. Manila: Ateneo de Manila University Press, 2000, pp. 22–24.

[7] For a discussion on the migration and settlements phenomenon, see Frederick L. Wernstedt and Paul D. Simkins, "Migrations and the Settlement of Mindanao," *Journal of Asian Studies*, Vol. 25, No. 1, November 1965, pp. 83–103.

[8] See Najeeb M. Saleeby, *Studies in Moro History, Law, and Religion*. Manila: Bureau of Public Printing, 1905; Abdulrasad Asani, "The Case of the Bangsa Moro People" in Permanent Peoples' Tribunal (ed.), *Philippines: Repression and Resistance*. Utrecht: Komite ng Sambayanang Pilipino, 1980.

who were otherwise divided by significant linguistic, geographic, and, to some extent, cultural barriers."[9]

When the United States passed governing powers in 1920 as part of preparations for eventual independence, Moro antipathy shifted to the Philippine administrators of the southern provinces who staffed *en masse* the Bureau of Non-Christian Tribes, created to administer the Moro provinces and modeled along the Bureau of Indian Affairs in North America.[10] Having secured power from the US colonial administration, the nascent Philippine state set about the task of Philippinizing the Moros: altering local cultural and religious laws and commandeering land, for instance. Intriguingly, frustrations at prejudice and discriminatory practices of these administrators from the north led Moros to clamor for a return to direct American rule (compared to Dutch and French colonial administrations in the Dutch East Indies and Indochina, respectively, American colonialism betokened a special sympathy for the Moro), which was a fate they preferred to being part of a sovereign Philippine territorial state. Needless to say, this set them at odds with the Philippine nationalists who looked to inherit the American colony in their entirety.

Following the formation of the Commonwealth of the Philippines in 1935, attempts by the newly formed Philippine government in Manila at assimilation of the Moro communities accelerated as imperial nemeses were replaced by an equally suppressive Philippine state. The pace of resettlement programs, in particular, gathered in earnest, as did the reallocation of resources away from Moro majority districts to settler areas. These programs continued apace after the interregnum of the Japanese occupation, and catalyzed further strains in relations between the indigenous population of the south and the central government authorities in Manila. Animus toward Philippine central authority deepened, leading to a number of Moro insurrections such as the rebellion in Sulu in the early 1950s and the Hajal Ouh movement of the early 1960s that sought to establish an independent Moro territory consisting of Sulu, Basilan, and Zamboanga by means of armed struggle. Nevertheless, it was in the 1960s that Moros managed to mobilize in a more organized fashion with the formation first of the Mindanao Independence Movement (MIM) in 1968 and, a year later, the MNLF against a Philippine government that was viewed as *"gobirno a sarwang a tao"* (foreign government). This marked the birth of the contemporary Moro separatist movement.

---

[9] McKenna, *Muslim Rulers and Rebels*, p. 132.
[10] Peter Gowing, *Mandate in Moroland*. Quezon City: New Day Publishers, 1983, p. 328.

The MNLF would soon be followed by the MILF and a host of other splinter organizations. The number of armed groups operating in southern Philippines has proliferated over the last two decades with the emergence of smaller groups such as the implacable Abu Sayyaf Group (ASG), Al-Khobar, the Pentagon Gang, and the Rajah Solaiman Movement (RSM). With the possible exception of RSM, however, these groups have for the most part been engaged in criminal activities, and their support base pales in comparison to more broad-based insurgent movements like the MNLF and the MILF, which remains by far the largest organization that claims to represent the collective interest of the Bangsamoro. As a consequence of internal opposition to negotiations with the state, new groups have emerged that splintered from the MILF, namely the Bangsamoro Islamic Freedom Movement (BIFM) and its armed wing, the Bangsamoro Islamic Freedom Fighters (BIFF).

To be sure, armed conflict has not been the only recourse for the Bangsamoro community seeking to assert their claims to greater political and cultural freedoms. Taking place alongside armed resistance, the emergence of several civil society groups and religious (and inter-religious) institutions that have been actively involved in the promotion of peace and development in southern Philippines have provided alternative channels through which to work toward the political aspirations of the Bangsamoro. More prominent among these initiatives have been the Bishops-Ulama Forum (BUF) formed by the Mindanao Catholic bishops and the *Ulama* League of the Philippines in 1996 (following the 1996 Peace Agreement), and the Mindanao Peoples Caucus that brings together grassroots leaders and activists from all ethnic and religious backgrounds from the region to work toward peace. Others include the umbrella civil society organization, Consortium of Bangsamoro Civil Society (CBCS), and Mindanano Peaceweavers (MPW).[11] Underlying the growth of these initiatives is both war weariness on the part of many Bangsamoro and the view that the articulation of the Bangsamoro cause was in no wise the exclusive domain of major insurgent groups, regardless of how powerful and influential they are.

Insofar as the MILF is concerned, arguably the foremost preoccupation for scholars and analysts who study the conflict in the southern Philippines today is several iterations of peace talks and negotiations between the MILF and the Philippine government that culminated in the Framework Agreement. Talks between Moro insurgent groups and

[11] The Consortium of Bangsamoro Civil Society brings together more than 160 Moro NGOs under one umbrella. It is the largest such organization in the southern Philippines and has been active in fostering peace and inter-faith dialogue among the local communities throughout Mindanao.

the Philippine government can be traced back to the GRP (Government of the Republic of the Philippines)–MNLF talks that began in 1976 and that resulted in the 1996 peace agreement leading to the formation of the Autonomous Region of Muslim Mindanao (ARMM). Talks between the MILF and the Philippine government were initiated in 1997 focusing on cessation of hostilities in order to lay the groundwork for more substantive negotiations. Since then, there have been several iterations of talks and agreements, including a seemingly successful conclusion of a Memorandum of Agreement on Ancestral Domains in 2008 that was eventually nullified by the Philippine Supreme Court on grounds that the (secretive) manner in which the agreement was arrived at was unconstitutional.[12] After a bout of violence between disgruntled segments of the MILF and government security forces following the Supreme Court's decision, both parties returned to the table for a new round of talks that led to the signal signing of the Framework Agreement on the Bangsamoro in October 2012.[13] In March 2014, leadership of the MILF and the government of President Benigno Aquino III signed the Comprehensive Agreement on the Bangsamoro, concluding seventeen years of negotiations and bringing an end to several decades of fighting between both parties.

In trying to understand the tone of state policy toward conflict in Mindanao, many scholars have rightly noted that the response of the Philippine state to Moro resistance has vacillated between hard line, militaristic policies such as martial law and "All-Out-War" to more tempered, conciliatory ones including dialogue and negotiation.

As highlighted earlier, since the formation of the Commonwealth of the Philippines before the Second World War, the central government's policies toward the south have been anchored on integration and assimilation, both cultural and political. Foremost, this led to the massive relocation of Filipinos to Mindanao and subsequent redistribution of Moro lands, dispossessing Moros of what they deem to be their "ancestral lands" and whitewashing Moro *adat* (customary law and practice) on land and resources along the way. It was only in the face of resilient armed resistance, by dint of the emergence first of the MNLF and later the MILF, that various governments pursued (with varying degrees of commitment) dialogue and negotiation. Even then, sandwiched between several decades of stuttering dialogue attempts were major military offensives – during the Estrada and Arroyo administrations in particular – designed to wipe out Moro resistance and achieve a conclusive battlefield

---

[12] Previous agreements reached were the Tripoli Agreement (2001), Implementing Guidelines on the Security Aspect (2001), and Implementing Guidelines on the Humanitarian, Rehabilitation, and Development Aspect (2002).
[13] See the discussion in Joseph Chinyong Liow and Joseph Franco, "Positive Signs for a Southern Philippines Peace," *Global Brief*, July 17, 2013.

victory. Predictably, these offensives served only to deepen resentment between centre and periphery.

In explaining the vacillation of state policy between discrimination and accommodation, as well as its inability to bring an end to the conflict despite the resources devoted to it, several issues stand out. One major problem is that of lingering mistrust between the Moro and Filipinos from elsewhere in the Archipelago. With respect to Bangsamoro perceptions, it is not surprising that conflict is essentially undergirded by very negative perceptions of both parties for each other, in particular the perceived strong bias and prejudice of Christians toward Muslim Moros. A Philippine congressman involved in the dialogue process with the MILF conceded as much when he described the relationship as one dictated by "centuries of Christian antipathy towards our Muslim brothers."[14] This view reinforced those of MILF chairman Al-Haj Murad Ibrahim, who opined that: "Christian prejudice and discrimination against Muslims is very deep, and ambitious politicians tap into it."[15]

Moros have expressed displeasure at historical stereotypes that continue to be used in contemporary times in reference to them. For instance, Cebuanos allegedly continue to pejoratively refer to the Muslims of Mindanao as "pirates" and "kidnappers", stereotypes that emerged as early as the days of Spanish colonialism.[16] More recent manifestations of this mistrust can be seen in how attempts to integrate Moro fighters into the Philippine police and military have frequently been plagued by obstacles.[17] Such obstacles include miscommunication and deep-seated suspicions.[18]

A second problem relates to the matter of policy consistency. The Philippine political process has often been defined as a semi-anarchy often given to contention and coalition building, frequently along personal lines. As described by one scholar, "the broad public space offered by Philippine democracy functions like an amplifier for all those groups that claim to be defenders of Philippine national identity and unity. Governments are structurally weak and have to rely on fragile and ever-changing alliances of political families and strongmen. Therefore, the government normally cannot act as a valid spokesman that can deliver her party's compliance."[19]

[14] Interview, Jakarta, February 11, 2015.
[15] Interview, Jakarta, February 12, 2015.
[16] E-mail interview, December 7, 2011.
[17] The integration of MNLF fighters into these state institutions was part of the 1976 Tripoli Agreement and the 1996 Final Peace Agreement.
[18] Details of these problems are discussed in Miriam Coronel Ferrer, "Integration of the MNLF Forces into the PNP and AFP: Integration without Demobilization and Disarmament." Unpublished Paper, 2000.
[19] Peter Kreuzer, "Enduring Civil War in the Philippines: Why the Way to Peace Always Leads to Renewed Warfare." Paper presented at World Convention of the Association

The fragmented and fluid nature of Philippine politics highlights a third consideration that has to do with what McKenna aptly describes as "disconnect between the state-level nature of the armed conflict and the fundamentally local issues that underlie it."[20] As the chapter will proceed to discuss in further detail later, feudalism and factionalism, often in the form of *rido* or blood feuds and clan wars, are rife in Mindanao and have been the subject of detailed study elsewhere.[21] The point to stress is that governance and legitimacy of the central government have long been a point of contention in Mindanao, and to large extents have crippled the state in terms of its ability to introduce sustainable policies in the south targeted at regaining the trust of local populations.

Identity: Who is a Bangsamoro?

Until the signing of the Comprehensive Agreement, the official goal of major Bangsamoro armed organizations had been the creation of an independent Moro state in southern Philippines. This objective is underpinned by an interpretation of history that sees the current struggle through the lens of the *longue durée* of Moro resistance against imperialism, whether Spanish, American, or Filipino. As one observer put it, "The present *Jihad Fiy Sabilillah* waged by the Bangsamoro people is a continuation of the struggle which had been fought by their ancestors and forebears demanding for freedom and independence."[22] In the case of the Bangsamoro struggle, the master frame has been the identity of the people, or, as some would describe it, Bangsamoroism.

From (Bangsa) Moro to Bangsamoro

For a self-determination movement that prided itself on its struggle for an independent state defined foremost by a unitary local indigenous identity, the tapestry of "Bangsamoroism" is actually remarkably diverse, and the concept itself, malleable. For starters, the concept of "Moro" or "Bangsamoro" is not an ethnic one in the sense that there is no single

---

for the Study of Nationalities, Columbia University, New York, April 23–25, 2009, p. 3.

[20] Thomas McKenna, "The Endless Road to Peace: Armed Separatism and Ancestral Domain in the Muslim Philippines." Paper presented at the conference Mobilization for Political Violence: What Do We Know? Oxford, University of Oxford, March 17–18, 2009, p. 6.

[21] Two of the most important books that have dealt with the issue of local politics and conflict in Mindanao are McKenna, *Muslim Rulers and Rebels*, and Abinales, *Making Mindanao*.

[22] Datuan Solaiman Panolimba, "The Bangsamoro Armed Struggle in the Philippines," *Maradika Online*, December 17, 2008. Available https://datspanolimba.wordpress.com/2008/06/15/the-bangsamoro-struggle-in-the-philippines-2/.

ethnic group that can be defined as "Moro" or "Bangsamoro." As a matter of fact, Moro people derive from at least thirteen separate and distinct ethnic groups, which can be differentiated by their languages. What binds them together into this entity termed "Moro," courtesy, as we saw previously, of American colonial classification – was their religious affiliation: these are Muslim societies.

This unity in religious faith is further supplemented by the historical and demographic fact that even though Moro people consist of different ethnic groups speaking their own language, they have enjoyed extensive interaction over time through inter-marriage, trade, and warfare. It is this record of interaction, coupled with their religious faith, that underpins the construction of Moro identity by nationalists. Even then, it should be noted that the term "Moro" itself is, according to conventional wisdom not a local one, but was instead a pejorative identity marker ascribed to them by the Spanish. In point of fact, the term "Moro" was first used by the Spanish not to describe the indigenous people of Mindanao, but rather the Muslims whom they met in Manila upon their conquest of the city in 1570, who shared religious faith and customs with the Moors back in Spain and also in North Africa.[23]

Yet, in order to demonstrate that the Moro resistance and self-determination movements possessed the credentials to govern the multi-ethnic and multireligious society that Mindanao had become over time, there was a need for an inclusive and all-encompassing collective identity marker (of the indigenous peoples). In other words, there was a requirement for a "national" identity that would also embrace non-Moro (non-Muslim) inhabitants of southern Philippines. This was particularly imperative for Moro groups fighting for independence as a means to demonstrate their readiness to incorporate the interests of non-Muslim inhabitants of southern Philippines into their imagined community, and in so doing reinforce the legitimacy and credibility of their claims for self-government. As Ghazali Jaafar, vice-chairman for political affairs for the MILF, once explained: "Residents of Muslim Mindanao, since time immemorial, are considered Bangsamoro, which includes Christians and Lumads.... They will be provided the same rights, privileges, and protection by the new political setup (of an automomous Bangsamoro state government)."[24]

Concomitantly, borrowing from a cognate language, "Moro" was prefixed with the word "Bangsa," roughly approximating "nation" in meaning in the Malay language, in order to expand the hitherto restrictive

---

[23] E-mail interview, December 7, 2011.
[24] "MILF: From ARMM to Bangsamoro State Government," *Philippine Daily Inquirer*, April 30, 2012.

conceptual boundaries of Moro (i.e., to be a Moro one had to be a Muslim) into a "national" identity that could conjure images of solidarity among those born in the land regardless of their religious affiliations.[25] On these pragmatic and egalitarian grounds, the concept of Bangsamoro was born. Accordingly, the MILF leadership has adumbrated that: "Our definition of Bangsamoro people is those who are native inhabitants of Mindanao, who have been living here since before the Spaniards came – regardless whether they are Muslims or non-Muslims. The Muslim Bangsamoro people we refer to as Moro. The natives (or Lumad) are included in our definition of Bangsamoro people."[26] Hence, it is on this basis that the MILF, and MNLF for that matter, proudly proclaims theirs to be a struggle for the collective rights of Bangsamoro – be they Muslim, indigenous Christian, or members of tribal groups.[27] Crucially, this view has anchored documents signed between the Philippine government and the MILF:

It is the birthright of all Moro and all indigenous people of Mindanao to identify themselves and be accepted as 'Bangsamoro'. The Bangsamoro people refers to those who are natives or original inhabitants of Mindanao and its adjacent island including Palawan and the Sulu archipelago at the time of conquest or colonization whether mixed or of full native blood, inclusive of all indigenous people living therein, subject to their freedom choice at the appropriate time.[28]

Moreover in recent times, the identity of Bangsamoro has found expression as geopolitical space, with the creation of a territorial and autonomous administrative entity called Bangsamoro as a consequence of the signing of the Framework Agreement in March 2014.

With the above considerations in mind, it stands to reason that the creation of Bangsamoro identity was in many respects a historical, social, and political construction on the part of Bangsamoro nationalists, but through a historical process that was closely tied to encounters with an American colonial administration that, as Michael Hawkins argues, in

---

[25] The term "Bangsamoro" is believed to have entered into the lexicon of Moro struggle in the late 1960s when MNLF leaders started making reference to it. See ibid.
[26] Tony Iltis, "Philippines: Moro People Demand Self-determination," www.greenleft.org.au, April 10, 2011. Available www.greenleft.org.au/node/47317. The Lumad consists of more than twenty non-Muslim ethno-linguistic groups scattered around Mindanao and the surrounding islands.
[27] Indeed, non-Muslim voices allegedly also have representation in the MILF's *Majlis al-Shura* (Consultative Assembly), which serves as an intermediary between the organization's legislative and executive branches. Interview, Cotabato City, July 16, 2005.
[28] See Preamble of The Memorandum of Agreement on Ancestral Domain of the GRP-MILF Tripoli Agreement of Peace of June 22, 2001. Available http://zamboangajournal.blogspot.com/2008/08/philippines-milf-memorandum-of.html.

fact fused the variegated ethnic identities into the concept of "Moro."[29] Likewise, while it is the Mindanao Muslims who most vocally agitate for their indigenous rights, the concept of Bangsamoro does not privilege those of the Muslim faith at the expense of others. It warrants noting as well that this re-definition and re-articulation of Moro identity was widely validated by Moro Islamic scholars. In fact, arguably the most eminent and recognizable of them, the late founding chairman of the MILF, Hashim Salamat, was a vocal champion of the inclusion of indigenous non-Muslims in his conceptualization of Bangsamoro identity.

The result of this process of recasting of identity, however, has been remarkable. What made the Bangsamoro struggle an ethno-nationalist one is the fact that it was an attempt to anchor it to a primordialist frame premised on the existence of a culture and identity totally distinct from the rest of the Filipino population, not to mention a shared collective memory of victimization. In other words, inasmuch as we can speak of a Bangsamoro "ethnicity," it is grounded on distinction and difference from what is otherwise known to be Philippine culture, as well as a shared colonial experience, more so than any self-evident similarities that Bangsamoro communities enjoy. Further underpinning this frame is a narrative, shared by nationalists of all strains, that the Bangsamoro nation predates the Philippines and includes both the Muslims and non-Muslim indigenous peoples, and possessed an ancestral homeland that encompasses the whole of Mindanao and its surrounding islands, despite the fact that as an explicit identity (or physical entity) Bangsamoro did not exist prior to the birth of the Philippine nation, nor did the collection of sultanates that the Spanish encountered on their arrival resemble anything of the modern unified territorial entity that Bangsamoro nationalists and romantics are wont to declare.

Yet, notwithstanding the seeming egalitarian shades of Bangsamoroism enumerated above, it remains a fact that a key feature of Bangsamoro discourses of history and identity is religion. The arid reality is that among Moro Muslims, Christians, and Lumads, those who have accepted and imbibed the Bangsamoro master frame and engaged in resistance on those grounds have by far been Muslims. This fact has not been lost on the Philippine central government, and hence it should hardly be surprising that "it is striking that these people (Moro) were mishandled (by the state), not as ethnicities, but as religious deviants."[30] Likewise, MILF

---

[29] See Michael Hawkins, *Making Moros: Imperial Historicism and American Military Rule in Philippines' Muslim South*. Dekalb, IL.: Northern Illinois University Press, 2012.
[30] Benedict R. O'G. Anderson, *The Spectre of Comparisons: Nationalism, Southeast Asia, and the World*. London: Verso, 1998, p. 328.

leaders themselves are cognizant of residual misgivings that non-Muslims have toward their agenda, regardless of how pluralist and egalitarian their definition of the concept of Bangsamoro has been. For instance, Ghazali Jaafar has acknowledged that he had been "looking for more ways that non-Muslim groups could help 'neutralize' the perceived apprehension of non-Muslims toward the MILF."[31] This view seems to be reinforced by those of Silvestre Afable, chief secretary for the state's peace panel, who informed American interlocutors in private meetings that some of Mindanao's Christian leaders "have been highly concerned that their localities would be handed to a new Muslim entity in a peace agreement. They were receptive to Muslim self government, including Zamboanga City Mayor Celso Lobregat, as long as their own municipalities were not included in the Muslim entity."[32]

History, and more specifically alternative and competing interpretations of history, loom large to explain the reticence of non-Muslims to the MILF's attempt to recast Bangsamoro identity in more egalitarian terms. The historical relationship between Lumad and the Moro Muslims, for instance, has always been difficult. Not unlike elsewhere in Southeast Asia, the Lumad hill peoples had historically been exploited by Muslim Moro lowlanders through relationships that ranged from asymmetric trading partnerships to outright predation that took the form of slave raiding and servitude. In fact, slave raiding by Muslim *datus* (clan chiefs) among the hill peoples continued well into the 1950s, and some would even suggest that in the case of Mindanao the practice lasted into the 1970s.[33] Not surprisingly, this history has led to continued prejudice on the part of Muslims against Lumad; it has also made Lumad wary of Muslim efforts to make common cause with them, even though they are aware that they share with Muslims similar grievances against the majority Christians and the Philippine establishment. As to the relationship between Muslims and Christians, there is no gainsaying that mutual mistrust runs just as deep, if not deeper. This owes no small measure to the difficult history documented earlier in this chapter, which in turn was exacerbated by decades of transmigratory policies that have seen a Muslim majority whittled down to a minority.

---

[31] "MILF Continues to Support Peace Process, Interested in Deeper Development Cooperation," *U.S. Embassy Manila Cable*, August 4, 2008. Available http://wikileaks.org/cable/2008/08/08MANILA1844.html.

[32] "Government Offers MILF 'Self-Determination' Instead of New Territory," *U.S. Embassy Manila Cable*, November 29, 2006. Available http://wikileaks.org/cable/2006/11/06MANILA4836.html.

[33] I thank Tom McKenna for pointing this out to me.

History, Sovereignty, Landlessness

For many Bangsamoro, the historical narrative that frames Bangsamoro-ism is also important in terms of the framing of resistance. This sentiment is captured in the following remarks of a Bangsamoro youth leader that betray a mood of despair: "We don't believe we are Filipinos. That's the essential problem.... The struggle of the Moro people has been going on for 500 years now. So this problem can't be solved in our time."[34] From this historical vantage, it is clear that what united otherwise disparate Moro clans and ethnic groups despite their long tradition of enmity toward each other was an even deeper enmity toward external occupiers. Put differently, historically the sultanates of Mindanao and Sulu shared one thing in common that could later be mobilized for purposes of collective identity construction – their encounters with and defiance of foreign rule.

Not only that, as noted above this collective resistance is also portrayed as a seamless struggle that has been ongoing for centuries, despite the fact that in truth, "over past 40 years the Philippine government and Muslim separatists have spent far more time talking to one another than in active armed conflict. It has, in fact, been primarily a history of long, slow peace negotiations punctuated by brief but fierce armed clashes."[35] Narratives not just of subjugation but also of extermination often accent historical frames of violent resistance in representations of Bangsamoro history as well. Referring to the slew of failed agreements between the MNLF and the Philippine government, a Bangsamoro scholar decried: "All agreements entered by and between the MNLF and GRP are only a showpiece of the Philippine government in order to smokescreen the oppression, colonization, exploitation and extermination of the Bangsamoro people."[36] These frames are reinforced through references to events such as the Jabaidah massacre, which precipitated the formation of mass-based armed separatist organizations, and the heavy-handed policies of several Philippine administrations

---

[34] Norimitsu Onishi, "In Philippines Strife, Uprooting is a Constant," *New York Times*, November 22, 2009.

[35] Thomas McKenna, "The Endless Road to Peace: Armed Separatism and Ancestral Domain in the Muslim Philippines." Paper presented at the conference Mobilization for Political Violence: What Do We Know?, Centre for Research on Inequality, Human Security, and Ethnicity, University of Oxford, March 17–18, 2009, p. 5.

[36] Datuan Solaiman Panolimba, "Armed Struggle of the Bangsamoro Muslims in the Philippines," *Reflections on the Bangsamoro*, June 8, 2009. Available https://datspanolimba.wordpress.com/2008/06/15/the-bangsamoro-struggle-in-the-philippines-2/.

that have become a part of Bangsamoro "national" and resistance narratives.[37]

Another equally important historical myth was the assertion that the Muslims have never been conquered, by either the Spaniards or the Americans, and that the Bangsamoro homeland had been unjustly annexed by Manila after independence.[38] Historically, however, it is known that in 1878, Sultan Jama ul-Azam of Sulu signed a peace treaty with the Spanish government, and in so doing agreed to bind his subjects to the Spanish king in exchange for autonomy. Likewise, Datu Utto of Cotabato had capitulated to Spain in 1887 and recognized the rule of the king of Spain.[39] Clearly, too, Mindanao was colonized by the United States after 1898. Indeed, it is precisely colonialism that the Bangsamoro armed struggle was pitched against. As the MNLF spokesman Asani reiterated: "Colonialism is the root cause of the Moro problem in the southern Philippines – a phenomenon that is not after all an exclusive preoccupation of Western nations. The present fighting in the area may be a fight against established but repressive government."[40]

Notwithstanding the narratives highlighted above, perhaps the most important feature of the Bangsamoro diagnostic frame is the matter of the loss of ancestral lands. In pre-colonial Philippines, the sultanates of Sulu and Maguindanao had exercised political sovereignty over Moro communities. Traditionally, Moros owned land communally, allowing *datus* to govern and dispose of land considered to be under their control. Because of the implementation of the Regalian doctrine during Spanish colonial rule, however, Moros and other indigenous peoples were denied what used to be free communal access to lands, forests, bodies

---

[37] The Jabaidah Massacre, which took place in 1968, involved the execution of Tausug trainees who were recruited by the Philippine Armed Forces for covert special operations training for the purpose of agitating among the people of Sabah and North Borneo in order to set the stage for annexation of the territory by the Philippines. When the Moros refused to undertake the mission, they were summarily shot for mutiny.

[38] The following excerpt from a pro-Bangsamoro website exemplifies this perspective: "There was neither rhyme nor reason for the Americans to give the Moro province to the Philippines to form a Philippine Republic in 1946. The Moro Province was NEVER a part of the Philippine Revolution of 1896 or 1898 or the Philippine Republic of Aguinaldo. A cursory glance at history – real history not the fiction of Most Filipino historians – shows that the Moros and Indios were never one people, never until 1946. But the various Moro rebellions and the MNLF and MILF wars show that the Moros are not satisfied with being a second-class citizen in the Philippine Republic." See www.quezon.ph/2008/08/15/greater-malaysia/.

[39] Agnes Brazal, "Beyond the Religious and Social Divide: The Emerging Mindanawon Identity," *Chakana: Intercultural Forum of Theology and Philosophy*, Vol. 2, No. 3, 2004, p. 14.

[40] Abdurasad Asani, "The Moro Problem in South Philippines," *The ASEAN Review*, August 1986.

of water, and other natural resources as these were now deemed Spanish property. During the last two decades of Spanish rule, moreover, the sultans of Sulu and Maguindanao were forced to recognize aspects of Spanish sovereignty. Rapacious colonial rule inevitably disrupted Muslim maritime commercial activities and systematically destroyed, depopulated, and isolated Muslim settlements, farms, and orchards from neighboring Muslim Malays colonized by the British and the Dutch. All of these consequently led to the demise of the sultanates of Sulu and Maguindanao.[41]

The situation was further compounded during the course of American colonial administration. Already excluded from administrative power – both national and regional – when Filipinos gradually assumed control of the state after 1920, Moro ownership of territory in Mindanao was compromised by policies emanating from the Bureau of Lands, which was in charge of issuing land titles.[42] Arriving on the back of a policy of migration from Luzon to Mindanao which gathered pace under the administration of Manuel Quezon, Christian settlers began commandeering lands hitherto possessed by Moros but which were dispassionately deemed "public" by the Bureau of Lands. Among other things, these lands, previously owned and occupied by Moros by virtue of customary land rights, were lost because of the unfamiliarity on the part of the Moros with the new regime of land registration.[43]

With the establishment of the Philippine Republic in 1946, socioeconomic conditions in Mindanao worsened with the influx of large multinational corporations which, as beneficiaries of state assistance and privilege, managed to gain extensive control and monopoly of the Mindanao economy, particularly in the export of pineapples, bananas, rubber, and sugar cane, and later in the mining industry as well. Land conflicts between settlers and Bangsamoro escalated in the 1950s and 1960s

---

[41] Cesar Adib Majul, "The Moro Struggle in the Philippines," *Third World Quarterly*, Vol. 10, No. 2, April 1988, p. 897; Astrid Tuminez, "This Land is Our Land: Moro Ancestral Domain and its Implications for Peace and Development in the Southern Philippines," *SAIS Review*, Vol. 27, No. 2, Summer–Fall 2007, p. 78.

[42] In order to integrate Moro territories into the larger framework of the Philippines, the American colonial authority passed the Land Registration Act in 1902 to determine the extent of private holdings in the country. This was soon followed by a series of Public Lands Acts (1911, 1913, 1914, and 1919). These legislations allowed the central government to commandeer Moro lands and claim them to be state property. At the same time, individuals were allowed to apply for private ownership. However, while Christian Filipinos were allowed to apply for private ownership of up to twenty-four hectares, non-Christians could only apply for a maximum of ten hectares. Thus began the phenomenon of legalized land grabbing in Mindanao.

[43] Similar tactics of administrative confusion were employed by the US government to dispossess native Americans of their traditional lands.

as a result of further government policies that systematically transmigrated tens of thousands of settlers to traditional Bangsamoro lands. Further compounding the strains was the fact that by local convention at the time, it was common for the Moro to own lands without title deeds. This made it that much easier for the government to define huge portions of hitherto Bangsamoro-owned lands as public property. Resettlement programs such as the National Authority for Reforestation and Rehabilitation Administration (NARRA), Land Settlement and Development Corporation (LASEDECO), and Economic Development Corporation (EDCOR) paved the way for massive and uncontrolled migration from northern Philippines to Mindanao and led to the establishment of Christian majorities in towns once dominated by Moros and Lumad.[44] Summarizing this gradual erosion of Bangsamoro sovereignty over their traditional lands, a Bangsamoro media platform averred: "What began in Mindanao as 'agricultural colonies' resulting in the unjust loss of the Bangsamoro ancestral domain are population transfers legitimized over the decades by political gerrymandering and plantation economy."[45]

Prognostic Frames: From Rebellion to Reconciliation

The changing conception of Bangsamoro nationhood and its place in the Philippine geobody and imagined nation discussed above accompanied a shift in Bangsamoro prognostic frames from armed rebellion and negotiations with the Philippine state. Indeed, while violence has been a definitive feature of politics in Mindanao even before the arrival of the Spanish, it has evolved over time and taken on various forms of armed resistance to attempts at subjugating the local populations to foreign rule. At the same time, there were also various attempts at conflict resolution through negotiations.

The MIM, organized in 1968, was the first movement that demanded outright secession of Mindanao, Sulu, and Palawan regions. It insisted on defending the Bangsamoro homeland through *jihad*. In order to accommodate and gain support from non-Moro inhabitants in the southern Philippines, the leadership of the MIM later changed the name of the

---

[44] Jamail A. Kamlian, *Ethnic and Religious Conflict in Southern Philippines: A Discourse on Self-Determination, Political Autonomy, and Conflict Resolution*. Atlanta, G.A.: Emory University, 2003.

[45] See "Weighing in Factors of State and Religion," www.tmchronicles.com, January 11–15, 2009. Available http://tmchronicles.com/vdbasee.php?idb=24&&dbase=Editorial&&type=3&&start=131&&end=140.

Prognostic Frames 79

movement to the Mindanao Independence Movement.[46] The MNLF, meanwhile, came to prominence soon after the declaration of martial law in 1972, after which violence in Mindanao escalated. It aimed to mobilize general Moro support recruit, train, and equip armed cadres to oppose what it perceived to be Philippine imperialism and procure international support for its cause. Through its military arm, the Bangsa Moro Army (BMA), the MNLF was successful in launching well-coordinated attacks against a number of military and police outposts in the provinces of Sulu, Cotabato, and Lanao. This was followed by more than two decades of armed insurgency in southern Philippines. The MNLF sought complete independence of the Bangsamoro people and Mindanao through the establishment of a Bangsamoro Republic. The objectives of the MNLF were explicitly stated in its manifesto:

> We, the five million oppressed Bangsamoro people, wishing to free ourselves from the terror, oppression, and tyranny of Filipino colonialism, that had caused us untold sufferings and miseries by criminally usurping our land, by threatening Islam through wholesale desecration of its places of worship and its Holy Book and murdering our innocent brothers, sisters and folks in genocidal campaign of terrifying magnitude. Aspiring to have the sole prerogative of defining and chartering our national destiny in accordance with our own free will in order to ensure our future and that of our children.[47]

The insurgency movement leveraged widespread grievances toward the central government's transmigration policies as well as national integration policies that sought to incorporate the southern islands into what Moro leaders considered a Catholic-dominated state. Encroachment of new non-Muslim settler populations in Mindanao, much of it through fraudulent manipulation of legal channels, sowed the seeds of discontent among the Muslim community.[48] Recourse to Muslim political elites

---

[46] The MIM wanted secession on four grounds: "(1) The establishment of the provincial and municipal governments undermined the status of the traditional leaders, dislocated the authority and communications set up, and negated the existing coalition formation patterns, so necessary in the cooperative and communal ventures that the Muslims were accustomed to. In operation, these governments were disruptive and not functional. (2) The imposition of a new legal system negated the judicial functions of the village elders. This caused a breakdown in social order and gave rise to a lot of social problems which exist up to this day. (3) It was in the field of education where irreparable dislocations were created. The public school organization systematically alienated the school children. They were forced to learn new sets of values that put down the cultural milieu in which they grew. (4) The transportation of settlers and land grabbers to Muslim provinces and the creation of agricultural colonies out of Muslim lands caused a lot of resentment in Muslim circles." In effect, this reduced the economic base of the Moroland. See Alunan Glang, *Muslim: Secession or Integration?* Manila: Cardinal Book Store, 1971, pp. 91–92.
[47] MNLF Manifesto, 1974.
[48] T.J.S. George, *Revolt in Mindanao*. Kuala Lumpur: Oxford University Press, 1980, p. 116.

who had been co-opted into the prevailing structure of national power failed to address many of their concerns. Because of this, the legitimacy of their traditional elite, the *datus*, waned in the eyes of the Muslim community. Others have ventured to argue that the Mindanao conflict is rooted as much in the various levels of contestation within the structure of Muslim society as it is a function of relations between them and the Filipino state, which in turn "exemplifies the political complexities found in similar political movements formed in postcolonial situations."[49] On the growth of popular Moro self-determination and the fissures it created in a Moro society hitherto obeisant to the traditional *datu* elite, Eric Gutierrez observed:

> The youths launched into a frenzied construction of images of their own 'nation' radically different from the 'homeland' offered by their untrustworthy, aristocratic and egocentric elders.... The fresh, new faces of non-traditional, youth-based leadership stirred the Moro re-awakening – Misuari, the intellectual; Salamat, the Islamic scholar and cleric; and Alonto, the aristocrat's son who found common cause with his generation. They set aside their differences, imagined and successfully engineered their own project, and broke away from traditional elite leadership. In so doing, they firmly established themselves as the alternative.[50]

Elaborating further on the dynamics that drove this rift within Bangsamoro Muslim society, Syed Serajul Islam argued that "(F)or traditional leaders, Muslim autonomy meant the recognition and reinforcement of their power. Misuari's vision of Muslim destiny, on the contrary, was to eliminate the old leaders and to install himself in their place."[51]

However, with the signing of the Tripoli Agreement on December 23, 1976, as well as the 1996 GRP-MNLF Peace Agreement under the auspices of the Organization of Islamic Conference (OIC), erstwhile obdurate MNLF demands for secession transformed to the slightly less disputatious call for political autonomy in Mindanao within the parameters of Philippine sovereignty and territorial integrity. The signing of the Tripoli Agreement, however, also resulted in the fragmentation of the MNLF. Former vice-chairman of the MNLF central committee, Salamat Hashim, founded the MILF, claiming in 1977 that the MNLF was

---

[49] This argument is made convincingly in McKenna, *Muslim Rulers and Rebels*, p. 5.
[50] Eric Gutierrez, "The Reimagination of the Bangsamoro," in Eric Gutierrez et al. (eds.), *Rebels, Warlords, and Ulama: A Reader on Muslim Separatism and the War in Southern Philippines*. Quezon City: Institute for Popular Democracy, 2000, pp. 312, cited in Mely Cabellero-Anthony, *Revisiting the Bangsamoro Struggle: A Tale of Contested Identities*. Unpublished paper, pp. 14–15.
[51] Syed Serajul Islam, "Ethno-communal Conflict in the Philippines," in Rajat Ganguly and Ian Macduff (eds.), *Ethnic Conflict and Secessionism in South and Southeast Asia: Causes, Dynamics, Solutions*. New Delhi: Sage, 2003, pp. 202–203.

moving away from its Islamic ideals and objectives and was morphing into a Marxist-Maoist movement, and that as its chairman Nur Misuari was personalizing policy planning and decision-making.

At its creation, the MILF declared its intent to continue the armed struggle for an independent home state for the Muslims of southern Philippines, but also to introduce a more Islamic flavor to the movement as the MNLF was deemed to be too secular in its outlook and strayed from the original aspiration for an Islamic state. At the same time, it also criticized the MNLF for abandoning the struggle in favor of the Philippine state's offer of the creation of an autonomous region, the expanse of which was determined by constitutional mandate and plebiscite. Later, the MILF would also reject the 1996 Peace Agreement between the Philippine establishment and the MNLF, this time brokered by Indonesia.

Since its formation, relations between the MILF and the Philippine political establishment have fluctuated between ceasefires and military clashes, the most notorious of which was President Joseph Estrada's 2000 policy of "All-Out-War" against the MILF.[52] Dialogue, however, resumed in 2002 and culminated in the signing of the Memorandum of Understanding on the Ancestral Domain (MOU-AD) on July 27, 2009. Building on the ARMM model, the agreement expanded the scope and depth of Muslim self-rule in the south. Nevertheless, non-Muslim politicians and local interests lobbied intensely against the MOU-AD. Meanwhile, the agreement was nullified by the Supreme Court on grounds that it was "unconstitutional," thereby setting the stage for a resumption of armed clashes between the MILF and Philippine security forces.[53] Even

---

[52] Estrada justified his policy of "All-Out-War" on the grounds that the MILF had never been serious about negotiations. He asserted: "One would think that with all these peace talks and ceasefires, a lasting peace would have been achieved already. But the MILF, with all due respect, has proven to be an organization that does not remain true to its word; a group that only uses ceasefires to regroup and strengthen their forces. We saw this in November 1999, when the MILF, in spite of a peace agreement, initiated heavy fighting in Central Mindanao and North Cotabato. We saw this again on January 10, 2000, when the MILF, in spite of a peace agreement, took over the Talayaan Municipal Hall in Magindanao. We saw this again on February 25, when the MILF, in spite of a peace agreement, bombed a ferry in Ozamiz City, killing 25 people. We saw this again on March 16 when the MILF, despite a peace agreement, occupied the Kauswagan Town Hall. And these are only a few of the hostilities initiated by the MILF in a period of less than six months. So after all these peace talks and ceasefires, it became clear that this was an organization that would neither respect the Philippine government nor salute the Philippine flag." See "Speech of Former President Estrada on the GRP-Moro Conflict" at the UP-HDN Forum on the GRP-Moro Conflict, September 18, 2008. Available http://hdn.org.ph/speech-of-former-president-estrada-on-the-grp-moro-conflict/.

[53] "MILF Warns SC Ruling could Lead to More Clashes," *Agence France-Presse*, October 15, 2008. The eighty-nine-page decision effectively concluded that "In sum, the

as the MILF central leadership tried to salvage the situation by agreeing to a new round of talks, factions within the organization, frustrated at the failure of the talks and the conciliatory position of the MILF leadership, broke ranks in order to continue armed struggle.

Notwithstanding an immediate upsurge in violence in Mindanao led by former MILF commander Ameril Umbra Kato, who formed the breakaway BIFM in the wake of the nullification of the MOU-AD, the central leadership of the MILF persisted in their attempts to revive dialogue with the central state. A new round of discussions began with a "secret meeting" between President Benigno Aquino III and Chairman Al-Haj Murad Ibrahim in Tokyo on August 4, 2011. This meeting paved the way for a series of exploratory talks facilitated by Malaysia, which culminated in the signing of the pathbreaking Bangsamoro Framework Agreement on October 15, 2012. In reaction to the failed MOU-AD, the Framework Agreement was deliberately left ambiguous, and details were to be outlined through a range of consultative mechanisms and annexes in time for the official creation of a Bangsamoro state in 2016. The Framework Agreement, however, set the tone for the evolution of Bangsamoro self-government with references to the "unacceptable" status quo, recognition of the right of Filipino Muslims to possess the "authority to regulate" their own society through the granting of "exclusive powers" to a Bangsamoro government, and, in a move clearly aimed at mitigating negative reactions from non-Muslims, that the *shari'a* would be applied as a template for governance but made only for affairs that related to Muslims.[54] Following several months of discussion and negotiation, four

---

Presidential Adviser on the Peace Process committed grave abuse of discretion when he failed to carry out the pertinent consultation process, as mandated by Executive Order (EO) No. 3, RA 7160, and RA 8371. The furtive process by which the MOA-AD was designed and crafted runs contrary to and in excess of the legal authority, and amounts to a whimsical, capricious, oppressive, arbitrary and despotic exercise thereof. It illustrates a gross evasion of positive duty and a virtual refusal to perform the duty enjoined." Moreover, "the Court held that respondents' failure to consult the local government units or communities constitutes a departure by respondents from their mandate under EO No. 3. Moreover, respondents exceeded their authority by the mere act of guaranteeing amendments to the Constitution. EO No. 3 defines the authority of the GRP Negotiating panel. The contents of the MOA-AD (more commonly known as the MOU-AD) are matters of paramount public concern involving public interest in the highest order, the Court noted. The Court stressed that the MOA-AD cannot be reconciled with the present Constitution and laws. Not only its specific provisions but the very concept underlying them, namely, the associative relationship envisioned between the GRP and the BJE, are unconstitutional, for the concept presupposes that the associated entity is a state and implies that the same is on its way to independence." See Jay B. Rempillo, "SC Declares MOA-AD Unconstitutional," October 2008. Available http://philippinecommentary.blogspot.com/2008/10/supreme-court-split-8-7-on-moa-ad.html.

[54] The Bangsamoro Framework Agreement can be accessed at www.gov.ph/the-2012-framework-agreement-on-the-bangsamoro/.

annexes – on transitional arrangements and modalities, on revenue generation and wealth sharing, on power sharing, and on normalization and the addendum on Bangsamoro waters – were eventually completed by January 25, 2014, leading to the signing of the CAB on March 27, 2014.

It remains to be seen if the momentum generated by the CAB can be sustained or whether it would be held hostage to the mistrust that has hitherto undermined every agreement signed between the Bangsamoro and the Philippine government. Indeed, the CAP has already hit stiff headwinds. It has yet to weather the fallout from an inadvertent clash between GRP and MILF forces on January 25, 2015, in Mamapasano, Maguindanao province, which triggered all-too-familiar sentiments of mistrust between the leaderships of both the Philippine state and the MILF, even though the incident has not led to the collapse of the agreement. At the same time, the fact that the CAB has also encountered resistance from elements within the Bangsamoro community should be borne in mind. This resistance has come from the militant BIFM led by Umbra Kato and the MNLF, with whom the creation of the ARMM was negotiated, and which is today widely seen to have failed in its own pursuit of the aspirations of the peoples of Muslim Mindanao.

The Motivational Frame of Islam

Given the protean character of Bangsamoro identity as described earlier, religion takes on greater currency in providing meaning and intelligibility to resistance. Indeed, as researchers of recruitment practices of the MILF have pointed out: "Religion, political ideology, and issues of Islamic identity, especially duty to Allah were all advanced as a strong motivational variable."[55]

The objectives of the MILF were articulated in decidedly religious terms: "All Mujahideen under the Moro Islamic Liberation Front adopt Islam as their way of life. Their ultimate objective in their *jihad* is to make supreme the word of Allah and establish Islam in the Bangsamoro homeland."[56] Salamat Hashim, the late founder-leader and in many respects the ideologue of the MILF, further expressed that "some personalities in the revolution advocate the idea that the sole and singular objective in our struggle is simply to liberate our homeland, giving no importance to the system of government that shall be established. We

---

[55] Alpaslan Ozerdem, Sukanya Podder, and Eddie L. Quitoriano, "Identity, Ideology, and Child Soldiering: Community and Youth Participation in Civil Conflict – a Study on the Moro Islamic Liberation Front in Mindanao, Philippines," *Civil Wars*, Vol. 12, No. 3, September 2010, p. 312.

[56] McKenna, *Rulers and Rebels*, p. 208.

want an Islamic political system and way of life and that can be achieved through effective *Da'wah, Tarbiyyah,* and *Jihad*."[57]

Cognizant of reticence on the part of non-Muslim indigenous groups, the MILF leadership have toned down their insistence on an Islamic political system and have instead thrown their weight behind the Bangsamoro Basic Law, which provides a blueprint for governance of Bangsamoro lands following the signing of the CAB between the Philippine state and the MILF in March 2014. It is worth noting that even as armed struggle was justified on religious grounds, it was a religious narrative that underscored with equal verve the MILF's pursuit of dialogue and eventual settlement of the conflict: "If people want peace, we as Muslims must give them peace."[58]

While the common perception is that the MILF was essentially a breakaway Islamic faction of the MNLF, it should be noted that not all of its senior leadership were religious clerics. Though the founding chairman, Salamat Hashim, and others like foreign affairs chief Abu Zahir, were recognized *ustadz* (religious scholars), others such as Al-Haj Murad Ibrahim, vice-chairman for military affairs and later successor to Salamat Hashim as MILF chairman, were not.[59] This of course raises questions as to how substantially "Islamic" the MILF's struggle has become following the passing of Salamat Hashim despite the existence of a *Majlis Shura* (consultative council) and presence of a considerable number of *ulama*, including Abdulaziz Mimbantas and Omar Pasigan, both household names in Mindanao, in the organization's central committee. Even so, careful scrutiny of the ideology behind the MILF reveals that it remains Salamat Hashim's ideology that best captures and represents the nature of the Islamic diagnostic and prognostic frames associated with the Bangsamoro struggle to construct a nation.

Despite the fact that he passed away more than a decade ago on July 13, 2003, the ideology behind the Bangsamoro movement today draws on the worldview, thought, and ideology of the late venerated Salamat Hashim.[60] Salamat Hashim was a student of Al-Azhar University, where he graduated in 1969 with a master's degree in religion and philosophy. To the Bangsamoro people, he is popularly known as Ustadz Salamat and *Amirul Mujahidin* (Commander of Muslims who take part in *jihad*). The

---

[57] Rigoberto Tiglao, "Peace in His Time: Ramos-Misuari Accord Has Structural Flaws," *Far Eastern Economic Review*, Vol. 159, No. 36, September 5, 1996, p. 25.
[58] Interview, Jakarta, February 12, 2015.
[59] I was informed by a Muslim scholar that the MILF Central Committee, which has about twenty members, has a roughly equal breakdown of leaders with religious and secular educational backgrounds. The interview was conducted in Manila, July 20, 2005.
[60] This was confirmed by several members of the MILF, including Central Committee members, during the course of my fieldwork in Cotabato in July 2005.

The Motivational Frame of Islam 85

guiding light of the Bangsamoro Islamic resistance, Hashim's ideology derives from his reputation as an established Islamic scholar, while his legitimacy stems from his standing as a *mujahid* (a person engaged in holy struggle) who has led the Moro struggle.

Notwithstanding Salamat's Islamist credentials, it is interesting to note that he always had a very keen sense of the historical and political contexts that framed the Bangsamoro rebellion. This was evident in the historically contextualized views he advanced:

> When the Philippine government was granted independence by America in 1946, the Bangsamoro people felt that instead of becoming free, they instead lost their freedom. Before the establishment of the Philippine government by western imperialists, the Bangsamoro people were independent. They had their sultanates or independent principalities in Sulu and Maguindanao which were united by alliance and cooperation. The Bangsamoro people felt that when their homeland was annexed to the Philippine government, the freedom they enjoyed was entirely lost. So this is the problem we want the Philippine government to address.[61]

In 1985, Salamat Hashim published *The Bangsamoro Mujahid* as a guide for the conduct of the MILF *jihad*. In it, he argued that *jihad* was necessary "to defend their (Bangsamoro) religion, the dignity of the Bangsamoro people, and regain their legitimate right to self-determination." Furthermore, the ultimate objective for the Bangsamoro resistance was, in his words, to "make supreme the word of Allah, which means – the establishment of a true Muslim community and a genuine Islamic system of government and the application of real Islamic way of life in all aspects of life."[62] Accordingly, Salamat Hashim proposed that it was through *dakwah* (proselytization) and *jihad* that the MILF Islamization agenda, which comprised the transformation of every Muslim in MILF "into a true and real Muslim whose beliefs... and his entire life is in conformity with the teachings of Islam derived from the Quran and Sunnah," of every MILF home into "real Islamic homes where the teachings of the Quran and Sunnah prevail," and of the community "into a truly Islamic one governed by the Sharia," would be realized.[63]

Salamat Hashim's conceptions of *jihad* rested on a belief that the world was divided between a *Dar al-Islam* (territory of Islam) and *Dar al-Harb* (abode of conflict). By his own account, "this material world is an arena of combat between *haqq* (truth) and *baatil* (falsehood), between *imaan* (faith) and *kufr* (apostasy), between *taqwaa* (piety) and

---

[61] Antonio Lopez, "The Muslim Separatist Rebel Leader Wants the East Timor Formula," *Asiaweek*, March 31, 2000.
[62] Salamat Hashim, *The Bangsamoro Mujahid: His Objectives and Responsibilities*. Mindanao: Bangsamoro Publications, 1985, pp. 8–9.
[63] Ibid., 9–11. To justify his arguments, Salamat cited the Quran, Surah 2:193 and 4:74.

kibr (pride), between justice and injustice, between the oppressed and oppressors.... (I)t is a battleground between Islam and all the manifestations and forces of *jahiliyyah* (the time of ignorance before the coming of Islam)."[64] In an address to the MILF youth, he issued the clarion call to that effect: "Are the Bangsamoro youth ready to join the Global Islamic Revival and Renaissance (GIRR)?... Either you are with Allah, His Messenger and the believers along with the GIRR, or with the enemies of Allah."[65] This perspective was indicative of the influence that radical Islamic scholars such as Syed Qutb (Muslim Brotherhood) and Syed Abul A'la Maududi (Jamaat-I-Islami) exerted on Salamat Hashim.[66]

At the same time, it should be pointed out that Salamat Hashim's conceptions of *jihad* can be distinguished from that of another militant Islamist group operating in southern Philippines, the Abu Sayyaf Group. While he noted that the Bangsamoro *jihad* included other aspects beyond militancy, the latter has argued that Muslims must engage in *Jihad Qital* (armed struggle) as it is *fard 'ayn* (individual obligation).[67] That said, Salamat Hashim has in fact explicitly called for armed *jihad* against the Philippine government on very few occasions, the most prominent being his call for retaliation in response to the Estrada administration's policy of "All-Out-War" from April to July 2000 and the February 2003 Buliok offensive of the AFP.

Up to this point, there should be little doubt that Salamat was also a proponent of the Islamic state. To him, this was the essential difference between the MILF and MNLF: "MNLF is more inclined to secularism, while MILF adopts the Islamic ideology and way of life... and believes in the Islamic concept of state and government."[68] He justified this belief on the basis that while a Muslim can and should perform his *ibadah*

---

[64] Salamat Hashim, Id el Fitr Message to the Bangsamoro Nation, Mindanao, December 16, 2001.

[65] Salamat Hashim, "Either You Are with Allah, or with the Enemies of Allah," address delivered at the *Bangsamoro* Youth National Peace Summit, Cotabato City, October 21, 2001.

[66] This was the view of Abhoud Syed M. Lingga, who was a close associate of the late Salamat Hashim. See Abhoud Syed Mansure Lingga, "The Political Thought of Salamat Hashim," M.A. dissertation, Institute of Islamic Studies, University of Philippines, 1995, p. 26.

[67] Julkipli M. Wadi, "State, Religion and Post-Nationalism in the Philippines." Paper presented at the International Conference on "State, Religion and Post-Nationalism: The Southeast Asian Experience," University of Malaya, Malaysia, February 23–24, 2001, p. 9. For a more detailed study on the Abu Sayyaf Group, see Mark Turner, "Terrorism and Secession in the Southern Philippines: The Rise of the Abu Sayyaf," *Contemporary Southeast Asia*, Vol. 17, No. 1, 1995.

[68] See "MILF Leader to 'Nida'ul Islam:' Perhaps the Moro Struggle for Freedom and Self-Determination is the Longest and Bloodiest in the Entire History of Mankind," www.islam.org.au, April–May 1998. Available www.islam.org.au/articles/23/ph2.htm.

(act of worship), if "the political authority to whom he owes obedience and allegiance does not recognize the supremacy of the Law of God, he has not perfected his worship to God."[69] The belief in Islamic governance has been given institutional expression in the context of the MILF structure of authority in the role of the *Majlis Shura* mentioned earlier. Even so, Salamat Hashim's position on the Islamic state, though robustly pursued, was never unequivocal. On other occasions, he had offered the following, more circumspect, analysis: "We have to accept the fact that most of the provinces here in the area are now dominated by non-Muslims. We can be satisfied with the provinces where the Muslims are still the majority. Regarding this Islamic State which people talk about, this idea did not come from us. What we want is to become independent. Regarding the system of government, that can be decided later."[70] This ambivalence doubtless sprang from a realistic assessment of how the demographics of Mindanao had changed over time, and arguably posed a large obstacle to Bangsamoro aspirations.

This more conciliatory approach has been shared by Salamat Hashim's successors. As to the matter of the continuity of Salamat Hashim's views, since his passing MILF leaders have continued to adopt a more calibrated stance on the issue of the Islamic state, suggesting instead that the specific type of administration for an independent Mindanao would be "decided by the people."[71] To understand this modulated outlook, one has to look at the politics surrounding the MILF struggle. As alluded to earlier, MILF leaders are fully aware that demographic trends in Mindanao work against their favor; hence, the discursive transformation of the nomenclature of resistance from "Moro" struggle to "Bangsamoro" struggle. Decades of resettlement have relegated the Muslim population to the status of minority.[72]

Clearly cognizant of demographic and political realities, the MILF's emphasis on Islam as the essence of their struggle was not emphasized at the expense of the participation of non-Muslims.[73] As noted earlier,

---

[69] Abhoud Syed Mansur Lingga, "Salamat Hashim's Concept of Bangsamoro State and Government," *Dansalan Quarterly*, Vol. 15, 1995, pp. 3–4.

[70] Salamat Hashim interview with BBC, Camp Abubakre As-Siddique, February 7, 1999 in Salamat Hashim, *Referendum: Peaceful, Civilized, Diplomatic and Democratic Means of Solving the Mindanao Conflict*. Edited and introduced by Nu'ain bin Abdulhaqq. Mindanao: Agency for Youth Affairs, 2002, p. 65.

[71] Interview with MILF member, Cotabato City, July 14, 2005; interview with MILF officials, Cotabato City, July 15, 2005.

[72] This also likely explains the early reluctance on the part of Salamat Hashim and other MILF leaders for a plebiscite.

[73] Muslims constitute only about 5 percent of the Filipino population and are a majority in only five provinces in southern Philippines. Statistics are available at CPRM Consultants, Institutional Strengthening of the Shari'a Justice System: Phase 1. Final Report

in their recent articulations of what constituted Bangsamoro identity and status, for instance, they have indicated that this will include non-Muslim indigenous tribal communities as well as indigenous Christians who were born in the geographical area. There is no gainsaying how this is a remarkable shift from earlier iterations of the Bangsamoroism encapsulated in the cognate concept of Moro, which was a status whose claims were restricted to Muslims born in the region. Likewise, MILF leaders have asserted that upon attaining political autonomy, they would not prejudice against non-Muslims, including settlers, who will be permitted the freedom to choose either a Bangsamoro identity (without prejudicing their religion) or that of settlers.[74]

At the heart of this seeming anomaly is the fact that despite the heavy use of religious references and the undoubted centrality of Islam as a motivational frame, the Bangsamoro struggle has to ultimately be appreciated against the context in which it evolved. As McKenna wisely cautioned: "The Muslim nationalist struggle for territory and a separate national identity has shaped (and continues to shape) what it means to be a Muslim in the Philippines, and has led to a search for a rationalized, self-conscious, and oppositional Islamic identity. But that more universal and rationalized identity has, in turn, been principally directed toward what is, in essence, a highly pragmatic political effort at nation-building."[75]

Islamic Schools

A critical vehicle through which the narrative contents of prognosis frames have been promulgated has been Islamic schools. Not unlike the case of southern Thailand (in the following chapter), Islamic schools in southern Philippines were not merely a repository of (religious) knowledge, but also played an instrumental role in sustaining Moro history and self-consciousness as the embodiment of cultural and political identity. At the same time, these institutions were for the most part viewed with suspicion and hostility on the part of the central state. This opprobrium was manifested not only in doubts as to the utility of religious education in equipping students for the modern world, but more fundamentally in the aspersions cast at them in the popular discourse of the larger Philippine body politic dominated by a Christian majority, particularly during the

---

on the SC-UNDP Project: PHI/01/001, June 2004, submitted to the Supreme Court of the Philippines. Available www.ombudsman.gov.ph/UNDP4/wp-content/uploads/2012/12/sharia-final-report1.pdf.
[74] Interview, Cotabato City, July 15, 2005.
[75] McKenna, "The Endless Road to Peace," p. 13.

colonial and early post-independence era. An all-too-familiar throwaway remark about Islamic schools in the context of September 11 captured the mood: "They are teaching their children, while still young, to wage a *jihad*. They will become the future suicide bombers."[76] Such exaggerations about the role of Islamic education institutions in the Philippines were unfortunately fairly pervasive in the discourse within many security-related agencies in the country, especially in the years immediately following the events of September 11.

Scholars have noted that while formal Islamic education institutions had begun appearing on the Mindanao landscape by the 1950s, it was the impulse of secessionism that in part gave new momentum to the growth of Islamic education, which in turn led to a proliferation of Islamic schools in the 1970s.[77] But to dress up this historical phenomenon as an ordained cosmic war between "Islamic Mindanao" and "Christian Manila" does little to advance proper understanding of the nature of the conflict. Beyond secessionism lay deeper issues of cultural negotiation and resistance, where Islamic schools stood at the forefront. The Islamic school in the southern Philippines stood to authenticate the cultural identity of the Moro by virtue of how it embodied the presumed (and constructed) common historical tradition, religious affinity, and cultural practices that accent the Moro nationalist narrative in resistance to attempts at subjugation by the colonial and national states. In essence, they were a reaction to the following:

American schooling replaced militant Spanish Catholicism as the weapon of choice in integrating Muslim Filipinos into an emerging Philippine state as a marginalized and subordinated minority stripped of all but a nominal Muslim identity. These policies, as well as the underlying conception of Muslim Filipinos as uncivilized, backward, and dangerous passed largely unchanged into subsequent independent governments. They were encoded in textbooks and curricula that virtually erased the history, experiences, customs and religion of Muslim Filipinos. Such policies presented Muslim Filipinos with a stark choice, a choice put rather bluntly in a history of the Commission on National Integration: 'In the process of helping them attain a higher degree of civilization, they have to discard some of their traditional values and customs'.[78]

---

[76] Thomas M. McKenna and Esmael A. Abdula, "Islamic Education in the Philippines: Political Separatism and Religious Pragmatism" in Robert W. Hefner (ed.), *Making Modern Muslims: The Politics of Islamic Education in Southeast Asia*. Honolulu, HI: University of Hawaii Press, 2009, p. 206.

[77] Manaros Borancing, Federico Magdalena, and Luiz Lacar, *The Madrasah Institution in the Philippines: Historical and Cultural Perspectives*. Iligan City: Toyota Foundation, 1987.

[78] Jeffrey Ayala Milligan, "Islamization or Secularization? Educational Reform and the Search for Peace in the Southern Philippines," *Current Issues in Comparative Education*, Vol. 7, No. 1, 2004, pp. 31–32.

If anything, it is this historical and cultural imperative that explains the resilience of this institution.[79] It also explains how complicated the process of reconciling education, identity, and integration has been when it comes to the southern Philippines:

> Efforts to Islamize public schools serving Muslim students represents a profound shift from ignoring or actively denigrating Islam to giving it a place of honor in the curriculum comparable to the place it holds in the larger Filipino Muslim community. This is likely to enhance the sense of self-worth and dignity of Muslim children as Muslims. But is it likely to do the same for their sense of being Filipino? Perhaps more importantly, Islamization policies do not address the curricular silence and bias regarding Muslim Filipinos in the education of the Christian majority. This raises the possibility that, to the extent the policy is effective in strengthen Islamic identity among Filipino Muslim schoolchildren, it may leave untouched, if not exacerbate, the gulf between Filipino Christians and Filipino Muslims that the integration policy was meant to eradicate.[80]

Unpacking the Narrative of Bangsamoro "Unity"

The core of the Bangsamoro narrative is the presumed unity and cohesion that existed among the Moro peoples in the face of foreign intrusion, namely, Spanish, American, and finally, Filipino colonialism. Accordingly, Islam provided a vocabulary through which to reconstruct their past on the basis of the flattering myth of Moro unity which passed for incontrovertible narratives of indigenous Moro history. Such a convenient interpretation of history to frame the present (or not so distant past) is of course understandable, for it is never the romantic nationalist's goal to strain after pedantic accuracy of fact. Rather, it points to the fiction invented to supply the ostensible foundation for the contemporary Bangsamoro struggle.

Yet the fact of the matter is that the received wisdom of Moro unity in a centuries-old resistance to external powers betrays a selective reading and transmission of the historical record. Moro nationalists and romantics gave short shrift to the animosity, discord, and treachery that were as much definitive features of Moro politics in the face of colonialism as animus toward the colonizer. The inconvenient reality is that unity among the Moro has always been elusive, and intra-Moro intrigues and conflict are legion. While one could draw attention to tension and differences within the MNLF which resulted in its split, and later the competition and rivalry between the MNLF and MILF, as a familiar

---

[79] Details on education policy with regards to the madrasah of southern Philippines are elaborated in Jeffrey Ayala Milligan, "Islam and Education Policy Reform in the Southern Philippines," *Asia Pacific Journal of Education*, Vol. 28, No. 4, 2008.
[80] Milligan, "Islamization or Secularization?" p. 35.

case in point, there are in truth many further examples to draw on as we cast our minds further back into history, some of which cast doubt at precisely the historical references that lie at the heart of the narratives of Bangsamoroism. On this score, it bears recollecting the point made earlier in the chapter that what passes as immutable identity in nationalist discourse is often actually colonial, or anti-colonial, invention. Put differently, notwithstanding attempts to frame the Bangsamoro struggle in transhistorical and transcultural terms, the myth of a united monolithic Moro resistance to colonization propounded by many nationalist leaders valorizes the Bangsamoro frame but downplays local diversity in the construction of identity and, more significantly perhaps, belies empirical evidence.

Until the creation of the Moro secessionist movements in the 1960s, the Muslim tribes in the southern Philippines were in fact not a unified group. As the historical record attests, they not only battled the Spaniards as separate sultanates, but also fought against each other. Upon their arrival, the Spanish were not met by unified resistance, regardless of the narrative spun by Moro discourses on history. Instead, what greeted them was a collection of Muslim polities that were engaged in conflict to undermine and discredit each other. Sultans were contesting, usurping, exacting revenge, and undermining the rule of their peers.[81]

During the period of Spanish colonization, the sultanates of Sulu, Maguindanao, and Buayan were beset by internecine dynastic rivalries and competition over economic resources. Notably, we are told that the dynastic wars between the *datus* of Buayan and Maguindanao occurred despite the fact that they were relatives. So acrimonious were these conflicts and rivalries, the Spanish seized the opportunity to advance their own interest by leveraging on Moro distrust of each other. They did so by, among other things, intervening in succession conflicts and recognizing the authority and legitimacy of certain Moro leaders who were amenable to supporting the Spanish.[82] As but one example, in the early 15th century, the Spanish sought to exacerbate rivalry between the *datu* of Maguindanao, Buisan, and the *datu* of Buayan, Sirungan, during a period when Buayan's traditional control of the Pulangi river, conduit of a major trade route in Mindanao, was being eclipsed by Maguindanao.[83] On their part, Mindanao sultans intrigued with colonialists, taking up

---

[81] In 1619–1621, the sultanates of Buayan and Maguindanao were locked in a bloody struggle for primacy in the Pulangi valley. In 1702, Sultan Shahab ud-Din killed Sultan Kahar ud-Din of Maguindanao for his throne.

[82] Jamail A. Kamlian, *Bangsamoro Society and Culture. A Book of Readings on Peace and Development in Southern Philippines*. Iligan City: Iligan Center for Peace Education and Research, 1999, p. 88.

[83] See Cesar Adib Majul, *Muslims in the Philippines*. Manila: University of the Philippines Press, 1999, pp. 139–140.

with them against fellow Moro rulers, including members of their own royal families, such as when Maputi dispossessed his nephew of his title as chief of Taulan in the 1600s, or when the sultan of Tamontaca, Muhammad Jafar Sadiq Manamir, enlisted Spanish protection in 1730 to fend off a challenge from his nephew Malinug, who had just proclaimed himself sultan of Slangan. In another instance, the sultan of Tawi-Tawi, Alimudin, signed a treaty with Spain in 1737, which among other things paved the way for Jesuit priests to spread Christianity on the island, in exchange for Spanish support of his drive to consolidate power and centralize authority in the sultanate against the feudal interests of the *datu*.[84]

In a similar fashion, some *datu* rose to power through American patronage. Conflict between the sultans and *datus* of Sulu and Maguindanao were particularly pronounced during this period. When General John C. Bates was appointed to the command of Mindanao in 1899, "he noticed that in Mindanao island there was no central figure of power. It was individual Sultans and *Datus* who independently ruled the territories, a clear sign of discord amongst the rulers that allowed the Americans to capitalize upon."[85] It has been recorded that during the era of American colonialism, while *Datu* Ali was fighting the Americans, *Datu* Piang was actively assisting them.[86] Similarly in Sulu, the sultan of Sulu proactively aided Americans in their offensive against Panglima Hassan who had waged conflict against American colonial forces in rejection of the Bates Treaty entered into by the sultan and the United States in August 1899. In Lanao, General Pershing was allegedly in possession of a list which carried the names of Maranao *datu* who were prepared to engage in subversion and spying for a fee. When the period of active military resistance was over, isolated encounters continued but *datu* who were now serving under the American flag vied with one another to please their new colonial masters.[87] What was noticeable during this period was the demonstration of strong ethnic interests among the Maranaos, the Maguindanaos, and the Tausugs, each of whom tried to vie for supremacy in the government service.[88]

The consequences of these contestations for unity among the Moro were portentous, particularly on the obstacles that would later prevent the emergence of a truly coherent Bangsamoro nationalism and undivided nationalist movement. As the Mindanao historian Samuel K. Tan

---

[84] Patricio N. Abinales, *Orthodoxy and History in the Muslim-Mindanao Narrative*. Manila: Ateneo De Manila University Press, 2010, p. 45.
[85] John Foreman, *The Philippines*, Second Series, Volume II (off print copy of the 1906 edition). Manila: Filipiniana Book Guild, 1980.
[86] Majul, *Muslims in the Philippines*, pp. 139–140.   [87] Ibid.   [88] Ibid.

explained: "The violent struggle between datuships and the system of intrigues which polarized interest and loyalties along trans kinship lines dominated internal politics of Muslim societies during the first half of the century. They prevented the Muslims as a people from forging a unified resistance to a formidable combination of external forces supported by modern logistics and technology. Indeed it was this disunity and internal conflicts that allowed the imperialist and colonial government to implement the divide and rule policy in their favour."[89]

In the post-independence era, mutual suspicion in Muslim Mindanao existed not just between the Manila government and the Muslim leaders in the south, or between the Muslim and Christian leaders, significant though these tensions were. Not unlike the situation during the colonial era, much of the unrest in the area can be attributed to misunderstandings among Muslim leaders, which is where the root of Muslim disunity lies.[90] Intra-Moro enmity was so intense on certain occasions that, for instance, in Cotabato City until the early 1950s, the Quirino and Tamontaka bridges formed boundaries for certain *datu* families; for them to venture beyond these bridges would be "courting trouble."[91] Until the 1970s there were frequent armed encounters between scions of rival *datu* families and clans in Cotabato City. Today, such rivalry for power and prestige is still a major part of the Mindanao problem. For instance, during elections in Sulu, the military was mobilized to keep order and prevent bloodshed given the power rivalry among the Maguindanao, Maranao, and Tausug ethnic groups.[92]

From May 1990 to July 1999, Patricio Abinales tallied sixty violent incidents that could be attributed to feuds or feud-related causes in Maguindanao, Lanao provinces, Basilan, Sulu, and Tawi-Tawi. In most of these instances, the feuds involved *datus* and sultans who were leaders of clans, some of whom have been fighting for decades. When violence flared, members of the organized armed separatist organizations, the MNLF and MILF, took sides not according to their organizations, but their clan loyalties.[93] As a result, there were frequent instances of members of the same separatist organization, but from different clans or linguistic groups, taking up arms against each other.[94] To further complicate the picture, it should also be pointed out that political rivalries existed not just between clans, but within clans as well.[95] In the decade

---

[89] Samuel K. Tan, *The Filipino Muslim Armed Struggle, 1900–1972*. Manila: Filipinas Foundation, 1977, p. 51.
[90] Ibid., p. 65.   [91] Ibid.   [92] Ibid.   [93] Ibid.
[94] Needless to say, this throws into question the effectiveness of the armed wings of the MNLF and MILF as fighting units.
[95] Ibid., p. 66.

of the 1990s, this happened in Magundanao, particularly in the Datu Piang, Maganoy, Sultan sa Barongis, Matanog, and Buluan-Lutayan areas.[96]

In some respects, the conflicts and contestations as well as pride and volatility that plague Muslim Mindanao have come to be captured in the concept of *rido*.[97] *Rido* has been defined as "a state of recurring hostilities between families and kinship groups characterized by a series of retaliatory acts of violence carried out to avenge a perceived affront or injustice."[98] The meaning of the concept is often simplified to feudal clashes or clan warfare, in order to spotlight the kin-focused and iterative nature of this violence. *Rido* has wider implications for conflict in Mindanao primarily because of the tendency for it to interact in unfortunate ways with separatist conflict and other forms of violence.[99] These disputes, most commonly between families, led to retaliatory acts organized along family lines as conflict spirals.[100] Family squabbles easily escalate into mini-wars due to the sheer number of people involved. The men of the clan are indoctrinated in the ideology of *rido* and the defense of the clan's interest and honor. The vicious nature of such conflicts are evident in the scale of family involvement, which often involves the extended family, but also the fact that the conflicts normally persist over a long period of time, during which there would be repeated acts of violence and murder by one clan against the other and vice-versa.[101]

Some consider *rido* to be rooted in the Mindanao Muslim culture of honor, although it is fair to say that such outbursts of retaliatory violence is prevalent in other cultures as well, not to mention also that in the

---

[96] Ibid., p. 68.
[97] Also known in local parlance as pangayaw, magahat, pagbunuh, mamauli, kasaop, pagbaos, and lido either among Lumad or Moro ethnic groups.
[98] According to June Prill-Brett, the logic of rido maintains that a harm done to a village member is considered a threat to the security and autonomy of the village itself. On such occasions, the village is expected to retaliate to assert its strength and defensive capacity, and not lose the respect of other villages. See June Prill-Brett, *Pechen: The Bontok Peace Pact Institution*. Baguio City: Cordillera Studies Center, College Baguio, University of the Philippines, 1987, p. 15.
[99] Wilfredo Magno Torres III, "Introduction," in Wilfredo Magno Torres III (ed.), *Rido: Clan Feuding and Conflict Management in Mindanao*. Manila: Ateneo de Manila University Press, 2014, p. 4.
[100] See "Durable Solutions Still out of Sight for Many IDPs and Returnees in Mindanao," *Internal Displacement Monitoring Centre*, June 10, 2011. Available www.internal-displacement.org/idmc/website/countries.nsf/(httpEnvelopes)/F11DCA748A6D58EFC125764F004C45E6?OpenDocument.
[101] These clan wars are exacerbated by conditions of poverty, poor governance, competition over resources, corruption, the proliferation of firearms, the lack of law enforcers, and an inefficient justice system. See Simone Orendain, "The Persistence of Blood Feuds in the Philippines," July 25, 2011. Available www.pri.org/stories/2011-07-25/persistence-blood-feuds-philippines.

Philippines such feuds predate the coming of Islam, meaning to say there is nothing "Muslim" about it.[102] Likewise, though cast as a cultural phenomenon, one should also consider that *rido* often takes place in the absence of (also in lieu of) an effective and legitimate justice system. *Rido* has periodically also come to be imbricated with insurgent and separatist violence in the southern Philippines. There have been several visible instances of this, such as in March 2012 when armed units under MNLF Commander Teo and MILF Commander Tarzan clashed over ownership of agricultural land in Sitio Maputi, or in May 2013 when troops under the command of Commander Mansur Imbong (MILF) and *Datu* Dima Ambil (MNLF) clashed in Matalam. More to the point, *rido* demonstrates how clan based identities defy, if not unravel, the master narrative of Moro Muslim unity in profound ways.

Rido is rooted in the feudal power struggles that have come to define much of Mindanao history, and shatters the myth of Moro unity. It has been estimated that since the 1930s, nearly 1,200 *rido* conflicts have occurred in Mindanao, resulting in the death of 5,000 people and the displacement of several tens of thousands, with at least 70,000 people being displaced in 2010 alone as a result of such conflicts.[103] The highest numbers of *rido* incidents have been reported in the following Mindanao provinces: Lanao de Sur, Maguindanao, Lanao del Norte, and Sulu.[104] With the receding of conflict between the Philippine government and the MILF since the signing of a ceasefire agreement in 2009, clan violence has represented the main cause of displacement in Mindanao.[105] Even so, the increasing number of clan conflicts still raises questions about the resilience of the peace agreement between the Philippine government and the MILF. This is because clan wars frequently expand into wider armed conflicts involving armed militias, the military, and armed separatist groups. In 2007, the head of the MILF truce panel said as much, conceding the fact that most of the fighting between the MILF and the government since 2003 in Mindanao had been triggered by *rido*, as warring families would petition either the separatist groups or the military for help.[106] This state of affairs is often not helped by the fact that in

---

[102] See "Philippines: Vendettas and Violence on Mindanao – Analysis," *IRIN*, June 24, 2009. Available www.irinnews.org/report/84979/philippines-vendettas-and-violence-on-mindanao-analysis.
[103] "Clan Wars (Rido) Regularly Cause Displacement in Mindanao (April 2011)."
[104] See "Philippines: Vendettas and Violence on Mindanao – Analysis," *IRIN*, June 24, 2009. Available www.irinnews.org/report/84979/philippines-vendettas-and-violence-on-mindanao-analysis.
[105] Haironesah Domado, "Mitigating Clan Violence in Mindanao Ahead of Midterm Elections," May 8, 2013. Available http://asiafoundation.org/in-asia/2013/05/08/mitigating-clan-violence-in-mindanao-ahead-of-midterm-elections/.
[106] "Clan Wars (Rido) Regularly Cause Displacement in Mindanao (April 2011)."

many instances, members of the warring family would also be members of either the groups or the military as well.

The point to be stressed thence, is that even though from the formation of the MNLF and after Moro armed resistance and separatist groups have claimed to have brought the disparate Moro clans together in the name of Islam, and in the process successfully constructed a collective identity of the Bangsamoro nation, the roots of division run deep in Moro society. Indeed, this at least in part explains the existence of factionalism in both the MNLF and MILF today, and the inability of the Bangsamoro to present a united front in pursuit of their cause.

In sum, the historical baggage from the pre-colonial and colonial eras has been carried forward to the present-day Muslim south. As Samuel Tan succinctly summarized:

> First is the problem of disunity. The Muslim struggle has not been freed from the ills of traditionalism, intrigues, collaboration, and ethnicism. Second is the problem of integration in three levels of social life... disunity in the local level is primarily due to individualistic tendencies and values which somewhat transcend ethnic values. Secondly, Muslim groups such as those from Lanao, Cotabato and Sulu maintain an ethnolinguistic rivalry which has kept them at a distance. Finally the most glaring disunity exists at the national level, which is rooted in the history of Filipino Muslims. This is primarily about integrating ethnically than at a wider societal level.[107]

Hence, as regards the hopes and aspirations of generations of Bangsamoro nationalists, the mitigating and centripetal potential of Islam was never realized in a way such that it could underpin the creation of the Bangsamoro nation in the Philippine south.

Finally, just as the diversity of identity signifiers and interests has frustrated attempts to orchestrate a singular pursuit of Bangsamoro self-determination, it has also prompted the reconceptualization and recasting of Moro history away from the "hegemony" of these very Bangsamoro discourses and narratives toward a recognition of its pluralist antecedents. As Miriam Ferrer observes:

> Other voices are coming out emphasizing the diversity among the 13 Islamized ethnolinguistic groups in Mindanao. They are concerned that official Bangsamoro history has downplayed the diversity in local histories and practices in the effort to compress Moro-ness into a single, historical timeline with attributes (events, features, personalities) largely drawn from the numerically and politically dominant Moro ethnic groups, namely, the Tausug, Maguindanao, Maranao. They are raising questions on the preeminence given to the sultanate as against the many more autonomous datus and councils of elders that shaped

---

[107] Tan, *The Filipino Muslim Armed Struggle, 1900–1972*, p. 151.

the evolution of Moro polities, and that could inform the charting of alternative political processes and arrangements.[108]

Conclusion

This chapter has outlined the contours of the struggle on the part of the Muslim minority in the southern Philippine islands of Mindanao and the Sulu Archipelago by casting light on the production and reproduction of discourses and meaning, in particular the conception (and reconception) of Bangsamoro identity. In terms of the diagnostic frames employed by agents of Bangsamoro nationalism, frustration about the loss of land has given rise to a Moro self-consciousness where local history was investigated and invented, national myths constructed, decay of local and religious culture deplored, and the glory of the pre-Spanish history celebrated. This in turn led to prognoses that turned on the need to regain loss land, not to mention pride and identity, which included the use of armed insurgency and rebellion. This has certainly been the case with organizations such as the MILF, for whom *jihad* resonates both in terms of political violence and political dialogue. The MILF has used Islamist ideology tied to historical memory to reaffirm Moro commitment to the cause, to generate meaning for the struggle, and to cement solidarity.

At the same time, the chapter has also identified the contours of change and how reframing has taken place in order for conflict narratives to remain pertinent and effective as vehicles of mobilization. This was evident in how discourses on Bangsamoroism – chiefly, what and who is a Bangsamoro – were framed and reframed in order to enhance its appeal, as well as how Islam became an increasingly salient feature of the narrative of local struggle.

Following the nullification of the MOA-AD in 2008, peace talks stalled and reactionary violence broke out in Central Mindanao. It was only after a "secret" meeting between President Benigno Aquino III and MILF Chairman Al-Haj Murad Ibrahim in Tokyo on August 4, 2011, that the impasse broke and talks resumed by way of informal and formal "exploratory" meetings that began in January 2012 and culminated in the signing of the landmark CAB in March 2014. Despite its successful completion, however, the devil remains in the details. While the Philippine state has acknowledged that the present status quo was insufficient to meet the aspirations of the Bangsamoro, it remains to be

---

[108] Miriam Coronel Ferrer, "Interrogating the Bangsamoro Master Frame," *ABS-CBN News*, October 30, 2009. Available www.abs-cbnnews.com/views-and-analysis/10/30/09/interrogating-bangsamoro-master-frame.

seen if the implementation of the CAB will succeed, or if it will meet the fate of the agreement reached with the MNLF almost two decades earlier, which led to the formation (and eventual failure) of the ARMM. Over and above that, the actions of spoilers such as the BIFM comprising rogue elements of the MILF continue their acts of political violence in Mindanao. Needless to say, these actions might well influence broader public opinion against government concessions to the Bangsamoro Muslims, bringing to the fore, yet again, the historically difficult relations between the faith and ethnic communities in Mindanao; difficulties built on frames and narratives that communities have come to be wedded to over decades and centuries.

3 Thailand's Southern Border Provinces
Constructing Narratives and Imagining Patani Darussalam

Thailand's southernmost provinces of Pattani, Yala, Narathiwat, and the Malay-speaking districts of Songkhla have a combined population of between 1.8 and two million people, of whom more than 1.5 million are ethnic Malays who profess the Islamic faith.[1] Once part of the independent kingdom of Patani (a historic kingdom not to be confused with the province of Pattani that exists today, although both are located in the same geographical area of the southern provinces), this distinctive ethnic-religious region has a history and identity that predate the imposition of centralized rule of the kingdom of Siam in the early 20th century.

The region is situated at the junction between predominantly Buddhist mainland and predominantly Muslim maritime regions of Southeast Asia. In cultural and linguistic terms, however, its occupants are at home in neither milieu. For instance, while Thai Malay-Muslims, known colloquially as *"Nayu,"* may share similar ethnic and cultural traits as their Malaysian-Malay counterparts, many who work across the border in northern Malaysia have in fact experienced alienation because of their association with the predominantly Buddhist Thai state, which they feel makes them less "Malay" in the eyes of their Malaysian neighbors.[2] It is for this reason that anthropologists and sociologists have written extensively on *Nayu* as being in possession of dual (and duelling) identities.

---

[1] The Malay-speaking Songkhla districts include Theba (Tiba in Malay), Saba Yoi (Sebayu), Na Thawi (Nawi), and Chana (Chenok).

[2] I have had this view expressed to me on many occasions by Thai Malay-Muslims who cross the border daily to work in northern towns of the Malaysian state of Kelantan in the course of random conversations during many visits to the southern provinces. Part of the problem lies in the fact that many Thai Malay-Muslims are illegal and unauthorized workers in northern Malaysia, particularly in the food and beverage industry. On the part of the Thai Malay-Muslims, many have also expressed admiration for the state of Malaysia, and especially Kelantan, which in their view has been able to practice the kind of "pristine Islam" denied to them and their fellow Malay-Muslims from the southern border provinces. This view is demonstrated by the immense popularity of Malaysian *ulama* such as the late Nik Aziz Nik Mat in Islamic circles in southern Thailand. Some locals even referred to the Malay-Muslims of southern Thailand as *"orang sakit di semenanjung Melayu"* ("The sick people of the Malay Peninsula").

In part because of the geographic position of this region at the margins of the Thai geobody, Thailand's nation-state constructs, along with its historical narrative and the centralized structure of the Thai state, have vacillated between accommodation and alienation of the unique identity and historical narrative of the Malay south. Resonating with what was discussed in the foregoing chapter on the southern Philippines, relative economic underdevelopment of the region has added further to the sense of alienation that over the decades has exercised the Malay-Muslim cause.

It is against this backdrop that the long-standing Malay-Muslim struggle to define and defend a conception of nationhood distinct from Thailand's official discourse of nationalism has been summarized succinctly by the Thai political scientist Michael Connors, who poignantly surmised: "The history of the South may well be written as a history of differentiated cyclical patterns of Malay resistance and rebellion and state accommodation and pacification."[3] As we shall see, driving this pattern is an ethno-nationalist cultural and historical narrative that has manifested religious overtones, which in turn have been used to frame a call to mobilization among disaffected youth toward the ends of resistance and opposition to the Thai state. A consequence of this clash of conceptions of nationhood, as suggested in Connors' reflections on the history of the region, has been the outbreak of periodic cycles of violence, the most recent of which has been raging for more than a decade and a half, with little sign of abating.

The ongoing violence in Thailand's southern border provinces has prompted learned disputes between scholars, commentators, and pundits divided over the causes of this violence, and more so, the identity of its perpetrators. This chapter does not intend to wade into the murky waters of that debate, for its interest lies not so much in the identity of the actors as the narratives that have been used to frame their actions.[4] Nevertheless, it argues that while the ongoing anarchic violence has elements to it that may be less about history and identity than they are about crime, politics, and vendettas, the existence of an insurgency amidst this anarchy, nourished by precisely these issues of history and identity, and that has found expression in armed violence, cannot be denied. In line with the framework of this book, what is of primary interest in this chapter is

---

[3] Michael K. Connors, "War on Error and the Southern Fire: How Terrorism Analysts Get it Wrong," *Critical Asian Studies*, Vol. 38, 2006, p. 151.

[4] I have addressed this issue in greater detail elsewhere. See Joseph Chinyong Liow, "International Jihad and Muslim Radicalism in Thailand? Toward an Alternative Interpretation," *Asia Policy*, Vol. 2, July 2006. While admittedly dated, I maintain the essence of the argument remains relevant a decade after the article was written.

the matter of how the place of the southern border provinces in the political history of Thailand has been conceptualized, and the central Thai state's inability to incorporate them into the imagined Thai geopolitical body despite numerous attempts that have ranged from accommodation to outright repression. This reality is all the more remarkable given the Thai state's relative success in gradually assimilating and integrating minority communities elsewhere along its borders, or even well within them (such as the Isan region of northeast Thailand).

To better understand the tangled roots of Thailand's restive south, one must invariably investigate subjective elements in the construction of nationalist discourse and movement such as memory, value, sentiment, myth, and symbol.[5] A central feature of these elements is the role of religion in the ethno-nationalist conceptions of nationhood that have framed resistance to the central state since 1909, perhaps even earlier.

Patani History as "Anti-Thai" History

Since the region's conversion to Islam, which most scholars speculate took place sometime in the 15th century, Thailand's southernmost provinces, then collectively known as Patani Darussalam or Patani Raya (Greater Patani), enjoyed various degrees of autonomy despite being forcefully incorporated into the sphere of influence of Siamese suzerainty in 1786.[6] As a tributary of Siam, Patani was obliged to supply soldiers for Siam's many wars with the neighboring kingdoms located in what is today Burma. More significant was the fact that the Patani kingdoms were expected to send *Bunga Mas* (Flowers of Gold), a symbol of obeisance, to the Siamese courts every two and a half years in a gesture of respect and deference. On several occasions, leaders of Patani refused to perform this gesture. Predictably, this defiance prompted Siamese recriminations that resulted in wars between Siam and Patani, which for the latter quickly entered into local folklore as wars of resistance. From these conflagrations, it was the 1786 conflict that stood out for how it considerably weakened Patani, forcing the once proudly independent kingdom into

---

[5] Ludger Mees, "Politics, Economy, or Culture? The Rise and Development of Basque Nationalism in the Light of Social Movement Theory," *Theory and Society*, Vol. 33, No. 3/4, June–August 2004, p. 312.

[6] Both terms were used interchangeably in local narratives of Patani history. See Wan Kadir Che Man, *Muslim Separatism: The Moros of Southern Philippines and the Malays of Southern Thailand*. Singapore: Oxford University Press, 1990, p. 34. According to Teeuw and Wyatt, the origins of the Islamic term Patani Darussalam could be traceable to the Islamization of the Patani region that occurred between the late 15th and early 16th centuries. See Andries Teeuw and David K. Wyatt, *Hikayat Patani*. The Hague: Martinus Nijhoff, 1970.

the sphere of influence of the court of Songkhla in 1809, itself a vassal of Siam at the time. Nothing symbolizes this troubled historical memory more vividly than the presence of the *Phaya Tani* (Seri Patani in Malay) cannon, the largest of forty-two cannons on display outside the Ministry of Defence building that according to the Malay-Muslim narrative was captured by the Siamese army during the 1786 conflict, in Bangkok today.[7] Several revolts by Malay-Muslims from Patani occurred, most notably in 1791, 1808, and 1931, but all were brutally crushed by Siam. In 1902, seven provinces were created out of the territory presumed to be the kingdom of Patani, each with a Raja appointed by the Siamese throne. In return, each province was required to provide an annual tribute in the form of money and/or military recruits for the Siamese king when the need arose.[8] These encounters have left scars on the landscape, scars that have yet to heal.

A great deal of tension and mutual distrust rooted in the assimilationist outlook and approach of the Siamese state has widened the chasm between the centre and the southern periphery. Geopolitical imperatives behind Siam's conquest of Patani outlined earlier were accompanied by a colonial disposition toward the southern provinces expressed in the central Siamese state's repeated disregard for local cultural and religious identity and practices during their administration of the region. Since the beginning of the 20th century, the royal Siamese court, the military, and the bureaucracy have instituted measures that sought to assimilate the Malay-Muslim provinces into the wider Siamese geopolitical body.[9] These measures continued to be pursued in earnest by subsequent Thai nationalist and military administrations following the end of absolute monarchy in 1925. Many of these measures were decidedly punitive and blatantly discriminatory in nature. Others, such as the exercise of juridical

---

[7] Legend has it that the *Phaya Tani* cannon was commissioned by the Patani kingdom to bolster its defense against Siamese invaders. It was believed to have been casted sometime between the 15th and 17th centuries. The significance of this cannon and what it represents is expressed in stories of how the cannon ended up in Bangkok. It is believed that the cannon was one of two massive weapons captured by invading Siamese forces during the 1786 conflict that resulted in the subjugation of the Patani kingdom. The cannons were purportedly drawn back to Bangkok as part of the commander of the Siamese forces Prince Sura Singhanat's strategy to demoralize the Malay-Muslim defenders. To many denizens of Patani, the cannon remains a symbolism of the humiliation of their historical kingdom at the hands of Siamese invaders. In response to local calls for the return of the *Phaya Tani* cannon, a replica was installed in Pattani in June 2013. Soon after its installation, it was bombed by militants. "Phaya Tani Replica Cannon Bombed," *Bangkok Post*, June 11, 2013.

[8] Nantawan Haemindra, "The Problem of the Thai-Muslims in the Four Southern Provinces of Thailand (Part I)," *Journal of Southeast Asian Studies*, Vol. 7, 1976.

[9] For a detailed account of the history and background behind Malay-Muslim separatism in southern Thailand, see Che Man, *Muslim Separatism*.

control drawn from British imperial strategies, studied with impressive detail by Tamara Loos, while arguably more subtle, were no less consequential.[10] In retrospect, they have had (and continue to have) a lingering caustic effect on relations between the central government and its ethnic Malay peripheries. It was from these encounters that enduring Malay-Muslim narratives of identity and resistance emerged.[11]

As a consequence of the heavy footprint that the Thai state left across the southern provinces, a litany of grievances gradually accumulated among the Malay-Muslim community in the region, which boiled over into civil protests and occasionally even violent confrontations with the state. The most significant of these was the April 1948 Dusun Nyor Rebellion, which remains fresh as collective memory and folk consciousness perpetuated by oral history.[12] By the 1960s, these sporadic outbursts and protests gave way to organized armed resistance with the formation of several separatist organizations, most notably the BNPP (*Barisan Nasional Pembebasan Patani* or National Liberation Front of Patani), BRN (*Barisan Revolusi Nasional* or *National Revolutionary Front*), and PULO (*Patani United Liberation Organization*).

Armed separatism in southern Thailand first peaked in the late 1970s and early 1980s, and was endorsed and supported by governments in the Middle East (particularly Libya and Syria), many of which provided financial aid, training, and ultimately refuge, thereby creating an activist Patani diaspora which provided material and ideological support for the insurgency. Additionally, European countries such as Sweden also provided refuge, and in so doing fostered a Patani political elite in exile that have since emerged lay claim to leadership of the present insurgency. Conventional wisdom contends that the separatist struggle had faded by the 1990s. As a matter of fact, violence continued, albeit with decreasing frequency. Thai officials have attributed this respite to the "success" of enhanced counterinsurgency efforts, a blanket amnesty for insurgent combatants, the introduction of civilian democracy that both precipitated

---

[10] See Tamara Loos, *Subject Siam: Family, Law and Colonial Modernity in Thailand*. Ithaca, N.Y.: Cornell University Press, 2006.

[11] For some specific examples of the policies of assimilation, particularly in terms of religion and language, see Joseph Chinyong Liow, *Islam, Education, and Reform in Southern Thailand: Tradition and Transformation*. Singapore: Institute of Southeast Asian Studies, 2009.

[12] Malay peasants had clashed with police forces of the Phibun Songgkram government in Kampung Dusun Nyor in the Rang-ae district of Narathiwat in violence, allegedly resulting in 400 Malay-Muslim and thirty police deaths. See Chaiwat Satha-Anand, "The Silence of the Bullet Moment: Violence and 'Truth' Management, Dusun-nyor 1948, and Kru-Ze 2004," *Critical Asian Studies*, Vol. 38, No. 1, March 2006. Through the perpetuation of this narrative as oral history, the mythology surrounding Dusun Nyor persists and replays in the minds of locals.

and facilitated greater Malay-Muslim representation in mainstream Thai politics, and even the presumed neutralization of international sympathy at the Organization of Islamic Conference after Thailand successfully obtained observer status in the organization in 1998.[13] Equally important but less well known, the ostensible success of a more balanced counterinsurgency strategy and the Thai government's diplomatic efforts also sowed rifts among leaders of armed resistance and separatist groups, contributing to factionalism and splits which further weakened the movement from within as insurgents were forced abroad and underground even as attempts to create an umbrella separatist organization failed.[14] But in truth, these were more tactical attempts to defuse conflict rather than strategic efforts to eliminate the underlying root causes.

While the 1990s did indeed witness a decline in armed resistance and violence, what set in was in fact a morose quiet that lulled the Thai state into a false sense of security.[15] As complacent authorities gradually shifted attention away from the provinces on the belief that the "security problem" had been solved, new opportunities for recruitment and mobilization opened up. Politico-cultural separatist organizations were reproduced, and splinter groups emerged in exile in Europe and closer to home across the border in neighboring Southeast Asian countries, taking various forms and guises. That the insurgency was not so much defeated as simply driven underground (or across borders and beyond the territorial reach of the state) meant that for insurgents intent on regrouping, new opportunities for consolidation and mobilization needed to be, and eventually were, found.

Conflict was eventually reignited with the advent of the administration of Thaksin Shinawatra, the most controversial political leader in recent Thai history. The year following his election victory witnessed a discernible spike in violence. In January 2004, armed assailants mounted

---

[13] After years of hardline counterinsurgency tactics, the governments of Prem Tinsulanonda (1980–1988) and Chavalit Yongchaiyudh (1996–1997) embarked on a major recalibration of counterinsurgency strategy in the south aimed not only at addressing the socio-economic and cultural grievances that drove the separatist insurgency. This included the establishment of key institutions such as the CPM-43 and the Southern Border Provinces Administrative Committee that fine-tuned military and civilian engagement tactics, respectively, and the implementation of an amnesty plan known as *Tai Rom Yen* or "South under a Cool Shade."

[14] Interview, Kelantan, January 28, 2008. In the 1990s, leaders of several separatist groups attempted to form an umbrella organization. Called Bersatu (meaning "united" in Malay), the organization never amounted to more than several gatherings of the respective leaderships.

[15] Thai military sources insist, however, it was because of budgetary cuts introduced by the democrat party leadership in the mid to late 1990s that counterinsurgency initiatives could not be sustained at an efficient and effective level.

an audacious raid on a military depot in the province of Narathiwat, in which 400 weapons were stolen and four Buddhist soldiers killed after they were separated from their Muslim counterparts. That attack was followed by an alarmingly swift escalation in violence. Over the course of Thaksin's terms in office, the situation was compounded by the hawkish outlook of his security advisors, many of whom prioritized the use of force to curb the growing trend of violence in the southern provinces.[16]

Notwithstanding the seemingly intractable nature of the violence today, what remains striking as one follows this conflict as it has meandered over the course of history is the remarkable familiarity and resilience of the narratives that have framed it even as the Thai state struggled to deal with the detritus from decades of failed policies at integration and assimilation.

"Anak Patani" as Subject or Citizen?

It is beyond the scope of this chapter to analyze in detail the historical backdrop to and origins of the current southern Thai conflict. This has received ample coverage elsewhere.[17] Nevertheless, for current purposes it remains important to consider the framing alignment of armed groups in terms of narratives that define the problem and are used to legitimize their struggle, as well as of the population in general for whom these narratives often resonate. To that end, an important element to the framing exercise of the Malay-Muslim resistance narrative has been the move to legitimize violence as a means of social and political change in order not only to right perceived historical wrongs, but also as a response to the majoritarian ethos of the Thai state that has refused to countenance or accommodate alternative identities as part of their official narrative of Thai nationalism.[18] In this manner, recurring themes of legitimacy deficit on the part of the central state in the eyes of the Malay-Muslims and

---

[16] This point was convincingly argued in Ukrist Pathmanand, "Thaksin's Achilles' Heel: The Failure of Hawkish Approaches in the Thai South," *Critical Asian Studies*, Vol. 38, No. 1, 2006.

[17] This issue has been taken up in Ibrahim Syukri, *History of the Malay Kingdom of Patani*. Athens, O.H.: University of Ohio, Center for International Studies, 1985; Surin Pitsuwan, *Islam and Malay Nationalism: A Case Study of the Malay-Muslims of Southern Thailand*. Bangkok: Thai Khadi Research Institute, 1985; Thanet Aphornsuvan, *Rebellion in Southern Thailand: Contending Histories*. Washington D.C.: East-West Center Washington, 2007.

[18] This is to be distinguished from the more tactical policies and gestures of accommodation on the part of various Bangkok-based governments, which are efforts to soften the edges of Thai policy but have little to do with the fundamental position that Thai nationalism and national identity leave little room for alternatives, meaning to say, minority nationalisms and national identities.

exclusion of this minority community in the state-building and nation-building process have continued to define the long-standing problems in Thailand's three southernmost provinces.

Historical contexts of cultural, communal, and national identity have always stood at the heart of the Malay-Muslim struggle in southern Thailand against central authority, and to a large extent continue to inform the content of the community's grievances today. The historical roots of rebellion can be traced to popular resistance to the legitimacy of Thai rule in the southern provinces as well as the desire to preserve important local cultural and linguistic practices threatened by the assimilation policies of various central administrations pursued in the name of "nation building" that is in turn premised on the cultural indivisibility of the country.

In consonance with Malay-Muslim historical narratives which nationalists, separatists, and insurgents continue to nourish and deploy for purposes of mobilization and legitimizing resistance, the kingdom of Patani Darussalam, which in their collective belief was coterminous with the territory of the three southern provinces today, was a stubbornly independent Malay polity that had thrived for centuries with a proud history.[19] All this was overturned, first with the subordination of Patani to Siamese rule in 1786, and later during the colonial era, epitomized most profoundly in the signing of the Anglo-Siamese Treaty of 1909. Yet while this narrative harks back to a Patani kingdom that encompassed present-day Pattani, Narathiwat, and Yala provinces (and, depending on whose historical account one is considering, portions of Songkhla), the Malay-Muslim conception and discourse of Patani nationhood are silent on the overlaps between the history of Patani and that of present-day northern Malaysian states, including a period in the mid-17th century when Kelantan exercised suzerainty over Patani.[20] Apropos this overlapping "Malaysian" and "Thai" history, the implications are that territorial borders that ring the Malay-Muslim "nation" conceived by nationalists and insurgents in southern Thailand would not in fact accord strictly by the "southern border provinces" known today, much in the same way that in the Philippines locally manufactured Moro histories (and mythologies) oftentimes differed from what actually transpired in the historical record.

---

[19] The classic narrative of this version of history in the English language can be found in Ibrahim Syukri, *History of the Malay Kingdom of Patani*. Translated by Conner Bailey and John N. Miksic. Athens, OH.: Center for International Studies, Ohio University, 1985.

[20] See Nathan Porath, "The Hikayat Patani: The Kingdom of Patani in the Malay and Thai Political World," *Journal of the Malaysian Branch of the Royal Asiatic Society*, Vol. 84, No. 2, 2011, pp. 52–54.

According to received wisdom contained in local narratives, the Anglo-Siamese treaty that forcibly incorporated seven Malay sultanates into Siam and effectively cemented the northernmost borders of the Malay-Muslim world between modern-day Thailand and Malaysia was nothing less than an act of subterfuge. Crucially, Malay-Muslims had little say in either the process or the outcome. This history is often juxtaposed in popular imagination with the "golden age" when Patani was a trading hub as well as an intellectual centre for Islamic studies, which British and Thai colonialists eventually contrived to eliminate.

After the signing of the Anglo-Siamese Treaty, the Patani kingdom was administratively subjugated and divided into the provinces collectively known today as the southern border provinces, namely Pattani (an administrative province not to be confused with the historical kingdom of Patani), Yala, and Narathiwat.[21] From the perspective of the metropole, the fragmentation of the old kingdom into these administrative provinces was deliberately done in order to prevent any coalescing of anti-Siamese forces against the government. To further entrench the capital's control of the provinces, Thai-Buddhists were dispatched from both Bangkok and the upper southern provinces to replace local Malay-Muslim elite in administrative positions. Cultural mores were also forcefully transformed as Malay-Muslims were compelled through various legislative means to abandon all measure of their cultural symbols – traditional names, traditional dress, and local language – in order to take on Thai names (in exchange for employment), learn the Thai language, and adopt Western styles.[22] The proud institution of the traditional Islamic boarding school – the *pondok* – was over time reduced to an outlier and anachronism by the modern education policies introduced by the state.

For the most part, these pressures on local Malay identity and their continued salience today are traceable to this unceasing drive on the part of the central Thai state to craft and assert a distinct and unitary Thai identity that encompassed various minority groups situated within its borders. This was undertaken under the guise of socioeconomic development (*pattanakarn*) and undergirded by a proud national narrative of how Siam adroitly navigated the predations of Western colonial powers in order to emerge from the colonial era as the only Southeast Asian state untouched, in form at least, by colonialism.

---

[21] The province of Satun is often included when the southern border provinces are mentioned. It has a different history, however. Satun was part of the Malay sultanate of Kedah, and was retained by Siam when it ceded Kedah, over which it enjoyed suzerainty, to Britain in 1909.

[22] For a detailed account of the history and background of the Malay-Muslim cause, see Che Man, *Muslim Separatism*.

But Thailand's ability to successfully elide colonialism was at least in part attributable to the Siamese state's quick adoption of Western social mores and administrative practices. Recognized as the father of modernization in Thailand, the rule of King Chulalongkorn (Rama V., 1868–1910) at the turn of the 20th century not only introduced bureaucratic reforms inspired by the West, but also Western conceptions of nationhood, specifically the creation of a nation-state on the premise of enforced conformity and the denial of differences. In Thailand, however, this attempt at embracing a "civic" identity in fact took the form of the categorical imposition of the dominant Thai identity, captured in the mantra of *Chat, Sasana, Phramahakasat* (Nation, Religion, King) promulgated by Chulalongkorn's son and successor, King Vajiravudh.

Not surprisingly, the period which saw the emergence of this conception of a superior, all-encompassing Thai-centric national identity in the early 20th century coincided with the genesis of unrest in the south. Vajiravudh's rule triggered a long struggle for autonomy by Malay-Muslims based precisely on local narratives of cultural identity and interpretations of history that the central state sought to assimilate (or according to these narratives, exterminate). As Surin Pitsuwan argued, Vajiravudh's rule marked "the beginning of a long and torturous struggle to widen the sphere and deepen the level of autonomy for the Malay-Muslims of Patani based on specific ethnic differences."

In keeping with the theme of this book, the factor of religion (*Sasana*) demands closer scrutiny. The concept of religion in Thai national discourse refers to Buddhism, which since the enunciation of the three pillars of Thai nationalism has operated as the *de facto* religion of the state. Commenting on this, Charles Keyes has intimated that "one of the underlying factors behind the virtual exclusion of... Muslims from national politics is the equation of Buddhism with the national religion."[23] Concomitantly, the monarchy had operated on the mistaken premise that the Thai people – including the Malay-Muslims of the southern provinces – had historically chosen Buddhism as their religion.[24]

At the same time that this Thai centric discourse on identity emerged, narratives of alternate identities such as "Khmer," "Lao," "Chinese," or "Malay" became actively discouraged.[25] Needless to say,

---

[23] Charles Keyes, *Thailand: Buddhist Kingdom as Modern Nation-State*. Boulder, CO. and London: Westview Press, 1987, p. 207.

[24] Walter F. Vella, *Chaiyo!: King Vajiravudh and the Development of Thai Nationalism*. Honolulu, HI: University of Honolulu Press, 1978, pp. 220–221.

[25] See Craig J. Reynolds (ed.), *National Identity and its Defenders: Thailand, 1939–1989*. Melbourne: Monash Papers on Southeast Asia, 1991; Yoko Hayami, "Redefining 'Otherness' from Northern Thailand. Introduction: Notes Towards Debating Multiculturalism in Thailand and Beyond," *Journal of Southeast Asian Studies*, Vol. 44, No. 2, 2006.

the consequences of this clash of identities have been played out vividly in the southern provinces. More recently, the dangers of a majoritarian identity emerging around the notion of "Thai-ness" have been compounded by a growing chorus of right-wing sentiments articulating how Buddhism in Thailand was coming under threat from the greater assertiveness on the part of the Malay-Muslims. This has resulted in the onset of a siege mentality. DVD-based comments expressed by a Bangkok-based monk suggesting this to be the case have been documented by Duncan McCargo:

> The separatists planned first to eliminate monks and temples, then make the region a forbidden area for Buddhists, who would be driven out of their homes and forced to move to other parts of the country. Eventually the south would be like Afghanistan, where huge ancient Buddha images had been blown up.... The strategy of the separatists was to rule the whole country using their religious laws. Muslims were now moving to many parts of the north and Isan and setting up *surau* (prayer facilities) and mosques everywhere, which would soon be as ubiquitous as Buddhist temples.[26]

Others have used even starker language to describe how the military has become, in the context of the southern Thailand conflict, "moral guardians, sacred avengers of the nation, not mere state servants, whose sacred duty is to uphold and protect the integrity of Thai Buddhism," implying an apparent blurring of the line between Buddhism and the Thai army that adds further to the climate of anxiety and the amplification of religious faultlines.[27] McCargo has also persuasively argued that "hardline nationalist discourse and anti-Muslim sentiments were becoming increasingly overt in the expression of Thai Buddhist identity and thinking."[28] Fraying Buddhist-Muslim relations have been further enervated by periodic attacks on monks and temples by the most extreme elements of the insurgency since the outbreak of full-scale violence in 2004.[29] Attacks on monks have been symbolic in this regard:

> Indeed, in my own research on Karen villages in northern Thailand (Mae Oo Soo Kee, Mae Kuang Luang, and Go Baw Ta), I had come across many instances where Karen living in this region referred to themselves as "Thai" despite the fact that they continue to speak the Karen language, don the Karen traditional dress, and celebrate Karen festivals.

[26] Duncan McCargo, *Mapping National Anxieties: Thailand's Southern Conflict*. Copenhagen: NIAS Press, 2012, p. 24.
[27] Jerryson, *Buddhist Fury*, p. 175.
[28] See Duncan McCargo, "The Politics of Buddhist Identity in Thailand's Deep South: The Demise of Civil Religion?" *Journal of Southeast Asian Studies*, Vol. 40, No. 1, February 2009, p. 32.
[29] Part of the problem, it seems, is because some Buddhist villagers have fled their villages and sought refuge in temples, after which militants resorted to attacking these temples. Interview, Pattani, January 12, 2011.

Attacks by militants upon monks are interpreted as attacks on the 'body-politic' as well as on the Buddhist Sangha. Indeed, Buddhism has never existed outside the state; it has served as a source and as a means of legitimation. Monks, as state agents, have promoted the sociopolitical objectives of reintegrating ethnic populations and creating moral communities of national belonging and solidarity. Monks are therefore seen as the 'enemy' even though they have no enmity toward Muslims. Ironically, monks cannot let go and detach from their political role and ethno-nationalist significations. They are identified as religious and national symbols, not as individual human beings.[30]

The Malay "Other"

How Malay-Muslim identity is viewed from the optic of Thai conceptions of nationhood is perhaps most profoundly, and uncomfortably, captured in the nomenclature used to identify and categorize them in the lexicon of the day. Several observations can be made in this regard, beginning with the term "*khaek*," which has frequently been employed in "official" Thai discourse to refer to the Malay-Muslims of the southern provinces.[31] On its surface, the meaning of "*khaek*" approximates "guests," and is used with reference not just to Malay-Muslims but many other minority ethnic groups within Thailand as well. The usage of this term in southern Thailand, however, has been and remains a controversial issue, and the controversy surrounding it speaks to the fact that it is highly context dependent.

As anthropologists have noted regarding how Muslims (not necessarily confined to those of Malay ethnicity) perceive the term: "It is acceptable to call themselves and be called by Muslims *kon khaek*, but if people of other faiths call them such, the meaning becomes derogatory as it marks them out as an exclusive community. This concept is more insulting in the three border provinces as it infers that Muslims living in the region of the former Patani Sultanate are not native."[32] In Thailand, this manner of ascribing identity to a minority community on the basis of difference

---

[30] Tim Rackett, "Putting Out the Fire in Southern Thailand: An Appeal for Truce Seeking," July 14, 2014. Available www.mei.edu/content/map/putting-out-fire-southern-thailand-appeal-truce-seeking. While the symbolism that Rackett points out in this quote is important to note, his point about monks not having enmity toward Muslims is an overstatement. The fact is that there are monks who are very anti-Muslim and are in fact trained soldiers in saffron robes specially deployed in the southern provinces.

[31] It is official in the sense that Thai officials often make reference to this term when they mention the Malay-Muslims.

[32] Amporn Marddent, "Interfaith Marriage Between Muslims and Buddhists in Southern Thailand" in Gavin W. Jones, Chee Heng Leng, and Maznah Mohamad (eds.), *Muslim-Non-Muslim Marriage: Political and Cultural Contestations in Southeast Asia*. Singapore: Institute of Southeast Asian Studies, 2009, p. 200.

is nothing short of a cognitive marginalization of the community in the discourse of the imagined Thai nation:

> While there is never a clear definition of what Thai-ness entails, Thais are often better able to identify what is un-Thai, thus defining the domain of Thai-ness from the outside. Often, reference to un-Thainess is done by creating an Other. One such un-Thai Other is codified in the term *khaek*. This term covers the peoples and countries of the Malay peninsula, the East Indies, South Asia and the Middle East without any distinction. *Khaek* also denotes Muslim. So we can see how, in defining Thai-ness, an unclear category, one side result is the creation of the Malay Muslims as un-Thai. And in the recent upsurge of violence in the south of Thailand, the Malay Muslim has become even more un-Thai by challenging the integrity of Thailand's borders and threatening national security.[33]

It is worth noting that the derogatory connotations here mirror certain Malay-Muslim majoritarian discourses regarding the place of non-Muslims in Malaysia, where these have taken on an ethno-religious and nationalist mien in the labeling of non-Muslims as *"pendatang,"* meaning "foreigners" or people who are not local.

If the etymology of *"Khaek"* with reference to the Malay-Muslims has proven problematic, the more officious (and comparatively more recent) term "Thai Muslim" or "Thai Islam," coined by the Thai state to apply to all Thais who confess the Islamic religion, but undoubtedly with a subtext related to the Muslims of the southern provinces, is equally freighted. At the heart of the notion of "Thai Muslim" is a recognition that religious identity co-exists with national identity, whilst at the same time denying the ethnic identity of Thailand's myriad Muslim communities so as to prevent the logic for a separate post-colonial national identity from taking root.[34] In this regard, it is striking that whereas ethnic Malay officials working for the state prefer to downplay their Malay identity by suggesting their preference for "Islam" rather than *"Melayu"* (Malay) or *"Nayu"* when referring to themselves, common folk in the southern provinces have no problems with the latter terms – indeed, I have come across some who very enthusiastically acknowledge that they are Malay – except when they are in conversation with or in the presence of state officials or soldiers.[35]

---

[33] Saroja Dorairajoo, "Peaceful Thai, Violent Malay(-Muslim): A Case Study of the 'Problematic' Muslim Citizens of Southern Thailand," *Copenhagen Journal of Asian Studies*, Vol. 27, No. 2, 2009, p. 70.

[34] Patrick Jory, "From '*Melayu Patani*' to Thai Muslim: The Spectre of Ethnic Identity in Southern Thailand," *South East Asia Research*, Vol. 15, No. 2, July 2007, p. 255.

[35] Ethnic Malays tend to get very nervous when the question of whether they are Malay is put to them. In one instance, an official shared with me his reluctance to be called Malay publicly even though he acknowledged that as his ethnicity. In another instance, a well-known ethnic Malay personality from the provinces was reluctant to speak in

There is another facet to the usage of the "Thai Muslim" or "Thai Islam" in reference to Malay-Muslims that warrants closer scrutiny. Because of the particular application of this term to the southern provinces, it tends to elicit interest as to the confessional character of the conflict. Yet an immediate point to note on that score is that there is scant evidence that Muslims elsewhere in Thailand (that is to say, residing outside of the southern provinces) identify in any substantive way with the plight of their co-religionists in the southern provinces – certainly not enough to prompt action on their behalf. On the contrary, there is ample anecdotal evidence suggesting that, like many non-Muslim Thais, Thai Muslims from regions outside of the border provinces favor a firm handling of the "problem" in the south. At best, they are either simply uninterested, or wary of being labeled as disloyal and sympathizers of violence. At the same time, there is also a tendency on the part of the Malay-Muslims from the south to denigrate their co-religionists from beyond the southern provinces for being "insufficiently devout and too deeply insinuated into Thai society."[36] Put differently, in contrast to the abstract notion of Islam's "universal" confessional appeal as expressed in the concept of the *ummah*, the reality among Thailand's Muslim co-religionists is that the plight of Malay-Muslims in the southern provinces has elicited remarkably little sympathy – if not an active desire to maintain distance – from their Muslim brothers and sisters residing elsewhere in the country.

The foregoing discussion is illustrative of how growing antagonism between the Thai state and its Malay-Muslim periphery was at its core driven by the fact that, in the official narrative of Thai nationalism to which they were subject, the Malay-Muslims of southern Thailand stood outside the conception of Thai nationhood and hence had to be brought back into the fold through assimilation. Significantly, assimilation policies have, as was the case with the Moros and the Philippine state, more often than not involved extreme measures that have had a corrosive effect on core–periphery relations. These included, *inter alia*, proscription of the local Malay language in the education curriculum and local administration (despite it being the language of the majority), circumscription of various Malay cultural and Islamic practices such as *shari'a* law, and, perhaps the most controversial of all, constant attempts by the state to police independent Islamic schools that have served for centuries as extensions of Malay-Muslim politico-cultural identity, and to regulate

---

Malay in public abroad, opining that "there may be 'Bangkok' (referring to government officials) anywhere." Interview, February 13, 2013.

[36] McCargo, *Tearing Apart the Land*, p. 5.

their curriculum. Increasingly, Malay-Muslims have also had to endure obloquy and suspicion in the course of their everyday lives. This has been worsened by the relocation of Thai-Buddhists to the southern provinces by writ, as noted earlier, that has been undertaken by various successive governments in Thailand, although, in comparison to the discussion in the previous chapter, nowhere on the scale that occurred in the case of Mindanao.[37]

As a consequence of the state's interdictions of pre-existing and deep-rooted cultural patterns, a litany of grievances gradually accumulated that eventually found expression in civil protests and even violent confrontations. Against this backdrop, populist nationalist policies of more recent administrations (most notably that of former Prime Minister Thaksin Shinawatra) constituted a new chapter in this combustible and circuitous pattern of local discontent and centre–periphery tensions, reigniting unresolved historical disconnects and opening old wounds.

It is further instructive to note that, in contrast to Bangamoro nationalism in the Philippines, ethno-cultural consciousness also had the effect of defining separatism in southern Thailand as an exclusive affair; the Malay-Muslim resistance was decidedly insular and rested exclusively on Malay-Muslim identity as its point of reference. At the heart of the matter, as Ruth McVey tells us, lay the tension "between Patani and those Muslims who do not share Patani's past."[38] The exclusivist subtext to southern Thai nationalism is often missed in many narratives of the conflict which tend to portray it as a phenomenon that covers the entire region of southern Thailand, including (problematically) the province of Satun.[39] Despite being a 67 percent or so Muslim majority, however, Satun's population is only 10 percent ethnic Malay. Again, historical antecedents and grievances had much to do with this.[40] For these

---

[37] This practice of settling Buddhists into the south continues today, and has been cited by separatists as a factor that has inflamed the insurgency. See Amy Chew, "Buddhists Move into Restive Southern Thailand," *South China Morning Post*, June 13, 2013.

[38] Ruth McVey, "Identity and Rebellion among Southern Thai Muslims" in Andrew D. W. Forbes (ed.), *The Muslims of Thailand, Vol. 2: Politics of the Malay-Speaking South*. Bihar, India: Centre for Southeast Asian Studies, 1989, p. 52.

[39] For instance, Andrew Holt, "Thailand's Troubled Border: Islamic Insurgency or Criminal Playground?" *Terrorism Monitor* (Jamestown Foundation), Vol. 2, No. 10, May 20, 2004. Holt writes that "The Thai provinces of Pattani, Narathiwat, Yala and Satun have long acted as a zone of Islamist discontent and violence."

[40] Unlike the other three provinces, which have retained their Malay ethnic and cultural heritage, Satun, which had for a long time been a district of the Malay state of Kedah known previously as Mukim Setul, has seen its authentic Malay population diluted as a result of migration and integration policies. Unlike the other three provinces, which were traditionally close to Kelantan, it was Kedah's close affiliations with Ayutthaya and later Siam under the Chakri dynasty that resulted in a practice of inter-ethnic marriage without religious reservations.

reasons, Satun has been distanced both geographically and ideationally from the separatist activity that has plagued the south.[41] This remains the case, as Satun has seen little violence in recent years compared to the other provinces.

The Pondok

The various policies enacted by the Thai state over the years to curb Malay cultural and religious expression have been felt most acutely in the realm of Islamic education, thereby deepening the reservoir of resentment among Malay-Muslim youth. To that effect, an important vehicle through which local narratives of Patani Malay-Muslim history and identity are reinforced and perpetuated are the region's ubiquitous Islamic schools.[42] Indeed, to the extent that there is a considerable disconnect between Thai and Malay perceptions of the meaning and significance of Malay-Muslim identity exists, it is in their respective and contrasting views on the institution of the *pondok* (traditional Islamic school, also known as *ponoh* in the local lexicon) that this disconnect is arguably most apparent.

For the Malay community of the southern provinces, Islamic schools have not only been merely a repository of religious knowledge, but a major social and cultural institution as well. Beyond that, it was also in the *pondok* Islamic schools that local narratives of Patani history were perpetuated via the oral tradition, and Malay language (in the form of the Jawi traditional Malay script and the Patani Malay dialect) kept alive.[43]

In sharp contrast to the institution's standing in Malay-Muslim eyes, Islamic schools have long been viewed with suspicion by the Thai state. Given their emphasis on religious knowledge, in the eyes of the state these

---

[41] A number of scholars have already documented this historical fact. See Astri Suhrke, "The Muslims in Southern Thailand."; Uthai Dulyakasem, "Education and Ethnic Nationalism: The Case of the Muslim-Malays in Southern Thailand," in Charles F. Keyes (ed.), *Reshaping Local Worlds: Formal Education and Cultural Change in Rural Southeast Asia*. New Haven: Yale University, 1991; Andrew Cornish, *Whose Place is This?: Malay Rubber Producers and Thai Government Officials in Yala*. Bangkok: White Lotus, 1997.

[42] For a more extensive treatment of Islamic education in southern Thailand, see Liow, *Islam, Education, and Reform in Southern Thailand*.

[43] Constraints of space preclude further elaboration of the structure of Islamic schools in the southern border provinces. In the interests of brevity, *pondok* is taken here to refer to Islamic schools in a generic sense, although in reality a distinction should be made between the *pondok*, which is a traditionalist boarding school, and the madrasah, which is a modernist educational institution. The *Pondok* is an Islamic boarding school run by traditionalist religious teachers known as *Tok Guru*. Until recently, it had little to no access to government funding. Madrasahs are private Islamic schools which, despite their nomenclature, are institutions funded in part or in full by the state. Many madrasahs are modernist in theological orientation. For a detailed study of the distinctions between the two institutions, see ibid.

schools were not providing the necessary training required to support the building of a modern economy. More to the point, these schools were viewed as progenitors of subversive narratives of Thai and Patani history, and by virtue of this their loyalty to the Thai state considered suspect. Finally, security officials are persuaded that Islamic schools have been key recruitment and indoctrination grounds for generations of Malay-based separatist movements, even though the evidence of this has been, at best, scant. These differences were amplified by the fact that there is an intimate correlation between Malay ethnicity and the Islamic religion, to the extent that Jawi script (and the accompanying Patani Malay spoken language), and not Arabic, is considered the "language of Islam" in the region.

According to those who have studied the current insurgency closely, the process of indoctrination through Islamic education has been taking place surreptitiously, involving highly decentralized and opaque processes that take place around small, unofficial study groups, or *halqah* in Islamic tradition, assembled by religious teachers who are either sympathizers or participants in the insurgency.[44] This was affirmed in an International Crisis Group study that reported the following:

Recruitment agents, often religious teachers, reportedly select youths who display three key characteristics: piety, impressionability, and agility. Agents recruit these youths into small groups, initially by befriending and inviting them to join discussion or prayer groups. Candidates are sounded out in conversations about Patani history. Those who seem receptive to liberationist ideology are invited to join the movement.[45]

Crucially, a distinction has to be drawn here between the *halqah*, which is in essence an informal, extra-curricular vehicle of Islamic education comprising students assembled by an individual teacher, and the classes of the Islamic school itself, which involved a formal curriculum.[46]

In addition to teachers, former separatist footsoldiers (who returned to their villages in the 1990s as a result of the amnesty policy) and adults who lived through historical events that have passed into Malay lore such as the Dusun Nyor incident of 1948; the disappearance of the popular Islamic teacher and *cause celebre* of the movement for local Malay autonomy, Haji Sulong Abdul Kadir, in 1954; the Patani Central Mosque demonstration of 1975; and the armed resistance from the 1960s to 1980s all played an instrumental role in ensuring mythologies and

---

[44] Interview, Bangkok, July 13, 2005.
[45] International Crisis Group, *Southern Thailand: Insurgency, Not Jihad*. ICG Asia Report no. 98, May 18, 2005, p. 26.
[46] This distinction is important because it differentiates the *halqah* as a venue of recruitment and indoctrination from the actual school where formal education is conducted.

resistance narratives were kept alive. In one particular instance, young men in their late teens from a weekend Islamic school recalled vividly how a *babo* (traditional Islamic religious teacher) preached passionately about how "*Anak Patani*" (children of Patani, usually used to refer to the Malay-Muslims of the region) had a moral obligation to "take back" Patani from the infidel Siamese. This religious functionary further demanded from them unquestionable loyalty to the cause of the liberation of Patani from the occupying forces.[47]

Clearly, then, the current armed insurgency in southern Thailand draws in no small measure from the discontent and dissatisfaction against the centripetal pull that has been a definitive feature of core–periphery relations between the region and the central Thai state. Not unlike the caricatured discourses on religious moderation and radicalism that have proliferated in recent times, the tendency among Buddhist Thai officials and politicians to refer to the insurgency as the work of "misguided youth" who had been taught the "wrong Islam," and extrapolating from this, that the conflict can be resolved once these youths are instructed in the "right Islam," has further alienated Malay-Muslims for whom religious creed is closely intertwined with ethnic identity and sense of history and belonging.

Prognostic Frames

Not unlike the struggle in southern Philippines, the primary prognostic frame among insurgents in southern Thailand has been armed struggle toward the objective of liberating the Malay-Muslim provinces.

Resistance to the central state peaked in the 1960s with the formation of organized armed separatist groups. Among the most prominent were the BRN, formed in 1963, and PULO, formed in 1968. Notably, the founding leaders of these two groups were both Islamic religious teachers. Groups such as BNPP and GMIP (*Gerakan Mujahidin Islam Pattani* or the Mujahidin Movement of Patani) would later emerge as the separatist movement metastasized. An attempt in the 1990s to form an umbrella organization with the intent of bringing these disparate groups together through the formation of Bersatu (also known in some sources as the United Front for the Liberation of Patani) was essentially stillborn, a victim of factionalism and competition both across its constituent groups as well as within some of them.[48]

---

[47] Don Pathan, "Alone in the Shadow of Militants," *The Nation*, May 21, 2006.
[48] For more information about the separatist movements active in southern Thailand, see International Crisis Group, *Southern Thailand: Insurgency, Not Jihad*.

Though there are clearly continuities between previous epochs of resistance and the contemporary insurgency, it has been the tactical discontinuities that have proven most striking. For one, the tactics adopted by the current generation of insurgents have been considerably more brutal and indiscriminate. This has been particularly so on the matter of targeting, where the conflict has witnessed a substantial amount of "collateral damage," mostly in the form of civilian victims of violence. In addition to this, the insurgency itself has transformed from a rural-based guerrilla struggle primarily based in the jungles to an urban resistance movement where insurgents blend easily into the population, thereby making intelligence gathering all the more difficult.

While a gradual upsurge in violence in southern Thailand was already discernible as early as mid-2001, the prevailing wisdom is that a new phase of insurgency effectively began with the audacious raid referred to earlier on a military base in Narathiwat on January 4, 2004, by an estimated hundred assailants. What was further striking about this operation was the fact that the armory raid was preceded that same night by arson attacks on nineteen schools throughout the province. The arson attacks were clearly diversionary in purpose, thereby indicative of meticulous planning, coordination, and execution on the part of the assailants. At the time, the scope and sophistication of the January 4, 2004, operations were on a scale far beyond the capabilities of any single known separatist group.[49]

Since January 2004, the conflict in southern Thailand has escalated to previously unseen levels as the insurgency (and violence more broadly) acquired fresh momentum – the death toll continues to escalate, bomb attacks have taken on new levels of sophistication, and civilian casualties are increasing at a disconcerting rate. Transformations in the insurgency's repertoire of contention have been equally profound, whereby large-scale, coordinated attacks on multiple targets bookend frequent occurrences of isolated yet surgical violence ranging from assassination of informants to arson and bomb attacks on schools and hotels, and ambushing of military and police convoys.

This current state of affairs could only have come about as a result of conscious attempts by at least some segments of preceding generations of insurgents to sow the seeds of rebellion that are currently being harvested. Underlying this is a belief that the prognosis involves violence in order to discredit the central state in the provinces, to undermine their claim

---

[49] For a detailed study on the tactical aspects of the insurgency, see Joseph Chinyong Liow and Don Pathan, *Confronting Ghosts: Thailand's Shapeless Southern Insurgency*. Sydney: Lowy Institute for International Policy, 2010.

to the land and its nation as part of the unitary Thai nation-state, and to reinforce, by way of arms, an alternative conception of nationhood for Malay-Muslims of southern Thailand distinct from Bangkok's imagined Thai community. To this end, at the heart of the conflict remains the struggle to resist Thai conceptions of nationhood on religious grounds, whilst at the same time conceptualizing the notion of the Malay-Muslim nation as a descendant of the historical kingdom of Patani.

Bearing in mind that little is yet known about the identity of leaders of the ongoing insurgency, many have argued that the BRN-Coordinate, which is a breakaway faction of the BRN separatist organization, is one of the most active groups today. Reeling from the costs of a decade of insurgency and unable to replenish its emaciated ranks, the original BRN broke into three factions in the early 1980s as a result of strategic and tactical differences – BRN-Congress, BRN-Ulama, and BRN-Coordinate. Unlike BRN-Congress, which sought to stay the course of armed struggle, the BRN-Coordinate consisted of leaders and members who agreed that there was a need to consolidate its ranks, particularly given the gradual erosion of support for the struggle. In hindsight, the strategy of BRN-Coordinate to rebuild through mobilization of *pemuda* (youth) proved the prudent one, for when the Thaksin administration inadvertently provided the right conditions with its heavy-handed overreaction to the initial upsurge of violence in 2004, it was they who were best placed to capitalize on the opportunities for recruitment. To the extent that there is a central leadership, the leaders of BRN-Coordinate are said to be ardent Patani Malay nationalists who have adopted an uncompromising position on insurgency as compared to other groups, which are believed to be more inclined toward negotiation and compromise.[50]

Aside from BRN-Coordinate, the other major known separatist group, PULO, also continues to operate in the south, albeit on a much smaller scale than it did in the 1970s and early 1980s, when it was at the peak of its strength.[51] As was the case with BRN, ideological and tactical differences resulted in a split in PULO in 1995, with a new, more militant faction splintering off into New PULO. The deepening sense of crisis was further aggravated by mass defections from the organization, brought about by the government's blanket amnesty policy, and, later, the arrest of prominent leaders of both PULO and New PULO in Malaysia in January 1998. Nevertheless, in the interest of rebuilding its reputation and reasserting its prominence on the landscape in southern Thailand, a major congress was held in Damascus in May 2006, in which PULO and New PULO leaders decided to reunite into a single organization. Toward these ends, a new leadership was elected in July 2009 with the mandate

---

[50] Interview, Bangkok, January 24, 2005.   [51] Interview, Kuala Lumpur, May 28, 2008.

to further PULO's role in the current struggle for self-determination, although the organization split again over differences on the matter of dialogue with the Thai state and idiosyncrasies of ambitious leaders.

Half-hearted attempts have thus far been made by the state to reach out to these groups through dialogue. Several initiatives have been attempted, beginning with one facilitated by former Malaysian Prime Minister Mahathir Mohamad in 2005. This was followed by several other ventures involving European NGOs and, most recently, yet another attempt by the Malaysian government which purportedly had established channels to the BRN-Coordinate. Notwithstanding these efforts, no headway has been made, and any resolution similar to what has happened in Mindanao remains a pipe dream. While part of the problem is the questionable commitment of elements in the Thai state, particularly the Thai military, toward resolution, the same can be said of the Malay-Muslim insurgents. Of those "leaders" who have emerged claiming to represent the Malay-Muslim cause in these dialogues, their credibility remains a point of contention.

The Legitimacy Question

The Thai polity sought to address the issue of its legitimacy deficit in the eyes of the local Malay-Muslim community by enhancing the representation of southern Malay interests in the political process. To this end, a political entity called Wadah was created in 1986 but rose to prominence in the 1990s as part of former Prime Minister Chavalit Yongchaiyudh's New Aspiration Party. Comprising ethnic Malay politicians sympathetic to the state, including Den Tohmeena, grandson of Haji Sulong, Wadah became self-proclaimed representatives of local interests of the southern border provinces, specifically, the ethnic Malay-Muslims. Needless to say, the formation of Wadah was supported by the political center as a means to bridge the trust deficit between the Thai state and the population of the southern border provinces.

Although members of Wadah made some initial headway as the presumptive representatives of Malay-Muslim interests, they suffered significant setbacks after being co-opted into Thaksin's Thai Rak Thai Party. At best, because of its obsequious posturing within Thai Rak Thai, Wadah was feckless in the face of the Thaksin administration's heavy-handed policy in response to the upsurge of violence that was escalating toward a full-blown armed insurgency. The devastating impotence of Wadah was driven home in the wake of the October 2004 Tak Bai massacre during which eighty-six unarmed Malay-Muslim protesters arrested at a rally died under the custody of security officials, when they were piled into army trucks and subsequently perished as a result of asphyxiation.

With resentment seething in the Malay-Muslim local communities, Wadah leaders were derelict in their presumptive role as community leaders even as the former dialed up pressure on them (to criticize the state for its handling of the protestors). As a consequence, Wadah all but discredited themselves in the eyes of those they were purportedly representing. Indeed, a less sympathetic analysis would suggest that by virtue of being part of the Thaksin government Wadah was even complicit in the formulation of policies that have further disadvantaged the Malay-Muslim population.

In the event, the legitimacy deficit confronting Thai authority in the southern provinces was accentuated as Wadah faded into irrelevance, its perfidy leading to the loss of its seats in the 2005 general election. The party eventually splintered into different groups that have since joined other political parties after Thai Rak Thai was itself disbanded. Tellingly, while candidates who were associated with the state (mostly through Wadah) have continued to lose at elections while standing in Malay-Muslim seats, there have been suggestions that, on the other hand, some candidates accused of being separatists or sympathetic to separatism were in fact catapulted to electoral victories precisely because of these accusations.[52]

Similar sentiments have been expressed toward the local Islamic committees. Though established to represent local religious and ethnic interests, Islamic committees have been dismissed in local opinion as an arena where narrow, idiosyncratic interests involving ideological and political persuasions have jockeyed for power and influence at the expense of the interests of their Malay-Muslim constituents.

Religious Narratives in the Southern Thailand Struggle

It is easily apparent that a key motivational frame for cultural, political, and eventually armed resistance toward central authority in southern Thailand has been religion. Indeed against the backdrop of Islamization trends globally, and closer to home in Malaysia, numerous conversations with locals throw up one common thread that binds different perspectives on the conflict – combatants are fighting to liberate their Islamic homeland from an illegitimate invading and colonizing force. But how, and to what ends, has religion manifested itself in this long-standing struggle?

Islam has provided the necessary language for militants and separatists to frame their historical struggle. By this token, one perspective uses the analogy of how Adam, the first prophet of Islam, originated from the soil

---

[52] See the discussion in McCargo, *Tearing Apart the Land*, pp. 60–72.

(the "dust"), in order to draw attention to the centrality of the land – "*tanah*" – to the identity of a people. The religious cleric who expressed this view with unction went on to weave from this analogy a didactic of religious nationalism that correlated to Patani history: "God made the Prophet Adam from the soil, and this soil is where we came from. We have a moral obligation to see that it remains under our rule. The movement is fighting for a liberated Patani, a historical Malay homeland. This is simple and straightforward. Islam permits armed struggle against unjust rulers and this is what we are doing. We do this to liberate our homeland."[53] According to this narrative, religious identity and a historical homeland are mutually imbricated, and have been critical to the framing of a nationalist struggle.

The role of religion in framing the narrative of nationalist struggle is further evident in how, as we established earlier, the chief vehicle of mobilization and recruitment for the current insurgency is widely believed to be the institution of the Islamic religious school. The following comments gleaned from an interview in Pattani provide some insight into this process:

Thai officials thought we had given up during the period of quietness. They were wrong. We came back in less than a decade and began to carry out attacks in late 2001. We are different from the previous generation, who camped out in the mountains as an army of guerilla fighters with clear structure and chain of command. That made them easy to be identified, tracked down, and suppressed by Thai security forces. Our new strategy is more community-based, operating from a cell in each village. About two-thirds of all the villages [in the southern border provinces] now have our cells set up, and we are expanding. Islam has become much more important for our fight [compared to the previous generation] as the guiding principle. My generation is much more educated in Islam. The guidance of Islam is uniting us together, and keeping all of us true to our cause – that is to fight to liberate our land from the infidel occupation. The recruitment process takes time and we want to be sure that they are really committed. We watch them for many years – often since they were studying in *tadika* (kindergarten) or *ponoh*. We only recruit those who are truly committed to Islam and their Islamic duty to fight for the liberation [of Patani Darussalam] to join us. They must be pious. We also welcome those from other [separatist] groups to join us as long as they agree to live and fight for our two guiding principles – [ethnic] Malay nationalism and Islam. There are many young men who would like to join but they are not committed to these principles. They wanted to do it out of resentment and anger. That is a personal matter. Our members must truly believe in their higher cause towards the liberation of our land and our people. This cannot, and will not, be compromised through any negotiations or any deals with the Thai state.[54]

[53] Interview, Narathiwat, October 30, 2013.   [54] Interview, Pattani, May 23, 2006.

Finally, religious motifs related to notions of religious governance and lifestyle have also been regularly mobilized in the course of conflict, where the resistance in southern Thailand is portrayed as a war to drive out Siamese "*kafir*" (unbelievers) and reinstate Islamic governance. Likewise, it has become increasingly common for insurgents to appropriate religious epithets to justify their struggle; the most common is the depiction of themselves as "*mujahidin*" carrying out a "*jihad*" – holy warriors carrying out a holy struggle. Not only that, common people in the region also often use these and other religious motifs to describe the conflict that has unfolded in the region.

Similar to the MILF struggle in the Philippines, the narrative of *jihad* – the Qur'anic injunction for believers to strive and struggle with their entire being in fulfillment of the commandments of God as part of their submission to God's will – features prominently in how the ongoing conflict in the southern Thai provinces has been framed. Be that as it may, it is arguably in southern Thailand that the discursive development of the *jihad* narrative as a lens through which to frame conflict has been comparatively most advanced in terms of how combatants attempt to explain why their conflict is or is not *jihad* in the religious sense. Part of this discursive landscape is defined by distinct differences among religious scholars from the southern provinces on whether the ongoing southern Thai conflict can justifiably be considered a *jihad* in accordance to Islamic scholarly traditions. Some, such as Ismail Lutfi, a respected Saudi-trained cleric and a prominent member of the local elite, are more circumspect. Lutfi has argued that to describe the ongoing conflict in southern Thailand as a religious struggle betrays "a very general and simplistic understanding of *jihad*."[55] Lutfi has written extensively on the topic in both Thai and Malay, and though he has often been associated with the Wahhabi school of Islam, his writings have in fact reflected classical Islamic thought in how it reminded that only recognized religious authority (*pemimpin agung bagi ummat Islam*) can declare a *jihad*, and even then, it can only be declared after other avenues of *dakwah* (proselytization) have been exhausted.[56] He further instructed that "Islam forbids the spilling of Muslim blood," and this view takes on particular currency in the context of ongoing violence in southern Thailand, which has witnessed the killing of fellow Muslims (including students of Islamic schools) purportedly by the insurgents who claim to be defending the Muslim cause.[57]

---

[55] Interview, Pattani, January 14, 2006.
[56] Ismail Lutfi Japakiya, *Islam: Agama Penjana Kedamaian Sejagat*. Alor Star, Kedah: Pustaka Darussalam, 2005, p. 76.
[57] The point should be made, however, that Ismail Lutfi has, and continues, to occupy senior positions within the Thai state. Some would suggest that this might have influenced his views on the ongoing conflict.

The equivocal views of scholars such as Lutfi are repudiated by more malignant perspectives on *jihad* and violence in southern Thailand that have also appeared on the discursive landscape. In sharp contrast to Lutfi's views, another religious leader pointedly insisted that *jihad qital* (armed struggle) had long been a calling for Muslims in southern Thailand because of their victimization at the hands of the repressive Thai state.[58] This cleric felt that an offensive *jihad* was necessary to ensure freedom, not just of religion but of Malay identity as well, in the southern provinces. Echoing a similar perspective, another cleric (linked to the GMIP) averred that the time for *jihad qital* had now descended upon the "*tiga wilayah*" (three provinces – referring to the local nomenclature for the Malay-Muslim provinces of Narathiwat, Pattani, and Yala).[59] This particular scholar challenged Ismail Lutfi's view that conditions were not present for a *jihad* to be waged, hastening to add that Lutfi's passivism stemmed from his "Saudi-oriented" perspective, which focused on developments in Islamic thought during the religion's expansive phase of the Prophet in Mecca ("*zaman nabi di Makkah*") and where the message focused on the spread of Islam peacefully ("*menyebarkan shari'a Islam dengan cara damai*") amidst opposition from various sources such as the aristocratic Quraiysh tribes who were sceptical of the new religion.[60] By his account, what bedevils Thailand's Malay-Muslims today are in fact conditions similar to those which confronted the followers of Islam during the Prophet's leadership of the community during the Medinan era ("*zaman nabi di Madina*"), which was defined, in his words, by the "assault and violation of Muslim lands by non-Muslims (*orang yang mencerobuhi bumi kita*)" from polytheistic Mecca. Under these conditions, *jihad qital* was not only warranted; it was obligatory. Similar perspectives that were equal and opposite to Lutfi's were echoed by another religious teacher who, when presented with the hypothetical situation in which he discovered that his students were active in militancy against the Thai state, opined that he would not stop them because they were engaging in a "legitimate struggle" that is several centuries old. When queried further what he thought of the fact that the Siamese did at various instances render aid and assistance to Patani, he reportedly responded: "Do you know how humiliating it is for the Malays to seek assistance from Siam?"[61]

As it suggests, insurgents justify the use of religious referents sketched out above on the grounds that Islam's Qur'anic injunction to fight the

---

[58] *Ustaz* interview, Pattani, May 8, 2006. [59] *Ustaz* interview, Pattani, May 10, 2006.
[60] Others have been more brazen in their dismissal of Lutfi, opinion that his passivism was essentially a pretense in order that he can further his own political ambitions away from the glare of suspicious eyes. Interview, Pattani, February 2010.
[61] This anecdote was shared by Don Pathan during a seminar at the S. Rajaratnam School of International Studies, Singapore, July 9, 2007.

oppression of Muslims resonates with the plight of the Malays in southern Thailand and the insurgents' objectives of liberating their historic homeland of the kingdom of Patani from unwelcome Siamese colonialism. Islam, they explain, legitimizes an "uprising against unjust rule."[62]

The social construction of religion as a motivational frame with which to conceptualize a stronger sense of identity has been a signal feature on the discursive plain of the long-drawn Malay-Muslim struggle for recognition of their identity in the context of Thai history and nationalism. Be that as it may, it also bears noting that the use of religion and theology to sanction acts of violence did not stem from established theological or juridical literature or sophisticated Qur'anic exegesis, but rather from the oral instruction that these religious teachers provide to their students. Again, the point needs to be stressed that unlike the situation in the southern Philippines or Indonesia, the armed conflict in southern Thailand does not appear to draw heavily from the teachings and writings of prominent clerics – there is no equivalent of an Abu Bakar Ba'asyir or Hashim Selamat to ideologically and intellectually advance the cause of resistance and rebellion, nor does one find any reference to Abdullah Azzam, the late Palestinian cleric who mentored Osama bin Laden, and whose theories on *jihad* were used to validate the Afghan *jihad* against the Soviet Union.[63] Nevertheless, the annals of Patani history do throw up one particular religious leader who, while he never openly championed separatism of Patani from Thailand or open armed conflict, nevertheless cogently articulated a coherent sense of identity for the Malay-Muslims of southern Thailand. This particular individual, Haji Sulong Abdul Kadir, continues to be held in totemic regard in southern Thai circles today, more than six decades after his mysterious disappearance.[64]

The Thai historian, Thanet Aphornsuvan, has described Haji Sulong's impact on the shaping of the narrative of religious nationalism in southern Thailand as such:

Politically, the appearance of Haji Sulong in the Muslim movement was very significant. . . . In this revival of Malay nationalism, a new formula had been created from which political autonomy based on the Islamic principles would be championed. . . . The Patani Muslim Movement spearheaded by Haji Sulong thus

---

[62] Interviews conducted with a member of the original BRN, and who was in charge of several cells involved in the contemporary insurgency and on condition of anonymity, in May 2006 (he also instructed that we were not to divulge where the meeting took place).

[63] This is not to say that there are no prominent clerics in southern Thailand. Rather, the point is that none have committed their thoughts on the legitimacy of violence to further the Malay-Muslim struggle to paper.

[64] He continues to be seen as the "heart and soul" of the Malay-Muslim people today. See Don Pathan, "A Short History of Southern Sultanates," *The Nation*, April 3, 2002.

became a mass movement and importantly was the first time that the leadership of the movement turned to the religious leader.[65]

Importantly, Haji Sulong was responsible for revitalizing the Malay struggle at a time when the nascent separatist movement was in danger of losing its momentum in the wake of hardline policies and repressive countermeasures from the authoritarian military government of Phibun Songgkram. Because of his leadership of the Malay-Muslim struggle, Haji Sulong has come to be venerated, accurately or otherwise, as the father of the Pattani independence movement.[66] While he never openly championed separation and independence, Haji Sulong was known to be a strong proponent of greater autonomy and preservation of Malay-Muslim culture, which for him was central to the Malay-Muslim sense of belonging in response to emergent Thai nationalism:

> We Malays are conscious that we have been brought under Siamese rule by defeat. The term "Thai Islam" with which we are known by the Siamese government reminds us of this defeat and is therefore not appreciated by us. We therefore beg of the government to honor us with the title of Malay Muslims so that we may be recognized as distinct from the Thai by the outside world.[67]

Given his standing in the community, Haji Sulong's arrest and trial in January 1948 and controversial disappearance in 1954 prompted widespread protests from the Malay-Muslim communities, and set the stage for the armed insurgency that was to follow. Despite his passing, Haji Sulong's influence remained undimmed. In point of fact, while in life Haji Sulong championed peace and non-violence in reaction to state aggression and provocation, it was his death that would raise a call to arms.

Haji Sulong's push for Islam as a vehicle to mobilize Malay-Muslims in denunciation of the repressive policies of the Thai government was significant in that it marked a departure from political activism of the Malay aristocrats – descendants of former Patani rulers, whose immediate objectives following the signing of the 1909 Anglo-Siamese Treaty to regain the traditional power of the raja lost to the court of Siam had overshadowed Islam as a motivating factor for resistance insofar as the local elite were concerned (not unlike the *datu* in Mindanao who were often

---

[65] Thanet Aphornsuvan, "Origins of Malay Muslim 'Separatism' in Southern Thailand." Asia Research Institute Working Paper Series No. 32. Singapore: National University of Singapore, October 2004, pp. 13–14.
[66] Pitsuwan, *Islam and Malay Nationalism*, p. 164.
[67] Numan Hayimasae, "Haji Sulong Abdul Kadir (1895–1954): Perjuangan dan Sumbangan Beliau kepada Masyarakat Melayu Patani." M.A. Thesis, Universiti Sains Malaysia, 2002, p. 83.

preoccupied with their own *rido* feuds, it should be added).[68] Following the emergence of Haji Sulong, Islam was no longer seen merely as an embodiment of rituals as previously emphasized in the teachings of the traditional religious institutions. Under Haji Sulong's tutelage it became, for Malay-Muslims, *ad-din* (a comprehensive way of life), governing both private and public life. Describing the qualitative shift of Malay-Muslim resistance to a more Islamic register under Sulong's influence, Wan Kadir Che Man postulated that it was "essentially Islamic reactions against alien domination. In some instances, Islam has become the fundamental ingredient of the struggle; in others, Islamic concepts and symbols are integrated into nationalist dogma ... to appeal to a wider population."[69]

During the height of armed separatist insurgency in the 1970s, even secular nationalist movements like PULO turned to religious metaphors to lend greater legitimacy to their actions. In his study of violence during the period from 1976 to 1981, Chaiwat Satha-Anand concluded that religion played an integral role in the propaganda of PULO. For example, frequent calls were made in PULO propaganda for the Malay-Muslims of southern Thailand to wage a *jihad*, and these calls were supported with citations from the Qur'an and Sunna in order to enhance their credibility and appeal.[70] Further references were made that juxtaposed, in provocative fashion, the Islamic faith with Buddhism, in order to stress not merely cultural differences but also, more significantly, polarization and conflict. Another major theme that emerged in the propaganda pamphlets that PULO produced during their prime was that Muslims were not to be governed by non-Muslims. It should not at all be surprising that this theme continues to resonate today.[71] Furthermore, not only have religious nationalists in the insurgency justified their struggle in the southern provinces in the emblematic name of Islam, there is, in comparison to Mindanao, a discernible absence of any attempt to articulate the need for conflict resolution using a religious discourse too.

---

[68] In fact, by the time Haji Sulong began to popularize his ideals in the late 1920s, the aristocratic elite had already either been co-opted into the Thai parliamentary system with positions of nominal power, fled to British Malaya in the hope that pressure could be put on London to intervene on their behalf to redraw the boundaries of southern Thailand, or retreated from the political scene altogether. See Aphornsuvan, "Origins of Malay-Muslim 'Separatism' in Southern Thailand," pp. 13–14.
[69] Che Man, *Muslim Separatism*, p. 12.
[70] Chaiwat Satha-Anand, *Islam and Violence: A Case Study of Violent Events in the Four Southern Provinces, Thailand, 1976–1981*. Gainesville, FL.: Florida University Press, 1987.
[71] See Duncan McCargo, "Patani Militant Leaflets and the Use of History," in Patrick Jory (ed.), *Ghosts of the Past in Southern Thailand: Essays on the History and Historiography of Patani*. Singapore: National University of Singapore Press, 2013, pp. 277–297.

The above observations seem to suggest that the insurgency in southern Thailand is essentially a religious conflict. Reinforcing this view, some have even drawn a causal connection between the conflict on one hand and rising Islamic consciousness and the purported growth of Islamism on the part of the Malay populace in southern Thailand on the other, implying the two latter phenomena somehow predispose Muslims to violence on the mistaken grounds that religious manifestations equate to a religious cause.

As far as the factor of religion is concerned, the critical takeaway is that this "holy struggle" is in fact taking place in a specific cultural, historical, and political milieu. Not unlike their predecessors, for the current generation of insurgents it remains the idea of Malay self-determination, or perhaps more accurately a Patani Malay-Muslim nationalism, upon which their cause is centered, and which serves as the standard under which the struggle is waged, even if this struggle can be conveniently couched in a religious language that provides further credibility and legitimacy. The most striking illustration of this is the fact that the geographical footprint of the struggle has not changed much since it first began several decades ago, although in recent years violence appears to have spread to Songkhla province. Insurgents remain uninterested in expanding the territorial parameters of insurgency beyond the provinces where Malay cultural identity enjoys preeminence, and where ethnic Malays form the vast majority of the population. Concomitantly, precepts and analogies carrying religious overtones are understood through local lenses, read alongside local narratives, and used to further animate long-standing resistance to the central state. The role of religious schools in the perpetuation of this nationalism is further instructive in this regard, considering how it is not Islamic studies that is used to indoctrinate and recruit, but narratives of local histories – in particular narratives of oppression and colonization. In other words, religion in the southern Thailand conflict needs to be properly contextualized.

Inventing Tradition

The perpetuation of the ethno-religious narrative of victimization and self-determination is frequently undertaken through local venues and vehicles. Poems read out at public gatherings in school and village compounds create powerful myths that allude to Patani's glorious past prior to its formal annexation of the region by Siam, and celebrate the exploits of Haji Sulong. Similarly, *"Bumi Patani"* (Land of Patani), ostensibly the unofficial national anthem of Patani, continues to be sung as a covert introit expressing resistance and patriotism in Islamic schools across the region, sometimes right under the noses of the watchful eye of the military. Recorded collections of these poems and songs are liberally circulated within the local communities and disseminated across the southern provinces.

The profound significance of this confluence of continuity and change, history and identity came out in dramatic fashion on April 28, 2004, when more than a hundred men conducted twelve coordinated predawn attacks and martyrdom operations on a series of police posts and security installations in Yala, Pattani, and parts of Songkhla with dense Malay-Muslim concentrations in a devastating dovetailing of religious and nationalist zeal (leading to 108 militants and five police and military officials being killed and seventeen arrests). The attacks culminated in the siege on the historic Krue Se (Krisek) Mosque in Pattani – the first mosque in Southeast Asia to be modeled after Middle Eastern architectural styles – by the Thai military. Their patience being exhausted, the military eventually unleashed a heavy but tactically reckless assault on the mosque, which resulted in the deaths of thirty-two assailants who had deliberately hemmed themselves in the house of worship.[72] In the aftermath of the denouement, it was revealed that some of the assailants were members of an Islamic group that engaged in mystic practices and believed themselves to be inured against bullets with the "holy water" they sprinkled on before waging battle.[73] The result was predictable: widespread condemnation in many quarters within the Malay-Muslim community, and worsening tension and suspicion between state and periphery. What was perhaps even more striking and pertinent about the event was the deliberate allusion to historical memory and cultural symbolism in the choice of this particular site for resistance culminating in martyrdom.

In Malay-Muslim folklore, the 400-plus year-old Krue Se Mosque has long been emblematic of Malay-Muslim identity. Legend tells of a Chinese lady of noble birth, Lim Ko Niew, who had come to southern Thailand 400 years ago in search of her brother, Lim Ko Thiam, a Chinese adventurer who settled in Patani in the 16th century and became a famous weaponsmith skilled in the manufacturing of cannons for the

---

[72] A detailed account of the devastating raid on the mosque can be found in Joseph Chinyong Liow, "Iron Fists without Velvet Gloves: The Krue Se Mosque Incident and Lessons in Counterinsurgency for the Southern Thai Conflict," in C. Christine Fair and Sumit Ganguly (eds.), *Treading on Hallowed Ground: Counterinsurgency Operations in Sacred Spaces*. New York: Oxford University Press, 2008, pp. 177–199.

[73] Liow and Pathan, *Confronting Ghosts*, pp. 39–40.

Patani Sultanate.[74] Upon finding out that her brother had married a local Muslim woman (he married the daughter of the governor of Patani), converted to Islam, and refused to return to China, she committed suicide, but not before allegedly laying a curse on the mosque then undergoing construction at the site of Krue Se that it would never be completed. Adding to the intrigue, legend also has it that it was none other than Lim Ko Thiam who had been contracted by Queen Hijau (1584–1616), one of the three queens who ruled over Patani during its golden era, to oversee the construction of the mosque. As it turned out, a sequence of wars between Patani and the kingdoms of Ayutthaya and Palembang (Indonesia) provided distractions that meant the mosque could never be completed. In 1935, Krue Se was made an official historical site, and the existence of an unfinished dome roof perpetuated the legend of the Lim Ko Niew curse. To round off the intriguing tale, as a gazetted historical site, no repairs or changes were allowed to be made to the site without permission from the Department of Fine Arts.

It bears noting that the folklore surrounding the Krue Se mosque summarized above remains prominent in local narratives of resistance today, and for mythopoetic Malay-Muslims of the southern provinces, served as a constant reminder of the presumed superiority of foreign cultures over local Malay-Muslim culture. This sentiment was further reinforced by the fact that the tomb of Lim Ko Niew, originally located some distance away, was paradoxically relocated to within 500 meters of the mosque.

As a historical site, the mosque has been a public space for visitors and tourists. Ironically, as a tourist attraction the curse of Krue Se is repeatedly reproduced as a commodity through advertisements and onsite walking tours.[75] To Muslims, however, the mosque is a sacred place to be used for prayer. In keeping with the sanctity and sobriety of the mosque, the reproduction of the curse placed upon Krue Se – expressed in the commercialism surrounding it – has been received by Muslims as untruthful and an affront to their religion and history. Local protests were registered through a series of demonstrations and rallies that took place between 1987 and 1990, when Muslims of all doctrinal persuasions (including *Shi'a* Muslims) demanded that the mosque be returned to its original status as sacred communal space and for the Lim Ko Niew shrine located

---

[74] Patrick Jory, "From '*Melayu Patani*' to 'Thai Muslim': The Spectre of Ethnic Identity in Southern Thailand," Asia Research Institute Working Paper Series No. 84. Singapore: Asia Research Institute, 2007, p. 5.

[75] Chaiwat Satha-Anand, *The Life of This World: Negotiated Muslim Lives in Thai Society*. Singapore: Marshall Cavendish, 2005, pp. 71–72.

next to the mosque to be removed. The Malay-Muslims felt that removing the official status of Krue Se would allow them to complete the mosque, thereby directly disproving the curse. Others, though, opine that the fact the mosque remains intact today despite the curse already demonstrates the resilience of the Islamic faith and Malay history of Patani in the face of persecution. Chaiwat Satha-Anand makes the argument that the curse rose in prominence in a time when Thai-Chinese had control of a large portion of Patani's economy. In these changed circumstances, the Muslims rallied, "trying to expand the cultural space of their own identity by contracting the Chinese space."[76]

Diverse local understandings of the history of Krue Se are nevertheless all associated with negative foreign influences, whether Siamese or Chinese. Because of the folklore surrounding the Krue Se curse as well as the role of the mosque as a stage for showcasing Malay-Muslim identity, one must recognize the grave importance of the historic mosque and the totemic place it occupies in hearts and minds of the local Muslim community. From the perspective of this local history, then, the choice of Krue Se Mosque as the site of a defiant stand on the part of the insurgents against the Thai government was hardly coincidental, and can only further perpetuate the mosque as a symbol of resistance.

There is a further significance to the Krue Se incident that needs to be registered as well. The decision by militants to mount attacks on April 28 was also striking in that several other incidences of rebellion against the Thai state have been recorded in the Malay-Muslim provinces on or around that date, the most prominent of which was the Dusun Nyor Rebellion of April 28, 1948.[77] The militants' choice of Krue Se as the site of resistance to the Thai state pointed to a calculated attack, meticulously orchestrated and executed in order to maximize symbolism and arouse Malay-Muslim fervor.

Notwithstanding this careful orchestration of violence to resonate with historical memories of victimization, the events of April 28, 2004, also heralded a new dimension to the southern Thai conflict, when the traditionally ethno-nationalist struggle had come to take on a patently discernible religious flavor. The sight of bloodstained floors and holy books inside Krue Se Mosque no doubt resonated with the Muslim population

---

[76] Ibid., p. 76.
[77] While it was doubtless the most significant, the Dusun Nyor Rebellion was not the only violence associated with April 28. On April 29, 1980, a noodle shop in Pattani was bombed, leaving fourteen injured. On April 28, 2003, a guerrilla unit armed with automatic rifles raided an armory of Thaksin Pattana 2 outpost in Narathiwat's Sukhirin district at 2:30 a.m., killing four soldiers before stealing more than thirty automatic rifles. Half an hour later, an outpost in Tharn Toh district, Yala, was raided, with twenty more guns stolen and many soldiers wounded.

in the south and further fueled resentment as Islam served as an increasingly potent avenue through which to comprehend, rally, articulate, and express resistance against the central state.[78] This was further reinforced by the purported discovery at the scene of the attacks of a manuscript titled "*Berjihad di Patani,*" which outlined in systematic fashion the religious motivations behind Malay-Muslim resistance by stressing a link between Islam and the Patani homeland, as well as the moral obligation that the Malay-Muslims of Patani had to liberate this homeland.[79]

This invention of tradition speaks to the essentializing of the identities of Malay-Muslims of southern Thailand on the part of not only some scholars who tend to caricature the Malay-Muslim of southern Thailand, but also the self-proclaimed Patani nationalists.[80] As alluded to earlier, sociologists and anthropologists have rightly highlighted the dual identities that Malays from southern Thailand possess, one in relation to their status as Thai citizens, and another in relation to their ethnic, cultural, and linguistic bonds to northern Malaysia. This duality has been highlighted succinctly by McCargo:

Malay Muslims in Thailand's Southern border provinces are very proud of an identity that they consider highly distinctive, as Malays, as Muslims, and as people of Patani, an ancient kingdom and center of Islamic learning and culture.... At the same time, Patani identity has an ambiguous relationship with the modern nation-state and with notions of citizenship. Almost all Patani people are citizens of Thailand, but for many of them this citizenship is a flag of inconvenience, a formal identity that they are obliged to adopt for pragmatic reasons. Numerous Malay Muslims, especially those living along the border between Kelantan and Narathiwat, hold flexible dual Thai and Malaysian citizenship. For many Malay Muslims, Malaysia offers an alternative to Thailand: a place to work, a place to earn additional income, and potentially as a land of refuge or exile.[81]

Even so, as was pointed out at the beginning of this chapter, for the Malay-Muslims of southern Thailand, this affinity does not translate automatically to acceptance or even sympathy from Malaysia. As one

---

[78] Events after April 28 gave further credence to concerns that the violence in the South was fast taking on a religious flavor. In July, three Buddhist temples in the south were desecrated in attacks that quickly reminded Thailand's Buddhist majority of the demolition of the Buddhas of Bamiyan by the Taleban in February 2001.

[79] Sugunnasil, "Islam, Radicalism, and Violence in Southern Thailand."

[80] See, for instance, the fine collection of essays in Michael J. Montesano and Patrick Jory (eds.), *Thai South and Malay North: Ethnic Interactions on a Plural Peninsula.* Singapore: National University of Singapore Press, 2008. During the course of a decade of fieldwork visits to the provinces, I have incurred the wrath and disdain of many a Patani Malay-Muslim with the suggestion that while the Islamic kingdom of Patani has a long and proud history, Patani itself was previously a Buddhist region and had a history that predates the arrival of Islam to the region.

[81] McCargo, *Tearing Apart the Land,* p. 4.

Patani Malay expressed with more than a hint of irony (and disillusionment): "nowhere do I feel more Thai than when I am in Malaysia."[82]

However, this is not to say that the pressures of co-identification stemming from affinity with Malays in Malaysia readily find expression in (political) separatism or irredentism. To be sure, this may not have always been the case. In the immediate aftermath of the Second World War for instance, Patani Malay nationalists attempted to leverage on Thailand's status as an ally of the Japanese imperial army to seek British support for the incorporation of the southern provinces into British Malaya. In the event, this endeavor failed to gather any significant momentum.

Such internal contradictions in local attempts at reconceptualizing identity spill over further into the question of how to understand – and, in the case of armed insurgents, how to justify – ongoing armed resistance to the Thai state. The presumed effectiveness and discipline of the armed insurgency, measured by the continued inability of the state to identify the perpetrators even after more than a decade of counterinsurgency measures and intelligence gathering, belie what is in effect a very disparate, fractious movement plagued by its own inherent inconsistencies. These have ranged from personality clashes among ambitious self-proclaimed "leaders" of the insurgency's movements and organizations that have led, for example, to the splitting re-uniting, and fracturing of PULO over the last decade and a half, to the different objectives that these movements have, ranging from cultural autonomy, political autonomy, independence, rectification of perceived injustices, or even the interpretation of the religious dimensions of Malay nationalism in the southern provinces.

Perhaps the most profound indication of the fractious relationships within the Malay-Muslim insurgent movement revolves around the acts of violence themselves, as perpetrated by a new generation of militants, and how the latter have sought to justify them with reference to religion. The following view of a leader of the older generation of Malay-Muslim resistance groups in response to the nature of the current armed insurgency, taken from Liow and Pathan's research into this issue based on interviews with those involved in the armed conflict, is poignant in this regard:

The problem with them (the younger generation of militants) is that their tactic is wrong and, besides, they don't seem to be going anywhere with what they are doing. They are accusing the Siamese of being *kafir* because they are Buddhists. We are not in the position to judge them or sentence anybody to death. Only god can do that. Most are good people and they have lived with us, even in the same villages, for many generations. Our children grew up together with them. They

---

[82] Interview, Kelantan, October 16, 2014.

have never done anything to obstruct our way of life or our religious practices. But today, our kids are killing them and burn their houses down. They are doing this to fellow Malays as well. They even killed Buddhist monks. That never happened when I was still fighting in the jungle. Buddhist monks are men of religion and cannot be harmed. But if that is not bad enough, these young *perjuang* are also persecuting our own people, accusing them of being *munafiq* who collaborate with Buddhist Thais. The judgements are often made hastily, carelessly, and unfairly. Many people have been shot or hacked to death in this way.[83]

Conclusion

While different assessments have been made of the identity of the perpetrators of ongoing violence in Thailand's southern border provinces and their intentions, there is no gainsaying that also at stake in the conflict are unresolved issues of identity and legitimacy that speak to how the Malay-Muslims of the southern provinces are imagined as a part of the Thai nation-state in the context of both Thai and Malay conceptions of nationhood.

Malay-Muslim identity has been cultivated and nursed by the construction of narratives that revolve around subjective elements of memory, sentiment, myths, and symbols, all of which are perceived to have been the subject of deliberate proscription by the state. Framed along religious lines, these narratives have easily gestated and emerged to foment an awareness of victimization and marginalization as well as nourish collective consciousness as a nation that, in turn, provides a wellspring of grievance for the insurgent narrative to draw on.

What is further striking about the context we find in southern Thailand is the fact that this process of articulating ethno-religious nationalist aspirations is further informed by the existence of an "other" in the form of an alien Buddhist-inspired nationalism imposed from Bangkok, and to which Malay are presumably forced to swear allegiance at the cost of their own political and cultural identity. Put differently, among the insurgent community in southern Thailand the brand of nationalism that is being articulated with reference to ethnic Malay and Islamic dialectics has been a reaction to not only the centrality that ethnic Thai referents and the Buddhist religion have assumed in the discourse and construction of Thai national identity in mainstream nationalist thinking, but also the perception that these norms and values are being forced upon them.

In many respects, it is this pattern of "othering" emanating out of the political center in Bangkok – for instance, its reluctance to accord to the Malay language the status of working language in the southern

---

[83] See Liow and Pathan, *Confronting Ghosts*, p. 34.

provinces – that has come to be viewed as a threat to the survival and preservation of the culture and identity of the southern Thai periphery precisely because of their ethno-religious disposition, and hence has fostered suspicions among its Malay minority communities and fanned the flames of resistance over the years. In contrast to the case of the relationship between the state in the Philippines and the Bangsamoro of Mindanao, the Thai state has been considerably more reluctant to entertain any possibility of either acknowledging the legitimacy of local narratives or accepting alternative conceptions of nationhood for a Malay-Muslim "nation without a state," and has instead prioritized control of a restive province peripheral to the national imagination, and the omission of its conception of identity from the "official" nationalism that dominates state discourse.

4 Malaysia
Religion, Ethno-Nationalism, and Turf-Guarding

Religious nationalism, as Chapter 1 pointed out, is premised on the idea that religiosity and patriotism can weave together in a manner that gives rise to a narrative which articulates a confessional perspective of nationhood. At its extreme, however, and in a climate where assertive religious claims dominate the narration of national identity and the institutions of the state, a heightened religious discourse potentially results in identity diffusion within the nation-state along religious lines, where confessional claims engender the creation of in-group and out-group identities. Malaysia provides a compelling case for how this process takes place.

In Malaysia, fault lines have formed over the issue of what it means to be a member of the Malaysian "nation" according to the official narrative of nationhood, and how this narrative has changed as erstwhile pluralist conceptions of national identity embraced by (and embracing) minority communities have been threatened, if not supplanted, by a religious discourse that seeks to rearticulate nationhood along narrow and exclusivist terms of a growing Malay-Islamic nationalism. If the previous cases of the Philippines and Thailand have demonstrated how religion offers a language and metaphor of resistance in the process of conceptualizing alternative nationhoods and national identities, in Malaysia it has taken the form of a hegemonic narrative of supremacy and exclusion dominated by religious vocabulary that is harnessed to reinforce, express, and institutionalize a narrowly interpreted narrative of *Ketuanan Melayu* – the dominance and lordship of the ethnic Malay-Muslims in multicultural Malaysia. Correspondingly, this has elicited responses from religious minorities who contest the legitimacy of this reframing of national identity and consciousness for reasons of the existential threat that they pose to their claims to be part of the "Malaysian nation."

The rise of religious conservatism among Muslim actors who dominate the discourse of Malaysian politics touches on issues of both national identity construction as well as political legitimacy. This is so because of how social-political entrepreneurs operating both within and outside the state threaten by dint of explicit religious referents to erode any semblance of shared history, common sense of belonging, and "deep horizontal comradeship" upon which pluralist conceptions of nationhood stand.[1] Questions of how, and by what measure, nationhood is or should be conceived have taken the form of conflicting narratives and debate as competing formulations of the nation are envisaged by conservative right-wing Malay ethno-religious nationalists (who, as we shall soon see, are also ardent religious nationalists), many of whom form the bedrock of Malay political class in control of the levers of state power, and an increasingly besieged Christian community which has mobilized resistance through alternative narratives and politics. Indeed, it is in the context of Muslim–Christian relations where competing and conflicting narratives of identity and belonging, rights and legitimacy have found most acute expression.

By way of the above as a point of entry, this chapter will focus on how Muslim groups have attempted to assert, and non-Muslim groups resist and negotiate, this Islamization process in the context of their own interpretations of Malaysian nationalism and national identity, and the tensions and conflicts this has generated. This has been captured most profoundly in debates and narratives on constitutional and citizenship rights, and beneath this, the more fundamental question of what constitutes the key essence of nationhood and identity in Malaysia. Two aspects to this social and political disaggregation need to be stressed in particular. First, race and ethnicity in Malaysia are imbricated with religion, where the link between "Malay" and "Muslim" is as intimate as it is unstable (for reasons that will be elaborated later). Second, the dynamics generated take place against the backdrop not only of state strength (in terms of authoritarian tendencies) but more so the matter of political legitimacy defined by the need to reinforce the predominance, if not outright supremacy, of one ethnic-religious group over others. Together, these twin dynamics have precipitated a crisis of nationhood in Malaysia defined by the contest between ethnic and civic forms of national identity and the clash of their accompanying narratives of nationhood, both of which have taken on increasingly religious hues in terms of the construction (and defense) of communal identity on one hand, and pursuit of political legitimacy on the other.

---

[1] Benedict Anderson, *Imagined Communities: Reflections on the Origin and Spread of Nationalism*, rev. ed. New York: Verso, 1991, p. 7.

A Brief Note on the Religious Imperative in Malay(sian) Nationalism

From its inception, anti-colonial nationalism in Malaysia (Malaya prior to 1963, and British Malaya prior to 1957) was already to varying degrees influenced by religious (Islamic) imperatives. Organized Islamist movements were very much part of the fabric of anti-colonial activism in the early 20th century, long before the creation of UMNO (United Malays National Organization), the dominant Malay-Muslim party today.[2] Foremost among these were the *Kesatuan Melayu Muda* (Young Malays Union), a collection of young, educated Malay intelligentsia who were influenced by modernist Islamic anti-colonial thought emanating from the Middle East. It was, however, after the Second World War that anti-colonialism in British Malaya gathered pace. Although the dominant narrative casts the spotlight on UMNO, which was formed to defend the status of the Malay sultans and interests of the Malay community in response to the British plan for a Malayan Union, parallel movements had also emerged which sought to align the nascent independence movement with Islamic and socialist ideals.[3] These views were represented by organizations such as the Malay Nationalist Party (successors to the *Kesatuan Melayu Muda*), *Majlis Agama Tertinggi Malaya* (the Supreme Religious Council of Malaya), and *Hizbul Muslimin* (also known as *Parti Orang Muslimin Malaysia* or the Muslim People's Party of Malaysia), all of which constituted what John Funston observed to be "the Islamic wing of Malay nationalism."[4] A notable point of departure with UMNO was the role envisaged for Islam in post-colonial Malaya. While UMNO under the leadership of Tunku Abdul Rahman was prepared to offer Islam token constitutional recognition, the Islamist socialists were of the view that Islam should be accorded a more prominent place. This is not to say that religion played no role in UMNO. On the contrary, mainstream nationalists of UMNO were also attempting to establish their own

---

[2] The role of Islam in early nationalism in Malaysia is discussed in the seminal work William R. Roff, *The Origins of Malay Nationalism*. New Haven, CT.: Yale University Press, 1967. See also Tim Harper, *The End of Empire and the Making of Malaya*. Cambridge: Cambridge University Press, 1999.

[3] For a comprehensive treatment of the Malayan Union, see A. J. Stockwell, *British Policy and Malay Politics During the Malayan Union Experiment, 1942–1948*. Kuala Lumpur: The Malaysian Branch of the Royal Asiatic Society, 1979 and Harper, *The End of Empire and the Making of Malaysia*.

[4] See John Funston, *Malay Politics in Malaysia: A Study of the United Malays National Organisation and Party Islam*. Singapore: Heinemann International, 1981, pp. 87–88.

religious identity and credentials by, *inter alia*, establishing an *ulama* wing, sponsoring Qur'an reading competitions and Islamic schools, hosting international Islamic conferences, and so on.

When UMNO eventually came to dominate the terrain of nationalism after the Second World War, it did so with the protection of Malay royalty and the Malay race as its *raison d'être*. Yet given the demographic constraints at the time of independence, when a substantial proportion of the population of British Malaya was non-Muslim, UMNO could not afford to take a dogmatic position on the matter of the role of religion in the post-independence state for fear of alienating this sizable constituency. More importantly, UMNO could ill afford to antagonize the British colonial administration, which demanded assurances that the former could oversee a moderate governing structure that would maintain multiracial stability. The result of this caution was a compromise struck between UMNO and key non-Muslim political allies, notwithstanding the agitation by vocal Islamist voices both within and outside the party, that while the religion of Malaya would be Islam it would not prejudice the secular orientation of the post-independence state.

At the same time, in an obvious concession to more radical Islamist elements in UMNO, the final constitutional document deliberately avoided characterizing Malaya as secular. This ambiguity was portentous, for it was precisely the constitution's ambivalence on the place of religion – and matters relating to religious freedom – that would eventually become a major point of contention among contrasting views of nationhood, citizenship rights and privileges, and questions of belonging, as religion became a focal point of national identity in the decades that followed. Subsequently, it was in the process of confronting complex challenges about rights and privileges in the context of the struggle to conceptualize a national identity that Islam emerged to play a key role, particularly in relation to the "rightful" place of non-Muslims in Malaysian society.

On this score, it has been relations between the politically dominant Malay-Muslim community and Malaysia's Christian minority that have by far been most testy and conflictual, given the growing limitations placed on non-Muslim expression and practice of their religious faith. Unlike the Muslim minorities in Thailand or the Philippines, however, the Christian minority has been the subject of considerably less scholarly attention in the case of Malaysia. It is in this vein that a closer look at this relationship would cast important and much needed light on these increasingly tense debates over the role of religion in the conception of Malaysian nationhood.

Christianity in Malaysia: History and Social Context

Malaysia is a Muslim majority country, where followers of the Islamic faith comprise about 60 percent of the total population.[5] In terms of ethnic groups, Malays form the largest number of Muslims (approximately 50 of the 60 percent). Indeed, in Malaysia, ethnic Malays are constitutionally and legally defined as Muslims, and this imbricated character of identity referents would have fundamental implications for conceptions of nationhood. Apart from ethnic Malays, ethnic Indians and, to a lesser extent, Chinese and other smaller denizen ethnic groups make up the remaining 10 percent of Muslims.

Among the other major religions, Christianity is arguably one of the most consequential today by virtue of the fact that according to statistics on religious identity, they form the majority in the East Malaysian state of Sarawak and are a growing segment of the population of Sabah, especially among the Bidayuh (Sarawak), Dayak (Sarawak), and Kadazan (Sabah).[6] As we shall see later in the chapter, the different religious profile of Sabah and Sarawak casts a somewhat different light on the dynamics of ethnicity and religious identity as they have played out in the conception of Malaysian nationhood.[7]

In total, Christians account for approximately 9 percent of the national population, although anecdotal evidence suggests the political and economic influence they command is incommensurate to their relatively small numbers. The Christian church is represented by a wide range of denominations, including the Anglican Church, the Roman Catholic Church, Methodists, Presbyterians, Lutherans, as well as a range of independent Evangelical and Pentecostal movements. It should also be noted that the spread of Christianity in Malaysia continues despite legal restrictions placed on proselytization by the Muslim-led incumbent government, restrictions that have arguably been exclusively targeted at the Christian church given its well-known prerogative to prioritize the conversion of non-believers.

---

[5] For official information on Malaysia's demographics, see www.statistics.gov.my/portal/index.php?option=com_content&id=1215.

[6] There are several available studies on Christianity in Malaysia. For example, Robert Hunt, Lee Kam Hing, and John Roxborogh, *Christianity in Malaysia: A Denominational History*. Petaling Jaya: Pelanduk Publications, 1990; Daniel Ho, "Malaysia," in Saphir Athyal (ed.), *Church in Asia Today: Challenges and Opportunities*. Lausanne: Asia Lausanne Committee for World Evangelism, 1996; John Roxborogh, *A History of Christianity in Malaysia*. Singapore: Armour Publishing, 2014.

[7] For a comprehensive study of Christianity in East Malaysia, see Liana Chua, *The Christianity of Culture: Conversion, Ethnic Citizenship, and the Matter of Religion in Malaysian Borneo*. New York: Palgrave MacMillan, 2012.

The arrival of Christianity in Malaysia (and Indonesia) can be traced as far back as the 7th century when the religion was brought to the region by Persian and Turkish traders. Nevertheless, Christian influences remained relatively marginal in a region more heavily influenced first by Indianization and, later, Islamization. In the 15th century, Catholicism was introduced by the Portuguese, while Protestantism appeared following the capture of Malacca by the Dutch in 1641. Protestantism gained further appeal during the colonial era of British administration in the 19th century in the Malay Peninsula as well as in Sabah and Sarawak, which together constitute East Malaysia.[8] The nature of Christianity's expansion during the colonial era doubtless contributed to widespread perceptions – to some extent still widely held today – that it was the "white man's religion" (despite the fact that the religion itself originated in what is today Palestine), and hence was a convenient veil for colonial domination. This would be a constant theme played up by Malay-Muslim nationalists of various stripes.

While colonialism proved the most potent vehicle for the introduction of Christianity since the 18th century, it was by no means the only one. Indeed, migrants also played a crucial role in facilitating the growth of Christianity in Malaysia. The role of Hakka Christians from China and South Asian migrants from the subcontinent was equally crucial in how they spread the religion through their transnational networks. In other instances, local networks such as the Borneo Evangelical Mission, which later morphed into the Borneo Evangelical Church (*Sidang Injil Borneo*), quickly sunk their roots and served as instrumental vehicles for proselytization among indigenous populations, especially in East Malaysia.

Aside from churches, the most visible manifestation of Christianity in Malaysian society can be found in the realm of education, where the influence of missionary schools remains strong. Missionary school networks such as the Anglo-Chinese School (ACS) found in Kuala Lumpur and Perak, the various St. Michael's Institution schools scattered across the country, and Selangor's prestigious Victoria Institution trace their heritage to various Christian denominations and foundations, and remain much sought-after educational institutions today, even among non-Christians who gain access on grounds of merit as such schools do not discriminate on the basis of race or religion. In addition, various uniform units such as the Boys Brigade and Girls Brigade movements continue to flourish in these missionary schools, imparting Christian

---

[8] John Roxborogh, *A Short History of Christianity in Malaysia*. Available http://roxborogh.com/sea/country/shmalaysia.htm.

values through extra-curricular activity.[9] Suffice to say, then, that the legacy of European (mainly British) missionary movements continued to thrive through these institutions long after the end of colonialism in Borneo (East Malaysia) and British Malaya. In more recent times, new networks of believers have surfaced to supplement the traditional networks of churches and educational institutions. Para-church organizations such as Fellowship of Evangelical Students (FES) and Graduate Christian Fellowship (GCF) provide venues through activities such as annual camps and conferences for Christian students, graduates, and young professionals to engage, network, discuss creedal beliefs through their bible study groups, and debate social issues of the day.

Despite strong institutional underpinnings and the fact that it is an essentially proselytizing religion, the growth of Christianity in Malaysia faces considerable obstacles. One of the reasons is the fact that members of the majority ethnic group in Malaysia – the Malays – are Muslims by birth. Both constitutionally and culturally, Malay-Muslims are prohibited from conversion to Christianity, or any other faith for that matter. Moreover, proselytization to Muslims is outlawed in the country. This lack of access to the Malay-Muslim community is further compounded by the fact that demographic trends in recent decades indicate a growing reduction of the non-Malay population relative to the Malay population. Yet, notwithstanding their minority status, Christians in Malaysia enjoy a very strong sense of community. In Peninsular Malaysia, anecdotal evidence suggests that Christians mostly consist of upper- and middle-class Malaysians from the ethnic Chinese and Indian communities, and tend to be better educated generally. This differs somewhat from the Christian community in East Malaysia, where they are spread across a larger number of ethnic groups. In fact, this overlay of class and ethnicity at least in Peninsular Malaysia has played no small part in contributing to the escalation of tension and conflict between Malay-Muslims and Christians by virtue of the perceived threat that the latter poses to the enshrined privileges of the former.

Ethnicity as Presumed Destiny

Scholars have argued that a significant change has taken place within Malaysia, whereby the outlook of large segments of the Muslim community has gradually shifted toward a more conservative register in terms

---

[9] In fact, anecdotal evidence suggests that quite a few Christian converts identify their membership in such groups during their school years as their initial exposure to the Christian faith.

of how social and political forces representing them have been asserting the prominence of Islam as a fundamental organizing principle for Malaysian society.[10] At issue is the intensification of an exclusivist narrative of Malay-Muslim supremacy that derogates religious freedom and rights of minority communities. For the most part, Malaysia's Christian community has reluctantly acquiesced to this shift. Even so, the gradual amplification of ethno-nationalist sentiments within segments of the Malay community that are increasingly couched in religious language has generated stiff headwinds for non-Muslim confessional communities, in particular the Christian community, against their freedom to exercise their faith and rendered diffidence increasingly difficult. This state of affairs has also set the backdrop for dramatic mobilization of both Malay-Muslim and non-Muslim groups. Two incidents stand out in this regard, in terms of how they triggered a deterioration of Muslim-Christian relations over the fundamental question of how Malaysian identity and nationhood is being conceived and articulated, reframed and reinvented.

First, in 2008 the Mufti of Perak, Harussani Zakaria, publicly fulminated that up to 260,000 Muslims in Malaysia had left the faith and converted to Christianity.[11] Despite the fact that no evidence was ever mustered to support his spurious claims, Harussani had no compunction about repeating his careless remarks, and in so doing catalyzed a backlash from many segments of the Malay-Muslim community as several civil society groups seized upon the opportunity to pressure the Malaysian government to "defend Islam."[12] This reaction foregrounded a growing sense of insecurity that attends certain segments of the Malay-Muslim community regarding their indigenous rights, a concern nursed by decades of political rhetoric on the part of UMNO about the presumed existential threat that non-Muslims posed to Malay-Muslim identity and interests.[13] This sentiment has also informed persistent talk of

---

[10] Recent scholarship on this topic includes Joseph Chinyong Liow, *Piety and Politics: Islamism in Contemporary Malaysia*. New York: Oxford University Press, 2009; Farish A. Noor, *The Malaysian Islamic Party PAS, 1951–2013: Islamism in a Mottled Nation*. Amsterdam: Amsterdam University Press, 2014.

[11] See http://helpvictor.blogspot.com/2011/10/christian-proselytization.html.

[12] Christian proselytization among the Malay-Muslim community was one of the immediate issues the post-independence government of Malaya sought to tackle, because of the latitude that the British colonial authorities afforded to Christian mission work. Since then, non-Muslim proselytization among the Malay-Muslim community has been banned by local religious authorities in almost all Malaysian states.

[13] This was a far cry from the relationship that the prominent Malay literary figure Munshi Abdullah had with the Christian missionary William Milne. As John Roxborogh noted: "Abdullah was never threatened in his own faith as a Muslim by his friendship with the LMS missionaries in Melaka and later in Singapore and his contribution to the rendering

cooperation between hitherto political opponents, UMNO and PAS (*Parti Islam Se-Malaysia* or the Pan-Malaysian Islamic Party), in the name of "Malay-Muslim unity." In response, the Muslim dominated state has encroached deeper into the lives of non-Muslims in the name of "defending Islam."[14] Using Islam as an ethnic boundary not only to differentiate themselves from non-Malays but also, more importantly, to reinforce a narrative of Malay-Muslim supremacy, a greater constriction of religious space for non-Muslim religious communities has taken place and, in turn, fanned the embers of the siege mentality that has taken root in the minority Christian community.[15]

Second, the usage of the term "Allah" by a Roman Catholic periodical, elaborated later in this chapter, sparked outrage in conservative quarters of the Malay-Muslim community possessed of a proprietary view that the term was the exclusive right of Muslims. Not only did events such as these precipitate mobilization of Malay-Muslim groups in defense of the primacy they ascribe to their faith, but also it prompted a discernible increase in political activism and mobilization from the Christian community, including rare open criticism of the state by religious leaders as well as ecumenical bodies such as the Council of Churches in Malaysia (CCM) and National Evangelical Christian Federation (NECF). At issue is the question of freedom of religion, which Malaysia's diverse Christian community has come to perceive as increasingly eroded in the wake of strong tides of Islamic conservatism that have infiltrated the Malaysian state.

Underlying this conservative turn is a domineering and heavily ethnicized political discourse that places great store on the notion of *Ketuanan Melayu*, or Malay lordship. A controversial concept which more often than not is misrepresented and misinterpreted, *Ketuanan Melayu* has nevertheless come to serve as the hegemonic master frame of Malaysian politics today, where the dominant discourse argues that Malaysia is, in essence, a Malay, and by extension Islamic, nation, and Malaysian nationhood must begin with an acceptance of this "reality." To get at the

---

of Christian scriptures into appropriate Malay was outstanding." See John Roxborogh, "Christianity in the Straits Settlements 1786–1842." Available www.academia.edu/4503922/Christianity_in_the_Straits_Settlements_1786_to_1842. See also Robert Hunt, "The History of the Translation of the Bible into Malay," *Journal of the Malaysian Branch of the Royal Asiatic Society*, Vol. 62, No. 1, 1989.

[14] See Judith Nagata, *The Reflowering of Malaysian Islam: Modern Religious Radicals and Their Roots*. Vancouver: University of British Columbia Press, 1984.

[15] Chong Eu Choong, "The Christian Response to State-led Islamization in Malaysia," in Bernhard Platzdasch and Johan Saravanamuttu (eds.), *Religious Diversity in Muslim-majority States in Southeast Asia: Areas of Toleration and Conflict*. Singapore: Institute of Southeast Asian Studies, 2014.

issue of challenges that Malaysia's Christians perceive to derive from this discourse, and their reservations toward these jeremiads in the context of their own negotiation of how nationhood is being conceived in Malaysia, it behooves to first establish the content of this dominant narrative of Malay-Muslim supremacy and how it has come to frame the national discourse on identity and politics.

The Master Frame of Malay-Muslim Dominance and Rise of Malay-Islamic Nationalism

During a lecture in Singapore in 1986, Abdullah Ahmad, then a Malaysian member of parliament and senior cadre of UMNO, famously exclaimed: "Let us make no mistake. The political system in Malaysia is founded on Malay dominance."[16] Following Abdullah Ahmad's statement, *Ketuanan Melayu*, as Malay dominance was translated, quickly entered into the lexicon as one of the paramount features of national discursive landscape in Malaysian society.[17] The profundity of what Abdullah Ahmad articulated cannot be overemphasized. According to the scholar of Malaysian Islam, Clive Kessler, these remarks all but triggered a major reconceptualization of the fundamental premises of Malaysian nationhood:

This was now a doctrine of explicit Malay political primacy and domination, one that went well beyond the NEP-era notion of simply the centrality of Malay culture to Malaysian national culture. That was one-half of the new approach. The other, and craftier, part was to assert that this notion of Malay ascendancy or domination was, and had been since 1957, part of the nation's foundational "social contract": that it had been an explicit or inherent part of the Merdeka agreements that had duly become embedded within the Federal Constitution itself. Radically revisionist, historically unfounded and even heretical when Abdullah Ahmad announced it, this idea was in following years powerfully promoted, and with insistent determination.[18]

---

[16] "*Dari Kacamata Melayu: Ucapan 'Malay Dominance' Abdullah Ahmad (1986) di Singapura.*" Available http://pesanan-pesanan.blogspot.com/2008/12/ucapan-malay-dominance-abdullah-ahmad.html.

[17] While the origins of the notion of Malay dominance as expressed in *Ketuanan Melayu* can be traced back to the pre-war anti-colonialist movement of the KMM, it has taken on several permutations since. Malay nationalists have used it to mobilize Malay support against the Malayan Union scheme (1946), the "Malaysian Malaysia" challenge from Lee Kuan Yew's Malaysian Solidarity Convention (1964), and the outcome of the May 1969 elections, which saw the Chinese opposition make significant inroads in Malaysian politics. Its more recent manifestations can be traced to the remarks alluded to here that were made by former UMNO stalwart Abdullah Ahmad.

[18] Clive Kessler, "Where Malaysia Stands Today," *The Malaysian Insider*, May 16, 2014. Available www.themalaysianinsider.com/sideviews/article/where-malaysia-stands-today-clive-kessler.

To this, we should hasten to add that while the notion that the Malay-Muslim population of Malaysia enjoys a status of primacy has never been seriously disputed, at the inception of the Malayan nation-state in 1957 this took the form of a "thin" conceptualization of *Ketuanan Melayu* where, for instance, the special rights and privileges accorded to the Malay population were understood to be time-bound: they were never envisaged to exist in perpetuity, and were to be pursued with careful appreciation of non-Malay interests and sensitivities toward their place in the nascent nation-state. Indeed, it was with this in mind that the architects of Malaya's constitution and "social contract" crafted a secular document that reflected the country's inherent diversity. What Abdullah Ahmad articulated in effect amounted to an invidious frontal assault on this edifice of Malaysian pluralism. It signaled a discursive shift that for all intents and purposes represented what was already gradually taking place, namely, a stronger emphasis on Malay rights and privileges at the expense of the interests of and discursive space for minorities. In other words, a shift from "thin" *Ketuanan Melayu* to "thick" *Ketuanan Melayu*, a major departure from what was originally envisaged by those who inherited the British colonial state at independence, had already begun.

Ketuanan Melayu is defined in Malaysian history textbooks as "the passion for anything related to the Malay race such as political rights, language, cultural heritage and customs, as well as the homeland."[19] According to the *Kamus Dewan* produced by the influential *Dewan Bahasa dan Pustaka* (Institute for Language and Literature), *Ketuanan* can mean "the right to rule or control a country (*Negara*), state (*Negeri*), or a district (*Daerah*), or sovereignty (*Kedaulatan*)." Its root word, *Tuan*, in keeping with this context, means "master" or "lord" (in relation to a servant or slave), or, in a related context, "owner" (in relation to property). Hence, literally, *Ketuanan Melayu* means Malay sovereignty or the lordship and ownership claim of the Malay on the *Tanah Melayu*, the land belonging to the Malays and everything in/on it. As with all nationalist discursive signifiers, the concept is often also heavily romanticized. Consider, in this regard, the following definition found in a Form Three textbook: "The love for whatever that is related to the Malay race such as political right, language, culture, heritage, customs and homeland. The Malay Peninsula (*Semenanjung Tanah Melayu*) is regarded as the ancestral land of the Malays."[20]

---

[19] See Yusu N. and Abu Chik A., *Eksel dalam PMR Sejarah*. Petaling Jaya: Pelangi Publishing Group Berhad, undated.

[20] Helen Ting, "Malaysian History Textbooks and the Discourse of Ketuanan Melayu," in Daniel P.S. Goh (ed.), *Race and Multiculturalism in Singapore*. New York: Routledge, 2009, p. 3.

What is more interesting, perhaps, is that despite the controversy surrounding it, the term *Ketuanan Melayu* itself does not appear in the Malaysian Constitution. At any rate, its underlying logic of according special rights to Malay interests is, in fact, constitutionally sanctioned. According to the Federal Constitution of 1957, while non-Malays were granted citizenship rights, Article 153 decrees that it is the responsibility of the King (*Yang di Pertuan Agong*) to safeguard the special position of the Malays and *Bumiputera* (indigenous groups), while also taking into account the "legitimate interests" of other communities.[21] In this way, the "special position" of the Malays and *Bumiputera* are codified. Rightly or wrongly, many Malay politicians, educationists, religious leaders, civil society activists, and culturalists have come to define this as Malay "*ketuanan*" over other segments of the population. In keeping with this definition, *Ketuanan Melayu* has become for them a legitimate organizing principle for Malaysian society by virtue of their view that the modern Malaysian state is built on the traditional Malay polity and anchored on the political culture and practices of its dominant ethnic group. The key questions, therefore, are to what extent this train of thought would or should be pursued to its logical conclusion in the process of imagining the Malaysian nation, and at what cost to the civic and pluralist conceptions of nationhood?

A critical feature of the discourse on *Ketuanan Melayu* is how the notion has been used to conceptualize the relationship between Muslim Malays and non-Malay citizens of Malaysia. Citing the following examples from history textbooks used in national schools, Ting points out how non-Malays are often cast in a negative light, and their citizenship – and, by extension, loyalty – called into question. Non-Malays are frequently referred to in such texts with depreciatory terms such as *anak dagang*, *golongan pendatang*, *pendatang asing*, or *imigran*, which she explicated to imply sojourners with no loyalty to the land, foreigners, aliens, or immigrants as opposed to *penduduk tempatan* or local inhabitants. It stands to reason that this is done to implicitly delegitimize their position in relation to Malay rights whenever the issue of citizenship is discussed. Moreover, the terms *orang dagang* and *golongan pendatang* are used in pejorative fashion to describe non-Malays in the context of Malay opposition to Malayan Union and advocacy of *Ketuanan Melayu*, thereby obliquely conveying the impression that any allusion to equal rights for non-Malays was essentially a threat to the position of the Malays. With

---

[21] Article 153(1) reads: "It shall be the responsibility of the Yang di-Pertuan Agong to safeguard the special position of the Malays and natives of any of the States of Sabah and Sarawak and the legitimate interests of other communities in accordance with the provisions of this Article."

this turn of phrase, *Ketuanan Melayu* became a zero-sum discourse with existential connotations for Malay-Muslim identity.

Needless to say, this view also carries religious connotations. Abdullah Zaik, president of *Ikatan Muslimin Malaysia* (Muslim Community Union of Malaysia), has argued that because non-Muslims are "immigrants," they should not be allowed a voice on the matter of whether and how Malaysia can be transformed into an Islamic state through the formulation and implementation of Islamic juridical strictures.[22] Malaysian national Islamic religious authorities which provide texts for the Friday sermons delivered in mosques throughout the country have regularly launched veiled attacks on Christians by alluding to "enemies of Islam" within the country who sought to confuse Muslims into believing that all religions are the same.[23]

This polarization of Malaysia's two largest confessional religious communities is compounded, Manickam further suggests, by referencing British colonialism and how non-Malays (namely, ethnic Chinese and ethnic Indians) were allied to the British and hence were beneficiaries of colonial rule, not to mention that unlike the Malays who claim themselves to be original inhabitants of the land, the ethnic Chinese and ethnic Indians were immigrants.[24] In sum, proponents of *Ketuanan Melayu* believe it to be a "timeless reality" which affords them the right to claim primacy and supremacy over other ethnic groups in the land even as the role of non-Muslims in the ascription of national identity and conceptualization of nationhood has been marginalized.[25] This train of thought is captured clearly in the writings of the former Prime Minister, Mahathir Mohamad, who stolidly opined that: "The Malays are the original or indigenous people of Malaya and the only people who can claim Malaya as their one and only country. In accordance with practice all over the world, this confers on the Malays certain inalienable rights over the forms and obligations of citizenship which can be imposed on citizens

---

[22] Dina Murad, "Abdullah Zaik: The Man behind Isma," *The Star*, May 22, 2014.
[23] See Clara Choi, "Friday Sermon Irks Local Church Leaders as 'Allah' Row Rages On," *The Malaysian Insider*, January 26, 2013. Available www.themalaysianinsider.com/malaysia/article/friday-sermon-irks-local-church-leaders-as-allah-row-rages-on/. The logic here is also somewhat flawed, as most confessional Christians do not in fact believe that all religions are the same.
[24] Sandra Khor Manickam, "Textbooks and Nation Construction in Malaysia," 2005. Available www.researchgate.net/publication/242203744_Textbooks_and_Nation_Construction_in_Malaysia.
[25] Historians and anthropologists have debated the indigenous status of Malays in the Peninsula. See, for instance, Tim Barnard (ed.), *Contesting Malayness: Malay Identity Across Boundaries*. Singapore: Singapore University Press, 2004. Needless to say, this argument is moot as far as political champions of *Ketuanan Melayu* are concerned.

of non-indigenous origin."[26] Despite his formal retirement from politics, Mahathir, in his studied disinterest, has continued to prod ultraconservative ethno-religious nationalist elements with this line of thinking.

As the definitive statement of claim for the supremacy of the Malay "race," *Ketuanan Melayu* has become arguably the most controversial concept that Malaysian society has to grapple with today. Given the assiduous myth-making that has surrounded the concept, the heavily racialized, ethno-religious nationalist discourse on *Ketuanan Melayu* can hardly be dismissed as merely a trope. While Malay politicians undoubtedly capitalize on the narrative of *Ketuanan Melayu* and the accompanying assumption that Malay interests and, indeed, survival are under threat and hence need to be defended, with far too much frequency, the fact of the matter is that this narrative continues to appeal to particular segments of the Malay community in Malaysia; and these segments are often large enough and influential enough to turn the tide of political contests in favor of ethno-religious nationalists. This is because the currency of the narrative of *Ketuanan Melayu* lies not only in its stress on the rights of denizens, but also the portrayal of non-Malays as a threat to these rights. Indeed, notwithstanding its seemingly innocuous role in outlining the markers of *Melayu* (Malay) identity as some scholars of Malay culture have argued, the etymology of the discourse has come to set more store by its political definition in relation to Malaysia's other ethnic communities, to wit: it implies that Malays are self-referenced "*tuan*" or "lords" and "masters" over other identities. "Thick" *Ketuanan Melayu*, then, is a narrative of special "birthright" and ethno-religious supremacy that in the view of non-Malays strikes at the very core of attempts to envision a civic and pluralist conception of nationhood despite the fact that the very notion of Malayness, which underpins *Ketuanan Melayu*, is a heavily contested concept.

Wrapped up in stereotypes and notwithstanding the conviction with which Malay-Muslim ethno-religious nationalist right-wing groups mobilize around the banner of *Ketuanan Melayu*, using it to justify the implementation of various affirmative action policies, discourses on this chief identity signifier in Malaysian society – the notion of *Melayu* or Malayness – are, as several recent scholarly collections have pointed out, highly ambiguous.[27] Be that as it may, promulgators of Malay supremacy

---

[26] Mahathir Mohamad, *The Malay Dilemma*. Kuala Lumpur: Times Books International, 1970, p. 133.

[27] See Barnard (ed.), *Contesting Malayness*; Yamamoto Hiroyuki, Anthony Milner, Kawashima Midori, and Arai Kazuhiro (eds.), *Bangsa and Umma: Development of People-Grouping Concepts in Islamized Southeast Asia*. Kyoto: Kyoto University Press, 2011; Maznah Mohamad and Syed Muhd Khairudin Aljunied (eds.), *Melayu: The Politics,*

would be quick to point out that the concept, or rather what it implies, has cultural and legal currency. This is captured in the special privileges guaranteed in the Federal Constitution. Specifically, reference is made to how the Constitution "expressly authorizes" certain "special provisions" such as the "special position" of the Malays and natives of Borneo (in the East Malaysian states of Sabah and Sarawak). This was promulgated in Articles 153 (1) mentioned earlier, and 153(2) of the Constitution, which states that:

> The Yang di-Pertuan Agong shall exercise his functions . . . necessary to safeguard the special provision of the Malays and natives of any of the States of Sabah and Sarawak and to ensure the reservation . . . of positions in the public service . . . and of scholarships, exhibitions and other similar educational and training privileges or special facilities given or accorded by the Federal Constitution.[28]

All this is doubtless true, except for the fact that, first, as this chapter pointed out, the term *Ketuanan Melayu* itself does not appear in the Constitution; second, the phrase "special provision" is hardly synonymous to "supremacy" or "lordship"; and, third, to the extent that it is implied in the Constitution, its coverage is clearly not limited to the "ethnic Malay" for it encompasses "natives of any of the States of Sabah and Sarawak" as well, a large number of whom are not, as it were, ethnic Malay.[29] Indeed, the amorphous nature of Malayness is captured in the concept of *"Masuk Melayu,"* which refers to how a person could "become" Malay upon conversion to Islam (which also implies that, at least in theory, a Malay may not have been a Malay at birth).[30] In

---

Poetics, and Paradoxes of Malayness. Singapore: National University of Singapore Press, 2011.

[28] The Constitution of the Federation of Malaysia can be found at http://confinder.richmond.edu/admin/docs/malaysia.pdf.

[29] Indeed, the conundrum of Sabah and Sarawak has remained poorly understood. The current Malaysian Constitution states that "the States of the Federation shall be Johore, Kedah, Kelantan, Malacca, Negeri Sembilan, Pahang, Penang, Perak, Perlis, Sabah, Sarawak, Selangor, and Terengganu." This, however, was not always the case. That phraseology contained in the latest Constitution, was revised in 1976. The original Constitution of September 16, 1963, mentions, in Article 1(2), that: "the states of the Federation shall be (a) the states of Malaya, namely Johor, Kedah, Kelantan, Malacca, Negeri Sembilan, Pahang, Penang, Perak, Perlis, Selangor, and Terengganu; (b) the Borneo States, namely Sabah and Sarawak; and (c) the State of Singapore." In other words, the original Federation of Malaysia was conceived as a conglomeration of three different but equal entities. This was further substantiated in the special provisions provided for Sabah and Sarawak, provisions that have over time been ignored and forgotten by the Malaysian state.

[30] A fine, though dated, article that covers this complexity is Judith Nagata, "What is a Malay? Situational Selection of Ethnic Identity in a Plural Society," *American Ethnologist*, Vol. 1, No. 2, May 1974, pp. 331–350.

point of fact, it is this that renders the implicit religious character of *Ketuanan Melayu* explicit.

Reframing the Narrative: From Ethnicity to Religion

Islam and Malay identity, already fused together constitutionally at the creation of independent Malaya, became even more intimately imbricated on the social landscape during the administration of former Prime Minister Mahathir Mohamad when *Sunni* Islam was embedded institutionally within the state, and formed the foundation for a growing Malay-Islamic nationalism. A central impetus to this process of Islamization was the escalating competition for Malay-Muslim votes that was taking place between Mahathir's UMNO party and the opposition Islamist party, PAS. Formed in 1951 by disillusioned members of UMNO's religious wing, the leadership of PAS took a decidedly religious turn in the early 1980s when the party replicated the Iranian example and voted in clerics into the top ranks of party leadership. Both parties subsequently became engrossed in the "Islamization race" that ensued, with UMNO using the levers of the state to bolster its Islamic credentials.[31] Needless to say, this uptick in religious politicking gave added impetus to the narrative of the primacy of Islam as religious credentials and the ability to "out-Islam" each other served as crucial source of legitimation for these Muslim political parties.

An outcome of this Islamization race was the amplification of a hegemonic discourse of both Islamic and Malay supremacy, which under the aegis of Mahathir's leadership took the form of the propagation of a brand of Islam that was articulated as progressive and modern, yet was distinctively conservative in praxis. Shaping this state-sanctioned Islamic landscape was the introduction of a host of Islamic programs on public television; Islamic banking; the building of mosques, Islamic schools, and the International Islamic University; and the proliferation of Islamic civil society organizations, many with close links to the ruling UMNO party. At the same time, activist Muslims began taking control of the levers of the state when the religious bureaucracy all but ballooned during this period.[32] Formed in 1968 as MKI (*Majlis Kebangsaan Hal*

---

[31] Joseph Chinyong Liow, "Political Islam in Malaysia: Problematising Discourse and Practice in the UMNO-PAS 'Islamisation Race,'" *Commonwealth and Comparative Politics*, Vol. 42, No. 2, July 2004; Joseph Chinyong Liow and Afif Pasuni, "Islam, the State and Politics in Malaysia," in Meredith Weiss (ed.), *Routledge Handbook of Contemporary Malaysia*. London: Routledge, 2015.

[32] For this topic, see Ahmad Fauzi Abdul Hamid, "Political Islam and Islamist Politics in Malaysia," *Trends in Southeast Asia*, No. 2, 2013; Mohd Azizuddin Mohd Sani,

Ehwal Ugama Islam Malaysia or the Malaysian National Association of Islamic Affairs) and incorporated into the Prime Minister's Office in 1974, JAKIM (*Jabatan Agama Kemajuan Islam Malaysia* or the Malaysian Department for Religious Development) and its affiliates that operated in the various states under the Malaysian federal system were endowed with extensive powers to define Muslim orthodoxy and orthopraxy in Malaysia. Accompanying this was a particularly disconcerting amendment in the Malaysian Constitution in 1988 that further empowered these religious authorities to police the practice of Islam.

Indeed, it is through these transformative processes that Islam has come to assume a prominent place in the Malaysian political psyche leading Malaysian national identity to be increasingly ascribed with religious (Islamic) markers, accompanied by a discomfiting puritanical rigidity on the part of a small but growing segment of the Malay-Muslim population. Even though freedom of worship is constitutionally guaranteed, Islam is enshrined in the Malaysian Constitution as the sole official religion of the country. Not only that, but also constitutional articles such as the controversial Article 121 1(A) accord Islamic *shari'a* law equal status with civil law on a range of jurisprudential matters concerning Muslims. Islam assumes further significance by virtue of the fact that, according to the Constitution, one of the chief criteria for the definition of "Malay" is that a person must be Muslim. As noted previously, the fact that converts to Islam in Malaysia are deemed to be "*Masuk Melayu*" is demonstrative of how ethnicity has blurred into religion on a level as fundamental as personal identity.[33]

While there may certainly be an element of brinkmanship and posturing in how the UMNO-led government has used religion to enhance its credibility and political legitimacy, it would be a mistake to presume that Islamization was merely sabre-rattling and politicking in religious

---

"Islamization Policy and Islamic Bureaucracy in Malaysia," *Trends in Southeast Asia* (Institute of Southeast Asian Studies), No. 5, 2015.

[33] Beyond this, the role of Islam as a core foundation of Malay identity has taken on further credence for the fact that the two other pillars upon which this identity is constructed, namely language and royalty, no longer carry the same weight as they used to as identity signifiers. The Malay language remains of consequence politically, but it is precisely because of this that led the state to formulate and implement an education policy based on its primacy in the national curriculum. What was the result? Simply put, knowledge of the Malay language was no longer an exclusive "Malay" prerogative. Similarly, royalty in Malaysia today has had a highly problematic relationship with the Malay ruling elite, where it is seen by the latter as a competitor to their legitimacy. Moreover, royalty have also further undermined their own legitimacy in the public eye as a result of a number of controversial episodes and scandals. For a study on Malaysia's constitutional monarchy, see Ali Fuat Gökçe, "Federal Parliamentary Democracy with a Constitutional Monarchy: Malaysia," *International Journal of Social Science*, Vol. 6, No. 5, May 2013.

guise. As a matter of fact, it strikes at the very essence of national identity and belonging. The combination of the factors discussed above, amplified by the prevalence of a state-orchestrated discourse of ethno-religious supremacy and narrative of rampant Malay-Islamic nationalism that politicians from the UMNO party and its affiliates enjoy free rein to engage in, has effectively ascribed to members of other ethnic groups and religions the status of "second-class" citizens in everything but name. Concomitantly, the fact that non-Muslims perceive this as a dereliction of the constitutional right to freedom of religion, enshrined in Article 11, appears to hold little sway as narrow exclusivist views carry the day amidst the deafening silence of the "moderates" in the Malay-Muslim establishment.

What is even more striking is the fact that while ethnicity has long been seen as the primary identity marker for Malays in Malaysia, recent research indicates that there may well be a shift in reference points away from ethnicity toward religion taking place today, with Malays prioritizing religious signifiers over ethnic ones.[34] According to this narrative, the centrality of Islam to Malay identity – and by extension, the Malay polity upon which the modern Malay(sian) state is built – becomes an inexorable ontological principle, disconnected from the pluralist social landscape comprising multiple "nations" bounded within the territorial state, or the constitutional rights which they lay claim to. While an *idea* of a Malaysian identity may exist, the hierarchical nature of the Malaysian political structure where power is essentially held in the hands of Malay-Muslim elite, and the dominant yet profoundly narrow narrative of nationhood they promulgate, weakens any effort at building Malaysian national identity as a collective whole, for fear that "a particular definition may favour the interests and identity of one sub-national group over another."[35] Consequently, the ascriptive identity of Malay-Muslim supremacy has gradually eroded the Malaysian political-constitutional identity that accommodates non-Muslim minorities, and that was envisaged by Malaysia's founding fathers.

Prognostic Frames: Christian Mobilization and Legal Recourse?

Since the 1980s, this exclusivist and restrictive conception of Malay-Muslim identity – bleeding into hegemony on grounds of religion and

---

[34] Carolyn Hong, "Increasing Religiosity in Malaysia Causes a Stir," *Straits Times*, September 5, 2006.
[35] Craig Calhoun, *Nationalism*. Minneapolis: University of Minneapolis Press, 1997, p. 98.

ethnicity – has been gathering momentum at the expense of religious freedom for non-Muslims in Malaysia. This constriction has been expressed in the activism of state Islamic authorities (including the policing of religious "practice" by these authorities, even when offenses involve non-Muslims), as well as the perpetuation of discriminatory laws and practices, such as the denial of the right to proselytize for Christians (a long-standing proscription), restrictions on permits for the construction of church buildings, obstacles to the importing of Christian literature, and the interference of zealous Muslim civil servants in the handling of issues pertaining to the Christian community.[36] So how has Malaysia's Christian community responded?

Unlike Muslim minorities in Thailand or the Philippines covered in previous chapters, the prognostic frames that Christians in Malaysia have chosen have not involved violence in any significant form but rather to emphasize citizen and belonging.[37] That is not to say, however, that the Christian community has demurred in the face of these exclusivist narratives promulgated by those favoring a more restrictive and "Islamic" interpretation of the fundamental tenets of Malaysian nationhood. In fact, Christian leaders have since independence sought to mitigate the effects of Islamization via quiet channels of dialogue with the state and its interlocutors.[38] Yet the increasing intrusion of the state into the non-Muslim sphere has provoked a shift from this traditional torpor. Concomitantly, previous practices of restraint, discreet dialogue, and lobbying have given way to more visible resistance and push-back in the form of deepening civil and political engagement for the cause of religious freedom and the mobilization of civil society groups and coalitions toward these ends.[39] The result has been the unfolding of high-profile legal cases which have cast a harsh light on religious freedom amidst an air of Malay-Muslim supremacy and dominance.

---

[36] See Peter Rowan, *Proclaiming the Peacemaker: The Malaysian Church as an Agent of Reconciliation in a Multicultural Society*. Oxford: Regnum Books, 2012; Chong Eu Chong, "The Christian Response to State-led Islamization in Malaysia," in Bernhard Platzdasch and Johan Saravanamuttu (eds.), *Religious Diversity in Muslim-Majority States in Southeast Asia: Areas of Toleration and Conflict*. Singapore: Institute of Southeast Asian Studies, 2014.
[37] Albert Sundadaraj Walters, *We Believe in One God? Reflections on the Trinity in the Malaysian Context*. Delhi: ISPCK, 2002, p. 59.
[38] Interview, Negri Sembilan, June 17, 2012.
[39] The formation of local ecumenical bodies was telling of the extent to which various Christian denominations perceived the intensification of state restrictions on religious freedom and freedom of worship for non-Muslims. This is because, while a universal religion, Christianity has always been plagued by doctrinal differences and different modes of church governance which have often proven impediments to unity and cooperation between churches and denominations.

As suggested earlier, the encroachment of rigid Islamization into the realm of creedal allegiance and worship has become more discernible over the years, resulting in the deepening of inter-religious and inter-ethnic cleavages. Permits for church buildings have become harder to come by as Christian communities began facing a raft of obstacles including the reduction of land for non-Muslim religious buildings and bureaucratic foot-dragging. As a consequence, many churches have resorted to renting commercial property or office premises for their worship. Smaller congregations were denied usage of the word "*gereja*" (church), and were only allowed to operate as "*pusat*" (center). More disconcerting is the fact that debates over conversions, particularly involving Muslims, have become rampant, amplified, and heated. Nowhere has this been more so in recent times than over the case of Lina Joy.

The case revolves around Azalina Jailani, a Muslim convert to Christianity who changed her name to Lina Joy in 1998. As Malaysian law requires all Muslim citizens to have their religion (Islam) reflected in their identity card, after her conversion Joy attempted on several occasions to have the word "Islam" removed. Her application was rejected by the National Registration Department on the grounds that she had to furnish written authorization from the *shari'a* court that officially declared her an apostate before such a change could be made.[40] The Federal Territories *Shari'a* Court, which she consulted in the issue, refused her request for the document, thereby denying her any right to leave the religion. Joy's appeal against the decision of the *shari'a* court in 2001 was likewise dismissed on grounds that civil courts had no jurisdiction over matters concerning religion. Finally, Lina Joy appealed the *shari'a* court decision to the Federal Court, the highest court in the land, on constitutional grounds, thereby setting the stage for a watershed decision.

On May 30, 2007, the Malaysian Federal Court finally made a much-awaited decision regarding the Lina Joy apostasy case. In a landmark pronouncement which reverberated across the Malaysian social-political landscape and set a legal precedence, the Federal Court ruled by a margin of two-to-one in favor of dismissing Lina Joy's appeal and upholding earlier legal decisions that her case had no standing in civil courts. The panel concluded that only an Islamic *shari'a* tribunal could certify her renunciation of Islam and, by virtue of that, the legality of her conversion. In other words, in the eyes of the Malaysian judicial system, Lina Joy

---

[40] According to the Malaysian Constitution and Malaysia's dual-track system of governance over religious issues, the state *shari'a* court is the final arbiter on all matters pertaining to a Muslim's practice of his/her faith. This includes matters of conversion.

remains a Muslim despite her public renunciation of the faith by virtue of her baptism into the Christian religion many years ago.

Predictably, the debate over apostasy lent itself to greater controversy precisely because of the multi-cultural and multi-religious nature of Malaysian society. Political expediency, coupled with a concern for the alleged proliferation of apostasy cases over the past few years, has forced the UMNO-led government's hand and pressured the state into engaging this controversial debate.[41] JAKIM stood at the forefront of the state's response by suggesting the possibility of a parliamentary bill on apostasy in 1998, the contents of which were never fully fleshed out. Following this, legislation was put in place that levied punishment in the region of a RM5,000 fine or a three-year jail term, or both, for the Islamic offense of *murtad* (apostasy).[42] In addition, these laws also clarified Article 11(4) of the Federal Constitution forbidding the proselytization of Muslims by other faiths in Malaysia.[43] In sum, this provision permits states to outlaw the propagation of any religious doctrine or belief among persons professing the religion of Islam, and to take penal action against non-Muslims caught proselytizing to Muslims.

The Lina Joy court ruling received extensive coverage in local and international media, and was predictably met with consternation within Christian circles in Malaysia and abroad. Within Malaysia, ubiquitous Christian bible study groups met in prayer for Joy, while Christian leaders concerned for the legal *cul-de-sac* of the Lina Joy ruling, mobilized to draw the Malaysian government's attention to constitutional guarantees of religious freedom. In an open letter, the CCM raised concerns that the sanctity of Article 11 of the Federal Constitution of 1957 had been severely diminished by the decision, and called on the Malaysian government to set in motion measures to protect religious freedom as originally intended in the document.[44]

Muslim-Christian antagonism in Malaysia escalated in January 2010 with a series of attacks on Christian churches, followed by seemingly retaliatory attacks on a couple of Muslim *surau* (prayer facilities). Though

---

[41] Patricia Martinez, "Mahathir, Islam and the New Malay Dilemma," in Ho Khai Leong and James Chin (eds.), *Mahathir's Administration: Performance and Crisis in Governance*. Singapore: Times Books International, 2002, p. 240.

[42] Norani Othman, "Islamization and Democratization in Malaysia in Regional and Global Contexts," in Ariel Heryanto and Sumit Mandal (eds.), *Challenging Authoritarianism in Southeast Asia: Comparing Indonesia and Malaysia*. London: RoutledgeCurzon, 2003, p. 128.

[43] Article 11(4) stipulates that "State law ... may control or restrict the propagation of any religious doctrine or belief among persons professing the religion of Islam."

[44] Rev Dr. Thomas Philips and Rev Dr. Herman Shastri, "Freedom of Religion Has Been Severely Diminished," in Nathaniel Tan and John Lee (eds.), *Religion Under Siege; Lina Joy, The Islamic State and Freedom of Faith*. Kuala Lumpur: Kinibooks, 2008, p. 26.

never conclusively proven, it was widely believed that the attacks on twelve churches were a direct response to a High Court ruling in December 2009 that permitted the use of the term *"Allah"* in the Malay language version of the Roman Catholic magazine, *Herald*, with the requisite disclaimer that such publications were for circulation among non-Muslims only.[45] The court ruling was met with widespread disapproval among the Malay-Muslim community, which viewed the use of the term *"Allah"* as the exclusive prerogative of Muslims.[46]

The consequences of a ban on the use of the word *"Allah"* by non-Muslims would have the greatest impact on Malaysian Christians from the Eastern states of Sabah and Sarawak, where most indigenous followers of the religion are illiterate in English and hence rely heavily on religious publications (bibles, religious tracts, hymnals) obtained from neighboring Indonesia, which are published in the cognate Indonesian language. The fact of the matter is that East Malaysian Christians have been using the word *Allah* for centuries without opposition from Muslims. In this regard, the attempt to ban the use of the word has been perceived as unwelcome regulation of their worship, thereby once again contravening constitutional rights to freedom of worship.

Traditionally, Christian representative bodies such as the CCM, NECF, and Churches of Federation of Malaysia (CFM) have occasionally lent their voice to the cacophony of electoral campaigns with generic calls for their followers to exercise responsible citizenship by voting for good governance, justice, and equity. Even so, Christian congregations have for the most part been apathetic in terms of active political participation, in that mass mobilization toward collective action in the form of a Christian "movement" in Malaysia has never materialized, nor had cause to. Likewise, preachers seldom preached on issues of nation-building, minority rights, or other potentially controversial topics over the pulpit.

All this has started to change. There has been a discernible shift away from this tradition of political indifference in the wake of anxiety over an Islamization process that has accelerated and deepened in recent years, and disenchantment over the inability of moderate Muslim and non-Muslim political leaders in the incumbent government coalition to arrest

---

[45] The case arose when customs officers confiscated 15,000 bibles translated into the Indonesian language (which is similar in many ways to Malay) in the last quarter of 2009. The rationale for the confiscation was the discovery of the use of the term "Allah" in these bibles, and attendant concern this would "confuse" Muslims in Malaysia.

[46] This was despite the fact that key religious scholars from the Islamist opposition PAS party, including its popular and respected spiritual leader Nik Aziz and president Abdul Hadi Awang, explaining that based on historical precedence followers of the Abrahamic faiths should be permitted to use the term.

the decline toward an exclusivist form of conservatism. Political quietism has given way to increasingly open vocal support for the cause of the political opposition.[47] Newly registered voters openly declared their allegiance to opposition parties, while older voters – many of them hitherto staunch supporters of the status quo – voiced disillusionment with the current non-Muslim component parties in the incumbent regime, whom they felt had perforce capitulated to the right-wing elements within UMNO.[48] Significantly, during the 2008 and 2013 election campaigns pulpits across the country were used to mobilize a "vote wisely" campaign, in which congregations were encouraged to vote with a critical mind. The hardly veiled subtext was for Christians to support the opposition.

Furthermore, in moves never previously witnessed in the country, churches across Malaysia actively facilitated voter registration, with some even offering their premises for such purposes. Since the 2008 election campaign, church pulpits have been frequently used as tools of mobilization, with sermons on national identity, nation building, and responsible citizenship taking place with regularity. The NECF rolled out its document titled "*Transform Nation Agenda*" which sought to establish a framework for Christian community activism.[49] A book titled "*Reflections on Christian Political Engagement in Malaysia Today: The Bible and the Ballot*" was also published, in which church leaders openly expressed that they would vote against the incumbent government.[50]

As suggested earlier, a key ecumenical Christian organization at the forefront of the discursive debate over the rights of minority religions has been the Christian Federation of Malaysia (CFM). Founded in 1985, CFM has been an umbrella body representing diverse Christian denominations in Malaysia in their dealings with the government. The component bodies of the CFM include the CCM, the NECF, and the Catholic Bishop's Conference of Malaysia. The CFM's charge is to serve as a platform for the expression of sentiments of the Malaysian Christian community on national issues of interest to them. The relationship between the CFM and the Malaysian state has grown testy in the last two decades. The denouement was reached with the *Kalimah Allah*: the matter of proprietary rights to the usage of the term *Allah*.

---

[47] I encountered this myself on numerous occasions in the course of fieldwork during the campaign period for the 2008 and 2013 general elections.
[48] Several church leaders interviewed for this chapter expressed similar sentiments on condition of anonymity.
[49] Eugene Yapp and Samuel Ang (eds.), *Transform Nation Agenda*. Selangor: NECF Malaysia Research Commission, 2009.
[50] Joshua Woo and Tan Soo-Inn (eds.), *The Bible and the Ballot: Reflections on Christian Political Engagement in Malaysia Today*. Singapore: Graceworks, 2011.

What's in a Name?

In December 1981, the Ministry of Home Affairs banned the printing, publication, sale, issue, circulation or possession of the Malay Bible (*Al-Kitab*) in Malaysia under Section 22 of the Internal Security Act (ISA) 1960, noting that it was prejudicial to the "national interest" and "security" of the country. The Christian community responded by filing an appeal. The order was subsequently amended in March 1982 to say that it would not apply to the possession or use of the Malay bible within church premises by Christians. Four years later, the Christian community faced another set of restrictions, when the government declared the words "*Allah*," "*Solat*," "*Ka'abah*," and "*Baitullah*" – words that hitherto appear in Malay language Christian publications – to be exclusive to Islam. CFM leaders did not openly protest against these directives for, after appealing to the authorities, they were given assurances by Prime Minister Mahathir Mohamad, and later his successor Abdullah Badawi, that it would not be an issue for the words to be used within the Christian community. According to Herman Shastri, General Secretary of the CCM, Christian leaders had refrained from stronger action as they were told by Mahathir that the issue was sensitive. However, in 2006, during the premiership of Abdullah Badawi, the Home Ministry began taking a tougher line on the usage of the word *Allah* in Christian publications. A Catholic weekly, *Herald*, began receiving letters from the ministry warning against the use of the word *Allah* in the publication. After receiving a sixth warning from the ministry and faced with the threat of revocation of its publishing license, the *Herald* sought redress through the courts. This process finally led to *Herald* filing for a judicial review in the Malaysian High Court on the Home Ministry's ban of its usage of *Allah*.

On December 31, 2009, the Malaysian High Court ruled that the Malaysian Home Ministry's ban was illegal, and that it was within the Catholic magazine's right to use the Arabic word *Allah* in reference to God in its Malay-language section. Predictably, Malay-Muslims took offense. Subsequently, public protests were organized, and the ruling challenged in several online chatrooms. This catalyzed further protests by vocal Malay ethno-religious nationalist right wing groups throughout the country that again mobilized "in defence of Islam." While these protests were for the most part peaceful, a hint of controlled violence lurked in the background as groups threatened to burn bibles as well as raid churches and the Malaysian Bible Society.[51] Meanwhile, moderate

---

[51] The Bible Society was indeed raided by Islamic religious authorities from the state of Selangor in January 2014.

voices within the Malay political establishment, careful not to go against the grain of popular sentiment stoked by these right wing Malay-Muslim groups, stayed conspicuously silent.

The controversy over proprietary claims to the word *Allah* has invariably triggered heated debate in Malaysia over the history and etymology of the term.[52] Malaysian Christians have pointed to the fact that the term *Allah* predates the founding of Islam, and has been used by Arab Christians and other Christians all across Southeast Asia for centuries. In Indonesia the term has been – and continues to be – used by both Catholics and Protestants since the arrival of Christianity in the Archipelago.[53] Yet in Malaysia, etymological and historical debates over the proprietary use of the term *Allah* among faith communities in the country (we should also note that the term features prominently in Sikh scriptures in the country as well) are, unfortunately, amplified, if not determined, by the political baggage that they carry. Even though freedom of worship is constitutionally guaranteed in Malaysia, Islam is enshrined in the Constitution as the sole official religion of the country. As the chapter pointed out above, constitutional articles such as the controversial Article 121 1(A) accord Islamic *shari'a* law equal status with civil law in jurisprudential matters in the private lives of Muslims. Islam assumes further salience in the Malaysian context by virtue of the fact that according to the Constitution one of the chief criteria for the definition of "Malay" is that a person must be Muslim, for both identity signifiers cohabit in a mutually reinforcing relationship. Because of these conditions, the claims of Malaysian Christians, particularly those residing in Eastern Malaysia, have been rejected by many Muslim organizations and leaders, including politicians, who betray a sense of insecurity in maintaining that allowing the term *Allah* to be used by non-Muslims would confuse Muslims and threaten their identity.

The controversy soon boiled over to public protests after Friday prayers at the National Mosque, which the government claimed they were unable to prevent.[54] Following this, several churches in Kuala Lumpur and Petaling Jaya were torched and fire-bombed, and threats were made online

---

[52] See Joseph Chinyong Liow, "No God But God: Malaysia's 'Allah' Controversy," *Foreign Affairs Online*, February 10, 2010. Available www.foreignaffairs.com/articles/malaysia/2010-02-10/no-god-god.

[53] Likewise, this common belief in a singular universal God also happens to be the factor that binds both Muslims and Christians (and Jews) so close together, as they come from the same Abrahamic tradition and believe in the same Prophets. And lest it be forgotten, the Prophet Adam was neither Muslim nor Christian, but simply a Prophet of *Allah*.

[54] "Najib: We Cannot Stop Friday's Protest." Available www.malaysia-today.net/najib-we-cannot-stop-fridays-protest/.

against members of the Christian community.[55] The Home Ministry filed an appeal against the court judgment. By that time, the *Kalimah Allah* controversy had become even more complicated as local Islamic religious authorities began taking the initiative to add more Arabic religious words to the list of the four words that the Home Ministry had initially deemed exclusive for Muslim usage.

In an attempt to break the impasse, some political leaders from UMNO ostensibly called for restraint, and for the issue to be resolved through interfaith dialogue. These gestures were however received a cold reception from many in the Christian community, whose sentiments can be summarized by the following response:

> The time for dialogue is over. Meaningful dialogue can only happen when all parties to the dialogue are treated as equals. In the current scenario, I'll wager that any 'dialogue' will involve non-Muslims acceding to the perceived 'sensitivities' and assumed rights of Muslims to own copyright to the word '*Allah*'. And mind you, the use of the word '*Allah*' is not a 'sensitive' issue, as top Umno leaders and the Umno-backed *Utusan Malaysia* are fond of restating repeatedly. It's a copyright issue. And there is nothing at all that gives Muslims in Malaysia, or elsewhere, the copyright to use the word to refer to God and deny others the right to do so.... an interfaith dialogue where non-Muslims are likely to be asked to compromise on their rights to protect the false sensitivities of some Muslim.[56]

One of the reasons why the non-Muslim community was not receptive to these calls for an interfaith dialogue to resolve the issue was the fact that the powerful Home Ministry had appealed the Federal Court's decision, thereby implying it was not merely an issue of confessional faith and belief, but one that spoke to the legitimacy and authority of the state as well as the constitutional right of religious minorities. In the event, the Home Ministry also changed its stand on its prohibition order concerning the Malay bible despite a compromise reached with Christian leaders on this issue in December 2005, which allowed the distribution of *Al-Kitab* on condition that the words "*Penerbitan Kristian*" (Christian Publication) along with the symbol of the cross was embossed on the cover.[57]

The controversy surrounding *Herald* was hardly happenstance. In March and September 2009, the port and customs authorities in Port Klang and Kuching seized a total of 15,000 Malay bibles that had arrived from Indonesia. About a year earlier the authorities had confiscated

---

[55] See "Allah Controversy in Malaysia: Church Burning has Happened." Available http://christianity.livejournal.com/3752432.html.

[56] See Jacqueline Ann Surin, "Allah Issue: Who Started It?" Available http://blog.limkitsiang.com/2010/01/13/allah-issue-who-started-it/.

[57] It is important that one bears in mind the difference between the Bible, which is for Christians a holy scripture, and *Herald*, which is a magazine.

Christian children's books in several bookshops in three states in Peninsular Malaysia (Johor, Negri Sembilan, and Perak). However, even as they protested these actions by state authorities, Christian leaders made it clear that they were prepared to work toward an amicable solution. In November 2009, when calling for the immediate release of the confiscated bibles, the Executive Secretary of the CFM Tan Kong Beng noted that "we (CFM) are open to and desire further discussion with officials so that this problem can be resolved."[58] Even in the matter of the court action on *Herald*, which was possibly the first instance of a Christian entity in Malaysia seeking legal recourse in a confrontation with the state, it was more of an act of last resort. Indeed until the case was brought before the High Court, the CFM and its components had clearly preferred a non-confrontational approach with the government, seeking dialogue with government officials and leaders (as in the compromise over the Malay bibles reached in December 2005) and keeping a low profile on disputes with the state, rather than escalating matters out into the public domain.

On January 12, 2011, the Home Ministry seized a further shipment of 30,000 Malay bibles at Kuching port. On the same day, the CFM released a statement signed by its head, Ng Moon Hing of the Anglican diocese, alleging that the "authorities are waging a continuous, surreptitious and systematic programme against Christians in Malaysia to deny them access to the Malay Bible in Malaysia."[59] It was the strongest statement yet from a leader of a minority religion against the state and conveyed the impression that the CFM had reached the end of its tether with the authorities. The CFM even began its statement saying that the organization was "greatly disillusioned, fed-up and angered" by the repeated seizure of Malay bibles. Confronted with such protests, the government relented on the impounded bibles but at the same time also seemed determined to have the final word. The decision was made to release the seized bibles, but not before they were marked with serial numbers and each copy stamped with the disclaimer: "*Peringatan: 'Al Kitab Berita Baik' ini untuk kegunaan penganut agama Kristian sahaja. Dengan perintah Menteri Dalam Negeri.*" ("Reminder: This Good News Bible is for the use of Christians only. By order of the Home Minister.").[60] Instead of

---

[58] Don Fisher, "Seizure of 15,000 Bibles in Malaysia Stuns Christians." Available www.christianheadlines.com/news/seizure-of-15-000-bibles-in-malaysia-stuns-christians-11616546.html, November 10, 2009.

[59] Eric Young, "30,000 Bibles Detained by Malaysian Government, Claim Christian Leaders," *The Christian Post*, March 11, 2011. Available www.christianpost.com/news/30000-bibles-detained-by-malaysian-govt-claim-christian-leaders-49377/#!

[60] Home Minister Hishamuddin Hussein provided a defense of his ministry's action by claiming that the stamping was done because the importer, the Bible Society of Malaysia

welcoming the Home Ministry's release of the impounded Malay bibles, Christian groups took offense at what they deemed to be the desecration of their holy books. The CFM issued another strong statement on March 17 condemning the Home Ministry's action as disingenuous and "wholly offensive to Christians," and challenged the state's contention that the bible in the Malay language was prejudicial to the national interest and the security of Malaysia.

After consultation within CFM, the two importers of the Malay bibles, namely Bible Society of Malaysia and The Gideons, chose not to collect the books on those terms, and instead demanded the unconditional release of the 30,000 Malay bibles together with another 5,100 bibles that had been detained earlier in Port Klang in March 2009. Later, on March 22, the Federal Government backtracked, this time using Idris Jala, a Christian senator from the state of Sarawak and a minister in the Prime Minister's Department, to offer a compromise whereby the government would no longer stamp or serialize imported Malay bibles but would require the words, "For Christianity," to be reflected on the bible covers. Although in its official response on March 30, the CFM did not reject the new proposal, it made it clear that it sought further concessions from the state in the form of assurances that they would "remove every impediment, whether legal or administrative" to the use of *Al-Kitab*, and requested them to revoke the order that Christian scripture posed a threat to national security. Apart from the CFM statement, the head of the Catholic Bishops Conference, Bishop Paul Tan, urged for a return to the previously agreed designation of "Christian publication" on each copy of the Malay bible noting that this phraseology was more neutral than the words "For Christianity" being proposed by state authority. (Bishop Tan who headed the CFM in the 1980s had, like Bishop Moon, publicly condemned the Home Ministry's serializing and stamping of the imported bibles as "flatly unacceptable" and a "crass form of censorship redolent of the communist era."[61])

Strains between Christian and Muslim communities worsened when the state's decision to release the bibles provoked outcry in many quarters of the vocal Malay-Muslim civil society. The influential Mufti of Perak, Harussani Zakaria, condemned the release of the Malay-language bibles

(BSM), had wanted the Malay bibles to be released quickly and that the action was based on practices adopted since former Prime Minister Mahathir's tenure. However, as the authorities had never before put serial numbers or their own stamp on seized bibles, their action was clearly perceived as offending the religious sensitivities of the Christian community.

[61] See "BN Turns Communist with Bible Conditions." Available http://malaysianjustice.blogspot.com/2011/03/bn-turns-communist-with-bible.html.

while *Angkatan Belia Islam Malaysia* (ABIM or Islamic Youth Movement) also registered its disapproval of the state's concession. In comments calibrated to contrive a link between the ascribed supremacy of Islam and the qualifications of Malaysian citizenship, Harussani, along with several other Islamic scholars, even suggested that the citizenship of those who questioned the ban on non-Muslim usage of the term *Allah* be revoked.[62] In the same vein, Ibrahim Ali, head of the ethno-nationalist Malay right-wing group Perkasa, threatened to burn bibles even as he brazenly warned Christians not to make "unreasonable demands" and "test the patience" of the Malay-Muslim majority.[63] In a baffling response to calls by non-Muslim political and religious leaders for Ibrahim Ali to be charged under the Sedition Act – a colonial era law that has been used frequently in contemporary times against those who are alleged to have threatened ethnic and religious harmony by questioning Malay supremacy and the primacy of Islam – for his incendiary remarks, the Malaysian Attorney-General retorted: "He (Ibrahim Ali) had no intention to create religious disharmony when he called for the burning of Bibles with the word 'Allah'. It is clear that his intentions were to defend the sanctity of Islam."[64]

As the controversy over impounded Christian scripture brewed, on October 15, 2013 the Court of Appeal reversed the December 2009 ruling of the High Court and retained the ban on *Herald*. According to Attorney-General Abdul Ghani Patail who elaborated on the decision, the primary consideration was national security. Abdul Ghani noted: "National security – that was the issue the government was concerned with. It had nothing to do with freedom of religion. It was only concerned with national security... The crux of the issue in the whole Kalimah Allah debate is whether it could be used to propagate Christianity to Muslims. It is not an issue of freedom of religion for Christians themselves."[65] Following this, attempts by the publishers of *Herald* to seek further legal redress were denied as the Federal Court, the highest court in the land, upheld the Court of Appeal decision and reinforced the ban by a four-to-three margin, thereby shutting the legal door to *Herald* and setting a precedent on the rights of Christian publications to use the term *Allah*.

---

[62] See "Revoke Citizenship of 'Allah' Fatwa Dissidents." Available http://malaysiansmustknowthetruth.blogspot.com/2014/01/revoke-citizenship-of-allah-fatwa.html, January 1, 2014.
[63] Boo Su-lynn, "Terrorising the Christian Minority," *Malay Mail*, October 17, 2014.
[64] Tan Yi Liang, "A-G: Ibrahim Ali's Bible-burning Remark not of 'seditious tendency,'" *The Star*, October 27, 2014.
[65] V. Anbalagan, "Ban on Allah in Herald a Matter of National Security, Says A-G," *The Malaysian Insider*, November 19, 2014. Available www.themalaysianinsider.com/malaysia/article/ban-on-allah-in-herald-a-matter-of-national-security-says-a-g.

164 Malaysia

The ruling however, did not seem to placate vocal Islamic NGOs, many of which have kept up the pressure on the state and the legal system to further restrict the public space available to Christians in the name of the defense of Islam. This is reflected in the comments by the leader of one such group: "We are dealing with aggressive, confrontational groups of Christians. Their demands over the Alkitab, kalimah Allah are connected to their attempts to spread Christianity ... They are using this strategy to tame Muslims, by using terms that we are familiar with in our own religion."[66]

East Malaysia

For the moment, friction between the Christian and Muslim communities in Malaysia have mostly been confined to the Peninsula. The social and political climate in the two Eastern Malaysian states of Sabah and Sarawak, geographically removed from the Malaysian mainland, have for the most part been insulated from the deterioration of Muslim-Christian relations and deepening restrictions on freedom of worship. On their part, political leaders – especially those associated with the incumbent coalition government – have repeatedly reassured Christians of East Malaysia that their religious freedom would not be undermined (ironically, the frequency of these assurances suggest a tacit acknowledgment that religious freedom of co-religionists in the Peninsula are indeed being undermined). Even Islamist opposition candidates from PAS have refrained from talking about *shari'a* and the Islamic state when campaigning in East Malaysia, to the extent of even introducing non-Muslim candidates.

Aside from geography, several other reasons account for how East Malaysia has been set apart. The growing power of the Islamic religious establishment, so visible and consequential in the Peninsula, has yet to penetrate the cultural and religious norms in East Malaysia. Indeed, it remains possible for Muslims to renounce their faith in East Malaysia, whereas that is all but impossible in West Malaysia given the rising conservatism of Islamic practice there. Further to that, unlike the constellation of power in the Peninsula, in Eastern Malaysia Christians have enjoyed greater access to office and positions of influence by virtue of the fact that many indigenous politicians and community leaders are Christians

[66] Shazwan Mustafa Kamal, "Pembela Blames 'aggressive Christians' for Muslim Siege Mentality," *The Malaysian Insider*, May 7, 2011. Available www.themalaysian insider.com/malaysia/article/pembela-blames-aggressive-christians-for-muslim-siege-mentality/.

(some are even pastors of congregations). By dint of the terms through which the states of Sabah and Sarawak were integrated into the Malaysian Federation in 1963, the access of these indigenous leaders to political and economic power in these states remain protected.[67] Moreover, as the chapter established earlier, Christians form the majority of the population in both these states. Therein lies an existential paradox, for their confessional allegiance as Christians has made it difficult for them in reality to claim the "rights and privileges" accorded to *Bumiputera*, an identity marker they as indigenous communities have legitimate right to at least in theory, because of the Malaysian state's move to extend their ethno-religious conception of nationhood and nation building to East Malaysia.

There are, however, indications that the insulation of East Malaysia from the intrusion of ethno-religious narratives of nationhood may be fraying at the edges. For starters, left unresolved, the *Kalimah Allah* controversy will doubtless have more profound effects on the Christians in East Malaysia than those in the Peninsula, given the reality that because of generally lower literacy levels, the former are more reliant on Indonesian language bibles and Christian literature as compared to their co-religionists in the Peninsula who are far more conversant in English and hence have access to English language scripture. Second, there is already an active effort by opposition political leaders who have drawn the attention of East Malaysian Christian religious and political leaders to the plight of their co-religionists in the Peninsula, and networks linking Christians to both sides of the South China Sea have begun to emerge.[68] In turn, this activism has increased awareness in East Malaysia of their rights as a religious minority. As a leader of *Perpaduan Anak Negeri Sabah* (PAN or Solidarity of the People of Sabah), Esther Golingi, asserted: "We want to worship God. We want to be united as Christians. With more than 30,000 Sabahans working in the peninsula, what happened to our religious freedom.... We need to uphold the Constitution of our land

---

[67] More importantly, in their accession to Malaysia in 1963 it was made clear constitutionally that the provision for Islam to be the official religion of the Federation does not extend to Sabah and Sarawak. Indeed, as Joshua Woo reminded me, whereas in West Malaysia public events oftentimes begin with an Islamic prayer, in East Malaysia such events frequently open with a Christian prayer.

[68] This is not to say that there was not already an awareness of the deterioration of freedom of worship for non-Muslims in the Peninsula. Rather, opposition politicians have taken to organizing prayer rallies in East Malaysia for the churches and congregations in the Peninsula. Some have even actively taken East Malaysian church leaders on "field trips" to the Peninsula where they interact with Christians from other states and are told firsthand of the restrictions and curbs they face.

and it says we have our freedom of religion. Freedom of religion means freedom of religion."[69]

More to the point, these percolating issues are gradually playing out against the backdrop of calls for greater autonomy within the Federation and growing assertiveness for denizen rights.[70]

The Hindu Community

To be sure, the Christian communities of Malaysia are not the only ones at the receiving end of these attempts by a politically influential segment of the Malay community and the Islamic religious establishment to redefine the terms of citizenship along religious lines. In 2007, the Hindu population mobilized a mass rally involving more than thirty ethnic and religious organizations, triggering a chain of events that culminated in the watershed general election result in 2008 when the incumbent UMNO-led coalition lost its hitherto customary two-thirds parliamentary majority.[71]

The ethnic Indian community in Malaysia, comprising those of South Asian descent, make up approximately 7 percent of the Malaysian population. While a significant minority are Christian and Muslims (particularly those of Pakistani descent), most of them are followers of the Hindu faith. Grievances of this ethnic Indian minority are, essentially, two-fold. Many nurse a grievance against Chinese and, by virtue of affirmative action policies, Malay dominance of the economy, which has seen the vast majority of ethnic Indians, who trace their roots to South Asian migrant labor imported to work in the railway and rubber plantation industries of the colonial economy, disadvantaged in terms of economic opportunity and social mobility.[72] Consequently, despite the existence

---

[69] Trinna Leong, "Sabah Christians Ban Together to Stop Conversion to Islam," *Malaysia Today*, January 23, 2014. Available www.malaysia-today.net/sabah-christians-band-together-to-stop-conversions-to-islam/.

[70] For a thorough discussion on the topic of the place of Sabah and Sarawak in the Malaysian Federation as well as the evolution of the relationship between East Malaysia and the central government, see Andrew Harding and James Chin (eds.), *50 Years of Malaysia: Federalism Revisited*. Singapore: Marshall Cavendish, 2014.

[71] Notwithstanding the role that the mobilization of widespread Hindu-based opposition played in eroding the parliamentary majority of the incumbent government, later moves by the latter to co-opt leaders of this segment of the opposition enervated the protest movement, leading to its eventual demise.

[72] The problem was further compounded by the fact that these rubber plantations were situated some distance from urban centers, and as a consequence, the children of ethnic Indian families located in these plantations had no access to modern education facilities. Their only option was vernacular schools created within the plantations themselves, which did little to prepare these students for a modern, industrialized economy.

The Hindu Community

of a small upper class, the bulk of the ethnic Indian population remains trapped in working-class poverty.

Economic displacement is but one side of the coin. Ethnic Indian grievance is also possessed of a decidedly religious dimension. Since the early 1990s, the urbanization of Malaysia had resulted in large swathes of rural land, many previously part of plantations, commandeered for redevelopment for modern industry and residences, particularly in the capital and its immediate outskirts of Klang Valley and Shah Alam. The process of demolition of the existing rural infrastructure involved the dismantling of numerous Hindu temples and shrines scattered across these lands. Despite protestations of the ethnic Indian Hindu community, the state proceeded with these demolitions on grounds that these temples, and the land on which they were built, lacked any legal status.[73] Needless to say, this move on the part of the state was seen as a deliberate marginalization of the religious rights of the Hindu community, for whom the temples and shrines were sacred spaces.

The Hindu narrative of marginalization became further entrenched with the increase in the number of cases of "body snatching" that were taking place. In present-day Malaysian local parlance, "body snatching" refers to the incidences when the bodies of deceased Hindus were forcefully taken – snatched – from their families on (usually substantiated) grounds that the deceased had at some point in life converted to Islam and hence had to be buried according to Islamic, not Hindu, funeral rights. The fact that these bodies are literally "snatched" by representatives of local Islamic authorities bearing a simple letter from the state *shari'a* court certifying the deceased to be Muslim only further compounded the sense of religious discrimination, not to mention the fact that the family would have no legal recourse as non-Muslim testimony has no standing in *shari'a* courts.

Because of the impotence and torpor of self-proclaimed representatives of ethnic Indian minority interests within the establishment, Hindu groups coalesced into the Hindu Rights Action Force (HINDRAF) and staged a major rally for minority rights on November 25, 2007. The rally was preceded by a countrywide road show that aimed to give voice to deepseated resentment and anger on the part of the Indian-Hindu community by framing it as victimization with no recourse for justice. Such frames identified injustices and grievances, and laid the responsibility for the plight of the Hindu community squarely at the feet of the state.

---

[73] The main problem was the absence of any land titles or deeds to prove that the land on which the temples were built actually belonged to the communities which claimed ownership.

Emotions articulated by the participants in the rally substantiated the value of framing as a trigger for collective action. For instance, words and phrases such as "fed up" and "life or death situation" were used by those who were present at the rally in demonstration of their deep sense of grievance against the state.[74]

Islamization and *Ketuanan* in Context and Retrospect

As we have established, the increasingly tempestuous climate that defines Muslim-Christian relations today is related to the processes of Islamization that have taken place over the past three decades, and that have seen the Malaysian government introduce a range of policies and institutions to govern the country according to Islamic norms and strictures, not to mention empower the Islamic religious establishment. Yet these have been but institutional expressions of a growing mindset where the Malay-Muslim public has become more conscious about the primacy of religion in their definition of identity, and where the bureaucracy, staffed mostly by ethnic Malays, have put these conceptions of identity into practice, for instance in how customs officers stop (or stall, as it were) shipments of non-Islamic religious material.

The clout of the Malay-Islamic nationalist narrative of *Ketuanan Melayu* perpetuated by UMNO and ethno-nationalist right-wing Malay civil society groups, and how it relates to Islamization, bears noting, to wit: this clout has grown precisely because of how *Ketuanan Melayu* has assumed religious dimensions that together with the discourse of threat has lent the narrative even greater currency. Because of the intimate, constitutionally enshrined relationship between Malay ethnic identity and the Islamic religion, it stands to reason that the UMNO logic on Malay "rights and privileges" segues into a discourse of the primacy of Islam – "*Ketuanan Agama*" – over other religions. Indeed, as some have noted, "the conjunction of ethnicity and religion in Malaysia dichotomizes the religious arena into a Muslim and non-Muslim field."[75] This is evident, among other things, in how numerous Muslim civil society organizations and political leaders view the controversial issue of public interfaith dialogue. While it is an initiative that has won endorsement and support from Malaysia's religious minorities, many Muslims have responded with apprehension, in some cases outright rejection, on the grounds that by

---

[74] K. Kabilan, "Fearless Indians Fight for Rights," November 26, 2007. Available www.malaysiakini.com/news/75289.
[75] Susan E. Ackerman and Raymond L. M. Lee, *Heaven in Transition: Non-Muslim Religious Innovation and Ethnic Identity in Malaysia*. Honolulu: University of Hawaii Press, 1988, p. 4.

virtue of its ascribed primacy, Islam should not be placed in a position that might entail compromises. As Azman Amin Hassan, Director General of the National Unity and Integration Department in the Prime Minister's Office, has conceded: "Interfaith dialogue is something new in Malaysia. Some religious groups do think that if they participate in an interfaith dialogue, they are giving way to other religions. There are also those who think that because Islam is the official religion, there is no need to initiate dialogue and explain why certain things are so."[76] Again, the sense of insecurity is not far from the surface of such thought, for central to concerns in many Malay-Muslim quarters is the perception that any dialogue on religion would threaten the sanctity of Islam.

The reality is that Islamization and the constriction of space for non-Muslims must be understood not through Islamic frames, but that of the overwhelming concern for the primacy of Malay ethnicity and interests on the part of Malay political stakeholders, the accompanying sense of insecurity which is abundantly clear in the discourse of "security threats" and "defence of the faith" that Malay-Muslim political and religious leaders provoke and engage in, and how these have intruded into every sphere of ordinary life in Malaysia. This brings us back to the concept of *Ketuanan Melayu*, how it has come to be ascribed by its promulgators as a core principle for the identity of the Malaysian nation and state, and the reaction among Christian communities to how the narrative has been seized upon by certain quarters of the Malay-Muslim population and political leadership to justify and perpetuate a hegemonic and exclusivist religious discourse. It is worth noting, too, that the fact that such an exclusive and "ethnicized" view of Islam goes against the grain of the religion's universalist principles has not stopped its proponents in Malaysia from imposing this interpretation of nationhood on the national discourse.

Through this discussion of Muslim–Christian relations, it is clear that *Ketuanan Melayu* has led to the marginalization, if not exclusion, of Malaysia's religious minorities from national discourses that directly bear on their constitutional rights as citizens of Malaysia.[77] For the Christian community in Malaysia, it is freedom of religion as a feature of citizenship and constitutional right that has been at stake. As one Christian minister put it in response to the ruling on the *Allah* issue: "It is more than just

---

[76] See "Time is Right for Inter-faith Dialogue," *The Star*, April 18, 2010.
[77] Peter G. Riddell, "Islamization, Civil Society and Religious Minorities in Malaysia," in K.S. Nathan and Muhamad Hashim Kamali (eds.), *Islam in Southeast Asia: Political, Social, and Strategic Challenges for the 21st Century*. Singapore: Institute of Southeast Asian Studies, 2005, pp. 172–174.

a word. It is about the fundamental right to worship God in the way we have been doing for generations without hindrance."[78]

Unpacking the Narrative of Ketuanan

Not unlike the Philippines where the concept of Bangsamoro is itself a contested one within the Bangsamoro community (as is the validity of a singular Moro-Muslim history and identity), the notion that *Ketuanan Melayu* should lie at the foundation of the Malaysian nation at the expense of non-Malays and non-Muslims is one that has been contested not only by ethnic and religious minorities, but within Malay-Muslim quarters as well.

Notwithstanding the foregoing discussion, the relationship between Islamization and the deterioration of Muslim–Christian relations is not axiomatic or teleological, and the expanding visibility and influence of Islam in everyday life need not automatically result in the constriction of social and cultural space for non-Muslims. It would be unreasonable, not to mention ill-informed, to assume that the Malay-Muslim community is monolithic and marching in tandem to the beat of the drums of provocative ethno-nationalist Malay groups bent on pressing an exclusive majoritarian view. Consider, for instance, the fact that the prominence of religious identity among Malay-Muslims today has invariably amplified the voice of the opposition Islamist PAS, even if the Islamization strategies put in place by the Mahathir administration was precisely aimed at diluting the PAS challenge. What is striking, in this respect, is that certain key quarters within the PAS party leadership have staked a position against the imposition of Islamic norms on non-Muslims.[79]

Indeed, during the *Kalimah Allah* controversy, the party even openly supported the right of Christians to use the term *Allah*, on grounds that according to Islamic history the term predated the revelation to the Prophet Muhammad.[80] Moreover, a progressive segment of the PAS

[78] See "Malaysian Christians and Religious Freedom in the Name of 'Allah,'" *Charisma News*, March 11, 2014. Available www.charismanews.com/world/43081-malaysian-christians-and-religious-freedom-in-the-name-of-allah.
[79] The question of the extent to which PAS should push the Islamist agenda in tandem with UMNO, however, has emerged as a major point of contention within the party itself. See Joseph Chinyong Liow, "Islamist Ambitions, Political Change, and the Price of Power: Recent Success and Challenges for the Pan-Malaysian Islamic Party, PAS," *Journal of Islamic Studies*, Vol. 22, No. 3, September 2011.
[80] The party's position on the *Allah* issue, for instance, only came about after an intense three-hour internal leadership discussion, and leaders who disagreed with the position have been allowed to publicly voice their contrarian views. See PAS TPJP, "Penjelasan oleh Ustz Taib Azzamuddin ttg kalimah Allah," PAS Taman Paya Jaras Permai, January 4, 2010. Available http://pastpjp.blogspot.com/2010/01/penjelasan-oleh-ustz-taib-azzamuddin.html; Roziyah Mahamad, "Guna Kalimah Allah: Bidang Kuasa

leadership, some of whom have since parted ways with the Islamist party, have worked closely with allies in the opposition coalition to purportedly present an alternative to UMNO's vision by articulating a Malaysian nation not built on Malay dominance but *Ketuanan Raykat*, the supremacy of the people.[81] In so doing, this perspective has demonstrated that Islam can provide an alternative conception of nationhood which can accommodate religious minority identities in a way the prevailing UMNO narrative, based on the conception of *Ketuanan Melayu* as the cornerstone of national identity, is reluctant or unable to.

Other non-partisan voices have also emerged to demonstrate that the conservative ethno-religious nationalism associated with the Malay-Muslim establishment and its civil society allies do not entirely dominate the discursive landscape. As but one example, twenty-five prominent former Malay senior civil servants – some of them with strong ties to UMNO – lent their names to a controversial letter published in the press on December 8, 2014, that called for a more measured and inclusive approach to discussions on religion and its place in Malaysian society, and which derided right-wing ethno-religious nationalist groups as: "Groups (which) clearly have low standards, poorly educated, intellectually challenged, incapable of seeing their own racism, intolerant, blindly obedient, and are destroying the fabric of our country's society."[82] Even UMNO itself is not entirely bereft of alternative voices that have attempted to ameliorate the over-bearing connotations of *Ketuanan Melayu*.

But these attempts to voice alternative conceptions of Malay and Muslim nationhood are, at best, fitful. The arid reality remains that more measured voices are often drowned out by the entrenched right wing and an overbearing Islamic religious establishment transfixed by inchoate fears yet presuming to claim the moral high ground (i.e., that Islam is under threat and they are protecting the faith). JAKIM, self-appointed adjudicators of what is permissible and not permissible in Malaysian Islam, frequently brings its Malay-Islamic nationalist zeal to bear on any, including senior officials and elected representatives, who dare to question its exercise of religious authority by invoking the threat of sedition, thereby drawing attention yet again to the profundity of the contradiction between supremacy and insecurity inherent in Malay-Islamic nationalism. Meanwhile, a nervously wavering political leadership, whose

---

Mahkamah Tak Jelas – Taib Azamuddin," Era Pakatan, January 3, 2010. Available www.erapakatan.com/berita/guna_kalimah_allah_bidang_kuasa_mahkamah_tak_jelas_-_taib_azamuddin/.
[81] It should be noted, however, that when he served in the Mahathir administration, Anwar was a chief proponent of Islamization and Malay supremacy. For instance, it was during his time as education minister that school syllabi were changed to reflect the theme of Malay supremacy more prominently.
[82] Razak Ahmad, "Open Letter by 25 Sparks Debate," *The Star*, December 17, 2014.

legitimacy depends precisely on the support of progenitors of narrow exclusivist Malay-Islamic nationalistic discourse, blanche when calls to defend Islam and the Malay race are directed at them. Perhaps most striking, and puzzling, about this state of affairs is that it is not so much that the purveyors of these exclusivist and obscurantist renditions of the primacy and "*ketuanan*" of the Malay race, ethnicity, and religion are large in numbers, but that they have been allowed to offer these views unchallenged in the corridors of power, and to articulate them with impunity.

In such testy discursive climes, it should hardly be a surprise that even alternative Malay-Muslim views would get – and have received – short shrift. Prospects for a discursive shift are at base imperiled by the fact that the Malay political class occupying state power, in league with religious authorities and vocal Malay-Islamic civil society groups, continues to perpetuate the siege mentality among the Malay-Muslim community by engaging in a discourse of threat, as typified by the following remarks articulated by a former cabinet minister that implicitly targeted at the Christian community: "The character and tradition of Islam, as well as its position as the official religion of Malaysia, has been challenged by various provocations with the intention of denting the pride of the religion."[83] Indeed, the dual, and dueling, narratives of (explicit) Malay-Muslim dominance and (implicit) Malay-Muslim insecurity have penetrated far too deep into Malay society through the extension of UMNO-led state institutions and the exertions of its civil society allies, such that the discursive point of reference is no longer that of accommodation as it was in the past, but dominance – how to assert it and defend it.

There is a further dimension to how identity is conceptualized and articulated within the Malay-Muslim community, to the point of exclusion of other groups, which should be taken into account. A less visible but no less poignant outcome of the emergence of a discourse premised on a hegemonic and exclusivist Malay-Muslim identity in Malaysia outlined in this chapter has been the assertion of religious orthodoxy in defining for the Muslim community what it means to be Muslim. This has created tense conditions that prevail over the issue of who is legitimately a Muslim, and by extension, the legitimate proprietors of this Malay-Muslim identity, as defined by the state and its religious functionaries. Foremost among these fault lines is that which exists between the

---

[83] See "Ex-minister Sees Christian Bigots a Threat to Najib's 'Moderation,'" *The Malaysian Insider*, November 9, 2014. Available www.themalaysianinsider.com/malaysia/article/christian-fanatics-abusing-moderation-for-themselves-says-ex-umno-minister.

dominant *Sunni* movement in Malaysian Islam, and a small but increasingly activist *Shi'a* community.

To be sure, events in the Middle East and Pakistan have promoted sharp divisions between *Shi'a* and *Sunni*, and catalyzed violence between the two predominant Muslim creeds. Be that as it may, in Malaysia the *Sunni-Shi'a* divide has primarily been driven by local conditions which include not only religious orthodoxy, but also *Sunni* hegemony in how the Islamic state of Malaysia is conceived and understood. A 1989 Islamic law and a 1996 *fatwa* (legal opinion issued by Islamic scholars) issued by Malaysia's top Islamic clerics banned the practice and teachings of *Shi'a* Islam, labeling it a "deviant" sect. Meanwhile, as part of its practice of policing Islam, JAKIM frequently distributes sermons that explicitly condemn *Shi'a* Islam.[84] Once again, the discourse of security threats was evoked as the *Shi'a* are demonized as a danger to national security on the basis of a circuitous argument regarding their alleged propensity to divide the Malay-Muslim population by way of their very existence. Although the details are far too lengthy to elaborate here, this same logic has been applied to legislate against other smaller "deviant" Muslim groups such as the *Ahmadiyah* and al-Arqam. Indeed, the drive to stress Malay-Muslim unity, particularly in the wake of encroachment of non-Muslims on perceived Malay-Muslim dominance wrapped in the language of rights and privileges, hews closely to the assertion of a coherent, uniformed religious identity. Therein lies the "deviancy" of fringe Islamic groups: it is not only deviation from Malaysia's Islamic theological orthodoxy as proclaimed by the mainstream religious establishment, but equally so a threat to Malay-Muslim homogeneity, if not unity. This logic is summarized with precision by Chandra Muzaffar in the following remarks:

> Establishment ulama in Malaysia have always seen themselves as the protector, the custodian of Islam and Muslims in the country. What this means is that they regard it as their right and responsibility to preserve the purity of not just Sunni Islam, but more specifically Sunni Islam of the Shafi'i legal school. Indeed, Shafi'i Sunni Islam is often perceived by the ulama and the Ummah as an essential attribute of Malay identity itself. And since protecting the community's identity is central to the national agenda, any 'deviant' tendency – especially if it has a religious orientation – will have to be suppressed.[85]

---

[84] Official mosques throughout Malaysia can only use sermons distributed weekly by JAKIM. These sermons regularly attack not only *Shi'a* Muslims, but Christians and Hindus as well.

[85] Chandra Muzaffar, "Foreword," in Karim D. Crow (ed.), *Facing One Qiblah: Legal and Doctrinal Aspects of Sunni and Shiah Muslims*. Bethesda, MD.: Ibex Publishers, 2005, p. ix.

Conclusion

The emergence and deepening of a narrative of Malay-Islamic nationalism that turns on an exclusivist ethno-religious narrative centered on the primacy – indeed, supremacy – of Malay-Muslim identity promulgated by the Malaysian state, the Islamic religious establishment, and its civil society allies dominate the discursive terrain in Malaysia today. This has seen the Malaysian nation conceived of as a "Malay" nation, framed axiomatically by a narrative of Malay ethnic dominance captured in the highly controversial concept of *Ketuanan Melayu*.

One of the most polarizing concepts in Malaysian national discourse, *Ketuanan Melayu* has time and again been evoked by Malay ethno-religious nationalists to anchor their narratives of Malaysian nationhood and legitimize their claims of primacy and dominance. Yet for the most part, it is not the concept itself that has been contested, but what is ascribed to it, and how it has been interpreted and implemented. At the heart of the political conflicts that have been triggered by the assertion of this narrative is the matter of religion and confessional identity. In turn, these forces have been emboldened by an Islamization process that has gathered decisive pace in the last three decades. Apropos to this, questions of legitimacy and religious freedom loom large behind the clashes between narratives of nationhood promulgated by Malay ethno-religious nationalists, who comprise a major segment of the state, and religious minorities, particularly the Christian community but also the Hindu community as we have seen briefly, in Malaysia. Beneath the intemperate remarks and dynamics of conflict lie a profound paradox: a growing sense of insecurity among the Malay-Muslim majority that is juxtaposed against a narrative of dominance and supremacy that has overwhelmed any discussion or attempt to renegotiate the conception of the Malay(sian) nation away from this dominant narrative.

Indeed, given this historical, cultural, constitutional, and functional backdrop that codifies Malay dominance in Malaysia, it is evident that Malay-Muslim identity cannot but determine the shape, contours, and trajectories of the state of politics and the politics of the state in the country. It is in this manner that political Islam has taken center stage in the competing conceptions of nationhood in Malaysia, for the objective of "safeguarding" Malay rights invariably means preserving and defending the status of Islam, a core marker of Malay identity.

5 Indonesia
Contesting Principles of Nationhood

Scholars of religion in Indonesia have consistently maintained that it is an exceedingly complex phenomenon not given to straightforward analysis or generalizations. The complexity of the topic is arguably captured in the concept of *aliran* (streams, referring to the different currents of Islam in Indonesia), which since its introduction to Indonesian studies by the anthropologist Cliffor Geertz has continued to provide a useful point of entry to the analysis of social and political trends in the country.[1] Originating in Geertz's study of Indonesian Islam, scholars of Indonesia had traditionally set great store by the notion of *aliran*, which speaks to the existence of multiple, dynamic, oftentimes competing streams that define the variegated nature of Indonesian society and politics. Even though the veracity of the concept has in recent times been critiqued and challenged, the evolution of autonomous regional and local histories and identities over time has doubtless also contributed to this diffused heterogeneity.[2]

Because Indonesian society has by and large managed to accommodate this diversity, it has acquired a reputation for pluralism and tolerance. The accuracy or aptness of this characterization, however, has been a matter of considerable debate. This debate notwithstanding, the main analytical assertion here is that issues of what constitutes the nation in terms of who should be included or excluded, and on what grounds, remain contested at the geographical as well as confessional margins, and the frequent occurrence of various forms of religious tension and conflicts serves as a prescient reminder of this.[3] Bearing this in mind, it is with caution that this chapter wades into the debate by focusing on

---

[1] Clifford Geertz, *The Religion of Java*. Chicago, IL.: University of Chicago Press, 1976.
[2] See, for example, Vedi Hadiz, "Indonesian Local Party Politics: A Site of Resistance to Neoliberal Reform," *Critical Asian Studies*, Vol. 36, No. 4, 2004; Saiful Mujani and R. William Liddle, "Leadership, Party, and Religion: Explaining Voting Behavior in Indonesia," *Comparative Political Studies*, Vol. 40, No. 7, 2007.
[3] Shamsu Rizal Panggabean, Rudi Harisyah Alam, and Ihsan Ali Fauzi, "The Patterns of Religious Conflict in Indonesia (1990–2008)," *Studia Islamika*, Vol.17, No.2, 2010.

what it is that is "religious" about religious conflicts in Indonesia, and how to conceptualize it against broader themes that define the process of negotiation and renegotiation of nationhood.

The study of communal or sectarian violence in Indonesia has long been a rich analytical and empirical field. An extensive literature is now available that explores the complex and multifarious dynamics that account for violence in Aceh, Papua, Sulawesi, Maluku, North Maluku, and Kalimantan. A careful scrutiny of this scholarship reveals a multiplicity of analytical frameworks and explanatory variables that includes ethnic identity, opportunism on the part of elites at local and national levels, terrorism and ideological and theological extremism, political transition as a result of the collapse of President Suharto's New Order government, resource competition, and criminality. Oftentimes, these explanations run sharply athwart each other. In reality, most of these conflicts appear to have combinations of factors rather than a single cause. Indeed, even in the case of deceptively isolated events, such as the outbreak of conflict in the town of Malifut in the province of North Maluku in August 1999, scholars have managed to tease out a raft of causes ranging from historical grievances to administrative restructuring, historical rivalries (between competing sultanates), and the machinations of conflict entrepreneurs and agent provocateurs.[4]

This chapter will pursue the theme of conflict in the name of religion and its conceptual underpinnings in relation to questions of identity and nationhood by focusing primarily on the violence between Christians and Muslims that engulfed Central Sulawesi, Maluku, and North Maluku during the period from 1999 to 2003. These conflicts have been chosen for the fact that, by most accounts, they have been portrayed as intuitive and self-evident cases of unbridled religious violence.

At the same time, the chapter will also discuss two other genres of "religious conflict" in Indonesia. First is the tension that has existed between Christian and Muslim communities from the era of Dutch colonialism to contemporary times over not only issues of access to power but also, more fundamentally, the nature and character of the post-independence state and the identity of its citizens. Second is the victimization of minority confessional groups within the same body of Muslim believers, as was evident in the conclusion of the previous chapter, between the dominant orthodox *Sunni* community on one hand, and the *Shi'a* and *Ahmadiyah* that claim to be adherents of Islam and

---

[4] See Chris Wilson, "The Ethnic Origins of Religious Conflict in North Maluku Province, Indonesia, 1999–2000," *Indonesia*, Vol. 79, April 2005; Christopher R. Duncan, *Violence and Vengeance: Religious Conflict and its Aftermath in Eastern Indonesia*. Ithaca, N.Y.: Cornell University Press, 2013.

members of the Indonesian Muslim nation, and seek to be recognized as such.

The chapter will not aim to provide complete accounts of the violence and conflicts in the cases it explores. To delve into the details of each conflict and their multifarious dimensions is beyond the scope here, and in any case, this information is available elsewhere. Rather, the chapter aims to explore and contextualize the religious dimension that, according to conventional accounts, is not only ostensibly evident in these conflicts, but also in some instances serves as their main drivers.

Religion, Nationalism, and Indonesia

Notwithstanding the dominance of secular nationalist narratives of Indonesian nationalism, religion has in fact always had a profound influence on the conception of the nation in Indonesia. Within that context, it has been Islam which has commanded most attention as a subject of inquiry, if only by virtue of the fact that it is the dominant religion in the archipelago.

There is no gainsaying the fact that Islam in Indonesia has always had multiple manifestations, and has never been given to any dominant "school of thought." This being the case, Islam's interaction with political and social forces in the archipelago was in many ways intertwined with internal debates taking place within its own body of believers in Indonesia, for instance between reformists (*Kaum Muda*) and traditionalists (*Kaum Tua*).[5] Such was the case within the anti-colonial movement, where scholars of the early origins of Indonesian nationalism have traced the roots of the notion of a "homeland" to Indonesian Muslims' encounters during travels to the holy land. In this respect, Michael Laffan's pathbreaking work argues for the role of transnational Islamic encounters – in particular, the *haj* pilgrimage – in codifying national identity among Indonesian Muslims.[6] For instance, in the 19th century, the Jawa of Mecca (a term commonly used during that time in Middle East and North African Islamic circles to refer to Muslims from archipelagic Southeast Asia, most of whom were from the islands

---

[5] R. E. Elson, "Islam, Islamism, the Nation, and the Early Indonesian Nationalist Movement," *Journal of Indonesian Islam*, Vol. 1, No. 2, 2007.

[6] Michael Francis Laffan, *Islamic Nationhood and Colonial Indonesia: The Umma below the Winds*. London: Routledge, 2003. According to Laffan, the *haj* was an ambivalent experience for the Jawa Muslims in the sense that it fostered seemingly contradictory ideas of both local and Islamic identities, and during their stay in Mecca, the Jawi pilgrims gained a heightened sense of their communal existence. Over the years, a realization of the strengths of that unity would develop into the form of an independence movement.

of Java, Sumatra, and the Malay peninsula) were extremely interested in the affairs of their Muslim brethren in Aceh.[7]

By way of a further example, in 1831 Islam began to be asserted among the Minangkabau as conflict in Sumatra transformed from what was initially a civil war to one of Minangkabau national resistance. As Laffan affirmed: "In many ways this conflict, and those of the Jawa War and later Aceh, form the backdrop to the later national struggle of Indonesia from the turn of the 1900s when Islam (traditionalist or reformist) would be reasserted as the rallying point for alterity against colonial rule."[8] Indeed, even before the emergence of Islamic organizations as expressions of a nascent anti-colonial movement, resistance to earlier epochs of Dutch colonialism had already assumed such forms of religious uprisings. Most notable of these were the Java War of 1825–1830 (also known as the Diponegoro Rebellion) and the Padri wars in West Sumatra during the period 1823–1837.

It was transnational encounters such as those associated with the *haj* that planted nascent ideas of nationalism, which were elucidated and disseminated via the medium of reformist Islamic journals printed in the neighboring British colony of Singapore in the early 20th century. In time, explicitly religious conceptions of nationhood in early Indonesian nationalist discourse came to be occasioned by the existence of a range of such journals that identified religion with patriotic and communal aspirations. These journals included *Al-Imam, Bintang Hindia*, and *Wazir Indie*. Like their counterparts in Malaya at the turn of the 20th century, they articulated a narrative of Islam as signifier of emerging national identity.[9] In Indonesia, this idea of nationalism framed in religious terms would later vie with more secular or religiously neutral nationalist ideals articulated by the secular nationalist movement that emerged in the late 1920s.

---

[7] Ibid., p. 27.   [8] Ibid., p. 31.

[9] William Roff, *The Origins of Malay Nationalism*. New Haven, CT.: Yale University Press, 1967. That said, the love of the homeland encouraged by journals such as *Al-Imam* was still a facet of religious division rather than an end in itself. Therefore the *Al-Imam* stressed a religious rather than primarily cultural identification with nationhood. Regardless of the secular Franco-Egyptian heritage of the modern *watan* (homeland), the term is associated with more "Islamic" than indigenous credentials. It was clear, then, that for the Muslims of the 1900s the terms *watan* and freedom were indispensable. The historiography, presented by *Al-Imam* then had many of the ingredients of a nationalist historiography but while it could address itself to the Malays, it lacked an appeal to a clearly defined *watan* – whether Malay or Jawi. What existed instead was a variety of *tanahs* and *rajas* joined by religion and language but separated by colonial and royal hegemonies. Thus, as in the past papers, in 1906 *Al-Imam* too was unable to be specific in defining Malay territory. That is, in the early 20th century, when a native was asked to define his or her nationality, a Malay or Javanese would more than likely have declared their primary *bangsa* to be Islam.

Discussions in the previous chapters on the Philippines, Thailand, and Malaysia drew some attention to the role of religious leaders or *ulama* at the forefront of resistance against colonialism (including "indigenous" colonialism) even as they provided leadership in their respective Muslim societies. The same holds true in the case of Indonesia, where many rulers were often at pains to seek Islamic legitimacy for their actions from the *ulama*. Many of these *ulama* and *hajis* (an honorific normally held by respected elderly Muslim men) themselves became heavily involved in the conflict in Aceh (1873–1910) where they helped lead a resistance against the Dutch after the collapse of the sultanate in 1874. There are many other cases of conflict involving *ulama*-led resistance, such as in Banten, where Yusuf al-Maqassari, who Dutch colonial authorities considered the most influential of the religious leaders in Banten, cast his lot with Sultan Ageng Tirtayasa in the struggle against the Dutch. Despite close supervision of the local Muslim populace by Dutch colonialists, personified in the controversial Arabist and advisor to the colonial government Christaan Snouck Hurgronje, *ulama* remained financially independent as the economic bases of their institutions were founded in support provided by the local populace.[10] Together with their religious credentials, the fact that they were not dependent financially on colonial authorities further enhanced their legitimacy as anti-colonial nationalists.

The unifying force of Islam was a major factor that was employed in service of the fledgling Indonesian nationalist movement in its early years. This role of confessional faith as catalytic agent was particularly salient in Indonesia, given the lack of other coalescing factors such as language,[11] culture, history, or sense of common territory. Indeed, this lack of universal binding agents was evident in the narrowness of early Indonesian nationalism, where speeches by leaders of Indonesia's first nationalist group, Budi Oetomo, as well as Sarekat Islam (another early standard bearer for Indonesian nationalism) could barely conceal their bias toward a distinctly Javanese identity and history. It was against this context that religion emerged as the bond which facilitated the creation of a discourse of resistance and identity assertion. Being a Muslim became synonymous with belonging and part of an expression of opposition to economic dominance, racial superiority, and political control imposed by the colonial regime. In this manner Islam became identified, both deliberately and obliquely, as a national symbol and sign of identification with the national community. It was this utility of Islam that resulted in

---

[10] Given that access to support from the Dutch colonial government was limited to Christian schools.

[11] Not until the advent of the Dutch did a universal language exist within Indonesia; thus, early Indonesian nationalists used Dutch in their writing and speaking.

it being endorsed by nationalist organisations such as the Sarekat Islam, which managed to some extent to overcome its Java-centric outlook, as an effective narrative for mobilization (before the organization itself started fragmenting in the 1920s). In so doing, religion provided an emotional basis for nationalism and an idiom of nationhood, albeit a still-imperfect idiom as the potential of its expansive and universal appeal was effectively curtailed with the expansion of Christianity, especially in the eastern islands of the archipelago.

Since the turn of the 20th century, Islamic organizations such as Sarekat Islam, Muhammadiyah, and Persis (Islamic Union or *Persatuan Islam*) have played an instrumental role in shaping the emergent nationalist discourse.[12] Another major organization that made a significant contribution in shaping Islamic and nationalist discourse in colonial-era Indonesia is Nahdlatul Ulama, currently the largest Islamic organization in Indonesia with a membership estimated at between forty and fifty million followers.[13] The founders of these organizations viewed their mission not only in terms of anti-colonial resistance but equally important, the education of their members to be devout Muslims and loyal citizens of a future Indonesian state.

By the late 1920s however, the role of Islam in nationalism would undergo transformative change. During this time, a hitherto elusive universal and coherent nationalist ideology and movement began emerging under the leadership of Sukarno, the *eminence grise* of the Indonesian nationalist movement. Concomitantly, the role of Islam, while remaining important, also began taking on a divisive character in the broader spectrum of Indonesian nationalism. This was because while Islam provided a crucial unifying premise for the early nationalist movement, it later became a major faultline between Islamic nationalists and counterparts who, while practicing Muslims, never desired an Islamic state. It was the latter group that eventually rose to dominate Indonesian nationalism. Indeed, this tension between differing conceptions of the post-colonial Indonesian nation would lay the ground for further competition and conflict over the fundamental premise of Indonesian nationhood later as the independent Indonesian nation-state came into being.

---

[12] Howard M. Federspiel, *Persatuan Islam: Islamic Reform in Twentieth Century Indonesia*. Jakarta: Equinox Publishing, 2009; Mitsuo Nakamura, *The Crescent Arises Over the Banyan Tree: A Study of the Muhammadiyah Movement in a Central Javanese Town, c.1910s–2010*. Singapore: Institute of Southeast Asian Studies, 2012.

[13] Saiful Mujani and R. William Liddle, "Muslim Indonesia's Secular Democracy," *Asian Survey*, Vol. 49, No. 4, 2009. Muhammadiyah has a membership of approximately thirty million followers.

Christianity in Indonesia

While the study of religious influences on Indonesian nationalism has by and large been engrossed in the role of Islam, Christianity also emerged to figure prominently in the shaping of decolonization, particularly in the eastern islands of the archipelago where large concentrations of Christians could be found.

Crucial to an understanding of the tone of Christian-Muslim relations as Indonesia transitioned into the post-colonial era is an appreciation of how Christianity was represented in the power structure especially the period beginning with the later era of Dutch colonialism, to wit: there is an anomaly in the distribution of political power in Indonesia during these periods, with Christians being granted power incommensurate to their numerical size, which at best accounted for around 15 percent of society in the Dutch East Indies. This translated to employment and educational opportunities and privileges that could be accessed through conversion to Christianity, which were otherwise denied to Muslims.[14] More to the point, for its newfound adherents and converts, "Christianity offered these Indonesians a future, not least the hope of escape from the lower caste status of colonial society."[15] Indeed, such was the dominance of Christians in various areas of Indonesian society extending from the late colonial era into the early years of independence, it should not be surprising to hear that they (Indonesian Christian leaders) "expressed the hope of winning all of Indonesia over to their faith."[16] At the same time, it should also be recognized that Christian dominance was not uniform, and access to positions of power and privilge during the colonial, and later the early independence, periods varied according to geography and ethnicity, resulting in certain groups within the Christian community enjoying greater influence compared to others. Indeed, this diversity conceivably contributed to the rise of secessionist sentiments in some regions such as Maluku, and not others, such as among Javanese Christians and the Christians in the Batak communities of North Sumatra.[17]

---

[14] Gerry van Klinken notes that it was the "embourgeoisement" of European Christianity which influenced Indonesian Christian nationalists.
[15] Gerry van Klinken, *Minorities, Modernity and the Emerging Nation: Christians in Indonesia, A Biographical Approach*. Leiden: KITLV Press, 2003, p. 238.
[16] Suzanne Shröter, "Introduction," in Suzanne Shröter (ed.), *Christianity in Indonesia: Perspectives of Power*. Berlin: Lit Verlag, 2010, p. 13.
[17] Because the Batak were and remain well represented in the colonial, and later Indonesian, bureaucracy and military, it was arguably more difficult for secessionist sentiments to gain any traction. This can be contrasted with the Christians of Maluku where, as this chapter will later discuss, secessionism posed a major challenge to the Indonesian state.

Today, Christians comprise approximately 9 percent of the Indonesian population, which translates to approximately twenty to twenty-five million followers.[18] They are the second largest faith-based community in the archipelago.[19] While Christians are dispersed across the country, they are concentrated mostly in the eastern islands of the archipelago, particularly Sulawesi, Maluku, and Papua, and form numerical majorities in regions and localities in Batak (North Sumatra), Minahasa (North Sulawesi), East Nusa Tenggara, areas of Maluku, and Papua. The Indonesian Christian population is also the second largest in Southeast Asia after the Philippines.

The arrival of Christianity in Indonesia can be traced to the Malay Peninsula and the Portuguese conquest of Malacca in 1511. Portugal's occupation of Malacca, a crucial port for intra-regional trade in the Indo-Malay World, paved the way for the colonial power's further expansion eastward. It was through this expansion that the Moluccas (present-day Maluku) and the Sultanate of Ternate saw active proselytization by Portuguese clergy that in turn had the effect of sowing the seeds of discord between a nascent community of converts to Catholicism and the predominantly Muslim local community. As the chapter shall later discuss, these seeds of discord would later sprout into outright violence between the two communities in modern times.

The Catholic-Portuguese presence was soon replaced by that of the Protestant-Dutch, for whom the entire Indonesian archipelago eventually became a vast and lucrative colonial empire. Even as the Dutch, and especially the Netherlands United East India Company (*Vereenigde Oost-Indische Compagnie*, or VOC), gradually expanded their influence in and control of the archipelago, unlike the Portuguese they initially deliberately eschewed active proselytization and conversion of indigenous populations in order to preserve nascent but gainful working relationships with the Muslim communities in the archipelago.[20] It was only in the wake of acts of Muslim resistance – in particular the Java War and the Padri wars – that the Dutch colonial administration began to consider religious conversion (to Christianity) as a means through which to foster a more pliant and cooperative local population.[21] By the turn of the 20th century, administration of the Netherlands East Indies had changed hands from the VOC

---

[18] Shröter, "Introduction," p. 9.
[19] While the Indonesian Constitution distinguishes between Protestants and Catholics, because we are not concerned for the doctrinal differences within Christianity this study will treat both as part of the body of confessional Christians in the country.
[20] Additionally, it should be noted that insofar as the practice of Christianity was concerned, the Dutch tolerated only Protestant Calvinism.
[21] van Klinken, *Minorities, Modernity, and the Emerging Nation*.

to the Netherlands government, and orthodox reformed Christian parties such as the Anti-Revolutionary Party, led by the reformed theologian Abraham Kuyper who also served as prime minister from 1901 to 1905, came to power. With the reformed church folded into government (and vice-versa), colonial authorities in the Dutch East Indies gradually intensified proselytization by not only Dutch but also German and North American missionaries and bible societies. From the point of view of the Dutch, the virtues of conversion were described as such: "Christian indigenes were loyal indigenes, as opposed to non-Christian ones."[22]

Although the expansion of Christianity in the pre-war years was viewed with suspicion in the eyes of Muslims in Indonesia, because of its glacial pace this expansion was not considered a significant threat to the place of Islam in traditional Indonesian society.[23] There was, nevertheless, latent resentment that was accumulating, and, as we shall soon see, these would eventually animate debates on how to conceptualize the post-colonial nation and state of Indonesia.[24] Not surprisingly, this antipathy between Muslims and Christians was especially targeted at the access that indigenous Christian converts enjoyed to the colonial administration.

As the Dutch East Indies entered into the era of anti-colonial struggle, the matter of Christian power and privilege fed deep-seated suspicion amongst the majority Muslim community. Against this backdrop, tension increased with the heightened religious consciousness and social activism of the conservative Muslim community that were already in evidence since the early years of the nationalist struggle facilitated, as we saw earlier, by growing transnational linkages to and awareness of developments in Islamic socio-political thought and activism in the Middle East and North Africa. Concomitantly, "the convergence of these two movements helped cause the development of mutual suspicions between Indonesian Muslims and Christians which affected the relationships between these groups in the early twentieth century and continued to influence the interactions between members of the two religious traditions from Indonesia's independence to the present time."[25] This state of affairs would later be compounded during the first two decades of Suharto's

---

[22] Ibid., p. 24.
[23] For a study of how traditional Muslim societies in Indonesia viewed Christianity, see Ismatu Ropi, "Muslim-Christian Polemics in Indonesian Islamic Literature," *Islam and Christian-Muslim Relations*, Vol. 9, No. 2, 1998.
[24] Andrée Feillard and Rémy Madinier, *The End of Innocence? Indonesian Islam and the Temptations of Radicalism*. Singapore: NUS Press, 2011, pp. 68–69.
[25] Alexander R. Arifianto, "Explaining the Cause of Muslim-Christian Conflicts in Indonesia: Tracing the Origins of Kristenisasi and Islamisasi," *Islam and Christian-Muslim Relations*, Vol. 20, No. 1, 2009, p. 75. See also Charles Farhadian, *Christianity, Islam, and Nationalism in Indonesia*. London: Routledge, 2005.

New Order rule when the state pursued policies that accorded privileges to Christians and nominal Muslims, while curbing the influence of those within the Muslim community that sought a more assertive place for their faith in the administration of the country.

In sum, the reality of the fragmentation of post-independence politics along separate religious lines would cast a long shadow as the architects of the Indonesian state sought to navigate between the concerns of the Christian and Muslim communities. The result of this was to foster tension and mutual suspicion between adherents of the Muslim and Christian faiths in Indonesia, a mutual suspicion that would be colored and animated by other socio-political dynamics that would emerge in the course of the country's anti-colonial and post-colonial history.

Negotiating the Bases of Nationhood and Statehood

Indonesia's Christian minority were acutely aware of the challenges confronting them as the task of constructing a sense of national identity out of the disparate identities that made up the Dutch East Indies gathered pace amidst the tumult of the Second World War. This sense of uncertainty only intensified against the backdrop of decolonization and the cauldron of revolution from which an Indonesian nation and political structure emerged, where Muslim fear of Christian proselytization and conversion, commonly known as "*Kristenisasi*" ("Christianization"), was met by Christian reservations toward pressures for the establishment of an Islamic state in newly independent Indonesia. On that score, a major point of contention which weighed heavily on the creation of the Indonesian state as well as the articulation of terms of citizenship and nationhood was the debate over content of the post-independence constitution.

At issue in the constitutional debate was whether an independent Indonesia would be an Islamic state ruled by *shari'a*, some form of secular state devoid of any reference to the divine, or, by way of compromise, a theistic, multi-confessional state. This debate came to be expressed most explicitly in the pressure that Islamist nationalists exerted on the BPUPKI (Committee for the Preparatory Work for Indonesian Independence or *Badan Penyelidik Usaha-usaha Persiapan Kemerdekaan Indonesia*), formed in March 1945 at the instruction of the Japanese military administration in the twilight of Japanese occupation in order to pave the way for Indonesian independence, for overt recognition of Islam as core to the national identity of post-colonial Indonesia.

To its proponents, the creation of an Islamic state in post-colonial Indonesia was a logical extension of the demographic reality where Islam was the dominant religion in the archipelago, Muslims formed the majority of the population, and Islam had played a pivotal role in the fledgling nationalist movement since its inception at the turn of the century. Because of differences among the sixty-two members of the BPUPKI, however, which had among its ranks advocates and opponents of an over recognition of Islam in the new constitution, a compromise was arrived at with Sukarno's intervention on June 1, 1945, to break the deadlock.

On June 1, 1945, President Sukarno enumerated five principles of the post-independence state in a speech to the BPUPKI. Collectively known as *Pancasila*, the five principles referred to (1) belief in a supreme God (*Ketuhanan yang Maha Esa*), (2) humanitarianism, (3) the unity of Indonesia, (4) consultative democracy, and (5) social justice.[26] Crucially, the principles of *Pancasila*, and in particular the first principle, was cast as an attempt to accommodate the aspirations of activist Muslim and Islamist nationalist counterparts who sought to articulate the post-independence Indonesian nation with specific reference to *shari'a*, yet simultaneously trying to avoid compromising the imperative of national unity. Significantly, the clause "with the obligation for the followers of Islam to practice *shari'a*" ("*dengan kewajiban menjalankan Syariat Islam bagi pemeluk-pemeluknya*," hereon known as the *shari'a* clause) was included in the preamble to the draft Constitution, which was based on the *Pancasila*. This preamble, known as the *Piagam Jakarta* or Jakarta Charter, was formalized on June 22 and approved by the BPUPKI, along with the accompanying seven-word *shari'a* clause as well as another making it compulsory that the president of Indonesia be a Muslim.

In August that year, the PPKI (Preparatory Committee for Indonesian Independence or *Panitia Persiapan Kemerdekaan Indonesia*), a committee established for purposes of the transfer of power from Japanese to Indonesian hands, discussed the possible adoption of the preamble and draft Constitution. During the PPKI meetings, the *shari'a* clause occasioned a rift between Islamists who sought a stronger legal Islamic identity for the nascent Indonesian state, and secular Muslims as well as non-Muslims who were more inclined to a less rigid assertion of the state's religious identity. Allied to the latter camp was a small but consequential group of Christians, many representing the eastern islands of the Indonesian archipelago which traditionally harbored misgivings toward excessive Javanese dominance, if not outright hegemony. In the final outcome of the deliberations, the PPKI overturned the BPUPKI's

---

[26] It should be noted that Sukarno's initial articulation on June 1, 1945, had the five principles appearing in a different order. Specifically, the reference to theism was the last of the five principles. After several discussions within the BPUPKI and PPKI, the reference to theism was moved to the top of the list.

initial position – namely, that the *Piagam Jakarta* be adopted wholesale – the day after Indonesian independence was declared on August 17, 1945. Consequently, the *Piagam Jakarta* was adopted but without the seven-word *shari'a* clause.

The removal of the *shari'a* clause was justified by Sukarno and his PPKI colleagues on grounds that the territorial integrity of post-independent Indonesia was their foremost priority. To that end, the concerns of those representing the eastern islands weighed heavily if only because the aspiration of the PPKI to inherit the entire expanse of the Dutch East Indies was threatened by a possible breakaway of the eastern islands, which was something representatives from these outer islands threatened to do if Indonesia "went Islamic."[27] Within the context of the PPKI's own deliberations, Christian concerns for the potential slide to Islamist statehood during this early post-independence period prompted them to lobby quietly but hard against proponents of the *shari'a* clause.[28] Because of this lobbying, the decision was taken to omit the clause in favor of the promotion of a more "generic" theism, that in any case was already captured in the original statement "Belief in one supreme God" (but without the accompanying statement on *shari'a* obligation), as the fundamental basis of nationhood and the post-independence state.[29]

Predictably, the rejection of the *shari'a* clause created resentment among Islamists, who were of the view that because Islam served as a major vehicle of anti-colonial resistance, it should be rightly accorded privileged status as the dominant religion in Indonesia (as opposed to Christianity, which was viewed as the religion of Dutch collaborators).[30] They also resented the fact that it was Christian pressure that led to the removal of the *shari'a* clause from the Jakarta Charter. This resentment would percolate.

[27] Ide Anak Agung Gde Agung, *Dari Negara Indonesia Timur ke Republik Indonesia Sarikat.* Jakarta: Gadjah Mada Press, 1985, talks about the State of East Indonesia. For a collection of brilliant essays on regional dynamics during the independence period, see Audrey Kahin (ed.), *Regional Dynamics of the Indonesian Revolution: Unity from Diversity.* Honolulu, HI.: University of Hawaii Press, 1985. For a detailed discussion in English of the debates over *Pancasila*, see B.J. Boland, *The Struggle of Islam in Modern Indonesia.* Leiden: Martinus Nijhoff, 1982.

[28] See the four volumes of documents for the preparation for the 1945 Indonesian Constitution collated in Muhammad Yamin, *Haskah Persiapan Undang-undang Dasar 1945.* Jakarta: Jajasan Prapantja, 1959.

[29] While secular Muslim nationalists such as Muhammad Hatta harbored their own reservations against the *shari'a* clause, they leveraged on non-Muslim concerns and the threat of secession to compel proponents of the clause to accept its omission.

[30] Yet, the debate over the Jakarta Charter presaged the re-emergence of these same issues first in 1957, and then again as Indonesia sought to find a new equilibrium after the fall of Suharto's New Order regime in 1998, when Islamist forces rallied to return the original Jakarta Charter to the agenda of national debate.

Among those in the Muslim community who harbored this resentment, the more radical elements refused to declare their allegiance to the new government, choosing instead to take up armed struggle for the creation of an Islamic Republic. The Darul Islam revolt spearheaded by the Islamic Army of Indonesia (*Tentera Islam Indonesia*, although they are in fact better known in the lexicon as Darul Islam) had its origins in West Java and soon spread to Central Java, South Sulawesi, South Kalimantan, and Aceh. The revolts triggered a backlash from the Indonesian state, which eventually managed to quell the rebellion in 1962 through a series of military operations throughout the archipelago, one of which led to the capture of the movement's leader, Sekarmadji Maridjan Kartosuwirdjo. Away from the battlefield, the Indonesian state circumscribed the activities of Islamic groups and political parties which continued to agitate for the Islamist agenda of the implementation of *shari'a* in Indonesia. The Indonesian state's relationship with Muslim social and political forces would remain on this testy course until the late 1980s and early 1990s.

Kristenisasi and the New Order

Amidst this tempestuous climate, it is not difficult to see how contending narratives of *Kristenisasi* or *Islamisasi* (Islamization) easily fueled hostility and catalyzed mobilization. Following the transfer of power from Sukarno to Suharto, Protestants and Catholics of almost all confessional persuasions made common cause with the latter's dirigiste New Order regime – especially the military – in much the same way they supported the colonial administration; this time, by supporting Suharto's narrative of nation building through national development. What is not commonly known is that religious identity and creedal confessions played an important part in the context of the violent political transition that began on September 30, 1965, which would further deepen mutual suspicions between Christians and Muslims.

At the height of the anti-communist purge that swept Suharto to power following the abortive communist coup of September 30, large numbers of nominal Muslim Indonesians had allegedly converted to Christianity in order to avoid suspicion and accusations of complicity with the communist movement.[31] Nevertheless, because many converted solely for purposes of escaping the dragnet of the anti-communist purge, a significant number would eventually revert back to Islam over time, when the

---

[31] Fatimah Husein, *Muslim-Christian Relations in the New Order Indonesia: The Exclusivist and Inclusivist Muslims' Perspectives*. Jakarta: PT Mizan Publika, 2005, pp. 120–121. See also *Sejarah Geredja Katolik di Indonesia*. Djakarta: Sekretariat Nasional K.M., 1971, p. 149.

existential threat posed by the purge subsided.[32] This religious reversion (from Christianity back to Islam) notwithstanding, the point is that with the advent of the New Order, Christians and nominal Muslim allies of the Suharto regime gained access to the corridors of power as well as key positions within the government and bureaucracy.[33] On the other hand, *santri* and conservative Muslim organizations, while well disposed of the New Order regime in its initial years, found themselves gradually marginalized by the regime.[34] As Suharto's suspicions of *santri* and conservative Muslim organizations grew, the New Order state slowly deepened its engagement of the Christian community in order to use it as a bulwark against conservative Muslim disquiet that was festering in opposition to the presidency of Suharto, thereby preventing it from morphing into a serious political movement. This led conservative Muslims to inveigh against Christian leaders for "fish(ing) in troubled waters" by taking advantage of political turbulence (via the threat of Islamist mobilization against Suharto) to increase their numbers in positions of influence and acquiring power at the expense of Muslims.[35]

In response to perceptions that this process of *Kristenisasi* was taking place and endorsed by the state, a discourse emerged in Muslim scholarly circles in the 1970s regarding the threat that it posed to Muslim interests. Mohamed Natsir, a former Prime Minister and stalwart of the Islamist Masyumi party that was disbanded by Sukarno in 1960 and prevented from reviving itself in the late 1960s by Suharto, castigated the popularity of foreign-funded and regime-approved Christian missionary activity which dwarfed Muslim efforts at religious propagation, likening it to a "cart" competing with an "express train."[36] Much in the same vein, the

---

[32] M.C. Ricklefs, *Islamisation and its Opponents in Java: c.1930 to the Present*. Singapore: National University of Singapore Press, 2012, pp. 138–150, provides a discussion on conversion among *abangan* Javanese up to the 1980s. For a discussion of Christians who actually either joined or were sympathetic to the communist party, see R.A.F. Paul Webb, "The Sickle and the Cross: Christians and Communists in Bali, Sumba, Flores, and Timor, 1965–1967," *Journal of Southeast Asian Studies*, Vol. 17, No. 1, March 1986.

[33] Some more prominent examples of this abangan/nominal Muslim alliance with the Christian community were the appointments of Johannes Leimena (from Maluku) by Sukarno as a deputy prime minister in the 1960s and Suharto's appointment of General Benny Moerdani as army chief of staff and defense minister in the 1980s.

[34] Traditional scholarship on Indonesian Islam had identified two broad categories of Javanese Muslims according to the degree of piety and adherence to Islamic social mores. *Santri* denotes those who actively practiced the faith, while *abangan* refers essentially to nominal Muslims.

[35] Alwi Shihab, "The Muhammadiyah Movement and its Controversy with Christian Mission." Ph.D dissertation, Temple University, 1995, pp. 306–307, cited in Arifianto, "Explaining the Cause of Muslim-Christian Conflicts in Indonesia," p. 81.

[36] Prawoto Mangkusasmito, "Rumus Pantja Sila dan Sedjarah Singkat Pertumbuhannya," *Kiblat*, No. 2, June 1968, pp. 48.

Muslim scholar Muhammad Rasjidi railed against Christian attempts to entice Muslims to convert through the use of material inducements such as money, schools, and hospitals.[37] Another Muslim scholar, Ismail al-Faruqi, drew an even starker picture, associating Christianity with what was arguably the most detested epithet of that day, neocolonialism: "I personally do not agree to discuss with anyone who argues that there is no neocolonialism today in . . . Indonesia. And what concerns us very much here is the linkage between the (Christian) missionary movement and neocolonialism."[38] Such narratives heightened the sense of indignation among Islamists and conservative Muslims who opposed the Suharto regime, engendering hostility toward Christianity and setting them on a collision course with the Christian community.

Kristenisasi needs also to be understood in the context of what was happening to Islamic social and political movements themselves during the same period. Under Sukarno and later Suharto, Islamic political parties such as Masyumi were banned by either or both of these leaders while Muslim leaders – both political and religious – were purged. In other instances, although they were not banned, Islamic organizations such as Parmusi and Nahdlatul Ulama were compelled to comply with New Order policies which constricted their authority and restricted their influence.[39] Because the circumscription of these Muslim organizations took place alongside the empowerment of the Christian community, it further deepened antipathy toward Christians (and the regime as well, it should be noted). This is not to say that the relationship between the New Order regime and the Indonesian Christian community was without its own problems. Points of contention did arise, such as when segments within the Christian community joined conservative Muslim organizations to express reservations toward Suharto's efforts to compel all religious organizations to adopt *Pancasila* as their sole doctrinal basis via law no. 8 of 1985.[40]

Be that as it may, it stands to reason that a concomitant sense of insecurity, born of the paradox of being part of a Muslim majority national

---

[37] Muhammad Rasjidi, "The Role of Christian Missions, the Indonesian Experience," *International Review of Mission*, Vol. 65, No. 260, October 1976.

[38] See "Discussion on Religious Freedom," *International Review of Mission*, Vol. 65, No. 260, October 1976, pp. 447–448. This was despite the fact that Indonesian Christians had also played a pivotal role in the independence movement against the Dutch. See van Klinken, *Minorities, Modernity, and the Emerging Nation*.

[39] Nahdlatul Ulama's political arm was forced to merge with Parmusi and *Partai Sarekat Islam Indonesia* (PSII) to form *Partai Persatuan Pembangunan* (PPP or United Development Party), one of the three approved political parties of the Suharto era, in 1973.

[40] See http://unpan1.un.org/intradoc/groups/public/documents/UN-DPADM/UNPAN 044239.pdf.

190 Indonesia

demographic but, compared to non-Muslims, with significantly less commensurate access to political and economic power, beset Islamists and conservative Muslims.[41] In this sense, there are some parallels to what we witnessed in Malaysia in the previous chapter, where the numerical majority has been accompanied by a "minority mindset" defined by insecurity toward the religious rights of the Muslim community, at least on the part of these Islamists and Muslim conservatives who sought – and were denied – a more assertive role for Islam in politics and national affairs.

Relations between the New Order and the Christian community, however, gradually changed in the late 1980s and early 1990s. Several factors accounted for this. First, Suharto had begun to actively seek out new bases of support to balance the military, which by then was becoming less complaint and increasingly viewed as a potential threat to the president's power base, a state of affairs compounded by the fact that the leader of the armed forces and Suharto's political rival, Benny Moerdani, was a Catholic. Second, Indonesia was not insulated from a rising tide of Islamization in the 1980s, which enhanced the popularity of Muslim organizations and threatened the interests and political position of Suharto's main political vehicle, Golkar. Third, Suharto himself was widely believed to have become more devout as he aged. Both in response to and as a consequence of these factors, Suharto adopted a more accommodating approach toward Muslim activists and Islamists, and in some instances even made common cause with them and proactively facilitated their return to prominence within the state and wider society. This period was characterized by the lifting of restrictions on Muslim activity and organizations; creation of a major new Muslim group (and vehicle for political power), ICMI (*Ikatan Cendekiawan Muslim Se-Malaysia* or Indonesian Association of Muslim Intellectuals); and greater integration of both Muslim conservatives and activists into the state at both national and regional levels.[42] Conversely, for elites from the nominal Muslim but especially the Christian communities, access to power and influence over affairs of state diminished considerably.[43] This was best epitomized in the cabinet of 1993, which excluded Christians from all

---

[41] For details of specific examples of *Kristenisasi* in recent times, see International Crisis Group, "Indonesia: 'Christianisation' and Intolerance," *ICG Asia Briefing*, No. 114, November 24, 2010.

[42] Suharto's creation of ICMI was especially significant. Formed in 1990, ICMI served to facilitate Muslim input into public policy. It eventually also provided senior bureaucrats and ministers for the Indonesian government.

[43] The diminution of Christian influence in the later New Order was also in part a function of the falling out between Suharto and hitherto Christian allies, foremost of whom was commander of the military forces and defense minister.

the major ministries while including several Muslim conservatives and activists.[44]

Having lost favor and finding themselves excluded from the center of power after enjoying positions of privilege from which they practiced discrimination against conservative Muslims, Christian concerns for their religious rights and access to patronage (which in the past allowed them to protect these rights) grew more acute. For Muslims, especially those of conservative stripe, this shift proffered political opportunities to redress the imbalance that had thus far tilted in the favor of Christians. What emerged was the articulation of an alternative vision of order in Indonesia that privileged its Islamic character. This narrative accelerated following the advent of the *Reformasi* period of political transformation and subsequent collapse of the edifice of Suharto's New Order. For Christians, non-Muslims more broadly, and indeed even fringe Muslim groups such as the *Shi'a* and the *Ahmadiyah*, the increasingly vocal mainstream conservative Islamic voice unleashed during the debates, renegotiation, and reconceptualization of nationhood and statehood in Indonesia that defined the *Reformasi* era was a cause of considerable consternation because of the threat of further marginalization, isolation, and exclusion. In a sense, these debates, renegotiation, and reconceptualization were mirrored in how the discourse and narrative of *Pancasila* itself were shifting subtely.

Pancasila: Secular Ideology?

Pancasila has been a chief organizing principle of Indonesian society, save possibly for a brief period immediately after the *Reformasi* period of the late 1990s when there was an attempt to discredit it as a device of the autocratic New Order state by political forces opposed to Suharto. As discussed earlier, under the leadership of nominal Muslims in the early post-independence years, *Pancasila* was cast as a notionally theistic ideology.[45] By the time of the New Order, it was widely seen, and articulated, as a secularist concept. According to this narrative, the notion of a "belief in a supreme God" as opposed to a belief in any specific deity in effect translated to secularism in terms of equal treatment and recognition of all accepted religions in Indonesia. This interpretation played well with the New Order regime on that score, given that it necessitated a strong state to manage any potential competition among religious

---

[44] See Arifianto, "Explaining the Cause of Muslim-Christian Conflicts in Indonesia," p. 84.
[45] Sunoto, *Mengenal Filsafat Pancasila*. Yogjakarta: BP FE UII, 1981; Sastrapratedja, *Pancasila Sebagai Ideologi*. Jakarta: BP-7 Pusat, 1991.

groups, so as to prevent any one religious community from ascending to a position of excessive power and influence relative to others.

This conventional conception of nationhood encapsulated in this interpretation of *Pancasila*, however, came under pressure as the tide of religious politics gradually started to turn and Islamists and conservative Muslims grew more assertive. The erosion with the collapse of the New Order regime of the erstwhile predominant role that nominal Muslim and their Christian political (and economic) allies played in Indonesian politics essentially laid the conditions for attempts to reinterpret *Pancasila* through religious frames.

When *Pancasila* was articulated during the apex of Indonesian nationalism in the months leading up to, and immediately after independence, Muslim organizations allied to the nationalist government were mobilized to cultivate the view that *Pancasila*'s first principle was in fact inspired by the Jakarta Charter and specifically the *shari'a* clause, even though in truth, the former actually preceded the latter. Even so, the accompanying view that *Pancasila* and the *shari'a* clause were reconcilable did gain some traction.[46] Because of this, even though some scholars have pointed out that the adoption of *Pancasila* marked the defeat of the Islamist goal of transforming Indonesia into an Islamic state, the concept itself may not have been the secular bulwark against attempts to introduce religion into the Indonesian state as its early progenitors would have argued.[47] On the contrary, *Pancasila* was in fact a religious signifier, albeit a necessarily ambiguous and, at the same time, multi-confessional one. For Islamists and conservative Muslims, the post-*Reformasi* era offered an opportunity to resolve the ambiguity.

While it is true that *Pancasila* was conceived to stave off more assertive religious forces, the concept itself was not entirely "secular." By virtue of its mention of a "supreme God" as its first article, the concept of *Pancasila* and the place it commands in Indonesian society (and history) speak rather to a theistic nationalism, or "godly nationalism" as Jeremy Menchik terms it, that has informed the conception of Indonesian nationhood since independence.

Yet within this framework of theistic nationalism a point of contention has emerged, which remains unresolved. This relates to the role of Islam in the context of the Muslim majority demographic in Indonesia, and its relationship with other theistic religions. In this respect, *Pancasila* did

---

[46] Robert W. Hefner, *Civil Islam: Muslims and Democratization in Indonesia*. Princeton, N.J.: Princeton University Press, 2000, p. 91.

[47] Moch Nur Ichwan, "Secularism, Islam and Pancasila: Political Debates on the Basis of the State in Indonesia," *Bulletin of the Nanzan Center for Asia and Pacific Studies*, Vol. 6, June 2011.

little to blunt the sharp edges of the discourses that political, religious, and community leaders engaged in along religious lines as each appropriated the concept to justify their own interpretation of the place of religion in the conception of Indonesian nation. As evidenced from our earlier discussion, this posturing has clearly been evident in how Muslim and Christian communities have pursued their retaliatory narratives of *Kristenisasi* and *Islamisasi* embedded in constitutive discourses of national identity respectively, how each have viewed the other's narrative with consternation and the symbiotic relationship that has resulted in terms of questions of rights and belonging as well as inclusion and exclusion.[48]

This ongoing, iterative tension between confession, constitution, and creed was evident in how the early post-New Order era saw attempts by Islamists to reorder Indonesian society with a return to the *Piagam Jakarta* in its original form, an issue that, as we saw, exercised nationalists at the time of independence in 1945. This time, the move was articulated by a new cast of Islamic political forces who sought a renegotiation of the Indonesian political and legal system toward a more Islamist political register, premised on the argument that the omission of the Charter's *shari'a* clause was merely a temporary compromise which could eventually be reneged.[49] Although the ideas associated with this new generation of advocates of the "shari'aization" of Indonesia ultimately failed to gain sufficient traction in the national parliament – it failed to be put to the vote nationally in the MPR (*Majelis Permusyawaratan Rakyat Republik Indonesia* or Indonesian Peoples' Consultative Assembly) in 2001 – regional parliaments, whose authority had been enhanced as a result of the passing of a new regional autonomy law in 2004, succeeded in getting elements of *shari'a* adopted as part of newly formulated regional regulations in West Java, West Sumatra, South Kalimantan, South Sulawesi, and Aceh.[50]

---

[48] This is not to say, however, that there were no avenues through which Christian and Muslim groups and actors have sought to build bridges in order to overcome the prolonged mistrust between their respective faith communities. While Islamist and conservative Muslim activism has gathered pace in the post-*Reformasi* years, this period also witnessed attempts to promote a pluralist version of Islam that could blunt suspicions, resolve conflict, and foster cooperation between Muslims and non-Muslims. These efforts revolved around the intellectual contributions of Muslim scholars such as Nurcholish Madjid (Muhammadiyah), Abdurrahman Wahid (Nahdlahtul Ulama), and Syafii Ma'arif (Muhammadiyah), and achieved some measure of success, for instance, when the Nahdlatul Ulama and Muhammadiyah lobbied for the rejection of the Jakarta Charter amendment.

[49] Marcus Mietzner, *Military Politics, Islam, and the State in Indonesia: From Turbulent Transition to Democratic Consolidation*. Singapore: Institute of Southeast Asian Studies, 2009, pp. 73–74.

[50] Michael Buehler, "The Rise of Shari'a By-laws in Indonesian Districts: An Indication for Changing Patterns of Power Accumulation and Political Corruption," *South East Asia*

The resurgence of a pro-*shari'a* narrative aside, arguably of greater concern to religious minorities was the upsurge in attacks on their houses of worship perpetrated by Muslim revivalist and vigilante groups. The Christian community was especially exercised by religiously inspired violence as Indonesia witnessed numerous acts of arson committed against churches, particularly during the period between 1998 and 2001. The combination of a more assertive mainstream Islamist narrative that has endeavored to reframe what constitutes the Indonesian nation and the alarming increase in violent activism of vigilante groups had corrosive effects for relations with an already beseiged Christian community. Nowhere was this more evident than in eastern Indonesia, where decades of lingering fears for *Kristenisasi* and *Islamisasi* that were playing out in Java eventually cascaded into the region.

"Religious Conflict" in Eastern Indonesia

Religious conflict is hardly a new phenomenon in Indonesia. To be sure, conflict between Muslims and Christians in Indonesia predated the interreligious strife between members of these two faith communities that occurred at the turn of the century with the demise of the New Order. For instance, inter-religious tension boiled over in the Makassar Incident (South Sulawesi) in October 1967, when a Christian preacher was believed to have blasphemed the Prophet Muhammad. The fact that this incident took place against the backdrop of plans for a major conference of the Indonesian Council of Churches compounded the backlash among Muslim communities, leading to further attacks on churches, schools, and dormitories and, eventually, to the spread of violence to Java. Even though violence was eventually brought under control, attempts at reconciliation mediated by the government and involving Muslim and Christian community leaders, which included an attempt to broker a consensual understanding of the limits of proselytization, failed.[51]

Notwithstanding events such as the Makassar Incident, it was the violence that beset several provinces in more recent times that brought home the volatility of inter-religious relations in the context of how each faith community conceived of its place in the imagined community of Indonesia. This was most emphatically demonstrated immediately after the fall of the New Order regime, when Indonesia experienced some of

Research, Vol. 16, No. 2, 2008; Robin Bush, "Regional Syari'ah Regulations: Anomaly or Symptom?" in Greg Fealy and Sally White (eds.), *Expressing Islam: Religious Life and Politics in Indonesia*. Singapore: Institute of Southeast Asian Studies, 2008.

[51] Jan Sihar Aritonang and Kareel Steenbrink, "The Ecumenical Movement," in Aritonang and Steenbrink (eds.), *A History of Christianity in Indonesia*. Leiden: Brill, 2008, p. 852–853.

the bloodiest violence since the anti-communist purge of 1965–1966. What was striking about this violence, especially what unfolded in the eastern parts of Indonesia, was the religious nature of some of this bloodshed. This was reinforced in extensive international media coverage of the events.[52]

Both the Sulawesi and Maluku islands (including the province of North Maluku formed in 1999) are constituent parts of what is commonly known as eastern Indonesia. Both islands share similar experiences in terms of their history and relationship to Java, the traditional center of power of the Indonesian archipelago. The culture and demographics of these islands are also markedly different from the main Indonesian islands of Java and Sumatra: considerable segments of the populations of both Sulawesi and Maluku are non-Muslim, and local culture retains elements of autonomy from the dominant Javanese cultural milieu. In recent years, both islands have unfortunately gained notoriety because of the violence that has occurred between Muslim and Christian segments of their populations. Hitherto at the margins of national affairs during the Suharto era, Maluku, and subsequently the newly created province of North Maluku as well, was thrust into the international spotlight almost overnight as the sites of extreme inter-religious strife.

Sulawesi lies at the junction of two historical streams of resistance to the central Indonesian state that were colored, though certainly not dictated, by issues of religion and specifically, the political expression of confessional alignments. From the south, the Darul Islam revolts that lasted from the 1950s to the mid-1960s saw the spillover of Islamist militancy that agitated for the creation of an Islamic state originating from south and southeast Sulawesi into the central regions. From the north, a Christian-led movement named Permesta (*Piagam Perjuangan Semesta Alam* or Universal Struggle Charter) emerged in the 1950s and was premised on a rejection of Javanese dominance and the creation of an autonomous Sulawesi. This movement, which intriguingly also drew some support from the Darul Islam in the late 1950s, gathered pace throughout the decade, culminating in the declaration of the autonomous state of North Sulawesi in June 1957.[53] Christian separatist sentiments

---

[52] Liz Sly, "Religious Violence the Latest Wrinkle in Indonesia's Woes," *Chicago Tribune*, December 1, 1998; Louise Williams, "Deepening Religious Divide Ripe for Political Exploitation," *Sydney Morning Herald*, December 5, 1998; Reuters, "New Violence Over Religion in Indonesia," *New York Times*, January 1, 2000. A lengthy list of reports from various broadsheets on the religious character of violence in Indonesia during this period can be found at www.reocities.com/CapitolHill/Senate/9388/religious_riots/religious_riots.htm.

[53] The revolt, which was suspected to have been emboldened by the United States, was eventually brought to an end by a combination of military operations and the further centralization of political authority, the very opposite of what the revolt hoped to achieve,

196   Indonesia

continue to percolate in North Sulawesi through the vehicle of Minahasa nationalism even after the rebellion was put down, which its proponents have taken to justifying with reference to biblical passages from the book of Galatians.[54]

Like Sulawesi, Maluku had over the course of Dutch colonialism developed along a trajectory that was substantially different from Java. In Maluku, Dutch colonialism facilitated the expansion of Christianity (specifically, Calvinism) at a rate far swifter than most other East Indies provinces. Part of the reason for the success of this expansion was the fact that it met with minimal local resistance. Instead, indigenous Maluku populations would provide a sizable number of professional soldiers for the Dutch colonial army, and they would go on to serve with distinction against the Japanese military during the Second World War. In April 1950, separatists loyal to Dutch colonial authority hastily proclaimed the formation of the Republic of South Moluccas (RMS or *Republik Maluku Selatan*), a move occasioned by resurgent religious identity and also opportunities that availed themselves as a result of military demobilization after the revolution. As with the case of the Permesta Rebellion, the venture was shortlived, and Indonesian military forces soon overwhelmed the separatists and absorbed the territory into the Indonesian Republic.

While Central Sulawesi has not been impervious to ethnic, communal, and religious conflicts in the years since Indonesian independence, it was the period between 1999 and 2001 which witnessed unprecedented violence, with more than a thousand deaths and many more wounded and displaced.[55] Most of the violence was centered on Poso. The violence was triggered by the now-infamous Christmas Eve incident in December 1998 – which coincidentally that year was also the month of Ramadhan – when a Christian man stabbed a Muslim.[56] The violence that followed was retaliatory and iterative, and soon involved extremist groups with external links such as the notorious Jemaah Islamiyah. Muslim mobs

in the hands of President Sukarno under "Guided Democracy." See Barbara S. Harvey, *Permesta: Half a Rebellion*. Ithaca: Cornell Southeast Asia Program Publications, 1977. I wish to acknowledge Greg Fealy for information about how Darul Islam elements had also supported the revolt.

[54] See www.indonesiamatters.com/758/minahasa-nationalism/. The region of Minahasa occupies the northern part of North Sulawesi province and contains the regencies of Minahasa, North Minahasa, South Minahasa, Bitung, Manado, Tomohon, and Bolaang Mongondow.

[55] For an insightful study on Christianity in Sulawesi, see Lorraine V. Aragon, *Fields of the Lord: Animism, Christian Minorities, and State Development in Indonesia*. Honolulu, HI: University of Hawaii Press, 2000.

[56] See "Indonesia Flashpoints: Sulawesi," www.bbc.co.uk, June 28, 2004. Available http://news.bbc.co.uk/2/hi/asia-pacific/3812737.stm.

attacked Christian and Chinese shops, purportedly to root out the sale of alcohol which was believed to have been the cause of the initial stabbing incident, while Christian militia were also mobilized to confront them. The ensuing violence resulted in the arrest and imprisonment of several leaders of the Christian militia accused of being provocateurs. The fact that no Muslims were arrested served only to further the perception which by then had already taken root in the Christian community that they were being discriminated against and marginalized.

A second wave of violence was triggered by yet another stabbing of a Muslim by a Christian, in April 2000, and more homes and shops, but also churches and schools, were attacked and burnt in retaliation. In turn, these events set the stage for the third wave of violence, which took the form of Christian "revenge" attacks. Ominously, the attacks were justified by a Christian narrative of "*mempertahankan kita punya wilayah*" ("in defence of our territory"), thereby speaking to perceptions of how (migrant) Muslims had purportedly transgressed indigenous Christian lands.[57]

Despite the eventual signing of the Malino Accords in December 2001 (brokered by Vice-President Jusuf Kalla) violence receded but was not entirely arrested.[58] In the years that followed, more attacks were seen, such as in 2003 when thirteen Christians were gunned down by unknown assailants, and 2005, when three Christian schoolgirls were beheaded allegedly by Muslim extremists, who in a provocative gesture deliberately placed one of the heads at the entrance of a local church. Following the conviction and execution of three Catholics in 2006 for masterminding

---

[57] David G. McRae, "Criminal Justice and Communal Conflict: A Case Study of the Trial of Fabianus Tibo, Dominggus da Silva, and Marinus Riwu," *Indonesia*, Vol. 83, April 2007, p. 84.

[58] The ten-point Malino Accord comprised the following terms:
1. To cease all conflicts and disputes;
2. To abide by due process of law enforcement and support the Government's efforts to impose sanctions on any wrongdoers;
3. To request the state to take firm and impartial measures against any violators;
4. To maintain the peaceful situation, the two sides reject civil emergency status and interference from outsiders;
5. To respect one another in an attempt to create religious tolerance;
6. That Poso is an integral part of Indonesia's territory. Therefore, any Indonesian has the right to come and live peacefully in Poso by respecting the local habits and custom;
7. To reinstate property to their rightful owners;
8. To repatriate refugees to their respective original places;
9. To rehabilitate, along with the Government, the economic assets and infrastructures of the area;
10. To respect all faith followers to implement their respective religious practices and beliefs as stipulated by the Constitution.

violence against Muslims in Poso in 2000, riots ensued in the predominantly Christian areas of Central Sulawesi. The riots were triggered by a Christian sense of injustice, as Muslim militants who were found to have been complicit during the same period of violence in Sulawesi were spared the death penalty and received only light prison sentences.[59]

In Maluku, corresponding violence had broken out around the same time. The atmospherics surrounding the violence in Maluku were similar to what was witnessed in Sulawesi, even as inter-communal tensions between different ethnic and confessional communities had been brewing for decades. Conventional explanations note that, as with Sulawesi, the demise of Suharto's New Order lifted the lid off these brewing tensions, leading to an outbreak of violence on an unprecedented scale.[60] Casualty figures, however, far exceeded those in Sulawesi, and whole communities and villages have been decimated. The extent of violence and how it spread was all the more remarkable given the trigger – a deceptively straightforward altercation between a Christian bus driver and a Muslim passenger that occurred in Ambon.[61] The violence that followed eventually cost an estimated 10,000 lives and displaced a further 700,000 people. Also iterative in nature, the cycles of violence in Maluku were often triggered by isolated events that quickly escalated as vigilante groups mobilized along religious lines.

Mirroring Sulawesi, the arrival of external groups such as Laskar Jihad (possibly in connivance with elements within the Indonesian military), KOMPAK, Laskar Mujahidin, and Jemaah Islamiyah in response to the perception that Christians were gaining the upper hand in the fight against Muslims further amplified polarization and tension.[62] The appearance of these groups deepened an already discernible shift in the religious discourse surrounding this second phase of conflict.[63] As Spyer observed: "This second phase of the conflict was characterized by a deepening of the religious definition of the opposing parties and the crystallization of relevant extremist discourses – to wit, that of militant Islam

---

[59] See "Executions Spark Indonesia Unrest," www.bbc.co.uk, September 22, 2006. Available http://news.bbc.co.uk/2/hi/5368922.stm.

[60] During the New Order era, the Indonesian government was not averse to using force and/or legislative tools to systematically control inter-communal tensions in Indonesia.

[61] Many have, however, suggested that the initial spark that triggered violence was to be found in Ketapang, Jakarta, where conflict took place among Christian and Muslim Ambonese gangs over parking at an entertainment center.

[62] John T. Sidel, *Riots, Pogroms, Jihad: Religious Violence in Indonesia*. Ithaca, N.Y.: Cornell University Press, 2006, pp. 183–184. See also Kirsten E. Schulze, "Laskar Jihad and the Conflict in Ambon," *The Brown Journal of International Affairs*, Vol. IX, No. 1, 2002.

[63] There was a massive gathering at the Monas monument in central Jakarta in early 2000 at which Amien Rais and Hamzah Haz both called for a *jihad* against Christians who were attacking Muslims in Ambon.

and *jihad*, represented by Laskar Jihad and the smaller, more covert Laskar Mujahidin, on the one hand, and that of nostalgic sovereignty and separatism, on the other, promulgated by the Christian FKM (*Fron Kedaulatan Maluku*, Front for Moluccan Sovereignty)."[64] The polarized state of intense religious fervor was further aggravated by the use of apocalyptic narratives by conflict actors, including purported sightings of Jesus Christ and the Virgin Mary among Christian militants, and on the part of their Muslim adversaries, sightings of angels on battle horses.[65] The repertoire of conflict also included forced conversions, and even forced circumcisions, of Christians at the barrel of the gun or blade of the machete.[66] Analogous images of the crusades were conjured by observations such as the following:

> Over the course of the conflict, local pastors, church ministries, and officials were responsible for choosing certain Biblical verses and religious texts for the Sunday sermons and other religious services, based on the socio-political context and adapting to developments. Generally pastors and church ministries selected popular Biblical verses in the Old Testament revolving around violence and the struggle of the Israelites against their enemies, from the Books of Genesis, Deuteronomy, Exodus, Joshua, Judges, Samuel (I, II), Kings (I, II), and Psalm. During the conflict, ordinary Protestants also recited these verses. Whenever they went to other places or to the battleground, they carried a small Bible in their pocket for self-protection, making it easier to recite selected verses and stoke the spirit of war.[67]

In North Maluku, a new province carved out from Maluku in 1999, conflict between indigenous Kao, which comprised mostly Christians but also some Muslims, and migrant Makian, who were Muslims, broke out on the island of Halmahera over local issues, namely the legal status of the land upon which Makian transmigrants had been residing for decades after they had been relocated from Makian island in the 1970s by the Indonesian government, and ownership of resources found in this land.[68] Armed vigilante groups very quickly joined in the violence and eventually also mobilized along religious lines. The violence peaked in

---

[64] Patricia Spyer, "Fire without Smoke and Other Phantoms of Ambon's Violence: Media Effects, Agency, and the Work of Imagination," *Indonesia*, Vol. 74, October 2002, p. 26.

[65] Nils Bubandt, "Malukan Apocalypse: Themes in the Dynamics of Violence in Eastern Indonesia," in Ingrid Wessel and Georgia Wimhöfer (eds.), *Violence in Indonesia*. Hamburg: Abera-Verlag, 2001, pp. 243–246.

[66] See "Maluku Refugees Allege Forced Circumcision," www.bbc.co.uk, January 31, 2001. Available http://news.bbc.co.uk/2/hi/asia-pacific/1146224.stm.

[67] Sumanto Al Qurtuby, "Christianity and Militancy in Eastern Indonesia: Revisiting the Maluku Violence," *Southeast Asian Studies*, Vol. 4, No. 2, August 2015, p. 315.

[68] The violence took place in August, two months before the inauguration of the new province of North Maluku. It then spread to the nearby islands at Ternate and Tidore after attacks by Kao triggered a mass exodus of the migrant Makian to these islands,

December 1999 and lasted through the first half of 2000, leading to the creation of Muslim and Christian enclaves and segregation of a society that had previously managed to co-exist in peace.

While we are interested for analytical and thematic purposes in the conflicts and the narratives that underlined them, it should also be acknowledged that the conflicts themselves were eventually brought under control. This process of conflict resolution was brought about in part by agreements brokered by senior office holders. For instance, as with Poso, violence in Maluku was gradually reduced with the signing of the government-sponsored Malino II Accord (modeled after the first Malino Accord signed a few months earlier) in February 2002 that established an eleven-point agreement to end conflict, restore the rule of law, protect the unitary state, establish freedom of movement, eliminate armed organizations, return displaced persons to their homes, rebuild infrastructure, maintain neutrality of security forces, and reconstruct an integrated university. Equally important were the role of religious communities in the conflict, whereby religiously framed narratives of conflict gave way to narratives of peace and reconciliation facilitated by civil society and popular movements, not unlike what transpired in the southern Philippines.[69]

However, as with Sulawesi, the Malino II peace agreement did not bring an immediate halt to hostilities. Instead, in the immediate aftermath of the signing of the agreement, conflict and violence took a different turn, away from incendiary religious imperatives toward more mundane drivers. As Sumanto Al Qurtuby observed: "After the signing of the Peace Accord in 2002, religious identities were in general no longer a vital ingredient for local religious militants. Some ex-combatants told me that they stopped attacking other religious groups once the security forces and political leaders and elite members of society intervened intensively and started to manipulate local discord and interreligious rivalry for their own political and economic interests."[70]

Unpacking the Religious Master Frame

It seems one of the foibles of media reporting on Indonesia, that whenever conflicts erupt between groups whose members are adherents of different religions, the immediate prognoses would be that some form of religiously inspired pogrom was taking place. Certainly in the case

where they subsequently launched reprisal attacks on the Christian communities on these islands.
[69] This has been argued in Sumanto Al Qurtuby, *Religious Violence and Conciliation in Indonesia: Christians and Muslims in the Moluccas*. London: Routledge, 2016.
[70] Al Qurtuby, "Christianity and Militancy in Eastern Indonesia," p. 332.

of conflicts in Sulawesi, Maluku, and North Maluku at the turn of the 20th century, broadsheets (and online media) have focused narrowly on religious cleavages between respective actors. To great extent, this perception was exacerbated by the involvement of extremist and vigilante Muslim groups such as Jemaah Islamiyah and Laskar Jihad in these conflict regions. When interviewed for instance, Ja'afar Umar Thalib, leader of Laskar Jihad, claimed that the formation of the group on January 30, 2000 was in response to revelations that Protestant churches in Eastern Indonesia were planning to form a breakaway Christian state comprising North Sulawesi, West Papua, and Maluku.[71]

One aspect to these conflicts that lent currency to the analytical lens of "religious war" was the fact that after the initial phases when violence was less systematic or organized, it became evident that mobilization was being undertaken through religious groups. This was palpable in the violence in Poso, Central Sulawesi, when large-scale violence during the period of May–June 2000 and later, in January 2001, involved groups such as the Central Sulawesi Christian Church (which was believed to have backed many of the Christian vigilante groups involved in the violence), *Gerakan Pemuda Sulawesi Tengah* (Central Sulawesi Youth Movement), Laskar Jundullah, and the Java-based Laskar Jihad which descended upon Poso in July 2001.[72] In the meantime, in both Maluku (in Ambon) and North Maluku (in Ternate), what initially began as conflicts between locals and migrants and/or different ethnic groups shifted quickly to a religious register as co-religionists who were otherwise of different ethnic origin coalesced against opposing faith communities (sometimes of the same ethnic origin).[73]

Perhaps more distressing was the deep polarization and segregation that creedal allegiances in the course of conflict created, where, as Nils Bubandt hastened to add, "the cascading of identity also meant the reconstruction of time and space . . . (where) social space was re-shaped according to religious affiliation" lingered after violence abated.[74] Districts began taking on a religious character as villages transformed into either Christian or Muslim enclaves as a consequence of forced migration brought about by conflict. Social institutions such as schools, hotels, and even public transportation further manifested these sharp divisions.

---

[71] Greg Fealy, "Inside the Laskar Jihad," *Inside Indonesia*, January–March 2001. Available https://www.library.ohiou.edu/indopubs/2001/07/24/0097.html.

[72] For a detailed discussion on the vigilante and militant groups operating during this period, see International Crisis Group, "Weakening Indonesia's Mujahidin Networks: Lessons from Maluku and Poso," *ICG Asia Briefing* No. 103, October 13, 2005.

[73] International Crisis Group, "Indonesia: The Search for Peace in Maluku," *ICG Asia Report* No. 31, February 8, 2002, p. 2.

[74] Bubandt, "Malukan Apocalypse," p. 238.

The observation had been made earlier regarding how the eruption of violence, at least in some areas in eastern Indonesia, coincided with religious holidays.[75] Writing on the Maluku violence, Lucien van Liere explained that: "Religion not only played an important part in distinguishing between friend and foe, but also in understanding what was going on and how to deal with the conflict. As a result, traditional theological language was used to indicate the victimhood of the in-group and to legitimate violence towards the out-group."[76]

So how should we understand these conflicts, and, in particular, their religious dimensions? What is striking about the conflicts in Sulawesi, Maluku, and North Maluku is the relative tranquility and harmony that hitherto apparently existed between the Christian and Muslim communities in all three cases. Indeed, just about every article that analyzes these conflicts never fails to preface their analysis with this observation. So, what happened? How and why did this inter-religious harmony unravel and descend into the depths of bloody inter-religious violence as swiftly as it did? And, importantly, what were the narratives underlying this phenomenon, and what explains their currency?

In attending to these questions, a few initial observations can immediately be made. The first point is that while there was much that was similar between these conflicts, they were also unique in significant ways, most noticeably in the way mobilization took place. Because the violence in both Sulawesi and Maluku (Poso and Ambon, for instance) took place in waves, mobilization processes differed even within a city or province, let alone across provinces, ranging from random violence to kinship and village networks to organized recruitment led by groups such as Laskar Jihad, Mujahidin KOMPAK, and Jemaah Islamiyah. Second, these conflicts were, importantly, not only about religion. Indeed, many other factors were at play, including clan, family, and personal conflicts that had little to do with a person's religious allegiance. Similarly, there were different, oftentimes contending, dynamics and processes of contention involved, not least of which was the incapacity and reluctance of security forces to intervene in order to bring violence under control.[77] Fingers have also been pointed at opportunistic local and national leaders for their complicity in fomenting violence in order to achieve narrow political ends, such as undermining the government of President Abdurrahman Wahid.

---

[75] Ibid., pp. 239–240.
[76] Lucien M. van Liere, "Fighting for Jesus on Ambon: Interpreting Religious Representations of Violent Conflict," *Exchange*, Vol. 40, No. 4, 2011, p. 323.
[77] This point is persuasively argued in Gerry van Klinken, *Communal Violence and Democratization in Indonesia: Small Town Wars*. London: Routledge, 2007.

Yet as this book has sought to argue, such instrumentalist logic does not tell the whole story, and we need still to get beyond them in order to ascertain the source of the appeal of religious idioms and metaphors.[78] As Lorraine Aragon rightly highlighted in her deep analysis of the conflict in Poso, Sulawesi, "to say that the Poso conflict was not originally about religion is not to say that religious ideologies and practices were not integral elements of both the history of the conflict and its process in 'daily life.' They were, and that is why partisan media stories and narratives about the violence were successful in further polarizing the population, and in intensifying the conflict process."[79] To that end, while several scholars have looked in depth at the processes through which actors were mobilized, the question remains as to how and why the mobilization process itself was framed in religious terms, the currency that religious narratives possessed, and why they resonated such that mobilization was successful.[80] It is in this regard that we must acknowledge that while there was clearly a religious dimension to the violence that broke out, it needs to be understood in its proper context.

One of the key factors that enabled conflict to take hold and escalate in Sulawesi and Maluku can be attributed to the demographic balance in these regions. Despite the fact that Muslims command an 88 percent majority nationwide in Indonesia, in both these regions there has traditionally been rough parity between Muslims and Christians, with neither commanding a sizable majority especially in urban centers. In recent decades, however, transmigration has tilted this balance in favor of Muslims.[81] This caused consternation among the Christian community on at least two counts: first, the privileges that the community had become accustomed to during colonialism and even after independence right up to the late 1980s were jeopardized; and, second, the demographic shift was taking place against the backdrop of greater Muslim assertiveness, including the use of force on the part of vigilante Muslim groups that surfaced in the climate of post-Suharto ferment. This being the case, it should hardly be a surprise to see these demographic realities create a sense of an existential threat, thereby catalyzing opportunism on

---

[78] Christopher Duncan implies the same point in "'The Other Maluku: Chronologies of Conflict in North Maluku, Eastern Indonesia," *Indonesia*, Vol. 80, October 2005.

[79] Lorraine V. Aragon, "Relatives and Rivals in Central Sulawesi: Grounded Protestants, Mobile Muslims, and the Labile State," in Susanne Schröter (ed.), *Christianity in Indonesia: Perspectives of Power*. Berlin: Lit Verlag, 2010, pp. 262–263.

[80] Two of the best studies in this genre are van Klinken, *Communal Violence and Democratization in Indonesia* and David McRae, *A Few Poorly Organized Men: Interreligious Violence in Poso, Indonesia*. Leiden: Brill, 2013.

[81] For example in the case of Poso, a hitherto Christian majority had by the turn of the century been reduced to a minority of 40 percent.

the part of local Christian elite who sought to play on fears and religious identity in order to mobilize.[82] Furthermore, the early 1990s also saw pressure from Muslim groups like ICMI to increase Muslim representation at senior levels of national and local governments, thereby upsetting previous Christian–Muslim power-sharing arrangements in places like Ambon.

A key driver behind these demographic changes, as suggested earlier, was transmigration. Transmigration had been a facet of the New Order regime's policy of economic development and nation building. During its tenure, the resettlement of Javanese was actively pursued as a means to "ethnically homogenize and boost the nation economically."[83] Such measures, however, posed a challenge by way of the need to balance the economic imperative with the impact that transmigration would have on indigenous communities who feared displacement as a consequence. In the event, during the Suharto administration transmigration policies resulted in many instances in increased competition for resources and local political power, predictably fostering resentment along the way. In Maluku, the movement of up to 100,000 Muslims, many from Sulawesi in fact, over several decades into the province overturned the rough equilibrium between Christian and Muslim communities. The shift caused a strain on indigenous interests as jobs that had traditionally been the preserve of the Christian elite throughout previous decades were taken over by migrants who were Muslims.

The transformation of the economic balance was followed by increased dominance of Muslims in local politics and administration. Jacques Bertrand's description of how the Muslim governor of Maluku, Akib Latuconsina, attempted to redress the imbalance in access to power between Christians and Muslims was instructive in this regard: "He accelerated the appointment of Muslims to the higher echelons of the bureaucracy, thereby displacing Christians from former strongholds. These nominations further politicized religious identities."[84] Needless to say, this rendered more acute the Christian perception that they were under siege and that their interests were being threatened. Because most of the transmigrants were Muslim while many indigenous communities were Christian, it stands to reason that certain quarters would construe

---

[82] See, for instance, Lorraine Aragon, "Communal Violence in Poso: Where People Eat Fish and Fish Eat People," *Indonesia*, Vol. 72, 2001.

[83] Lorraine Aragon, "Reconsidering Displacement and Internally Displaced Persons from Poso," in Eva-Lotta E. Hedman (ed.), *Conflict, Violence, and Displacement in Indonesia*. Ithaca, N.Y.: Cornell University Southeast Asia Program, 2008, p. 175.

[84] Jacques Bertrand, "Legacies of the Authoritarian Past: Religious Violence in Indonesia's Moluccan Islands," *Pacific Affairs*, Vol. 75, No. 1, Spring 2002, p. 68.

conflicts over land and resource allocation or employment opportunities as religious conflicts by virtue of the religious affiliations of the competing parties and communities involved.[85] The uncertainty and heightened insecurity among indigenous communities were aggravated by further movement of people as a consequence of conflict from South Sulawesi to Ambon (in Maluku), and later to Ternate in northern Maluku. In other words, conflict bred more conflict.

A measure of how issues of land rights quickly took on religious undertones was evident in the North Maluku conflict between migrant Muslim Makianese on one hand and Jailolo and Kao Protestant Christian locals on the other over the legal status of land occupied by Makian settlers who were relocated from Makian island to Malifut by the state. Conflict erupted when the Makianese claim to legal status and land ownership on grounds that their relocation was permanent was refuted by the indigenous Kao. This fault line overlapped with historical rivalry between the Sultan of Ternate, who was aligned with the indigenous population and Protestant groups, and Sultanate of Tidore and his Muslim followers.[86] What was striking about the North Maluku conflict was the fact that during its early stages violence was waged not along religious lines but between indigenous Christian and Muslim Kao against Makianese settlers over the proposed creation of a new *kecamatan* (subdistrict), in Malifut. From there, violence cascaded to the islands of Ternate and Tidore, which witnessed the wholesale decimation of Christian villages. The escalating conflict later took a decisive turn toward a more religious register in Halmahera when Kao and Makianese Muslims set aside their differences and made common cause against indigenous Christians in response to the circulation of propaganda, purportedly issued by the leadership of the Maluku Protestant Church (GPM or *Gereja Protestan Maluku*), calling for a holy war against Muslims.

Rumors, Mythologies, Narratives

As with the case of the conflict in Thailand's southern provinces, the role of mythology and rumors was crucial in amplifying the religious dimension of these conflicts in Indonesia. The most obvious case was the bloodletting against Christians in North Maluku, which was provoked by the appearance of an inflammatory letter allegedly issued by the Head

---

[85] Bugis traders from South Sulawesi were particularly aggressive in expanding their stake in local informal economies, much to the resentment of Christian small businesses.
[86] Smith Alhadar, "The Forgotten War in North Maluku," *Inside Indonesia*, July–September 2000.

of the Maluku Synod of the GPM.[87] The letter, which was widely circulated, purported to exhort Christians to consolidate their superiority in numbers in the North Maluku and Central Halmehara regions, as it linked the Christian struggle in North Maluku to religious violence in Ambon. Despite denials of culpability by the very Christian organizations implicated in the letter, its intemperate contents still provoked outrage in Muslim circles. At a deeper level, the invective letter resonated because its contents essentially reflected the Muslim community's historical encounters with Christian counterparts and reinforced negative perceptions of Christian intent. This was captured in how a local Muslim respondent explained reactions to the letter to Christopher Duncan: "People believed the letter was real because it proved what they had seen historically. The letter itself may have been a forgery, but its content showed the true nature of Christian plans to take over the province."[88]

The provocative contents of the letter were used as a pretext for mobilization of the Muslim community along religious lines and unleashed violence first in Tidore and then Ternate over a period between October and December 1999, which correspondingly led to the exodus of large numbers of Christians from the province. While the conflict was initially rooted in competing perspectives of claimant ethnic groups over rights to the land, because ethnic identity easily (though not perfectly) reflected religious allegiances, not to mention the combustible potential of religious narratives, religious metaphors and idioms were quickly used to inject deeper meaning to the conflict on the part of both the Christian and Muslim communities. Further exacerbating matters was the fact that during this period of violence, religious allegiances were also manifested in the security services that were mobilized to bring the conflict under control, with the police siding with Christians while the military sided with Muslims.

In sum, the weight of totemic narratives – whether constructed by Muslims or Christians – in shaping a climate of conflict cannot be underestimated. Patricia Spyer's remarks illustrate this powerfully:

Too little heed is given to the work of the imagination and the construction of knowledge in all of this and, specifically, to how these compel and propel particular actions and shape those who carry them out. The mobile, dense, and murky terrain in which something that is waiting to happen does, in fact, happen is built on spirals of information, misinformation, and disinformation, on the revamping of criteria of credibility, customs of trust and accountability, and on

[87] For a detailed discussion of this letter, see Duncan, *Violence and Vengeance*. An alternative view on the role of the letter is provided in Chris Wilson, *Ethno-Religious Violence in Indonesia: From Soil to God*. London: Routledge, 2012, pp. 84–95.
[88] Ibid.

knowledge forms that blur the boundaries between what is seen and what is heard, what is known and what is suspected, what is feared and what is fantasized, what is fact and what is fiction.[89]

What Lies Beneath the (Religious) Master Frames

The foregoing discussion highlights an essential point to bear in mind: in assessing religious conflicts, we have to consider not just the religious affiliation of vigilante groups that mobilized but also, equally importantly, the claims they make. Put differently, a distinction must be made between what is being mobilized (religious identity and allegiance, in this case) and why it is being mobilized. To that end, it is argued that many of these groups mobilized around a narrative of indigeneity, rights, and belonging, which were of immediate concern, and which religious identity amplified and animated.

Closely tied to the loss of land discussed earlier was the erosion of long-standing cultural identities and affiliations by the divisive effects of transmigration. Spyer writes, for example, of the sanctity that local Malukan communities attached to traditional land rights that were not necessarily aligned to religious communities, which were subsequently ignored if not undermined by new migrants. Van Klinken makes a similar point in his assessment of how traditional avenues of cross-cultural exchange which used to underpin harmony between Christian and Muslim communities in Maluku were subsequently quashed by *fatwa* issued by the Indonesian Ulama Association that forbade Christians to participate in Islamic activities.[90] Much in the same vein, the traditional practice of *pela-gondong*, an oath of allegiance that previously bonded Christian and Muslim villages in a mutual help relationship, fell apart with the demographic changes and outbreak of conflict. Even traditional village heads and elders who previously commanded respect in their local communities could no longer assert any significant authority as a consequence of the restructuring of bureaucratic hierarchies that relegated them to the bottom of the totem pole of local power.[91]

---

[89] Spyer, "Fire Without Smoke and Other Phantoms of Ambon's Violence," p. 24.
[90] Gerry van Klinken, "The Maluku Wars: Bringing Society Back In," *Indonesia*, Vol. 71, 2001.
[91] Sidney Jones explains that this was because changes in Indonesian law "essentially turned local traditional village heads into the lowest rung of the Indonesian bureaucratic administration. So once the conflict broke out, it could not be controlled because the traditional authority of local figures had gradually been sapped and they then constituted the lowest rung of the bureaucracy. Traditional village heads then had much less influence over their followers." See Sidney Jones, "Causes of Conflict in Indonesia," *Asia Society*, 2002. Available http://asiasociety.org/causes-conflict-indonesia.

The fact that these demographic shifts were taking place against a backdrop of dramatic political change at a national level cannot be discounted either. Two points can be registered in this regard. First, any serious analysis of regional political developments in Indonesia at the turn of the 21st century cannot avoid discussing the impact of political transformation at the center. Indeed, the demographic shifts elaborated previously were taking place against the backdrop of a turbulent period of political transition triggered by a concatenation of events that conspired to bring an end to the Suharto regime's thirty-two-year rule. This is not to imply that the process of democratization unleashed "ancient hatreds," which broke out in communal conflicts across the archipelago. Such a caricature would be both conceptually and empirically unsound. Nevertheless, it stands to reason that as the political system sought out a new equilibrium after more than three decades of authoritarian rule, political entrepreneurs mobilized along religious lines, playing up latent tensions and mutual suspicions among faith communities to incite violence. Underlying this was a process of renegotiation of the fundamental premises of nationhood. This was epitomized in reticence toward *Pancasila* as an organizing principle for Indonesian society because of its association with the New Order. The uncertainty was felt most acutely by Christians and ethnic Chinese, who often found themselves at the receiving end of unrest as the social-political fabric came under strain.

Second, there was a shift in political power and access between Muslims (specifically conservative Muslims and Islamists) and Christians hitherto favored historically during the colonial administration and later under the first couple of decades of Suharto's New Order. By way of illustration, in a place like Poso where established local structures of religious authority and identity were already coming under strain as a result of political changes at the national level, these shifts in how political power and authority were being realigned along religious lines set the conditions for the outbreak of violence:

[T]he location and timing of religious violence in Poso were associated with a local conjuncture that threatened to undermine the foundations of religious authority in the regency. This local conjuncture was one in which the dominant structures of religious authority faced unprecedented uncertainty as to their strength, their solidity, and their claims on the local population, in the face not only of unsettling sociological trends but also of sudden political change. Under the Suharto regime, Protestant and Muslim hierarchies of authority had been subordinated to, and partially submerged within, a highly centralized authoritarian state, beneath which they found shelter, stability, and patronage.[92]

[92] Sidel, *Riots, Pogroms, Jihad*, p. 161.

It is this underlying uncertainty in the wake of structural changes that precipitated responses such as that which were witnessed in reaction to the politicking around local elections, when Muslims sought to contest political offices that Christians deemed to have traditionally been their preserve.

At this point, we should also recognize that while there were obvious local dynamics at play in the conflicts that took place in Sulawesi and Maluku, in both instances conflict actors were also part of networks that could be traced back to Jakarta, thereby indicating these conflicts were also influenced by structural changes. The appointment of Akib Latuconsina as Governor of Maluku in 1992, which heightened Christian consternation, could not have happened without Jakarta's approval. Likewise, his rival, Freddy Latumahina, a Christian, received support from various segments of the Golkar ruling party. In the same vein, the involvement of groups like Laskar Jihad in the conflict introduced another permutation of the structural overlay, where Jakarta-based networks exerted influence on regional conflicts in Sulawesi and Maluku.[93]

The demise of the New Order also opened the way for a recalibration of loyalties as regional identities – long kept in check by the centripetal forces it generated through Suharto's exercise of power and patronage – returned to the fore. This was evident in various moves to carve out new territories premised on old identities, such as in the case of North Maluku, which overlapped with and was exacerbated by differences between indigene and migrant identities with their respective claims to ownership of the land, not to mention the control over political and commercial activities that transmigrant Muslim communities started to assert. It is apparent from the previous discussion that within these contexts the factor of religion also entered into the fray in rough congruence with the ethnic identities of indigene and migrant communities. Transmigration and competition for resources and political power amplified differences and created in-group and out-group mentalities while also undermining conceptions of identity and belonging in indigenous communities when it challenged traditional understandings of what it meant, for instance, to be Kao in Maluku.

In effect, while conflicts in Sulawesi, Maluku, and North Maluku might have primarily originated as the outcome of resource competition, they all had an underlying emotive dimension which ensured the dueling narratives could be easily reframed in order to take on religious hues

---

[93] Here it is important to register the fact that paramilitary groups like Laskar Jihad and others were also financed by the Indonesian army, at least until Megawati Sukarnoputri came to power.

so as to further tap into these emotions. At the heart of the competition over resources and identity was the question of rights and belonging – contention over who belonged, who owned the land, and what identity defined "ownership."

Subversive Narratives within the Indonesian *Ummah*: The *Ahmadiyah* Question

The assertiveness of mainstream Islamist political actors and vigilante groups that have endeavored to reframe what constitutes the Indonesian nation has had corrosive effects not only for relations with the Christian community. The hegemony of these mainstream conservative and Islamist groups has also impinged on relations among self-professing Muslim groups.

Violence against *Ahmadiyah*, and to a lesser extent *Shi'a*, communities in Indonesia has been well-documented by both the international and local (Indonesian) mainstream media. This has in turn spawned a growing literature on *Ahmadiyah* in Indonesia.[94] However, most, if not all, of this literature approaches these issues from the perspective of either the Indonesian state or mainstream Islamic identity (in terms of theological consistency within the broadly accepted Islamic tradition of thought) in Indonesian society. Concomitantly, analysis has revolved around questions of state policy toward religious minorities (and Islamic sects) and how Indonesia's orthodox Muslim-majority mainstream have responded to the emergence of these religious communities. Significantly less is known about how these communities locate themselves within the larger Indonesian nation-state and the narratives that dominate discourses of nationhood in Indonesia.

While physical and doctrinal attacks on the *Ahmadiyah* minority and their confession by mainstream Indonesian Muslims have been the subject of fairly extensive analysis, the reasons behind them remain a subject of debate. Since the first *Ahmadiyah* missionary was recorded to have visited Sumatra in 1925, the *Ahmadiyah* had co-existed with other Muslim groups for decades until the end of the New Order era, and were

---

[94] For recent studies of this issue, see Ahmad Najib Burhani, "Hating the Ahmaddiya: The Place of 'Heretics' in Contemporary Indonesian Muslim Society," *Contemporary Islam*, Vol. 8, No. 2, 2014; Ahmad Najib Burhani, "Treating Minorities with *Fatwas*: A Study of the Ahmaddiya Community in Indonesia," *Contemporary Islam*, Vol. 8, No. 2, 2014; Jeremy Menchik, *Islam and Democracy in Indonesia: Tolerance without Liberalism*. New York: Cambridge University Press, 2015. Burhani documents how the *Ahmadiyah* went from a tolerated Muslim fringe to a condemned heretical sect, while Menchik explores the limits of religious tolerance among mainstream Indonesian Islamic organizations like the Muhammadiyah and the Nahdlatul Ulama.

relatively unharassed during this time despite being viewed with suspicion by mainstream Muslim groups. In this regard, it is worth noting that though a *fatwa* on the *Ahmadiyah* had been issued by the *Majelis Ulama Indonesia* (MUI or Indonesian Ulama Association) in June 1980 declaring them outside the fold of Islam, it was never implemented and the presence of the *Ahmadiyah* continued to be tolerated, thereby giving them something that approximated recognition.[95] This climate of tolerance changed, however, with the collapse of the New Order regime, when a call for the ban was repeated by MUI through another *fatwa* issued in July 2005, under pressure from mainstream Muslim groups perceiving an increase in *Ahmadiyah* activity.[96] This time, the *fatwa* received vocal support from vigilante groups like *Fron Pembela Islam* (FPI or Islamic Defender's Front) and *Majelis Mujahidin Indonesia* (MMI or Indonesian Mujahidin Council).[97] Quickened by this *fatwa*, FPI militants attacked an *Ahmadiyah* village in Cianjur, West Java, in 2005. The attack was followed shortly by another MUI *fatwa* which reinforced its earlier position that the *Ahmadiyah* was a deviant group. The MUI *fatwa* further emboldened other mainstream Islamic groups, and several coalesced to orchestrate a new round of attacks on the *Ahmadiyah* community as well as those Muslim groups that came to their defense.[98]

Up to that point, in an attempt to brandish liberal and democratic credentials it seemed that President Susilo Bambang Yudhoyono was prepared to demonstrate sympathy for the *Ahmadiyah*. Yet in a bizarre turn of events in which continued violence against the *Ahmadiyah* by Muslim vigilante groups played no small part, President Yudhoyono vacillated and eventually buckled under pressure from vocal segments of Indonesia's conservative religious establishment, and the government eventually issued a joint decree signed by the Minister of Religious Affairs, Minister of Home Affairs, and the Attorney-General that outlawed the *Ahmadiyah*.[99] Even though the decree only explicitly curtailed publicly visible activity on the part of adherents to the *Ahmadiyah* sect and skirted

---

[95] Khoiruddin Nasution, "Fatwa Majelis Ulama Indonesia (MUI): On Ahmadiyah." Available http://journal.uii.ac.id/index.php/Millah/article/viewFile/351/264.

[96] A copy of the *fatwa* that was issued in 2005 is available at: "*Salinan Fatwa MUI Ttg Kesesatan Ahmadiyah*," *NAHIMUNKAR*, April 30, 2008. Available www.nahimunkar.com/salinan-fatwa-mui-ttg-kesesatan-ahmadiyah/.

[97] The two *fatwa*, however, were different in the following sense: whereas the first *fatwa* did not explicitly mention the consequences that should follow from alleging that the *Ahmadiyah* were "deviant," the second *fatwa* cited law no. 1/PNPS/1965 related to desecrating and insulting of Islam to call on Muslims to take firm action on the *Ahmadiyah*, and on the state to immediately ban the movement.

[98] See "Hard-liners Ambush Monas Rally," *Jakarta Post*, June 2, 2008.

[99] See "Indonesia: Reverse Ban on Ahmadiyah Sect," *Human Rights Watch*, June 10, 2008. Available www.hrw.org/news/2008/06/10/indonesia-reverse-ban-ahmadiyah-sect.

the question of whether they were free to practice their faith in private (and hence cannot be interpreted as a ban on private *Ahmadiyah* activity), it nevertheless enjoined the broader Muslim community to report instances of propagation of *Ahmadiyah* belief and paved the way for regional adminstrations to enact their own penal legislation against the *Ahmadiyah*, a move that triggered even more attacks on the latter by mainstream Muslim vigilante groups.

Of interest is the fact that the *Ahmadiyah* response to the doubt surrounding the veracity of their religious identity was couched not in terms of doctrine, theology, or apologetics, but rather in terms of national identity, citizenship, and rights. *Ahmadiyah* leaders evoked the concept of "*Bhinneka Tunggal Ika*" (Unity in Diversity), a principle drawn from Javanese history and which has since been used to articulate the Indonesian state's policy of pluralism, to justify their right to hold the confessional identity that they do. On October 17, 2003, Abdul Basit, the national Amir of the *Ahmadiyah*, met Sidarto Danusubroto, Speaker of the People's Consultative Assembly, to reaffirm that "like other Indonesian citizens, Ahmadis would like to contribute and play an active role in the community in accordance with the *Ahmadiyah* motto of obeying God and obeying the constitution of Indonesia," to which Sidarto responded "(members of) the *Ahmadiyah* community are Indonesian citizens whose rights and obligations are the same as other citizens, and they are also entitled to play an active role in the development of Indonesia. All understanding of the *Ahmadiyah* should be referred to the nation's constitution."[100] Needless to say, melancholic reaffirmation of the *Ahmadiyah*'s place in the Indonesian nation such as that attempted by Abdul Basit above failed to break the impasse or prevent the MUI *fatwa* that followed. Indeed, such voices were quickly drowned out by the chorus of orthodoxy. Nor could it avert further violence against the *Ahmadiyah*, or the government's subsequent move to ban the movement. All this despite the *Ahmadiyah*'s fulminations that the victimization of its followers contravened the principles of *Pancasila*, the Indonesian Constitution, the International Convention of Civil and Political Rights, and the United Nations Declaration of 1981 on the elimination of all forms of intolerance and of discrimination on the basis of religion or belief.[101]

---

[100] See "*Ahmadiyah Ingin Luruskan Kesalahpaham di Ruang Publik.*" Available www.mpr.go.id/berita/read/2013/10/17/12759/ahmadiyah-ingin-luruskan-kesalahpaham-di-ruang-publik.

[101] See "*Komisi Hukum Nasional Republik Indonesia*," www.komisihukum.go.id, January 19, 2013. Available www.komisihukum.go.id/index.php?option=com_content&view=article&id=158:arti-pengesahan-dua-kovenan-ham-bagi-penegakan-hukum&catid=162&Itemid=622.

Nationhood and Narratives

In April 2015, *Warta Ahmadiyah* (*Ahmadiyah News*) published an article entitled *"Ahmadiyah 100% Islam Tidak Sesat dan Menyesatkan"* ("Ahmadiyah: 100% Islam; Not Deviant and Misleading"). The article was based on a presentation by a preacher from *Ahmadiyah* Priangan Timur, H. Muhammad Syeful Uyun, which he delivered during a meeting with officials from the MUI at the organization's Kota Banjar office on March 19, 2015. The article presented the view of the *Ahmadiyah* with regard to their status as members of the (Islamic) nation of Indonesia, and amounts to a stalwart attempt to defend the fringe group's narrative claim to inclusion. Its main elements are worth summarizing here.[102]

The article asserts that the *Ahmadiyah* recognizes Indonesia to be a *"Negara Kebangsaan"* (a state based on nationality), not a state based on religion. Furthermore, it acknowledged that the basis of the state is *Pancasila* and the 1945 Constitution. Indonesia is a nation-state that is built upon pluralism and respects pluralism. Indonesian pluralism is captured in the mantra of *Bhineka Tunggal Ika*. Indonesia is a state that guarantees the freedom of its population to embrace their religion and to worship according to their religion and beliefs (based on Articles 29(1) and (2) of the Constitution). As such, Indonesia should be considered a safe home for all religions, including Islam, Christianity, Catholicism, Hindu, Buddhist, and Confucianism. It should also be welcoming to religious organizations that represent these religions, such as Nahdlatul Ulama, Muhamadiyah, Ahmadiyah, *Shi'a*, Persis, and so on.

According to the *Ahmadiyah* narrative of their identity, they are an Islamic organization no different from Nahdlatul Ulama, Muhammadiyah, or Persis.[103] The *Ahmadiyah* is neither a religion nor a political party. Rather, it is only "a platform for the struggle to revive, uphold, and proclaim the religion of Islam." The *Ahmadiyah* in Indonesia enjoys legal status in accordance to a Ministry of Justice decree (No. JA.5/23/13 dated March 13, 1953, supplement to the Republic of Indonesia official gazette no. 26 of March 31, 1953). What the *Ahmadiyah* interprets this to mean is the *Ahmadiyah* of Indonesia possesses a legal identity and hence has the right to exist within the territories of the Republic of Indonesia.

---

[102] H. Muhammad Syeful Uyun, *"Ahmadiyah 100% Islam Tidak Sesat dan Menyesatkan,"* *Warta Ahmadiyah*, March 24, 2015. Available http://warta-ahmadiyah.org/ahmadiyah-100-islam-tidak-sesat-dan-menyesatkan/.

[103] The point was also made that the movement took on the name *Ahmadiyah* not because the founder's name was Ahmad. The name was taken from the other name of the prophet Muhammad, namely Ahmad. Hence, according to Muhammad Syeful Uyun, the name *Ahmadiyah* was chosen with the intention of encouraging its followers to emulate the character of the Prophet.

Interestingly, the article further moved to document the *Ahmadiyah*'s contribution to Indonesia's revolutionary struggle and independence. The *Ahmadiyah* was, according to Muhammad Syeful Uyun, "an organization that was born before the independence of Indonesia, and together with other components of the nation, it participated in the struggle for independence." Following independence, the *Ahmadiyah* involved itself in "building the nation, specifically in relation to Indonesia's mental and spiritual development." It was further highlighted that the Indonesian national anthem, *Indonesia Raya*, was composed by Wage Rudolf Supratman, an *Ahmadiyah* activist, and was an example of the *Ahmadiyah*'s "contribution to the nation and state of the Republic of Indonesia."[104]

The plight of the *Ahmadiyah* – specifically the denial of recognition of their full rights as a "nation" of Indonesia – is instructive at several levels. In the first instance, it is clearly a matter of confessional differences that have been taken to the extreme by virtue of an assertive majoritarian mindset on the part of the Muslim mainstream as evidenced in attempts to enact punitive legislation, not to mention the intimidation and exertion of pressure from vigilante groups. Yet at issue here is not merely the aggressive assertion of majoritarianism or of theological differences, but, drawing from the earlier discussion of Muslim–Christian relations, "a broader effort by civil society and the state to constitute the nation through belief in God. In that respect, contemporary intolerance of (religious minorities) is merely the most recent manifestation of a long-standing effort to promote godly nationalism while dislodging secular or Islamic alternatives."[105]

The act of declaring movements like the *Ahmadiyah*, or *Shi'a* for that matter, *aliran sesat* (deviant sects) is premised on the view that these movements undermine a fundamental premise of the Indonesian nation, namely that every Indonesian is to declare adherence to one of six official religions *recognized* by the state. By this measure, the Indonesian state's denial of legitimate standing to the *Ahmadiyah* is an extension of the mainstream Muslim community's rejection of claims by the *Ahmadiyah*

---

[104] The article also elaborated on the confessional beliefs of the *Ahmadiyah*, which Muhammad Syeful Uyun maintained was in line with mainstream Islamic belief. This included the existence of only two sources of religious knowledge (the Qur'an and Sunnah of the prophet), the belief that Muhammad was the last of all the prophets, the six pillars of Iman, the five pillars of Islam, that Islam is the final religion of Allah, and that the Qur'an contained the final revelations of Allah. The point was also stressed that Mirza Ghulam Ahmand, the founder of the *Ahmadiyah* movement, was not the "new prophet" and harbinger of "new scripture" that detractors of the *Ahmadiyah* claim.

[105] Jeremy Menchik, "Productive Intolerance: Godly Nationalism in Indonesia," *Comparative Studies in Society and History*, Vol. 56, No. 3, 2014, p. 595.

to be members of the Muslim *ummah*, ergo, Muslims. The crux of the matter is the prerogative that mainstream Islamic groups endorsed and supported by the state exercise in defining what is and what is not "Islam" on the basis of adherence to what they define and impose as the principle teachings of the faith. Conversely, the existence of fringe groups claiming to be part of the *ummah* are deemed to undermine the religious identity of Indonesian Muslims, and the national identity of the nation.

The point of the *Ahmadiyah* plight being one that also encompasses a struggle to claim inclusion in the nation is illustrated –but also obfuscated – in the curious case of how the *Ahmadiyah* declare their religon as "Islam" on their identity cards. Here Daniel Bottomley has found that, unlike others for whom the compulsory act of declaring one's religion is merely a ritual to fulfill what is deemed an administrative requirement regardless of actual belief or practice, for followers of the *Ahmadiyah* it has become an important means through which they assert their identities as Muslims and members of the Indonesian nation, through an act that is in fact legislated by the Indonesian state.[106] In so doing, they become, for all intents and purposes, literally "card-carrying Indonesian Muslims." This tension is captured in the following remarks:

Because the Indonesian government classifies the Ahmadis as deviant Muslims, but offers its deviant citizenry constant reminders of their non-deviance as well as their legally recognized place in the Indonesian nation, we can see underlying tensions in which contradictory edicts designed to perpetuate the Indonesian national identity foster an ambiguous national community.[107]

To this, we can hasten to add that in Indonesia, religious nationalism has been manifested as "an imagined community bound by a common, orthodox theism and mobilized through the state in cooperation with religious organizations in society. As long as citizens believe in one of the state-sanctioned pathways to God, they become full members of civil society and receive state protection and other benefits of citizenship."[108] The conflict between mainstream Islam and the *Ahmadiyah* in Indonesia, then, is about much more than the principles and practice of faith; it speaks to fundamental issues regarding the boundaries of Indonesian nationhood and how it is contested between inclusion in and exclusion from the Indonesian nation on grounds of religious belief.

[106] Daniel C. Bottomley, "The KTP Quandary: Islam, the Ahmadiyya, and the Reproduction of Indonesian Nationalism," *Contemporary Islam*, Vol. 9, No. 1, 2015, pp. 10–12.
[107] Ibid., p. 13. [108] Menchik, "Productive Intolerance," p. 594.

Conclusion

Attention in this chapter has focused on conflicts in eastern Indonesia between Muslim and Christian communities, although they are by no means the only examples of such conflicts, as well as within the community of Muslim believers in Indonesia between mainstream Islamic groups and fringe movements such as the *Ahmadiyah*.[109] What can be surmised from the foregoing analysis is the fact that religion has been and remains a key identity marker of competing constituencies in Indonesia. Because of this, religious allegiances played an important role in sharpening differences in times of crisis, thereby undermining any hitherto religious "harmony" that might have existed in relations between confessional communities. Nils Bubandt aptly describes the effect of this:

> As violence takes shape around religious or ethnic identity, a process known as cascading often occurs: the overproduction and conspicuous consumption of particular markers of identity. Religious cascades thus involve a shift from religiously neutral to religiously charged activities and the adoption by key entrepreneurs of highly emotional symbols of religious identity, which transform the imagined religious differences into visible, social divisions.[110]

Oftentimes, however, the differences between these groups themselves had less to do with matters of faith or creed than they had with questions of the underlying (unresolved) principles of nationhood in terms of who is included or excluded, and on what terms.

In eastern Indonesia, it is apparent that religious conflict was at its essence an expression of anxieties in response to structural strains on the fundamental premises of nation and state. By way of example, the end of the New Order created uncertainties in peoples and communities over their place in the new Indonesia. In the face of these uncertainties, they often fell back on identities as the terms of nationhood viewed through local lenses were reconceptualized and renegotiated through the rebalancing of political power, representation, access, and authority between communities which were predominantly Christian and/or Muslim.

In sum, religious conflict in contemporary Indonesia cannot be understood divorced from the process of democratization that ushered in the end of the New Order era. The opening up of political space has generated pressures on multinational conceptions of the nation in Indonesia. Reflecting on the effects of such pressures at a theoretical level, Michael Walzer noted: "But bring the 'people' into political life and they will

---

[109] There have been numerous cases of attacks on Christian churches not only elsewhere in eastern Indonesia, but even in West Java, such as in Bogor and Bekasi in the period between 2011 and 2013.

[110] Bubandt, "Malukan Apocalypse," p. 237.

arrive, marching in tribal ranks and orders, carrying with them their own languages, historical memories, customs, beliefs, and commitments – their own moral maximalism."[111] Developments in Indonesia since the fall of Suharto have clearly illustrated this.

---

[111] Michael Walzer, *Thick and Thin: Moral Argument At Home and Abroad*. Notre Dame, I.N.: University of Notre Dame Press, 1994, p. 65.

Conclusion

In the conclusion to his 1963 study on religion and nationalism in Southeast Asia, the eminent political scientist Fred R. von der Mehden proposed that: "twentieth-century Southeast Asia is an excellent laboratory in which the relationship of religion to politics can be assessed against changing political and social backgrounds. The past fifty years have seen peoples lacking political, economic, and social cohesion assume nationhood and finally statehood."[1] Forty years later, in a quantitative article published in 2004 that collated data from the Minorities at Risk and State Failure datasets, Jonathan Fox found that since 1980, religious nationalist groups were responsible for more cases of conflict (specifically armed violence) than non-religious nationalist groups.[2] These two observations may seem unrelated, but they provide important points of entry, as well as bookends, for this study as it draws to a conclusion.

In a sense, this book has picked up the Southeast Asian story where von der Mehden left off. It has done so by unpacking several conflicts in Southeast Asia that have commanded widespread popular attention recently, and that appear religious in nature by virtue of the frequent use of religious symbols, metaphors, and narratives to describe them on the part of media, academia, and, most significantly, conflict actors themselves. Rather than treading the beaten path to pinpoint whether or not these conflicts are "religious" in the strict sense of the term, this book has chosen to offer an alternative interpretation of religious conflicts in Southeast Asia. The search for a different approach provoked a series of questions. How do we understand the element of religion in the contemporary intrastate conflicts that have arisen in Southeast Asian societies? Indeed, why have these conflicts even taken on a confessional nature and found religious expression? How should we understand the veracity of their religious contents and claims? These questions are of

---

[1] von der Mehden, *Religion and Nationalism in Southeast Asia*, p. 206.
[2] Jonathan Fox, "The Rise of Religious Nationalism and Conflict: Ethnic Conflict and Revolutionary Wars, 1945–2001," *Journal of Peace Research*, Vol. 41, No. 6, November 2004.

Conclusion

signal importance because of their analytical novelty in the sense that no one else has asked these questions substantively of Southeast Asian intrastate conflicts, certainly not in the context of a comparative study contained in a single volume.

The book has set out the basic premise that religious identity and discourses have been important in the framing of political conflicts in Southeast Asia. Indeed, in all the cases investigated here, conflict actors have themselves often framed their actions in religious terms in one way or another. As one scholar reflected on his research:

> The 'grassroots people' of the Maluku province and Ambon city who took part in the violence and whom I interviewed, namely Christian warriors and Muslim jihadists, were not interested in issues of migration, political ambitions, the market, democratization, decentralization, and the like. While outside observers and religious moderates claim that creed was a camouflage for greed, the 'foot soldiers,' the masses engaged in the warfare, declared that political and economic issues were actually just a mask for the true religious goals of the strife.[3]

Reflexive responses on the part of such conflict actors certainly give pause. Care should be taken that such views are not willy-nilly dismissed as bluster but instead engaged analytically. The fact of the matter is that ideas, narratives, and mythologies do matter: be they related to mythopoeic Bangsamoro unity, the immutability of Patani Muslim identity, contrived Malay-Muslim supremacy, or the existential challenges posed by *Kristenisasi* or, for that matter, from minorities within the (Muslim) faith. Mindful that the fervor and zeal of religious "warriors" cannot and should not be brushed aside since religion obviously matters in religious conflicts, it nevertheless behooves us to throw new light on the questions of precisely why, how, and to what end religion matters.

If media reports and political statements are any indication, on the face of it religious conflicts in Southeast Asia are nothing short of the incendiary acts of extremist religious groups waged against each other, or the wholesale rejection of modernity by such groups. These perspectives are ventriloquized in keynote speeches and populist literature, where elegant explanations are predicated on clichés and catch-phrases such as "anti-modernity," "cosmic wars," "clash of civilizations," and "inter-religious conflicts." But such explanations (rather, statements) do little more than obscure and caricature what are very complex issues. More to the point, they are conceptually vacuous, epistemologically unsound, and oftentimes empirically erroneous. This is because they confuse (and conflate) the issue of how religious conflicts have materialized with the

---

[3] Sumanto Al Qurtuby, "Christianity and Militancy in Eastern Indonesia: Revisiting the Maluku Violence," *Southeast Asian Studies*, Vol. 4, No. 2, August 2015, p. 319.

more important and pertinent question of why religion matters in the context of these conflicts. In other words, their argument is based on circular logic, and their conclusion is a logical fallacy – they infer that drivers of religious conflicts must be religious because the conflicts themselves take on religious forms. As this study has argued, on closer inspection the case can be made that while religious differences can either cause or exacerbate some conflicts in Southeast Asia, it is oftentimes not what the conflicts are fundamentally about.

A detailed look at how actors use histories and narratives to frame conflicts has gone some length toward showing that these religious conflicts are, at a deeper level, a result of competing conceptions of nationhood rather than the "cosmic wars" or "clash of civilizations" they are often made out to be. This argument proceeds from the observation that many conflicts in Southeast Asia have taken on religious hues because of how strong identities, nationalist discourses, and conceptions of nationhood have evolved. The crucial point is that discourses and narratives of nationalism draw on religious motifs, symbols, and histories to demonstrate cultural authenticity, reinforce social solidarity, sanction political views, and mobilize populations.

Moreover, because religion is a key component of individual and collective identity, it stands to reason that religion therefore plays an important role in providing a framework for interpreting political events and a normative language for articulating moral purpose. The use of religious narratives in fact speaks to broader concerns that relate not so much to confessional beliefs or doctrine, but to questions of identity, nationhood, legitimacy, and belonging. Extrapolating from this, the chapters in this present study have shown in considerable detail how conflict occurs when religiously defined conceptions of nationhood clash. It is by way of this observation that this book considers the process of national identity and consciousness framing and construction fundamental to understanding the religious character of some political conflicts and contestations in the region.

Religion, Nationalism, Modernity

In his work assessing the emergence of religious nationalism during the maelstrom of the Cold War and decolonization, von der Mehden provided valuable analysis as to why religiously oriented nationalists were essentially eclipsed by Marxists and secular nationalists in the rivalry to obtain paramount positions in national politics. Deliberately or otherwise, in making the observation that religious nationalists failed to gain traction during the decolonization process, his argument made common epistemological cause with those who have pressed the decoupling of religious identity and national identity in the liberal West against the onslaught of a radically secularizing world. Yet the notion that religion is somehow "out of sync" with the development of a modern society in the face of industrialization, science, and technology and hence can be tossed unto the proverbial scrapheap of history betrays a tendency in Western scholarship to take a teleological view of religion's decline in the shadow of secularism's ascendance, a phenomenon which in European history found its ultimate expression in the creation of the modern nation-state that replaced the church. But, as our conceptual framework has maintained, religion is not merely a matter of faith; it is pregnant with social and political meaning; and inasmuch as this is the case, it follows that religion does not exist in a vacuum, and is not devoid of context. If one bears this in mind, the situation in Southeast Asia, as we have seen, throws up a completely different, far more complex picture.

In Southeast Asia, religion shares a complicated and intricate conceptual relationship with the nation. Confessional faith has played a considerable – indeed, vital – and dynamic role in the process of the imagination and construction of the nation, as well as in motivating conflict that results from competing conceptions of nationhood. The basis of this has been the consequential role of religion in the cultural and historical narratives through which identity is interpreted and mobilized. That religion has proven imperative in the forming and sustaining of the nation through its shaping of national identity, often serving as a bedrock for nation building, is evident in the cases of Thai, Malaysian, and Indonesian "official" nationalism, with the Philippines being a possible exception.[4] At the same time, however, confessional identities can also emerge to challenge and undermine "the nation" as defined by the post-independence state. This has been shown in how intrastate conflicts framed in religious language have played out, and the strains they have created, in all four cases. Intriguingly, the logic can even work at cross-purposes for minority communities depending on context and circumstance – juxtapose, for example, the inconvenience of necessary loyalty to the Thai flag for the Malay-Muslim residing in Thailand's southern

---

[4] The Philippine case is more ambivalent because of how the Catholic clergy was in fact associated with Spanish colonial power and hence became a target of nationalist sentiments, giving rise to anticlericalism rather than outright opposition to religion per se. Having said that, in the post-independence era the Catholic Church quickly began to serve as an important political institution that was used by the state to legitimize its consolidation of the Philippine nation. Indeed, it is the latter phenomenon, among other things, that set relations between the Philippine state and the Moro populations of Mindanao on a collision course.

province with the convenience of Indonesian citizenship for a member of the *Ahmadiyah* in Indonesia.

The manner in which confessional identity negotiates, competes with, and coheres to conceptions of nationhood in the modernist (and modernizing) project of imagining the nation within the territorial state documented in the preceding chapters points to the fact that religion is hardly the antithesis of modernity that secularist scholars would make it out to be. Instead, non-Western societies such as those in Southeast Asia have melded their cultural cores (ergo, religious identities) with Western modernity in the process of imagining identity as a nation.[5] Nor should it be inferred that by adapting, these societies have arrived at "the end of history" any more than Western societies themselves. Far from it, for religious nationalism can be as divisive as modernity itself. But the more important point to stress is that religious conflict is not a visceral primordial reaction to modernity. Rather, it is the very outcome of the process of adaptation, where attempts to conceive of and reconcile nationhood and statehood are defined, negotiated, and contested in the language of religion and with religiously defined conceptions of identity as the referent.

There is a further logic to take cognizance of regarding the role of religion in informing national consciousness. Even if von der Mehden was right five decades ago that religious nationalism could not obtain in its early efforts to define or appropriate the "official" narrative of nationalism at the point of independence, it is arguable if its influence has since diminished. On the contrary, it appears to have endured, and manifests itself in how it has given substance to majoritarian national identities on one hand, as in the case of Malay-Muslim assertiveness in Malaysia and Muslim political consciousness in Indonesia, and on the other, reinforced minority identities, as in the case of the Bangsamoro and Malay struggles in the Philippines and Thailand.

Competing Conceptions of Nationhood and Legitimacy

While Benedict Anderson may be right when he observed that in Southeast Asia, the model of official nationalism assumes its relevance above all at the moment when revolutionaries successfully take control of the state, and are for the first time in a position to use the power of the state in pursuit of their nationalist visions, yet there is also every possibility that competing visions among outlier communities located on the peripheries

---

[5] Partha Chatterjee, *The Politics of the Governed: Reflections on Popular Politics in Most of the World*. New York: Columbia University Press, 2004.

of the imagined community exist, that do not conform to the characteristics of these established models of nationhood that have facilitated entry into membership in international society, and that have become entangled in this incomplete process of nation and state building.[6] Herein lies further significance of religious nationalism to our understanding of religious conflicts in Southeast Asia. If religion is instrumental to how the identity of a nation is conceived, then it can be argued that a conflict waged in the name of religion – whether in the form of physical violence, detention, denial of constitutional or citizenship rights, marginalization, or discrimination – can be understood as an expression of "othering," a process by which notions of inclusion and exclusion define how the parameters of the nation are conceptualized.

The previous point is a particularly poignant one given how religion is often inextricably linked to other identity signifiers (e.g., other aspects of ethnicity) and plays an important role in the construction and collective mobilization of these identities, where the symbolic building blocks of confessional faith allow religious communities to reinforce their identity through conflict with the "out" group.[7] Something of this was expressed in how religious metaphors and language were used to reinforce "in" and "out" group identities in Sulawesi and Maluku as indigenous Christian communities perceived their identity and status as rightful occupants of their lands to be under threat from Muslim migrants. Indeed, all manner of religious invocations were mobilized in the conflicts that ensued as both parties staked their claim against the backdrop of an uncertain environment created by the collapse of the New Order.

Competing identities aside, the process of self-identification and self-understanding inherent in the construction of national identity has also evolved to reflect changing notions of legitimacy as an outcome of the process through which nationhood is conceived. Let us return for a moment to the discussion of Malaysia, where the task of constructing national identity has proven to be onerous despite the fact that tensions between competing conceptions of nationhood have yet to break out into open hostilities (unlike the other examples covered in this book). In Malaysia, the fundamental premise of state (political parties aligned along ethnic

[6] Anderson, *Imagined Communities*, p. 159.
[7] In the study of nationalism, religion is often depicted as possessing currency because of how it overlaps with ethnicity. This overlap can take three forms: religion can be subsumed in ethnicity in how religious labels and identity become signifiers for ethnic groups, it can have additive effects in how distinction and group solidarity of both markers reinforce each other, or it can be interactive when dynamic and emergent properties collaborate to create a complex relationship. See Joseph Ruane and Jennifer Todd, "Ethnicity and Religion: Redefining the Research Agenda," *Ethnopolitics*, Vol. 9, No. 1, 2010.

lines such that identity differences are actually formally institutionalized and perpetuated) and society (policies of ethnic compartmentalization going as far back as the colonial era) renders the task almost insurmountable given how legitimacy is built on the blatant assertion of a majoritarian identity to the point of outright marginalization and discrimination. Indeed, these obstacles have led a prominent scholar of Malaysia to the conclusion that the country cannot claim with any confidence to be in possession of a "national identity."[8] This is despite the fact that public discourse is replete with celebratory salutes to Malaysian multiculturalism in the form of slogans such as *Bangsa Malaysia* (Malaysian nation) and "1 Malaysia."

An added element that further complicates the already complex exercise of national identity formation in Malaysia is the fusion of ethnic and religious identity that has deepened over the past two decades in a country where ethnic boundaries are already heavily politicized, and where the dominant Malay community continues to grapple with the bipolar paradox of a sense of supremacy born of a presumed right to claims of dominance on one hand and an acute (if somewhat misguided) perception of vulnerability and insecurity on the other. The challenge that this poses has been compounded by the existence of a monological, as opposed to dialogical, ideal of nationhood which increasingly denies the claims of those who are not members of the Malay-Muslim nation to equal status within the Malaysian state. Although not as explicit or as "official," a somewhat similar script is playing out in Thailand, where the terminology of "*Khaek*" continues to be used by Thais to refer to Malay-Muslims from the southern provinces, and in Indonesia, where the place (and rights) of followers of the Muslim *Ahmadiyah* sect as members of the Indonesian nation are being contested on grounds of their "unorthodox" understandings of the faith.

In essence, then, religious nationalists have recognized the value of religious identity and history and seek to harness their emotive power on the basis that their conception of nationhood needs to be defended and perpetuated. This, however, should not be mistaken for mere instrumentalism or opportunism on their part, for the emotive power upon which rests the mobilizing potential of religious nationalism was not conjured by them, but rather exists as the collective memory of the people. The instrumentalist logic turns on the Benthamite view that suggests decisions are taken in a disparate manner based on a disembodied utilitarian calculus. Yet decisions made in this manner still have to make sense, and for the common people – for the collective nation, as it were – this sense

---

[8] Edmund Terence Gomez, "Introduction," in Edmund Terence Gomez (ed.), *Politics in Malaysia: The Malay Dimension*. New York: Routledge, 2007, p. 3.

is found precisely in its narratives that are superimposed on historical events to give depth and meaning to their reality. And because narratives are socially constructed and marginally bound by fact, the mythopoeic faculty of nationalists allows them to make vertiginous leaps in order to create, sustain, and reshape the sense of self and others (thereby creating the "othering" effect mentioned earlier). That is why nationalists and political leaders invest much attention and energy to constantly invent and reinvent the past even as they frame (and reframe) the future in order to accomplish their manifest destiny.

To be sure, this is not to suggest that elements of opportunism and "politics by any means" were absent in how narratives were constructed to facilitate mobilization. As Gerry van Klinken observed in his authoritative study of conflict in Poso:

> The reason why this conflict kept on expanding as a religious war was not because farmers in Poso were more preoccupied with their religious identities than their material needs for land, but because armed conflict requires organization and brokers. The religions on both sides of the war were simply better organized, with better connections in the corridors of power, than land-hungry subsistence peasants.[9]

Nevertheless, the mere existence of such intent to play the politics of opportunity is insufficient as an explanation of the appeal and mobilizing potential of a narrative. This is because it matters to what or to whom, and for what reason, people in a polity give their allegiance. Indeed, it is precisely because there is substance, intelligibility, and meaning in how religious identity is conceived, and the recollection of grievances this process provokes, that makes its narrative an appealing mobilizing vehicle which politicians and nationalists can draw on. To that end, it is precisely because of the role that religion plays and what it invokes in the collective memories of post-colonial societies that it is used as an idiom of nationhood through narratives that access these wellsprings of identity and difference.

Narratives, Contexts, and Contingencies

It bears repeating that in Southeast Asia, religiously inspired and referenced narratives that frame conceptions of nationhood have taken various forms. Some are part of "national" histories sanctioned by the state, while others express "subaltern" histories. Some are articulated explicitly, while others implicitly. Narratives have changed and been reframed, whether to legitimize resistance or discredit it. But they all point to one thing – the

---

[9] van Klinken, *Communal Violence and Democratization in Indonesia*, p. 140.

use of religion in the narrative itself to trigger collective memory and experiences. Likewise, the narratives are also contextualized and mobilized toward different ends. In both Mindanao and the southern provinces of Thailand, contrary to the unfounded speculations of alarmist pundits, what is being liberated by the Bangsamoro and Malay nationalist is not some vague transnational caliphate but a historical territorially and culturally bounded entity, imagined or otherwise. Furthermore, the reason for the move to liberate these kingdoms lies in the perceived illegitimacy of the central state, measured by their inability or reluctance to accept the Bangsamoro and the Malay-Muslims as separate nations within the territorial state, and by their treatment as inferior members of the respective politico-social entities. Put differently, conflict has been a response to the struggle or reluctance of "official" Thai and Philippine nationalism to accommodate local conceptions of nationhood, or even to countenance a "nation without [a] state."

In Mindanao, religious discourse has been used to frame grievances over land loss and marginalization. Yet at the same time, references to confessional faith and creed have also been reframed by the leadership of the MILF to rationalize and explain the decision to bring hostilities against the Philippine state to an end despite falling short of the objective of the creation of an Islamic state in the dogmatic sense of the term, an objective for which a Moro *jihad* was purportedly waged for decades, if not longer. An analogous phenomenon, albeit within a different context and with its own twist, can be discerned in the Malay-Muslim narratives that frame conflict in Thailand's southern provinces. According to these narratives, conflict with the Thai state flows from historical narratives of conquest and subjugation at the hands of a hegemonic central state portrayed as a Buddhist colonial power, and resistance has essentially been framed with reference to cultural identity and ethnic distinctiveness which religion serves to amplify. It appears, then, that the struggle is cut from the same cloth of anti-colonial resistance movements prevalent during the Cold War, only this time it is using religion as an idiom of nationhood.

At any rate, because religious identity – specifically, Islamic identity in both Mindanao and southern Thailand – weighs so heavily in their histories as well as the ethnic and cultural self-conceptions and collective memories of the respective communities, it should hardly be surprising to find that religion has been employed to animate historical narratives. Yet equally evident is the fact that, despite the universalistic appeal of the Islamic faith, in Mindanao and the southern Thai provinces the scope of religious conflict has been decidedly limited, and remarkably parochial in the latter case. Not only that, but also the fact that there are at times also degrees of variation within the collective's own narratives of religious nationalism further indicates that the phenomenon itself is far more complex than simple recourse to piety. In other words, Bangsamoro and Patani mythopoeia belies the absence of a singular Bangsamoro or Malay-Muslim narrative.

The preceding point highlights the reality that the construction of identity along religious lines is also contested within the in-group, as is evident in the dissonances within the religious nationalist movements and narratives discussed in the preceding chapters. Heretofore, nationalists will claim to speak for the communities they represent, and oftentimes present the identities and narratives that frame them as coherent and consistent.[10] In truth, the situation is often far more ambiguous, and even resistance frames may be – and oftentimes are – contested from several quarters within the communities they purport to represent. The point to stress here, again, is the interactive and transactional nature of conceptions of nationhood, where this dynamic and contingent feature of religion belies modernist attempts to dismiss its purported antediluvian and primordial nature.

Contextualization can be observed in the other two cases in Malaysia and Indonesia, albeit expressed in different forms. In Indonesia with regard to the dynamics between *Islamisasi* and *Kristenisasi*, resistance was triggered by the perception that indigenous rights of a Muslim-dominant society were being undermined with the conjunction of interests between the New Order state its Christian (and nominal Muslim) allies up to the late 1980s, whereas political transition was seen to offer up opportunities to rectify this imbalance, indeed to renegotiate the place of religion in Indonesian conceptions of nationhood in terms of its primacy. In Malaysia, on the other hand, Malay-Islamic nationalists have essentially commandeered the instruments of the state and seek to use it as a vehicle to impose their conception of nationhood and legitimacy onto (non-Malay-Muslim) minorities on grounds that Malay-Muslim dominance is the cornerstone of the Malaysian nation and state. In both instances, majoritarian Muslim impulses to renegotiate and recast the fundamental premises of nationhood have in turn prompted counter-mobilization in defense of minority rights as equal citizens and members of the nation, amplifying tensions in the process.[11]

---

[10] To be sure, this tendency is not merely limited to nationalists and politicians. Scholars, too, have a propensity toward generalization.
[11] Non-Muslim rejection of the legitimacy of this state-sanctioned discourse and practice of Islamization was expressed most devastatingly in the exodus of their support for the ruling coalition at the general elections of 2008 and 2013.

So What Does It All Mean?

Southeast Asia provides fertile analytical ground for this investigation into how nations and nationalism have reflected some degree or other of a religious character, giving rise to intrastate conflict.[12] The region contains a rich sample of cases where religious identity has shaped – and continues to shape – conceptions of nationhood, giving rise to conflicts in the process. In many Southeast Asian states, centrifugal forces generated by minority groups that challenge the creation of a unitary nation-state and that press for a variety of forms of self-determination have often found expression in religious vocabulary. On another level, we also witness how, in the course of centralized state-building projects on the part of nationalists who have inherited the colonial state, conceptions of nation have also found reference in religion. In both instances, a major political differentiation has taken place along religious lines.

Yet at the same time, it is argued that what is frequently mistaken for religious conflicts is oftentimes more deeply embedded in identity contestations, many of which involve ethnicity and religion as a marker. This is possible because of how religion has been woven into the fabric of identity and society in Southeast Asian history. For instance, religious identity remains a signifier of ethnicity in Southeast Asian societies and vice-versa, and narratives of ethno-religious identity continue to weigh heavily on attempts to imagine into creation national identities that cohere with the territorial boundaries of the post-colonial state.[13] At its most rudimentary, then, religion appears to amplify the appeal of ethnic nationalism, and to serve as a subtype of the main concept (ethnicity). Morgan Oddie sheds further light on this with the following observation regarding the construction and instrumentalization of religious identity: "Religion often plays a crucial role in ethnic definition, as many of the quarrelling nationalist groups are too similar in ethno-linguistic features to be separated by criteria other than religious affiliation. Religion is thereby utilized in a secondary function as a cultural characterization, rather than a purely spiritual alignment and religious community."[14]

---

[12] von der Mehden, *Religion and Nationalism in Southeast Asia*; Brown, *The State and Ethnic Politics in Southeast Asia*; Terence Chong, "Nationalism in Southeast Asia: Revisiting Kahin, Roff, and Anderson," *Sojourn: Journal of Social Issues in Southeast Asia*, Vol. 24, No. 1, April 2009, pp. 1–17.

[13] For a theoretical discussion on the nexus between religion and ethnicity, see William Safran, "Language, Ethnicity, and Religion: A Complex and Persistent Linkage," *Nations and Nationalism*, Vol. 14, No. 1, 2008; Ruane and Todd, "Ethnicity and Religion."

[14] Morgan Oddie, "The Relationship of Religion and Ethnic Nationalism in Bosnia-Herzegovina," *Religion in Eastern Europe*, Vol. XXXII, No. 1, February 2012, p. 34.

Having said that, there are also instances where religion binds people of different ethnicities. So while there is a potential link and overlap, both religion and ethnicity are also conceptually distinct categories. It would be useful, to that end, to dwell for a moment on the link between ethnicity and religion in conceptions of national identity in Southeast Asia.

Modernist theories of the nation contend that post-colonial states strive to construct a shared sense of citizenship and national identity among their disparate, and at times fractured, populations. In many Southeast Asian states, though, such identity construction is wrought with contradictions, if not heavily contested. Not only is this evident in the large number of minority separatist and secessionist groups that emerged in the process of nation and state building in the post-independence era, some still active today, but these contradictions are also evident in the narratives of "official nationalism," of which some, as in the case of Malaysia and Thailand for example, are decidedly prejudiced in favor of one particular ethnic and religious group, to the extent of promoting cultural and religious chauvinism.

Religion further resonates in the discourse of ethno-religious master frames because of how it accentuates identity and marginalization. Indeed, these emerge as recurrent themes in all self-reflections of self-determination movements. Like religious nationalism, ethno-religious master frames also privilege the construction and mobilization of primordialist accounts which are then passed on as popular "immutable truths." We have already witnessed how religious identity frames are often given to dogmatic and atavistic narratives that reinforce the perception of deep attachments, for which the claim of immutable ethnic affiliation has proven deeper than most, precisely because of its paradoxical tendency toward ascription. The same can be said of narratives of ethnic identity. As Horowitz avers: "The putatively ascriptive character of ethnic identifications imparts to ethnic conflicts its intense and permeative qualities. It also accounts for some special difficulties ethnic conflicts pose for democratic politics. And ascription is what makes interethnic compromise so difficult in divided societies, for those who practice compromise may be treated with the bitter contempt reserved for brothers who betray a cause."[15] This view is further accented by Tarrow, who notes that the deep attachments they inspire are "almost certainly why nationalism and ethnicity or religion have been more reliable bases of movement organization."[16]

---

[15] Donald L. Horowitz, *Ethnic Groups in Conflict*, 2nd edition. Berkeley, CA.: University of California Press, 2000, pp. 53–54.
[16] Tarrow, *Power in Movement*, p. 6.

By focusing on the emotional and instinctive pull of ethnic and religious identity, often cast as indigenous people frames, movements construct and draw on the emotive powers that flow from the in-group notion that members of a nation are united by a shared faith.[17] For this reason, Brubaker and Laitin have observed how ethnic identity has often become the default referent for political conflict: "Even without direct positive incentives to frame conflicts in ethnic terms (there has been) a marked ethnicisation of violent challenger-incumbent contests as the major non-ethnic framing for such contests has become less plausible and less profitable."[18] Because ethnic and religious identities illuminate and set priorities, it augurs that while ethnicity and religion may not always be the source of violent conflict, these conflicts nevertheless tend to be "ethnicized" or "sacrilized" and framed in such terms.

In addition, Brubakar and Laitin further note that the increasing significance of diasporic social formations and the growing number of international and non-governmental organizations have meant that support for such claims has increased (consider, as an example, the role of the Organization of Islamic Conferences in sympathizing with and supporting the struggles of Muslim minorities in the Philippines, Thailand, and Myanmar, as well as that of international Evangelical Christian networks in the case of the challenges confronting co-religionists in Malaysia and Indonesia), and this sometimes provides a further incentive for groups to frame conflicts in such terms.[19]

Much like their ethnicity-based cousins, religiously defined self-determination movements also often construct frames of marginalization on the grounds of discrimination, especially in the case of minority religious communities. Together, their narratives argue that communities are denied political representation in national affairs, a local voice in local governance, and a share of economic wealth on the ground of their ethnic and/or religious identity. The significance and implications of this reside on two levels. First, there is a material alienation, whereby minorities are denied access to political and economic goods. Second, there is also the matter of an ideational alienation. This pertains to the hegemony of a state-defined discourse and the rejection of alternative and contrarian discourses premised on cultural history (or even a different interpretation of "national history"). Needless to say, this proposition

---

[17] In this sense, ethnic and "indigenous people" frames are underlined by the belief in primordial identities. For a study of this and other aspects of ethnic conflict, see Horowitz, *Ethnic Groups in Conflict*.

[18] Rogers Brubaker and David Laitin, "Ethnic and Nationalist Violence," *Annual Review of Sociology*. Vol. 24, 1998, p. 425.

[19] Ibid.

presupposes the presence of a prevailing and dominant national narrative – official nationalism(s) – that serves as a diligent reminder of the existence of core–periphery dynamics which attempt to forcefully draw minority identities into the ambit of the state (core) that on its part denies the existence and validity of any alternative local and subaltern narrative. In that sense, counter-narratives, mostly referenced to ethnicity, religion, and ethno-religious histories, challenge and undermine the legitimacy of the central state and in so doing compel the latter to respond, leading to conflict and contestation over meaning and authenticity.

In different but cognate ways across the Philippines, Thailand, Indonesia, and Malaysia, religion has provided an appealing vocabulary for understanding and articulating difference. It has informed conceptions of nationhood that enabled self-identification that segments the political realm to include some and exclude others that lie outside the collective identity schema of the "nation" as viewed from the center. In turn, the consequent religious conflicts that these processes have spawned, conditioned by history and circumstance, have been part of the wider, complex context of nation building and nationalism, and need to be understood as such. Imbued with a religious content and meaning that have tendentiously informed majoritarian ethos and minority identities, nationalism has served to divide as much as unite the societies of Southeast Asia.

Bibliography

Abinales, Patricio N. *Making Mindanao: Cotabato and Davao in the Formation of the Philippine Nation-State*. Manila: Ateneo de Manila University Press, 2000.

———. *Orthodoxy and History in the Muslim-Mindanao Narrative*. Manila: Ateneo de Manila University Press, 2010.

Ackerman, Susan E., and Raymond L. M. Lee. *Heaven in Transition: Non-Muslim Religious Innovation and Ethnic Identity in Malaysia*. Honolulu, HI: University of Hawaii Press, 1988.

Agung, Ide Anak Agung Gde. *Dari Negara Indonesia Timur ke Republik Indonesia Sarikat*. Jakarta: Gadjah Mada Press, 1985.

Ahmad, Razak. "Open Letter by 25 Sparks Debate." *The Star*, December 17, 2014.

"Ahmadiyah Ingin Luruskan Kesalahpaham di Ruang Publik." *Majelis Permusyawaratan Rakyat Republik Indonesia*, October 17, 2013. www.mpr.go.id/berita/read/2013/10/17/12759/ahmadiyah-ingin-luruskan-kesalahpaham-di-ruang-publik.

Al Qurtuby, Sumanto. "Christianity and Militancy in Eastern Indonesia: Revisiting the Maluku Violence." *Southeast Asian Studies* 4, No. 2 (August 2015): 313–339.

———. *Religious Violence and Conciliation in Indonesia: Christians and Muslims in the Moluccas*. London: Routledge, 2016.

Alagappa, Muthiah. "The Bases of Legitimacy." In *Political Legitimacy in Southeast Asia: The Quest for Moral Authority*, edited by Muthiah Alagappa, 39–41. Stanford, CA.: Stanford University Press, 1995.

Alhadar, Smith. "The Forgotten War in North Maluku." *Inside Indonesia* 63 (2000): 15–16.

Anbalagan, V. "Ban on Allah in Herald a Matter of National Security, Says A-G." *The Malaysian Insider*, November 19, 2014. www.themalaysianinsider.com/malaysia/article/ban-on-allah-in-herald-a-matter-of-national-security-says-a-g.

Anderson, Benedict. *Imagined Communities: Reflections on the Origin and Spread of Nationalism*. 3rd ed. London: Verso Books, 2006.

———. *The Spectre of Comparisons: Nationalism, Southeast Asia, and the World*. London: Verso, 1998.

Andre, Virginie. "From Colonialist to Infidel: Framing the Enemy in Southern Thailand's 'Cosmic War'." In *Culture, Religion and Conflict in Muslim*

Bibliography

Southeast Asia: Negotiating Tense Pluralisms, edited by Joseph Camilleri and Sven Schottmann, 109–125. London: Routledge, 2013.

Aphornsuvan, Thanet. Origins of Malay Muslim "Separatism" in Southern Thailand. Asia Research Institute Working Paper Series No.32. Singapore: National University of Singapore, 2004.

——. *Rebellion in Southern Thailand Contending Histories*. Washington, D.C.: East-West Center, 2007.

Appleby, Scott. *The Ambivalence of the Sacred: Religion, Violence, and Reconciliation*. New York: Rowman & Littlefield, 2000.

Aragon, Lorraine V. "Communal Violence in Poso: Where People Eat Fish and Fish Eat People." *Indonesia* 72 (2001): 45–79.

——. *Fields of the Lord: Animism, Christian Minorities, and State Development in Indonesia*. Honolulu, HI: University of Hawai'i Press, 2000.

——. "Reconsidering Displacement and Internally Displaced Persons from Poso." In *Conflict, Violence, and Displacement in Indonesia*, edited by Eva-Lotta E. Hedman, 173–205. Ithaca, N.Y.: Cornell University Southeast Asia Program Publications, 2008.

——. "Relatives and Rivals in Central Sulawesi: Grounded Protestants, Mobile Muslims, and the Labile State." In *Christianity in Indonesia: Perspectives of Power*, edited by Susanne Schröter, 259–290. Berlin: Lit Verlag, 2010.

Arifianto, Alexander R. "Explaining the Cause of Muslim-Christian Conflicts in Indonesia: Tracing the Origins of Kristenisasi and Islamisasi." *Islam and Christian–Muslim Relations* 20, no.1 (2009): 73–89.

Aritonang, Jan Sihar and Kareel Steenbrink. "The Ecumenical Movement." In *A History of Christianity in Indonesia*, edited by Jan Sihar Aritonang and Kareel Steenbrink, 852–853. Leiden: Brill, 2008.

Armstrong, John A. *Nations Before Nationalism*. Chapel Hill, N.C.: University of North Carolina Press, 1982.

——. "Religious Nationalism and Collective Violence." *Nations and Nationalism* 3, no.4 (1997): 597–606.

Asad, Talal. *Genealogies of Religion: Discipline and Reasons of Power in Christianity and Islam*. Baltimore, MD.: Johns Hopkins University Press, 1993.

Asani, Abdulrasad. "The Case of the Bangsa Moro People." In *Philippines Repression & Resistance: Permanent Peoples' Tribunal Session on the Philippines*. Ultrecht: Komite ng Sambayanang Pilipino, 1980.

As I See It Blog. http://helpvictor.blogspot.com/2011/10/christian-proselytization.html (2011).

Atran, Scott. *In Gods We Trust: The Evolutionary Landscape of Religion*. New York: Oxford University Press, 2002.

Avalos, Hector. *Fighting Words: The Origins of Religious Violence*. Amherst, N.Y.: Prometheus Books, 2005.

Bangsa Moro Blog. https://bangsamoro.wordpress.com/category/mnlf-milf/page/2/.

Barnard, Frederick M. "National Culture and Political Legitimacy: Herder and Rousseau." *Journal of the History of Ideas* 44, no.2 (1983): 231–253.

Barnard, Timothy, ed. *Contesting Malayness: Malay Identity Across Boundaries*. Singapore: National University of Singapore Press, 2004.

234 Bibliography

Béland, Daniel and André Lecours. "Sub-State Nationalism and the Welfare State: Québec and Canadian Federalism." *Nations and Nationalism* 12, no.1 (2006): 77–96.

Bendix, Reinhard. *Kings or People: Power and the Mandate to Rule*. Berkeley, CA.: University of California Press, 1978.

Benford, Robert D. and David A. Snow. "Framing Processes and Social Movements: An Overview and Assessment." *Annual Review of Sociology* 26 (2000): 611–639.

Berger, Peter, ed. *The Desecularization of the World: Resurgent Religion and World Politics*. Grand Rapids, MI.: Wm. B. Eerdmans Publishing, 1999.

Bertrand, Jacques. "Legacies of the Authoritarian Past: Religious Violence in Indonesia's Moluccan Islands." *Pacific Affairs* 75, no.1 (2002): 57–85.

"'Indigenous Peoples' Rights as a Strategy of Ethnic Accommodation: Contrasting Experiences of Cordillerans and Papuans in the Philippines and Indonesia." *Ethnic and Racial Studies* 34, no.5 (2011): 850–869.

Bertrand, Jacques and André Laliberté, eds. *Multination States in Asia: Accommodation or Resistance*. Cambridge: Cambridge University Press, 2010.

Boland, B.J. *The Struggle of Islam in Modern Indonesia*. Leiden: Martinus Nijhoff, 1982.

Borancing, Manaros, Federico Magdalena, and Luiz Lacar. *The Madrasah Institution in the Philippines: Historical and Cultural Perspectives*. Iligan City: Toyota Foundation, 1987.

Bottomley, Daniel C. "The KTP Quandary: Islam, the Ahmadiyya, and the Reproduction of Indonesian Nationalism." *Contemporary Islam: Dynamics of Muslim Life* 9, no.1 (2015): 1–16.

Brass, Paul R. *Language, Religion and Politics in North India*. New York: Cambridge University Press, 1974.

Brazal, Agnes. "Beyond the Religious and Social Divide: The Emerging Mindanawon Identity." *Chakana: Intercultural Forum of Theology and Philosophy* 2, no.3 (2004): 7–26.

Breuilly, John. *Nationalism and the State*. Chicago, IL.: University of Chicago Press, 1994.

Brinkley, Joel. "Islamic Terror: Decentralized, Franchised, Global." *World Affairs* 176, no.2 (2013): 43–44.

Brown, David. *The State and Ethnic Politics in Southeast Asia*. London: Routledge, 1997.

Brubaker, Rogers. *Citizenship and Nationhood in France and Germany*. Cambridge, MA.: Harvard University Press, 1992.

"Religion and Nationalism: Four Approaches." *Nations and Nationalism* 18, no.1 (2012): 2–20.

Brubaker, Rogers and David Laitin. "Ethnic and Nationalist Violence." *Annual Review of Sociology* 24 (1998): 423–452.

Bubandt, Nils. "Malukan Apocalypse: Themes in the Dynamics of Violence in Eastern Indonesia." In *Violence in Indonesia*, edited by Ingrid Wessel and Georgia Wimhöfer, 243–246. Hamburg: Abera-Verlag, 2001.

Buehler, Michael. "The Rise of Shari'a By-Laws in Indonesian Districts: An Indication for Changing Patterns of Power Accumulation and Political Corruption." *South East Asia Research* 16, no.2 (2008): 255–285.

Burhani, Ahmad Najib. "Hating the Ahmaddiya: The Place of 'Heretics' in Contemporary Indonesian Muslim Society." *Contemporary Islam* 8, no.2 (2014): 133–152.

"Treating Minorities with Fatwas: A Study of the Ahmaddiya Community in Indonesia." *Contemporary Islam* 8, no. 2 (2014): 285–301.

Bush, Robin. "Regional Syari'ah Regulations: Anomaly or Symptom?" In *Expressing Islam: Religious Life and Politics in Indonesia*, edited by Greg Fealy and Sally White, 174–191. Singapore: Institute of Southeast Asian Studies, 2008.

Calhoun, Craig. *Nationalism*. Minneapolis, MN.: University of Minnesota Press, 1997.

Carr, John E. "Ethno-Behaviorism and the Culture-Bound Syndromes: The Case of Amok." In *The Culture-Bound Syndromes: Folk Illnesses of Psychiatric and Anthropological Interest*, edited by Ronald C. Simons and Charles C. Hughes, 199–223. Dordrecht: D. Reidel Publishing Company, 1985.

Cavanaugh, William T. *The Myth of Religious Violence: Secular Ideology and the Roots of Modern Conflict*. New York: Oxford University Press, 2009.

Chatterjee, Partha. *The Nation and its Fragments: Colonial and Postcolonial Histories*. Princeton, N.J.: Princeton University Press, 1993.

The Politics of the Governed: Reflections on Popular Politics in Most of the World. New York: Columbia University Press, 2004.

Che Man, Wan Kadir. *Muslim Separatism: The Moros of Southern Philippines and the Malays of Southern Thailand*. Singapore: Oxford University Press, 1990.

Chew, Amy. "Buddhists Move Into Restive Southern Thailand." *South China Morning Post*, June 13, 2013.

Choi, Clara. "Friday Sermon Irks Local Church Leaders as 'Allah' Row Rages on." *The Malaysian Insider*, January 26, 2013. www.themalaysianinsider.com/malaysia/article/friday-sermon-irks-local-church-leaders-as-allah-row-rages-on/.

Chong, Terence. "Nationalism in Southeast Asia: Revisiting Kahin, Roff, and Anderson." *Sojourn: Journal of Social Issues in Southeast Asia* 24, no.1 (2009): 1–17.

Choong, Chong Eu. "The Christian Response to State-Led Islamization in Malaysia." In *Religious Diversity in Muslim-Majority States in Southeast Asia: Areas of Toleration and Conflict*, edited by Bernhard Platzdasch and Johan Saravanamuttu, 290–320. Singapore: Institute of Southeast Asian Studies, 2014.

Christianity Community Live Journal, 2010. http://christianity.livejournal.com/3752432.html.

Chua, Liana. "Clan Wars (RIDO) Regularly Cause Displacement in Mindanao (April 2011)." In *Philippines: Durable Solutions Still Out of Sight for Many IDPs and Returnees in Mindanao*. Geneva: Internal Displacement Monitoring Centre, 2011. www.internal-displacement.org/assets/library/Asia/Philippines/pdf/Philippines-June-2011.pdf.

The Christianity of Culture: Conversion, Ethnic Citizenship, and the Matter of Religion in Malaysian Borneo. New York: Palgrave MacMillan, 2012.

Coakley, John. "Religion and Nationalism in the First World." *Ethnonationalism in the Contemporary World: Walker Connor and the Study of Nationalism* 21 (2002): 206–225.

Cohen, Paul A. *History and Popular Memory: The Power of Story in Moments of Crisis*. New York: Columbia University Press, 2014.

Cole, Juan. "How the United States Helped Create the Islamic State." *Washington Post*, November 23, 2015.

Conde, Carlos H. "On Mindanao, Jihad Looms if Peace Talks Fail." *New York Times*, October 11, 2004.

Connor, Walker. *Ethnonationalism: The Quest for Understanding*. Princeton, N.J.: Princeton University Press, 1994.

Connors, Michael K. "War on Error and the Southern Fire: How Terrorism Analysts Get it Wrong." *Critical Asian Studies* 38, no.1 (2006): 151–175.

Cornish, Andrew. *Whose Place Is This?: Malay Rubber Producers And Thai Government Officials In Yala*. Bangkok: White Lotus Press, 1997.

Crawford, Beverly. "The Causes of Cultural Conflict: An Institutional Approach." In *The Myth of "Ethnic" Conflict: Politics, Economics, and "Cultural" Violence*, edited by Beverly Crawford and Ronnie D. Lipschutz, 3–43. Berkeley, CA.: University of California-Berkeley, 1998.

Crippen, Timothy. "Old and New Gods in the Modern World: Toward a Theory of Religious Transformation." *Social Forces* 67, no.2 (1988): 316–336.

Dari Kacamata Melayu Blog, 2008. http://pesanan-pesanan.blogspot.com/2008/12/ucapan-malay-dominance-abdullah-ahmad.html.

Department of Statistics Malaysia, Official Portal. "Discussion on Religious Freedom." *International Review of Mission* 65, no.260 (1976): 447–452.

"Population and Demography." Last modified January 29, 2014. www.statistics.gov.my/index.php?r=column/ctwoByCat&parent_id=115&menu_id=L0pheU43NWJwRWVSZklWdzQ4TlhUUT09.

Domado, Haironesah. "Mitigating Clan Violence in Mindanao Ahead of Midterm Elections." *Asia Foundation*, May 8, 2013. http://asiafoundation.org/in-asia/2013/05/08/mitigating-clan-violence-in-mindanao-ahead-of-midterm-elections/.

Dorairajoo, Saroja. "Peaceful Thai, Violent Malay (-Muslim): A Case Study of the 'Problematic' Muslim Citizens of Southern Thailand." *Copenhagen Journal of Asian Studies* 27, no.2 (2009): 61–83.

Duara, Prasenjit. *Rescuing History from the Nation: Questioning Narratives of Modern China*. Chicago, IL.: University of Chicago Press, 1995.

Dulyakasem, Uthai. "Education and Ethnic Nationalism: The Case of the Muslim-Malays in Southern Thailand." In *Reshaping Local Worlds: Formal Education and Cultural Change in Rural Southeast Asia*, edited by Charles F. Keyes, 131–152. New Haven, CT.: Yale University Press, 1991.

Duncan, Christopher R. "The Other Maluku: Chronologies of Conflict in North Maluku." *Indonesia* 80 (2005): 53–80.

Violence and Vengeance: Religious Conflict and Its Aftermath in Eastern Indonesia. Ithaca, N.Y.: Cornell University Press, 2013.

Eisenstadt, Shmuel Noah (S.N.). "Multiple Modernities." *Daedalus* 129, no.1 (2000): 1–29.

"Introduction." In *Multiple Modernities*, edited by Shmuel Noah Eisenstadt. New Brunswick, N.J.: Transaction Publishers, 2002.

Elegant, Simon, Andrew Perrin, Robert Horn, and Mageswary Ramakrishnan. "The Road to Jihad." *Time International*, October 5, 2004.

Elson, R.E. "Islam, Islamism, the Nation, and the Early Indonesian Nationalist Movement." *Journal of Indonesian Islam* 1, no.2 (2007): 231–266.

Estrada, Joseph. "Executions Spark Indonesia Unrest." *BBC News*, September 22, 2006. http://news.bbc.co.uk/2/hi/5368922.stm.

"Speech of Former President Estrada on the GRP-MORO Conflict." Speech presented at UP-HDN Forum on the GRP-MORO Conflict, University of Philippines, School of Economics Auditorium, Philippines, September 18, 2008. http://hdn.org.ph/speech-of-former-president-estrada-on-the-grp-moro-conflict/.

Farhadian, Charles. *Christianity, Islam, and Nationalism in Indonesia*. London: Routledge, 2005.

Fealy, Greg. "Inside the Laskar Jihad." *Inside Indonesia*, January–March 2001. www.library.ohiou.edu/indopubs/2001/07/24/0097.html.

Federspiel, Howard M. *Persatuan Islam Islamic Reform in Twentieth Century Indonesia*. Jakarta: Equinox Publishing, 2009.

Feillard, Andrée and Rémy Madinier. *The End of Innocence? Indonesian Islam and the Temptations of Radicalism*. Singapore: National University of Singapore Press, 2011.

Ferrer, Miriam Coronel. "Integration of the MNLF Forces Into the PNP and AFP: Integration Without Demobilization and Disarmament." Unpublished Paper, 2000.

"Interrogating the Bangsamoro Master Frame." *ABS-CBN News*, October 30, 2009. www.abs-cbnnews.com/views-and-analysis/10/30/09/interrogating-bangsamoro-master-frame.

Fisher, Don. "Seizure of 15,000 Bibles in Malaysia Stuns Christians." *Christian Headlines*, November 10, 2009. http://www.christianheadlines.com/news/seizure-of-15-000-bibles-in-malaysia-stuns-christians-11616546.html.

Fitzgerald, Timothy, ed. *Religion and the Secular: Historical and Colonial Formations*. London: Equinox Publishing Ltd, 2007.

Fong, Jack. "Sacred Nationalism: The Thai Monarchy and Primordial Nation Construction." *Journal of Contemporary Asia* 39, no.4 (2009): 673–696.

Ford, Liz. "Philippines: Where Catholics, Condoms And Conservatism Collide Over Health." *The Guardian*, May 30, 2013.

Foreman, John. *The Philippines*. Second Series, Vol. 2. Manila: Filipina Book Guild, 1980.

Fox, Jonathan. "The Rise of Religious Nationalism and Conflict: Ethnic Conflict and Revolutionary Wars, 1945–2001." *Journal of Peace Research* 41, no.6 (2004): 715–731.

Freedman, Lawrence. *Strategy: A History*. New York: Oxford University Press, 2013.

Friedland, Roger. "Religious Nationalism and the Problem of Collective Representation." *Annual Review of Sociology* 27 (2001): 125–152.

Fukuyama, Francis. *The End of History and the Last Man.* New York: Free Press, 1992.
Fuller, Thomas. "Elderly Woman's Killing Lays Bare Myanmar's Religious Divisions." *New York Times*, November 9, 2013.
Funston, John. *Malay Politics in Malaysia: A Study of the United Malays National Organisation and Party Islam.* Singapore: Heinemann International, 1981.
Garner, Roberta. *Contemporary Movements and Ideologies.* New York: McGraw-Hill, 1996.
Geertz, Clifford. *The Interpretation of Cultures.* New York: Basic Books, 1973.
The Religion of Java. Chicago, IL.: University of Chicago Press, 1976.
George, T.J.S. *Revolt in Mindanao.* Kuala Lumpur: Oxford University Press, 1980.
Gellner, Ernest. *Nations and Nationalism.* Ithaca, N.Y.: Cornell University Press, 1983.
Gilman, Nils, Michael Grosack, and Aaron Harms. "Everyone is Special." *The American Interest* 8, no.4 (2013): 18–19.
Glang, Alunan. *Muslim: Secession or Integration?* Manila: Cardinal Book Store, 1971.
Gökçe, Ali Fuat. "Federal Parliamentary Democracy with a Constitutional Monarchy: Malaysia." *International Journal of Social Science* 6, no.5 (2013): 327–346.
Gomez, Edmund Terence. "Government Offers MILF 'Self-Determination' Instead of New Territory." *U.S. Embassy Manila Cable*, November 29, 2006. http://wikileaks.org/cable/2006/11/06MANILA4836.html.
"Introduction." In *Politics in Malaysia: The Malay Dimension*, edited by Edmund Terence Gomez, 1–24. New York: Routledge, 2007.
Gowing, Peter. *Mandate in Moroland.* Quezon City: New Day Publishers, 1983.
Green, Elliott D. "Understanding the Limits to Ethnic Change: Lessons from Uganda's 'Lost Counties.'" *Perspectives on Politics* 6, no.3 (2008): 473–485.
Griffin, Larry J. "Narrative, Event-Structure Analysis, and Causal Interpretation in Historical Sociology." *American Journal of Sociology* 98, no.5 (1993): 1094–1133.
Guibernau, M. Montserrat. *Nations Without States.* Cambridge: Polity Press, 1999.
Gutierrez, Eric. "The Reimagination of the Bangsamoro." In *Rebels, Warlords, and Ulama: A Reader on Muslim Separatism and the War in Southern Philippines*, edited by Eric Gutierrez, 35–48. Quezon City: Institute for Popular Democracy, 2000.
Gutierrez, Eric and Saturnino Borras Jr. *The Moro Conflict: Landlessness and Misdirected State Policies.* Policy Studies No. 8. Washington, D.C.: East-West Center Washington, 2004.
Gutmann, Amy. *Identity in Democracy.* Princeton, N.J.: Princeton University Press, 2003.
Hadden, Jeffrey K. "Toward Desacralizing Secularization Theory." *Social Forces* 65, no.3 (1987): 587–611.
Hadiz, Vedi R. "Indonesian Local Party Politics: A Site of Resistance to Neoliberal Reform." *Critical Asian Studies* 36, no.4 (2004): 615–636.

Haemindra, Nantawan. "The Problem of the Thai-Muslims in the Four Southern Provinces of Thailand (Part One)." *Journal of Southeast Asian Studies* 7, no.2 (1976): 197–225.

Halverson, Jeffry R., Steven R. Corman, and H.L. Goodall Jr. *Master Narratives of Islamist Extremism*. New York: Palgrave Macmillan, 2011.

Hamid, Ahmad Fauzi Abdul. "Political Islam and Islamist Politics in Malaysia." *Trends in Southeast Asia*. Institute of Southeast Asian Studies no.2 (2013).

Hamilton, Mark. "New Imaginings: The Legacy of Benedict Anderson and Alternative Engagements of Nationalism." *Studies in Ethnicity and Nationalism* 6, no.3 (2006): 73–89.

Harb, Mona and Reinoud Leenders. "Know Thy Enemy: Hizbullah,'Terrorism' and the Politics of Perception." *Third World Quarterly* 26, no.1 (2005): 173–197.

"Hard-Liners Ambush Monas Rally." *Jakarta Post*, June 2, 2008.

Harding, Andrew and James Chin, eds. *50 Years of Malaysia: Federalism Revisited*. Singapore: Marshall Cavendish, 2014.

Harper, Tim. *The End of Empire and the Making of Malaya*. Cambridge: Cambridge University Press, 1999.

Harrison, Peter. *The Bible, Protestantism, and the Rise of Natural Science*. Cambridge: Cambridge University Press, 1998.

Harvey, Barbara S. *Permesta: Half a Rebellion*. Ithaca, N.Y.: Cornell Modern Indonesia Project, Southeast Asia Program, Cornell University, 1977.

Hashim, Salamat. *The Bangsamoro Mujahid: His Objectives and Responsibilities*. Mindanao: Bangsamoro Publications, 1985.

"Either You Are With Allah, or With the Enemies of Allah." Speech delivered at the Bangsamoro Youth National Peace Summit, Cotabato City, October 21, 2001.

"Id el Fitr Message to the Bangsamoro Nation." Speech from Mindanao, Philippines, December 16, 2001.

Referendum: Peaceful, Civilized, Diplomatic and Democratic Means of Solving the Mindanao Conflict. Mindanao: Agency for Youth Affairs – MILF, 2002.

Hastings, Adrian. *The Construction of Nationhood: Ethnicity, Religion, and Nationalism*. Cambridge: Cambridge University Press, 1997.

Hatta, S. Mohamed. "A Malay Crosscultural Worldview and Forensic Review of Amok." *Australian and New Zealand Journal of Psychiatry* 30, no.4 (1996): 505–510.

Hawkins, Michael. *Making Moros: Imperial Historicism and American Military Rule in the Philippines' Muslim South*. Dekalb, IL.: Northern Illinois University Press, 2012.

Hayimasae, Numan. "Haji Sulong Abdul Kadir (1895–1954): Perjuangan dan Sumbangan Beliau kepada Masyarakat Melayu Patani." M.A. thesis, Universiti Sains Malaysia, 2002.

Hefner, Robert W. *Civil Islam Muslims and Democratization in Indonesia*. Princeton, N.J.: Princeton University Press, 2000.

Herbst, Jeffrey, Terence McNamee, and Greg Mills, eds. *On The Fault Line: Managing Tensions and Divisions within Societies*. London: Profile Books, 2012.

Hinchman, Lewis P. and Sandra K. Hinchman. *Memory, Identity, Community: The Idea of Narrative in the Human Sciences*. New York: SUNY Press, 1997.
Hiroyuki, Yamamoto, Anthony Milner, Kawashima Midori, and Ari Kazuhiro, eds. *Bangsa and Umma: Development of People-Grouping Concepts in Islamized Southeast Asia*. Kyoto: Kyoto University Press, 2011.
Ho, Daniel. "Malaysia." In *Church in Asia Today: Challenges and Opportunities*, edited by Saphir Athyal, 257–287. Lausanne: Asia Lausanne Committee for World Evangelization, 1996.
Hobsbawm, Eric. "Introduction." In *The Invention of Tradition*, edited by Eric Hobsbawm and Terence Ranger, 1–14. Cambridge: Cambridge University Press, 1983.
Holt, Andrew. "Thailand's Troubled Border: Islamic Insurgency Or Criminal Playground?" *Terrorism Monitor* 2, no.10 (2004): 4–6.
Hong, Carolyn. "Increasing Religiosity in Malaysia Causes a Stir." *Straits Times*, September 5, 2006.
Hoppenbrouwers, Frans. "Winds of Change: Religious Nationalism in a Transformation Context." *Religion, State and Society* 30, no.4 (2002): 305–316.
Horowitz, Donald L. *Ethnic Groups in Conflict*, 2nd ed. Berkeley, CA.: University of California Press, 2000.
Hunt, Robert A. "The History of the Translation of the Bible into Bahasa Malaysia." *Journal of the Malaysian Branch of the Royal Asiatic Society* 62 no.1 (1989): 35–56.
Hunt, Robert A., Kam Hing Lee, and John Roxborogh. *Christianity in Malaysia: A Denominational History*. Petaling Jaya, Malaysia: Pelanduk Publications, 1990.
Husein, Fatimah. *Muslim-Christian Relations in the New Order Indonesia: The Exclusivist and Inclusivist Muslims' Perspective*. Jakarta: PT Mizan Publika, 2005.
Ichwan, Moch Nur. "Secularism, Islam and Pancasila: Political Debates on the Basis of the State in Indonesia." *Bulletin of the Nanzan Center for Asia and Pacific Studies* 6 (2011): 1–43.
Ileto, Reynaldo C. *Magindanao, 1860–1888: The Career of Datu Utto of Buayan*. Pasig City: Anvil Publishing Inc, 2004.
Iltis, Tony. "Indonesia Flashpoints: Sulawesi." *BBC News*, June 28, 2004. http://news.bbc.co.uk/2/hi/asia-pacific/3812737.stm.
"Indonesia: Reverse Ban on Ahmadiyah Sect." *Human Rights Watch*, June 10, 2008. www.hrw.org/news/2008/06/09/indonesia-reverse-ban-ahmadiyah-sect.
"Philippines: Moro People Demand Self-Determination." *Greenleft Weekly*, April 10, 2011. www.greenleft.org.au/node/47317.
International Crisis Group (ICG). *Indonesia: The Search for Peace in Maluku*. Jakarta: International Crisis Group, 2002.
Southern Thailand: Insurgency, Not Jihad. Singapore/Brussels: International Crisis Group, 2005.
Weakening Indonesia's Mujahidin Networks: Lessons From Maluku and Poso. Jakarta: International Crisis Group, 2005.

Indonesia "Christianisation" and Intolerance. Jakarta: International Crisis Group, 2010.
Islam, Syed Serajul. "Ethno-Communal Conflict in the Philippines: The Case of Mindanao-Sulu Region." In *Ethnic Conflict and Secessionism in South and Southeast Asia: Causes, Dynamics, Solutions*, edited by Rajat Ganguly and Ian Macduff, 195–224. New Delhi: Sage, 2003.
James, Paul. *Nation Formation: Towards a Theory of Abstract Community.* London: Sage Publications, 1996.
Japakiya, Ismail Lutfi. *Islam: Agama Penjana Kedamaian Sejagat.* Alor Star, Kedah: Pustaka Darussalam, 2005.
Jerryson, Michael K. *Buddhist Fury: Religion and Violence in Southern Thailand.* New York and Oxford: Oxford University Press, 2011.
Jervis, Robert. *Perception and Misperception in International Politics.* Princeton, N.J.: Princeton University Press, 1976.
Johnston, Hank. "Verification and Proof in Frame and Discourse Analysis." In *Methods of Social Movement Research*, edited by Bert Klandersmans and Suzanne Staggenborg, 62–91. Minneapolis, MN.: University of Minnesota Press, 2002.
Johnston, Hank and Bert Klandermans, eds. *Social Movements and Culture.* Minneapolis, MN.: University of Minnesota Press, 1995.
Jones, Sidney. "Causes of Conflict in Indonesia." *Asia Society*, 2002. http://asiasociety.org/causes-conflict-indonesia.
Jory, Patrick. "From 'Melayu Patani' to Thai Muslim: The Spectre of Ethnic Identity in Southern Thailand." *South East Asia Research* 15, no.2 (2007): 255–279.
Juergensmeyer, Mark. "Is Religion the Problem?" *Hedgehog Review* 6, no.1 (2004): 1–9.
Kabilan, K. "Fearless Indians Fight for Rights." *Malaysiakini*, November 26, 2007. www.malaysiakini.com/news/75289.
Kahin, Audrey, ed. *Regional Dynamics of the Indonesian Revolution: Unity From Diversity.* Honolulu, HI: University of Hawaii Press, 1985.
Kamal, Shazwan Mustafa. "Pembela Blames 'Aggressive Christians' for Muslim Siege Mentality." *The Malaysian Insider*, May 7, 2011. www.themalaysianinsider.com/malaysia/article/pembela-blames-aggressive-christians-for-muslim-siege-mentality/.
Kamlian, Jamail A. *Bangsamoro Society and Culture: A Book of Readings on Peace and Development in Southern Philippines.* Iligan City: Iligan Center for Peace Education and Research, 1999.
——— *Ethnic and Religious Conflict in Southern Philippines: A Discourse on Self-Determination, Political Autonomy, and Conflict Resolution.* Atlanta, GA.: Emory University Press, 2003.
Katznelson, Ira and Gareth Stedman Jones, eds. *Religion and the Political Imagination.* Cambridge: Cambridge University Press, 2010.
Kaviraj, Sudipta. "On Thick and Thin Religion. Some Critical Reflections on Secularization Theory." In *Religion and the Political Imagination*, edited by Ira Katznelson and Gareth Stedman Jones, 336–355. Cambridge: Cambridge University Press, 2010.

Keppel, Gilles. *Jihad: The Trail of Political Islam*. Cambridge, MA.: Harvard University Press, 2002.
Kessler, Clive. "Where Malaysia Stands Today." *The Malaysian Insider*, May 16, 2014. www.themalaysianinsider.com/sideviews/article/where-malaysia-stands-today-clive-kessler.
Keyes, Charles. *Thailand: Buddhist Kingdom as Modern Nation-State*. Boulder, CO.: Westview Press, 1987.
Kimball, Charles. *When Religion Becomes Evil*. New York: HarperCollins, 2008.
Kinnvall, Catarina. "Globalization and Religious Nationalism: Self, Identity, and the Search for Ontological Security." *Political Psychology* 25, no.5 (2004): 741–767.
Klandermans, Bert. *The Social Psychology of Protest*. Oxford: Blackwell, 1997.
Kreuzer, Peter. "Enduring Civil War in the Philippines: Why the Way to Peace Always Leads to Renewed Warfare." Paper presented at World Convention of the Association for the Study of Nationalities, New York, Columbia University, April 23–25, 2009.
Kuhnt-Saptodewo, Sri, Volker Grabowsky, and Martin Grossheim, eds. *Nationalism and Cultural Revival in Southeast Asia: Perspectives from the Centre and the Region*. Wiesbaden: Otto Harrassowitz Verlag, 1997.
"Komisi Hukum Nasional Republik Indonesia." *Komisi Hukum*, January 19, 2013. www.komisihukum.go.id/index.php?option=com_content&view=article&id=158:arti-pengesahan-dua-kovenan-ham-bagi-penegakan-hukum&catid=162&Itemid=622.
Laffan, Michael Francis. *Islamic Nationhood and Colonial Indonesia: The Umma Below the Winds*. London: Routledge, 2003.
Langan, John. "Nationalism, Ethnic Conflict, and Religion." *Theological Studies* 56, no.1 (1995): 122–136.
Larana, Enrique, Hank Johnston, and Joseph Gusfield, eds. *New Social Movements: From Ideology to Identity*. Philadelphia, PA.: Temple University Press, 1994.
Lawrence, Paul. *Nationalism: History and Theory*. Harlow: Pearson Education, 2005.
Lee, Shi-Ian. "Ex-Minister Sees Christian Bigots a Threat to Najib's 'Moderation.'" *The Malaysian Insider*, November 9, 2014. www.themalaysianinsider.com/malaysia/article/christian-fanatics-abusing-moderation-for-themselves-says-ex-umno-minister.
Leheny, David. "Terrorism, Social Movements, and International Security: How Al Qaeda Affects Southeast Asia." *Japanese Journal of Political Science* 6, no.1 (2005): 87–109.
Leifer, Michael, ed. *Asian Nationalism*. London: Routledge, 2000.
Leong, Trinna. "Sabah Christians Ban Together to Stop Conversion to Islam." *Malaysia Today*, January 23, 2014. www.malaysia-today.net/sabah-christians-band-together-to-stop-conversions-to-islam/.
Leopold, Joan. *Culture in Comparative and Evolutionary Perspective: EB Tylor and the Making of Primitive Culture*. Berlin: Dietrich Reimer Verlag, 1980.
Lewis, Bernard. *The Crisis of Islam: Holy War and Unholy Terror*. New York: Random House Trade Paperbacks, 2004.

Liang, Tan Yi. *Lim Kit Siang for Malaysia Blog*. http://blog.limkitsiang.com/2010/01/13/allah-issue-who-started-it/.

"A-G: Ibrahim Ali's Bible-Burning Remark Not of 'Seditious Tendency.'" *The Star*, October 27, 2014.

Lingga, Abhoud Syed Mansur. "Salamat Hashim's Concept of Bangsamoro State and Government." *Dansalan Quarterly* Vol.15 (1995): 3–4.

"The Political Thought of Salamat Hashim." M.A. thesis, Institute of Islamic Studies, University of the Philippines, 1995.

Liow, Joseph Chinyong. "Political Islam in Malaysia: Problematising Discourse and Practice in the UMNO–PAS 'Islamisation Race.'" *Commonwealth & Comparative Politics* 42, no.2 (2004): 184–205.

"International Jihad and Muslim Radicalism in Thailand?: Toward an Alternative Interpretation." *Asia Policy* 2, no.1 (2006): 89–108.

Muslim Resistance in Southern Thailand and Southern Philippines: Religion, Ideology, and Politics. Policy Studies 24. Washington, D.C.: East-West Center, 2006.

The Politics of Indonesia-Malaysia Relations: One Kin, Two Nations. London: Routledge, 2006.

"Iron Fists without Velvet Gloves: The Krue Se Mosque Incident and Lessons in Counterinsurgency for the Southern Thai Conflict." In *Treading on Hallowed Ground: Counterinsurgency Operations in Sacred Spaces*, edited by C. Christine Fair and Sumit Ganguly, 177–199. New York: Oxford University Press, 2008.

Islam, Education, and Reform in Southern Thailand: Tradition & Transformation. Singapore: Institute of Southeast Asian Studies, 2009.

Piety and Politics: Islamism in Contemporary Malaysia. New York: Oxford University Press, 2009.

"No God But God: Malaysia's 'Allah' Controversy." *Foreign Affairs Online*, February 10, 2010. www.foreignaffairs.com/articles/65961/joseph-chinyong-liow/no-god-but-god.

"Islamist Ambitions, Political Change, and the Price of Power: Recent Success and Challenges for the Pan-Malaysian Islamic Party, PAS." *Journal of Islamic Studies* 22, no.3 (2011): 374–403.

Liow, Joseph Chinyong and Don Pathan. *Confronting Ghosts: Thailand's Shapeless Southern Insurgency*. Sydney: Lowy Institute for International Policy, 2010.

Liow, Joseph Chinyong and Joseph Franco. "Positive Signs for a Southern Philippines Peace." *Global Brief*, July 17, 2013.

Liow, Joseph Chinyong and Afif Pasuni. "Islam, the State and Politics in Malaysia." In *Routledge Handbook of Contemporary Malaysia*, edited by Meredith Weiss, 50–59. London: Routledge, 2015.

Little, David. "Belief, Ethnicity, and Nationalism." *Nationalism and Ethnic Politics* 1, no.2 (1995): 284–301.

Llobera, Josep. *The God of Modernity*. Providence, R.I.: Berg, 1994.

Loos, Tamara. *Subject Siam: Family, Law, and Colonial Modernity in Thailand*. Ithaca, N.Y.: Cornell University Press, 2006.

Lopez, Antonio. "The Muslim Separatist Rebel Leader Wants the East Timor Formula." *Asiaweek*, March 31, 2000.

Mahamad, Roziyah. "Guna Kalimah Allah: Bidang Kuasa Mahkamah Tak Jelas – Taib Azamuddin." *Era Pakatan*, January 3, 2010. www.erapakatan .com/berita/guna_kalimah_allah_bidang_kuasa_mahkamah_tak_jelas_-_ taib_azamuddin/.

Malaysian Justice Blog, http://malaysianjustice.blogspot.com/2011/03/bn-turns-communist-with-bible.html.

"Malaysian Christians and Religious Freedom in the Name of 'Allah.'" *Charisma News*, March 11, 2014. www.charismanews.com/world/43081-malaysian-christians-and-religious-freedom-in-the-name-of-allah.

Malaysians Must Know the Truth Blog, http://malaysiansmustknowthetruth .blogspot.com/2014/01/revoke-citizenship-of-allah-fatwa.html.

Majul, Cesar Adib. *Muslims in the Philippines*. Quezon City: University of Philippines Press, 1973.

"The Moro Struggle in the Philippines." *Third World Quarterly* 10, no.2 (1988): 897–922.

Malesevic, Sinisa. "Maluku Refugees Allege Forced Circumcision." *BBC News*, January 31, 2001. http://news.bbc.co.uk/2/hi/asia-pacific/1146224.stm.

Identity as Ideology: Understanding Ethnicity and Nationalism. New York: Palgrave Macmillan, 2006.

Mangkusasmito, Prawoto. "Rumus Pantja Sila dan Sedjarah Singkat Pertumbuhannya." *Kiblat* no.2 (1968): 46–48.

Manickam, Sandra Khor. "Textbooks and Nation Construction in Malaysia." *Asia-Pacific Forum* 28 (2005): 78–89. www.rchss.sinica.edu.tw/capas/publication/newsletter/N28/28_01_04.pdf.

Marddent, Amporn. "Interfaith Marriage Between Muslims and Buddhists In Southern Thailand." In *Muslim-Non-Muslim Marriage: Political and Cultural Contestations in Southeast Asia*, edited by Gavin W. Jones, Heng Leng Chee, and Maznah Mohamad, 190–218. Singapore: Institute of Southeast Asian Studies, 2009.

Martinez, Patricia. "Mahathir, Islam and the New Malay dilemma." In *Mahathir's Administration: Performance and Crisis in Governance*, edited by Ho Khai Leong and James Chin, 215–251. Singapore: Times Books International, 2002.

McAdam, Doug, John D. McCarthy, and Mayer N. Zald. "Introduction." In *Comparative Perspectives on Social Movements: Political Opportunities, Mobilizing Structures, and Cultural Framings*, edited by Doug McAdam, John D. McCarthy, and Mayer N. Zald, 1–22. Cambridge: Cambridge University Press, 1996.

McCargo, Duncan. *Tearing Apart the Land: Islam and Legitimacy in Southern Thailand*. Ithaca, N.Y.: Cornell University Press, 2008.

"The Politics of Buddhist Identity in Thailand's Deep South: The Demise of Civil Religion?" *Journal of Southeast Asian Studies* 40, no.1 (2009): 11–32.

Mapping National Anxieties Thailand's Southern Conflict. Copenhagen: NIAS Press, 2012.

"Patani Militant Leaflets and the Use of History." In *Ghosts of the Past in Southern Thailand: Essays on the History and Historiography of Patani*, edited

by Patrick Jory, 277–297. Singapore: National University of Singapore Press, 2013.
McKenna, Thomas. *Muslim Rulers and Rebels: Everyday Politics and Armed Separatism in the Southern Philippines.* Berkeley, CA.: University of California Press, 1998.
"The Endless Road to Peace: Armed Separatism and Ancestral Domain in the Muslim Philippines." Paper presented at the conference Mobilization for Political Violence: What Do We Know? Oxford, University of Oxford, March 17–18, 2009.
McKenna, Thomas and Esmael A. Abdula. "Islamic Education in the Philippines: Political Separatism and Religious Pragmatism." In *Making Modern Muslims: The Politics of Islamic Education in Southeast Asia*, edited by Robert W. Hefner, 205–236. Honolulu, HI: University of Hawaii Press, 2009.
McLoughlin, William G. *Revivals, Awakenings, and Reform: An Essay on Religion and Social Change in America, 1607–1977.* Chicago, IL.: University of Chicago Press, 1978.
McRae, David. "Criminal Justice and Communal Conflict: A Case Study of the Trial of Fabianus Tibo, Dominggus da Silva, and Marinus Riwu." *Indonesia* 83 (2007): 79–117.
A Few Poorly Organized Men: Interreligious Violence in Poso, Indonesia. Leiden: Brill, 2013.
McVey, Ruth. "Identity and Rebellion Among Southern Thai Muslims." In *The Muslims of Thailand: Politics of the Malay-Speaking South*, edited by Andrew D.W. Forbes, 33–52. Bihar, India: Centre for South East Asian Studies, 1989.
Mees, Ludger. "Politics, Economy, or Culture? The Rise and Development of Basque Nationalism in the Light of Social Movement Theory." *Theory and Society* 33, no.3–4 (2004): 311–331.
Menchik, Jeremy. "Productive Intolerance: Godly Nationalism in Indonesia." *Comparative Studies in Society and History* 56, no.3 (2014): 591–621.
Mietzner, Marcus. *Military Politics, Islam, and the State in Indonesia: From Turbulent Transition to Democratic Consolidation.* Singapore: Institute of Southeast Asian Studies, 2009.
Mihelj, Sabina. "Faith in Nation Comes in Different Guises: Modernist Versions of Religious Nationalism." *Nations and Nationalism* 13, no.2 (2007): 265–284.
"MILF Continues to Support Peace Process, Interested in Deeper Development Cooperation." *U.S. Embassy Manila Cable*, August 4, 2008. http://wikileaks.org/cable/2008/08/08MANILA1844.html.
"MILF Leader to 'Nida'ul Islam': Perhaps the Moro Struggle for Freedom and Self-Determination is the Longest and Bloodiest in the Entire History of Mankind," www.islam.org.au, April–May 1998. Available www.islam.org.au/articles/23/ph2.htm.
"MILF Warns SC Ruling Could Lead to More Clashes." *Agence France-Presse*, October 15, 2008.
"MILF: From ARMM to Bangsamoro State Government." *Philippine Daily Inquirer*, April 30, 2012.

Milligan, Jeffrey Ayala. "Islamization or Secularization? Educational Reform and the Search for Peace in the Southern Philippines." *Current Issues in Comparative Education* 7, no.1 (2004): 30–38.

"Islam and Education Policy Reform in the Southern Philippines." *Asia Pacific Journal of Education* 28, no.4 (2008): 369–381.

Mohamad, Mahathir. *The Malay Dilemma*. Kuala Lumpur: Times Books International, 1970.

Mohamad, Maznah and Syed Muhd Khairudin Aljunied, eds. *Melayu: The Politics, Poetics, and Paradoxes of Malayness*. Singapore: National University of Singapore Press, 2011.

Montesano, Michael J. and Patrick Jory, eds. *Thai South and Malay North: Ethnic Interactions on a Plural Peninsula*. Singapore: National University of Singapore Press, 2008.

Mujani, Saiful and R. William Liddle. "Leadership, Party, and Religion: Explaining Voting Behavior in Indonesia." *Comparative Political Studies* 40, no.7 (2007): 832–857.

"Muslim Indonesia's Secular Democracy." *Asian Survey* 49, no.4 (2009): 575–590.

Muslim Mindanao. "The Muslim Separatist Rebel Leader Wants 'the East Timor Formula.'" *Asiaweek*, March 31, 2000.

"Philippine Muslim Communities." 2011. www.muslimmindanao.ph/Islam_phil2.html.

Murad, Dina. "Abdullah Zaik: The Man Behind Isma." *The Star*, May 22, 2014.

Muzaffar, Chandra. "Foreword." In *Facing One Qiblah: Legal and Doctrinal Aspects of Sunni and Shiah Muslims*, edited by Karim D. Crow, vii–xii. Bethesda, MD.: Ibex Publishers, 2005.

Mydans, Seth. "Thailand Set to Make Buddhism the State Religion." *New York Times*, May 24, 2007.

Nagata, Judith A. "What is a Malay? Situational Selection of Ethnic Identity in a Plural Society." *American Ethnologist* 1, no.2 (1974): 331–350.

The Reflowering of Malaysian Islam: Modern Religious Radicals and Their Roots. Vancouver: University of British Columbia Press, 1984.

"Open Societies and Closed Minds: The Limits of Fundamentalism in Islam." *ICIP Journal* 2, no.2 (2005): 1–19.

"Najib: We Cannot Stop Friday's Protest." *Malaysia Today*, January 7, 2010. www.malaysia-today.net/najib-we-cannot-stop-fridays-protest/.

Nakamura, Mitsuo. *The Crescent Arises Over the Banyan Tree: A Study of the Muhammadiyah Movement in a Central Javanese Town, c. 1910–2010*. Singapore: Institute of Southeast Asian Studies, 2012.

Nasution, Khoiruddin. "Fatwa Majelis Ulama Indonesia (MUI): On Ahmadiyah." *Millah* 7, no.2 (2009): 1–18. http://journal.uii.ac.id/index.php/Millah/article/viewFile/351/264.

Nicholas, Ralph W. "Social and Political Movements." *Annual Review of Anthropology* 2 (1973): 63–84.

Noor, Farish A. *The Malaysian Islamic Party PAS, 1951–2013: Islamism in a Mottled Nation*. Amsterdam: Amsterdam University Press, 2014.

O'Leary, Brendan. "On the Nature of Nationalism: An Appraisal of Ernest Gellner's Writings on Nationalism." *British Journal of Political Science* 27, no.2 (1997): 191–222.

O'Toole, Gavin. *The Reinvention of Mexico: National Ideology in a Neoliberal Era.* Liverpool: Liverpool University Press, 2010.
Oddie, Morgan. "The Relationship of Religion and Ethnic Nationalism in Bosnia-Herzegovina." *Religion in Eastern Europe* 32, no.1 (2012): 34–42.
Oliver, Pamela and Hank Johnston. "What a Good Idea! Ideologies and Frames in Social Movement Research." *Mobilization* 5, no.1 (2000): 37–54.
Onishi, Norimitsu. "In Philippines Strife, Uprooting Is a Constant." *New York Times*, November 22, 2009.
Oquist, Paul and Alma Evangelista. *Peace-Building in Times of Institutional Crisis: Ten Years of the GRP-MNLF Peace Agreement.* Makati City: United Nations Development Programme, 2006.
Orendain, Simone. "The Persistence of Blood Feuds in the Philippines." *Public Radio International*, July 25, 2011. www.pri.org/stories/2011-07-25/persistence-blood-feuds-philippines.
Othman, Norani. "Islamization and Democratization in Malaysia in Regional and Global Contexts." In *Challenging Authoritarianism in Southeast Asia: Comparing Indonesia and Malaysia*, edited by Ariel Heryanto and Sumit Mandal, 117–144. London: RoutledgeCurzon, 2003.
Ozerdem, Alpaslan, Sukanya Podder, and Eddie L. Quitoriano. "Identity, Ideology and Child Soldiering: Community and Youth Participation in Civil Conflict–A Study on the Moro Islamic Liberation Front In Mindanao, Philippines." *Civil Wars* 12, no.3 (2010): 304–325.
Palatino, Mong. "Don't Let the Flames of Nationalism Engulf Southeast Asia." *The Diplomat*, April 6, 2013.
Panggabean, Samsu Rizal, Rudi Harisyah Alam, and Ihsan Ali Fauzi. "The Patterns of Religious Conflict in Indonesia (1990–2008)." *Studia Islamika* 17, no.2 (2010): 239–298.
Panolimba, Datuan Solaiman. "The Bangsamoro Armed Struggle in the Philippines." *Maradika Online*, December 17, 2008. https://datspanolimba.wordpress.com/2008/06/15/the-bangsamoro-struggle-in-the-philippines-2/.
"Armed Struggle of the Bangsamoro Muslims in the Philippines." *Reflections on the Bangsamoro*, June 8, 2009. https://datspanolimba.wordpress.com/2008/06/15/the-bangsamoro-struggle-in-the-philippines-2/.
Pas Taman Paya Jaras Permai Blog. http://pastpjp.blogspot.com/2010/01/penjelasan-oleh-ustz-taib-azzamuddin.html.
Pathan, Don. "A Short History of Southern Sultanates." *The Nation*, April 3, 2002.
"Alone in the Shadow of Militants." *The Nation*, May 21, 2006.
Pathmanand, Ukrist. "Thaksin's Achilles' Heel: The Failure of Hawkish Approaches in the Thai South." *Critical Asian Studies* 38, no.1 (2006): 73–93.
Petersen, William. "Philippines: Vendettas and Violence on Mindanao – Analysis." *IRIN*, June 24, 2009. www.irinnews.org/report/84979/philippines-vendettas-and-violence-on-mindanao-analysis.
Ethnicity Counts. New Brunswick, N.J.: Transaction Publishers, 2012.
Philips, Thomas and Herman Shastri. "Freedom of Religion has Been Severely Diminished." In *Religion Under Siege. Lina Joy, The Islamic State and Freedom of Faith*, edited by John Lee and Nathaniel Tan, 26. Kuala Lumpur: Kinibooks, 2008.

Philpott, Daniel. "The Religious Roots of Modern International Relations." *World Politics* 52, no.2 (2000): 206–245.

Pickel, Gert. "Contextual Secularization–Theoretical Thoughts and Empirical Implications." *Religion and Society in Central and Eastern Europe* 4, no.1 (2011): 3–20.

Pitsuwan, Surin. *Islam and Malay Nationalism: A Case Study of Malay-Muslims of Southern Thailand*. Bangkok: Thai Khadi Research Institute, 1985.

Ploughshares. "Philippines-Mindanao (1971 – first Combat Deaths)." Last modified June 2015. http://ploughshares.ca/pl_armedconflict/philippines-mindanao-1971-first-combat-deaths/.

Polletta, Francesca. *It Was Like a Fever: Storytelling In Protest and Politics*. Chicago, IL.: University of Chicago Press, 2006.

Porath, Nathan. "The Hikayat Patani: The Kingdom of Patani in the Malay and Thai Political World." *Journal of the Malaysian Branch of the Royal Asiatic Society* 84, no.2 (2011): 45–65.

Preamble of the Memorandum of Agreement on the Ancestral Domain Aspect of the GRP-MILF Tripoli Agreement on Peace, June 22, 2001. http://zamboangajournal.blogspot.com/2008/08/philippines-milf-memorandum-of.html.

Preston, Peter Wallace. *Political/Cultural Identity: Citizens and Nations in a Global Era*. London: Sage Publications, 1997.

Prill-Brett, June. *Pechen: The Bontok Peace Pact Institution*. Baguio City: Cordillera Studies Center, College Baguio, University of the Philippines, 1987.

Pye, Lucian and Mary W. Pye. *Asian Power and Politics: The Cultural Dimensions of Authority*. Cambridge, MA.: Harvard University Press, 1985.

Rackett, Tim. "Putting Out the Fire in Southern Thailand: An Appeal for Truce Seeking." *Middle East Institute*, July 14, 2014. www.mei.edu/content/map/putting-out-fire-southern-thailand-appeal-truce-seeking.

Rasjidi, Muhammad. "The Role of Christian Missions: The Indonesian Experience." *International Review of Mission* 65, no.260 (1976): 427–447.

Rempillo, Jay. "SC Declares MOA-AD Unconstitutional." *Philippine Commentary*, October 14, 2008. http://philippinecommentary.blogspot.com/2008/10/supreme-court-split-8-7-on-moa-ad.html.

Renan, Ernest. "What is a Nation?" In *Nation and Narration*, edited by Homi Bhabha, 8–22. London: Routledge, 1990.

Reuters. "New Violence over Religion in Indonesia." *New York Times*, January 1, 2000.

Ricklefs, M.C. *Islamisation and its Opponents in Java: c.1930 to the Present*. Singapore: National University of Singapore Press, 2012.

Riddell, Peter G. "Islamization, Civil Society and Religious Minorities in Malaysia." In *Islam in Southeast Asia: Political, Social and Strategic Challenges for the 21st Century*, edited by K.S. Nathan and Mohammad Hashim Kamali, 162–190. Singapore: Institute of Southeast Asian Studies, 2005.

Rieffer, Barbara-Ann J. "Religion and Nationalism Understanding the Consequences of a Complex Relationship." *Ethnicities* 3, no.2 (2003): 215–242.

Robertson, Bruce Carlisle, ed. *The Essential Writings of Raja Rammohan Ray*. Delhi: Oxford University Press, 1999.

Roff, William R. *The Origins of Malay Nationalism*. New Haven, CT.: Yale University Press, 1967.
Ropi, Ismatu. "Muslim-Christian Polemics in Indonesian Islamic Literature." *Islam and Christian-Muslim Relations* 9, no.2 (1998): 217–229.
Rousseau, Jean-Jacques. "On the Social Contract." In *Basic Political Writings*, edited by Donald A. Cress, 141–227. Indianapolis, IN.: Hackett Publishing, 1987.
Rowan, Peter. *Proclaiming the Peacemaker: The Malaysian Church as an Agent of Reconciliation in a Multicultural Society*. Oxford: Regnum Books, 2012.
Roxborogh, John. "Christianity in the Straits Settlements 1786–1842." 1990. www.roxborogh.com/sea/country/SSET1786%20update%2009.pdf.
A History of Christianity in Malaysia. Singapore: Armour Publishing, 2014.
Roy, Olivier. *The Failure of Political Islam*. Cambridge, MA.: Harvard University Press, 1994.
Globalized Islam: The Search for a New Ummah. London: C. Hurst & Co., 2004.
Ruane, Joseph and Jennifer Todd. "Ethnicity and Religion: Redefining the Research Agenda." *Ethnopolitics* 9, no.1 (2010): 1–8.
Sabra, Samah. "Imagining Nations: An Anthropological Perspective." *Nexus* 20 (2007): 76–104.
Safran, William. "Language, Ethnicity and Religion: A Complex and Persistent Linkage." *Nations and Nationalism* 14, no.1 (2008): 171–190.
Saleeby, Najeeb M. *Studies in Moro History, Law, and Religion*. Manila: Bureau of Public Printing, 1905.
"Salinan Fatwa MUI Ttg Kesesatan Ahmadiyah." *Nahimunkar*, April 30, 2008. www.nahimunkar.com/salinan-fatwa-mui-ttg-kesesatan-ahmadiyah/.
Sani, Mohd Azizuddin Mohd. "Islamization Policy and Islamic Bureaucracy in Malaysia." *Trends in Southeast Asia* 5 (2015).
Sastrapratedja. *Pancasila Sebagai Ideologi*. Jakarta: BP-7 Pusat, 1991.
Satha-Anand, Chaiwat. *Islam and Violence: A Case Study of Violent Events in the Four Southern Provinces, Thailand, 1976–1981*. Gainesville, FL.: Florida University Press, 1987.
The Life of this World: Negotiated Muslim Lives in Thai Society. Singapore: Marshall Cavendish, 2005.
"The Silence of the Bullet Monument: Violence and 'Truth' Management, Dusun-Nyor 1948, and Kru-Ze 2004." *Critical Asian Studies* 38, no.1 (2006): 11–37.
Schulze, Kirsten E. *Sejarah Geredja Katolik di Indonesia*. Djakarta: Sekretariat Nasional K.M., 1971.
"Laskar Jihad and the Conflict in Ambon." *The Brown Journal of World Affairs* 9, no.1 (2002): 57–70.
Selengut, Charles. *Sacred Fury: Understanding Religious Violence*. New York: Rowman & Littlefield Publishers, 2008.
Shaery-Eisenlohr, Roschanack. *Shi'ite Lebanon: Transnational Religion and the Making of National Identities*. New York: Columbia University Press, 2008.
Sheridan, Greg. "Jihad Archipelago." *The National Interest* (2004): 73–80.
Shröter, Suzanne, ed. *Christianity in Indonesia: Perspectives of Power*. Berlin: Lit Verlag, 2010.

Sidel, John T. *Riots, Pogroms, Jihad: Religious Violence in Indonesia*. Ithaca, N.Y.: Cornell University Press, 2006.
Sly, Liz. "Religious Violence the Latest Wrinkle in Indonesia's Woe." *Chicago Tribune*, December 1, 1998.
Smith, Anthony D. *The Ethnic Origins of Nations*. Oxford: Blackwell, 1988.
——. "The Myth of the 'Modern Nation' and the Myths of Nations." *Ethnic and Racial Studies* 11, no.1 (1988): 1–26.
——. *Chosen Peoples: Sacred Sources of National Identity*. Oxford: Oxford University Press, 2003.
——. *The Antiquity of Nations*. Cambridge: Polity Press, 2004.
Smith, Wilfred Cantwell. *The Meaning and End of Religion*. Minneapolis, M.N.: Fortress Press, 1991.
Snow, David A. and Robert D. Benford. "Ideology, Frame Resonance, and Participant Mobilization." *International Social Movement Research* 1, no.1 (1988): 197–217.
Snow, David A., E. Burke Rochford Jr., Steven K. Worden, and Robert D. Benford. "Frame Alignment Processes, Micromobilization, and Movement Participation." *American Sociological Review* 51, no.4 (1986): 464–481.
Snyder, Jack L. *From Voting to Violence: Democratization and Nationalist Conflict*. New York: W.W. Norton & Company, 2000.
Spyer, Patricia. "Fire Without Smoke and Other Phantoms of Ambon's Violence: Media Effects, Agency, and the Work of Imagination." *Indonesia* 74 (2002): 21–36.
Steinberg, Marc. "Tilting the Frame: Considerations on Collective Action Framing From a Discursive Turn." *Theory and Society* 27, no.6 (1998): 845–872.
Stockwell, A. J. *British Policy and Malay Politics During the Malayan Union Experiment, 1942–1948*. Kuala Lumpur: The Malaysian Branch of the Royal Asiatic Society, 1979.
Stone, Jon R., ed. *The Essential Max Muller: On Language, Mythology, and Religion*. New York: Palgrave, 2002.
Su-Lynn, Boo. "Terrorising the Christian Minority." *The Malay Mail Online*, October 17, 2014.
Sugunnasil, Wattana. "Islam, Radicalism, and Violence in Southern Thailand: Berjihad di Patani and the 28 April 2004 Attacks." *Critical Asian Studies* 38, no.1 (2006): 119–144.
Suhrke, Astri. "The Muslims in Southern Thailand." In *The Muslims of Thailand: Politics of the Malay-Speaking South*, edited by Andrew D.W. Forbes, 1–18. Bihar, India: Centre for South East Asian Studies, 1989.
Sunoto. *Mengenal Filsafat Pancasila*. Yogyakarta: BP FE UII, 1981.
Surin, Jacqueline Ann. "Allah Issue: Who Started It?" http://blog.limkitsiang.com/2010/01/13/allah-issue-who-started-it/.
Swearer, Donald. *The Buddhist World of Southeast Asia*. New York: SUNY Press, 2010.
Syukri, Ibrahim. *History of the Malay Kingdom of Patani*. Athens, OH.: Ohio University, Center for International Studies, 1985.
Tambiah, Stanley J. *Leveling Crowds: Ethnonationalist Conflicts and Collective Violence in South Asia*. Berkeley, CA.: University of California Press, 1996.

Bibliography

Tan, Samuel K. *The Filipino Muslim Armed Struggle, 1900–1972.* Manila: Filipinas Foundation, 1977.

Tannen, Deborah, ed. *Framing in Discourse.* New York: Oxford University Press, 1993.

Tarrow, Sidney G. *Power in Movement: Social Movements, Collective Action and Politics.* Cambridge: Cambridge University Press, 1998.

Teeuw, Andries and David K. Wyatt. *Hikayat Patani.* The Hague: Martinus Nijhoff, 1970.

Tiglao, Rigoberto. "Peace in His Time: Ramos-Misuari Accord has Structural Flaws." *Far Eastern Economic Review* 159, no.36 (1996): 24–26.

Tilly, Charles and Sidney Tarrow. *Contentious Politics.* New York: Oxford University Press, 2006.

"Time is Right for Inter-Faith Dialogue." *The Star*, April 18, 2010.

Ting, Helen. "Malaysian History Textbooks and the Discourse of Ketuanan Melayu." In *Race and Multiculturalism in Malaysia and Singapore*, edited by P.S. Goh Daniel, Matilda Gabrielpillai, Philip Holden, Gaik Cheng Khoo, 36–52. New York: Routledge, 2009.

Tonnesson, Stein, and Hans Antlov, eds. *Asian Forms of the Nation.* London: Curzon, 1996.

Torres III, Wilfredo Magno. "Introduction." In *Rido: Clan Feuding and Conflict Management in Mindanao*, edited by Wilfredo Magno Torres III, 3–27. Manila: Ateneo de Manila University Press, 2014.

Tuminez, Astrid. "This Land is Our Land: Moro Ancestral Domain and its Implications for Peace and Development in the Southern Philippines." *SAIS Review* 27, no.2 (2007): 77–91.

Turner, Brian. "Religious Nationalism, Globalisation and Empire." Keynote address at the Conference on Transnational Religions: Intersections of the 'Global' and 'Local', Cambridge, July 19–20, 2004.

Turner, Mark. "Terrorism and Secession in the Southern Philippines: The Rise of the Abu Sayaff." *Contemporary Southeast Asia* 17, no.1 (1995): 1–19.

Uyun, H. Muhammad Syeful. "Ahmadiyah 100% Islam Tidak Sesat dan Menyesatkan." *Warta Ahmadiya*, March 24, 2015. http://warta-ahmadiyah.org/ahmadiyah-100-islam-tidak-sesat-dan-menyesatkan.html.

van der Veer, Peter. *Religious Nationalism: Hindus and Muslims in India.* Berkeley, CA.: University of California Press, 1994.

"The Secular Production of Religion." *Etnofoor* 8, no.2 (1995): 5–14.

van Klinken, Gerry. "The Maluku Wars: Bringing Society Back In." *Indonesia* 71 (2001): 1–26.

Minorities, Modernity and the Emerging Nation: Christians in Indonesia, A Biographical Approach. Leiden: KITLV Press, 2003.

Communal Violence and Democratization in Indonesia: Small Town Wars. London: Routledge, 2007.

van Liere, Lucien M. "Fighting for Jesus on Ambon: Interpreting Religious Representations of Violent Conflict." *Exchange* 40, no.4 (2011): 322–335.

Vella, Walter F. *Chaiyo!, King Vajiravudh and the Development of Thai Nationalism.* Honolulu, HI: University Press of Hawaii, 1978.

Vendley, William and David Little. "Implications for Religious Communities: Buddhism, Islam, Hinduism, and Christianity." In *Religion, the Missing Dimension of Statecraft*, edited by Douglas Johnston and Cynthia Sampson, 306–315. Oxford: Oxford University Press, 1994.

Vermeersch, Peter. "Backdoor Nationalism: EU Accession and the Reinvention of Nationalism in Hungary and Poland." Paper presented at the Association for the Study of Ethnicity and Nationalism, London, April 1–3, 2009.

von Der Mehden, Fred R. *Religion and Nationalism in Southeast Asia: Burma, Indonesia, the Philippines*. Madison, WI.: University of Wisconsin Press, 1963.

Wadi, Julkipli M. "State, Religion and Post-Nationalism in the Philippines." Paper presented at the International Conference on State, Religion and Post-Nationalism: The Southeast Asian Experience, University of Malaya, Malaysia, February 23–24, 2001.

Wagemakers, Joas. "Legitimizing Pragmatism: Hamas' Framing Efforts from Militancy to Moderation and Back?" *Terrorism and Political Violence* 22, no.3 (2010): 357–377.

Walker, Simon. "Between Church and Crown: Master Richard Andrew, King's Clerk." *Speculum* 74, no.4 (1999): 956–991.

Walters, Albert Sundadaraj, *We Believe in One God? Reflections on the Trinity in the Malaysian Context*. Delhi: ISPCK, 2002.

Walzer, Michael. *Thick and Thin: Moral Argument at Home and Abroad*. Notre Dame, IN.: University of Notre Dame Press, 1994.

Warren, James Francis. *The Sulu Zone, 1768–1898: The Dynamics of External Trade, Slavery, and Ethnicity in the Transformation of a Southeast Asian Maritime State*. Honolulu, HI: University of Hawaii Press, 1981.

Watzlawick, Paul, John H. Weakland, and Richard Fisch. *Change: Principles of Problem Formation and Problem Resolution*. New York: WW Norton & Company, 1974.

Webb, R.A.F. Paul. "The Sickle and the Cross: Christians and Communists in Bali, Sumba, Flores, and Timor, 1965–1967." *Journal of Southeast Asian Studies* 17, no.1 (March 1986): 94–112.

"Weighing in Factors of State and Religion." *TMChronicles*, January 11–15, 2009. http://tmchronicles.com/vdbasee.php?idb=24&&dbase=Editorial&&type=3&&start=131&&end=140.

Wellman Jr., James K. and Kyoko Tokuno. "Is Religious Violence Inevitable?" *Journal for the Scientific Study of Religion* 43, no.3 (2004): 291–296.

Wernstedt, Frederick L. and Paul D. Simkins. "Migrations and the Settlement of Mindanao." *Journal of Asian Studies* 25, no.1 (1965): 83–103.

Willford, Andrew C. and Kenneth M. George, eds. *Spirited Politics: Religion and Public Life in Contemporary Southeast Asia*. Ithaca, N.Y.: Cornell University Press, 2005.

Williams, Louise. "Deepening Religious Divide Ripe For Political Exploitation." *Sydney Morning Herald*, December 5, 1998.

Wilson, Chris. "The Ethnic Origins of Religious Conflict in North Maluku Province, Indonesia, 1999–2000." *Indonesia* 79 (2005): 69–91.

Ethno-Religious Violence in Indonesia: From Soil to God. London: Routledge, 2012.

Woo, Joshua and Soo-Inn Tan, eds. *The Bible and the Ballot: Reflections on Christian Political Engagement in Malaysia Today.* Singapore: Graceworks, 2011.

Wood, Elisabeth Jean. *Insurgent Collective Action and Civil War in El Salvador.* Cambridge: Cambridge University Press, 2003.

"The World's Muslims: Religion, Politics and Society." *Pew Research Center*, April 30, 2013. www.pewforum.org/2013/04/30/the-worlds-muslims-religion-politics-society-overview/.

Wright, Matthew and Tim Reeskens. "The Pious Patriot. Establishing and Explaining the Link Between Religiosity and National Pride among European Mass Publics." Paper presented at the 19th International Conference of the Council for European Studies, Boston, Massachusetts, March 22–24, 2012.

Yamin, Muhammad. *Haskah Persiapan Undang-undang Dasar 1945.* Jakarta: Jajasan Prapantja, 1959.

Yapp, Eugene and Samuel Ang, eds. *Transform Nation Agenda.* Malaysia: NECF Malaysia Research Commission, 2009.

Young, Eric. "30,000 Bibles Detained by Malaysian Government, Claim Christian Leaders." *The Christian Post*, March 11, 2011. www.christianpost.com/news/30000-bibles-detained-by-malaysian-govt-claim-christian-leaders-49377/#.

Yusu, N. and A. Abu Chik. *Eksel dalam PMR Sejarah.* Petaling Jaya: Pelangi Publishing Group Berhad, undated.

Zubrzycki, Geneviève. "National Culture, National Identity, and the Culture(s) of the Nation." In *Handbook of Cultural Sociology*, edited by John R. Hall, Laura Grindstaff, and Ming-Cheng Lo, 514–529. London: Routledge, 2010.

"Religion and Nationalism: A Critical Re-examination." In *Sociology of Religion*, edited by Bryan Turner, 611–619. Sussex: Blackwell Publishing, 2010.

Index

Aceh, 176, 178, 179, 187, 193
activism, 12, 137, 153, 157, 165, 183, 194
  Muslim activism, 54, 193
  political activism, 54, 125, 143
adat, 68
Africa, 3, 24, 71, 177, 183
agrarian societies, 33
aliran, 175, 214
Allah, 83, 85, 86, 143, 155–156, 157–160, 163–164, 165, 169–170
Anderson, Benedict, 32, 33, 222
anti-colonial movements, 137, 177–180
anti-colonialism, 183–184
  anti-colonial resistance, 186, 226
Aquino, Benigno, 62, 68, 82, 97
armed insurgency, 15, 79, 97, 116, 119, 125, 132
ascription, 9, 26, 147, 229
  ascriptive identity, 8, 12, 22, 27, 30, 48, 152
  ascriptive meaning, 30, 37

Bangladesh, 28
Bangsamoro, 16, 43, 55, 62–63, 67–88, 90–91, 92, 96–98, 134, 170, 219, 222, 226–227
  Bangsamoro community, 67, 83, 170
  Bangsamoro identity, 72–74, 83, 87–88, 97
  Bangsamoro Islamic Freedom Fighters, 67
  Bangsamoro Islamic Freedom Movement, 67
  Bangsamoro nationalism, 97
  Bangsamoro nationalists, 63, 72–73, 96
  Bangsamoroism, 70, 73, 75, 88, 91, 97
  Framework Agreement on the Bangsamoro, 62, 68
Barisan Nasional, 103
belief systems, 11, 50
Bosnia, 30

Buddhism, 31, 99, 108–110, 126, 226
  activist Buddhism, 31
  Buddhist Sangha, 6, 110
  Buddhists, 1, 105, 107, 109, 113, 116, 132–133, 213
Burma. *See* Myanmar
Bush administration, 28

Catholicism, 1, 67, 79, 89, 140, 157–159, 162, 182, 187, 190, 197, 213
  Roman Catholic Church, 23, 31, 46, 139, 143, 156
centre–periphery relations, 16, 38, 113
Christianity, 17, 23–24, 28, 48, 64, 92, 139–141, 142, 154–155, 160, 161, 180–181, 182, 183, 184, 186–189, 196, 213, 230
  Christian communities, 17, 72, 77–78, 88–90, 136, 138, 141, 153–154, 166, 169, 176, 184, 190, 216, 223
  Christian community, 141–142, 143, 160, 169, 172, 174, 194–195, 210
  Christianization, 15, 184
  Christian–Muslim relations, 69, 74, 93, 183, 187–189, 192–193, 202–204, 207–209, 214, 227
  Christian–Muslim violence, 17, 176, 196–202, 205–206
  Christians, 15, 30, 48, 65, 73–74, 88, 90, 139–141, 144, 147, 153, 156–159, 161–165, 166, 170, 181, 182, 184, 185, 190, 191, 219
citizenship, 10, 131, 146, 147, 156–157, 163, 166, 169, 184, 212, 215, 229
  citizenship rights, 136, 138, 146, 223
  Indonesian citizenship, 222
  Malaysian citizenship, 131, 163
clash of civilizations, 2, 3, 219, 220
Cold War, the, 15, 220, 226
collective action, 10, 12–13, 16, 22, 29, 51–56, 57–59, 156, 168
  collective mobilization, 12, 22, 223

Index

collective identity, 6, 32, 36, 41–42, 71, 75, 96, 220, 231
collective consciousness, 10, 133
collective representation, 44
colonialism, 15, 23, 24, 34, 64–66, 76, 79, 90, 107, 108, 124, 140–141, 176–179, 203
   American colonialism, 92
   American colonization, 64, 65
   anti-colonialism, 137
   British colonialism, 147
   colonial enterprise, 24–25, 26
   colonial power, 28, 64, 107, 182, 226
   colonial rule, 38, 65, 76, 77, 147, 178
   colonizer, 24, 90
   decolonization, 15, 181, 184, 220
   Dutch colonialism, 176–178, 181, 196
   neocolonialism, 189
   post-colonial nations, 38, 111, 183
   Spanish colonialism, 69
community, 5–7, 9–11, 25, 27, 29–30, 39, 44–45, 52, 58–59, 63, 67, 85, 106, 110, 111, 114, 118, 119–120, 121, 123, 125, 133, 164, 173, 179, 182, 184, 193, 203
   Bangsamoro community, 83, 170
   Christian community, 136, 143, 153, 157–158, 159–160, 169, 174, 181–182, 188–190, 194–195, 197, 203, 210
   confessional communities, 17, 142, 198, 216
   Hindu community, 166–168, 174
   imagined community, 33, 39, 71, 215, 223
   Malay community, 137–138, 148, 224
   Muslim community, 1, 17, 79, 80, 85, 90, 103, 128, 130, 141–143, 147, 156, 160, 170, 172–173, 176, 182, 187, 206, 211–212, 214, 216
   political community, 41
   religious community, 48, 52, 192, 228
comparative politics, 41
conflict, 1–4, 8–12, 13–16, 17, 19–23, 26, 37, 38, 39, 42–43, 54, 62–65, 67–70, 75, 77–78, 80, 84, 89, 90–95, 97, 101, 102, 104–105, 109, 112, 113, 116–118, 120–122, 124, 126–127, 130, 132–133, 136, 141, 174, 175–178, 179, 180, 194, 198–203, 204–210, 215–216, 218–221, 223, 225–226, 228, 230–231
   ethnic conflicts, 229

intrastate conflicts, 1–3, 14, 58, 60, 218–219, 221, 228
nationalist conflicts, 42
political conflicts, 2, 8, 18, 174, 230
religious conflicts, 1, 2, 9–10, 13, 15, 16, 18, 21–23, 26, 45, 176, 194, 196, 207, 216, 218–220, 222–223, 226, 228, 231
constructivism, 33–34
conversion, 36, 101, 139, 141, 149, 154–155, 181, 182, 183, 184, 199
Cordillerans, 55
corruption, 23, 63
culture, 6–7, 21–25, 27, 30, 32–33, 39, 42, 43, 46–47, 48–49, 51, 55–56, 73, 94, 129, 131, 134, 144–146, 179, 195
   cultural values, 10, 41, 60
   Malay culture, 148
   Muslim culture, 94, 125, 129
   religious culture, 97

datu, 74, 76, 80, 91–94, 95, 96, 125
democratization, 1, 42, 208, 216, 219
discrimination, 8, 26, 29, 42, 48, 66, 69, 102, 153, 223–224, 230
   religious discrimination, 49, 140, 167, 191, 197, 212

economic inequality, ix, 63
education, 33, 62, 90, 107, 112, 140, 141, 146, 149, 180–181
   Islamic education, 88–89, 114–115
   mass education, 33, 35
elite, 26, 42, 50, 51, 60, 79–80, 122, 125, 176, 190, 200
   Christian elite, 203–204
   Malay-Muslim elite, 107, 152
   Muslim elites, 65
   political elite, 103
ethnicity, 12, 26, 28, 29, 33, 35, 41–42, 50, 73, 136, 139, 141, 150, 151–153, 168, 172, 181, 223, 228–231
   ethnic group, 7, 70–71, 75, 93, 96, 110, 139, 141, 146, 201, 206
   ethnic groups, 141, 147, 152
   ethnic identity, 36, 111, 116, 168, 176, 206, 216, 229, 230
   Malay ethnicity, 110, 115, 169
ethnies, 34–35, 36, 39
Eurocentrism, 35–38
Europe, 3, 5, 7, 24, 37, 51, 59, 103, 104, 119
   European colonialism, 24, 34, 65, 141
   European history, 33, 221

256   Index

extremism, 20, 25, 176
religious extremism. *See* religious radicalism

faith, 2, 4, 10, 18, 21–22, 30, 39, 43, 46, 48–49, 54, 85, 98, 110, 141–143, 154–155, 159–160, 166, 169, 171, 181–182, 184, 212, 215–216, 219, 221, 224, 230
confessional faith, 5, 8–10, 19–20, 36, 42, 47, 160, 179, 221, 223, 226
faith communities, 194, 201, 208
interfaith dialogue, 168–169
Islamic faith, 1, 17, 73, 99, 126, 130, 139, 226
religious faith, 32, 44, 138
framing, 2, 7, 8, 9, 10–12, 13–14, 15, 16, 22, 39, 49, 51–56, 57–59, 62, 75, 85, 90–91, 97, 100–101, 105, 120, 121, 122, 124, 133, 135, 142, 144, 150, 167, 168, 174, 178, 194, 200, 203, 209, 210, 219–220, 221, 225–227, 230
frames, 4, 9, 51–56, 59, 70, 73, 75–76, 78, 84, 88, 97–98, 116, 120, 153, 167, 169, 192, 227, 229–230

Geertz, Clifford, 43, 175
Gellner, Ernest, 26, 33–34
Golkar, 190, 209
governance, 26, 49, 70, 82–84, 122, 156, 230
Islamic governance, 87, 122

identity, 4–6, 8–12, 17, 18–23, 25–26, 28–30, 32, 35–37, 40–42, 43–49, 52, 55–57, 58–60, 63, 70–75, 88–91, 96, 97, 99–100, 103, 107–111, 118, 121, 123, 124, 127–128, 130–132, 133–134, 139, 144, 148–150, 154, 159, 165, 168–170, 172, 176, 179, 201, 209, 210, 213, 215–216, 220–224
Bangsamoro identity, 83, 88, 97
collective identity, 6, 42
cultural identity, 112
ethnic identity, 116, 206, 216, 230
Islamic identity, 83, 88, 185, 210
Malay-Muslim identity, 110, 113, 114, 128, 142, 147, 152, 174
Moro identity, 65
Muslim identity, 65
national identity, 6, 9, 15–16, 18, 37, 39–40, 43, 49–50, 63, 69, 88, 106, 111, 135–136, 138, 142, 147, 151–152, 157, 171, 177–178, 184, 193, 212, 215, 224, 229
religious identity, 9–10, 12, 18, 23, 31, 39, 52, 102, 111, 121, 138, 139, 170, 185, 187, 196, 204, 207–208, 212, 215, 216, 219, 224–231
ideology, 6, 15, 24, 27, 31–32, 33, 37, 46, 49, 51, 54, 83–85, 94, 103, 115, 118, 120, 124, 176, 191
Islamic ideology, 86, 97
nationalist ideology, 33, 180
imagination, 32, 33, 50, 56–57, 78, 80, 101, 107, 111, 206, 226, 228
imagined community, 33, 39, 71, 118, 194, 215–216, 223
national imagination, 146, 222
nationalist imagination, 11, 18
religious imagination, 20
imperialism, ix, 24–25, 34, 54, 64, 70, 79, 85, 93
India, 30, 43, 48, 182
Indian nationalism, 48, 51
Indians, 139–140, 141, 147, 166–167
Indonesia, 1, 15, 17, 31, 49–51, 55, 81, 124, 129, 140, 156, 159, 165, 175–203, 205, 207–208, 210–217, 221–222, 224, 227, 230–231
Indonesian nationalism, 51
industrialisation, 33, 37, 221
inequality
economic inequality, ix, 63
intolerance, 25, 212, 214
religious intolerance, 1
Iraq, 28
irrationality, 4, 24
Islam, 6, 16–17, 20, 27–28, 46, 51, 54–55, 65, 73, 79–81, 83–90, 94–97, 101, 104, 107, 111–112, 120–131, 133, 140, 141–144, 147, 150–155, 158–160, 162–166, 167–174, 175, 176–181, 183–194, 195–196, 198–199, 201, 202, 207–208, 210–211, 213–216, 226–227, 230
Islamic education, 112–116
Islamic faith, 1, 99, 139
Islamic groups, 31
Islamic nationalism, 135–138
Islamist militancy, 48
Islamization, 156

jihad, 1–2, 3, 54, 70, 78, 83–84, 85–86, 89, 97, 122–124, 126, 198–199, 201, 202, 209, 219, 226

kafir, 122, 132

Index

Kaum Tua, 177
Kenya, 28
Ketuanan Agama, 55, 168
Ketuanan Melayu, 16, 55, 135, 143–150, 168–170, 171, 174
kinship, 32–33, 93–94, 202

land rights, 77, 205, 207
language, 7, 11, 21, 32, 34–35, 39, 41–42, 45, 51, 58, 59, 71–72, 107, 109, 115, 120, 135, 145, 156, 165, 173, 179, 217, 220, 223
   Malay language, 112, 114, 133, 156, 158, 162–163
   primary language, 52–53
   religious language, 1, 15, 127, 142, 202, 221–222
   Thai language, 107
legitimacy, 6, 8–11, 15, 16, 30, 36, 40–42, 43, 45, 48–50, 53, 55, 70, 71, 80, 85, 91, 105–106, 119–120, 126–127, 133–134, 135–136, 160, 172, 174, 179, 220, 223, 224, 227, 231
   illegitimacy, 226
   Islamic legitimacy, 179
   legitimacy claims, 27
   legitimation, 30, 40, 110, 150
   political legitimacy, 136, 151
Lumad, 71, 72, 73–74, 78

majoritarianism, 1, 17, 41–42, 105, 109, 111, 170, 214, 222–224, 227, 231
Malay dominance, 144, 166, 171, 174
Malay supremacy, 148, 150, 163
Malay-Muslims, 102–104, 105–109, 112–120, 124–134, 140–145, 152–153, 158–159, 221–222
Malaysia, 1, 6, 15, 17, 31, 50, 55, 82, 99, 107, 111, 118, 120, 131–132, 135–149, 150–174, 179, 190, 222–224, 227, 229–231
Maluku, 15, 17, 176, 181–182, 195–196, 198–206, 207, 209–210, 219, 223
Manila, 62, 66, 71, 76, 89, 93
masses, 49, 50, 66, 118, 125, 156, 166, 219
McCargo, Duncan, 109, 131
McKenna, Thomas, 65, 70, 88
Mecca, 123, 177
Middle East, 3, 20, 24, 103, 111, 128, 137, 173, 177, 183
MILF, 15, 16, 62, 67–69, 71–74, 80–88, 90, 93, 95–96, 97–98, 122, 226
militancy, 20, 86, 89, 123
   Christian militants, 199

Islamic militancy. *See* Islamic militancy
Islamic militants, 198, 211
Islamist militancy. *See* Islamist militancy
militant groups, 20, 83, 86, 118
militants, 20, 56, 110, 120, 128, 130, 132, 200
Muslim militants, 15
Mindanao, 15–16, 62–63, 65, 66–75, 76–83, 84, 87, 89, 91–98, 113, 119, 125–126, 134, 226
minorities, 7, 41, 48, 54, 63, 101, 110, 133, 135, 145, 176, 190, 218, 227
   Christian minority, 138, 141, 143, 184
   minority communities, 110, 142, 221
   minority groups, 1, 107, 228, 229
   minority identity, 222, 230–231
   minority populations, 50
   minority rights, 156, 227
   Muslim minority, 16, 74, 87, 89, 97, 106, 138, 152–153, 230
   religious minority, 157, 160–161, 165–171, 174, 194, 210, 214, 219
MNLF, 63, 66–68, 72, 75–76, 79–81, 83, 84, 86, 90, 93–96, 98
mobilization, 2, 3, 4, 8–13, 15, 17, 21–22, 28–30, 33, 42, 47, 49, 51–52, 54, 56–57, 61, 66, 75, 79, 93, 97, 100, 104, 106, 118, 121–122, 125, 136, 142, 143, 148, 153, 155–157, 158, 166, 180, 187–188, 192, 196, 197, 202–204, 206–207, 215, 220–221, 223, 224–226, 227, 229
   political mobilization, 9
   religious mobilization, 2, 198, 199–201, 208
modernism, 32–37
modernity, 2, 5–7, 12, 25–27, 37–40, 43–44, 73, 88, 93, 107, 131, 146, 152, 167, 182, 219–222
   modernism, 4, 38–39, 43, 137, 150, 222, 227, 229
   modernization, 3, 19, 51, 108, 115, 222
Moro, 62–66, 71–80, 88–92, 95–97, 106, 112, 170, 226
   Moro nationalism, 55
   Moro resistance, 15, 62, 66–71, 83–85
Moro Islamic Liberation Front. *See* MILF
Moro National Liberation Front. *See* MNLF
mujahideen, 83–85, 116, 122, 198, 199, 202, 211
Muslim–Christian relations, 2, 48, 136, 142, 155, 164, 168–170, 214

Muslims, 1–2, 15–17, 20, 27, 31, 48, 62–66, 67–69, 71–77, 79–88, 89–91, 93, 100, 105, 109–112, 122–124, 135–139, 146–147, 150–151, 153–157, 159–160, 162–164, 166–169, 176–195, 196–212, 214–216, 219, 223, 224, 230
  Malay-Muslims, 135, 148, 150, 169–174, 224, 227
  Muslim activism, 54
  Muslim communities, 54
  Muslim identity, 219
  Muslim supremacy, 219
  Muslim world, 54
Myanmar, 1, 6, 49–50, 230
myth, 7, 11, 29, 34, 51, 55–57, 76, 90–91, 95, 97, 101, 127, 129, 133, 148, 225, 227
mythology, 64, 106, 115, 205, 219

Narathiwat, 99, 105, 106–107, 117, 123, 131
narratives, 2, 4–6, 7–9, 11, 13–16, 28–29, 37, 39, 43, 48, 49, 52–53, 55–59, 60, 63–64, 73, 75, 76, 88, 90–91, 95, 96–98, 100, 102, 103, 105–108, 112–116, 121, 122, 127, 133–134, 135–137, 142–143, 144, 148, 150, 152–153, 168, 169, 171, 172, 174, 178, 180, 187, 189, 191, 193–194, 199–200, 202–203, 206, 207, 209–210, 213, 218–220, 224–227, 228–231
  historical narratives, 75, 100, 221, 226
  local narratives, 127
  nationalist narratives, 89, 124, 168, 177, 187, 222
  religious narratives, 51, 84, 124, 127, 165, 167, 174, 197, 206, 220
  resistance narratives, 76, 116, 129
national imagination, 133–134
nationalism, 2, 3, 5–9, 11–13, 14–17, 18, 26, 31–47, 49–52, 55, 59–61, 63, 88, 90, 91, 92, 100–101, 106, 110, 111, 118, 121, 130, 131, 133–134, 137–138, 140, 142, 145, 150, 152, 158, 163, 183, 192–193, 196, 214, 218, 220, 225, 228–231
  Arab nationalism, 54
  Bangsamoro nationalism, 72–73, 97
  Indonesian nationalism, 177, 178–181, 192
  Islamist nationalism, 184–185
  Malay nationalism, 132, 170, 226
  Moro nationalism, 55, 64, 71, 89
  nationalist discourse, 109
  nationalist imagination, 11, 18
  nationalist movements, 54, 56–58, 92
  nationalist narratives, 59, 168, 177, 220
  Philippine nationalism, 66, 226
  religious nationalism, 31, 32, 43–48, 54, 121, 126–128, 133, 135–136, 148, 171–172, 174, 215, 218, 220–223, 224, 226–227
  Thai nationalism, 102, 105, 108, 112–113, 124–125
nationhood, 5–13, 14, 18, 29, 31, 34, 35–40, 41, 44, 45, 47, 49, 50–51, 55, 59–60, 78, 100–101, 106, 108, 110, 112, 118, 133, 134, 136, 138–139, 142, 143–144, 146, 147–148, 152–153, 165, 169, 171, 174, 176, 178, 180, 184, 186, 191–192, 208, 210, 215–216, 218, 220–228, 231
nation building, 12, 54, 88, 106, 156, 157, 165, 187, 204, 221, 231
national consciousness, 10, 37, 222
national culture, 39, 48–49, 144
national symbols, 110, 179
nations without states, 10, 40–41, 47
nation-state, 6–7, 8–9, 16, 17, 18, 26, 28, 29, 32, 35–37, 38, 40, 48, 60, 63, 100, 108, 118, 131, 133, 135, 145, 180, 210, 213, 221, 228
non-Muslims, 1, 15, 17, 72, 73–74, 82, 87–88, 111, 123, 126, 138, 142–143, 147, 152–153, 155–156, 159–160, 169, 170, 173, 185, 190, 191
non-Western world, 23, 25
non-Western cultures, 24
non-Western societies, 30, 222

othering, 22–23, 133, 223, 225

Palawan, 16, 72, 78
Pancasila, 31, 50, 185, 189, 191–193, 208, 212–213
Panglong Agreement, the, 50
Papua, 176, 182, 201
  Papuan culture, 55
  Papuans, 55
Parti Islam Se-Malaysia. *See* PAS
PAS, 143, 150, 170–171
Patani, 99, 101–102, 103, 106–108, 110, 113–118, 121, 123–132, 219, 227
patriotism, 7, 44, 128, 135, 178
Pattani, 99, 128. *See* Patani
perennialism, 32, 34

Index

Philippines, 1, 15–16, 31, 43, 48, 55, 62–70, 71–79, 80–86, 88–90, 91, 94–98, 100, 106, 112–113, 116, 122, 124, 134, 135, 138, 153, 170, 179, 182, 200, 221, 222, 226, 230–231
  Philippine nationalism, 226
piety, 2, 4, 22–24, 85, 115, 227
political order, 11, 27
politics, 2, 8, 18, 20, 22, 23, 26–27, 30–31, 39
  contentious politics, 13, 15, 22
  identity politics, 19
  secular politics, 23
population, 6, 7, 16, 28, 46, 50, 56, 62–65, 70, 73, 78, 79, 99, 105, 113, 117, 119, 126, 127, 138–141, 145, 146, 165, 166, 167, 182, 185, 195–196, 203, 213, 220, 229
  ethnic population, 110
  indigenous population, 65, 66, 182, 205
  local population, 78, 208
  Muslim population, 63–64, 87, 120, 130, 145, 151, 169, 173
post-independence, 89, 93, 191, 229
  post-independence nation-state, 16, 29
  post-independence politics, 18, 184–186
  post-independence state, 31, 138, 176, 221
prayer, 109, 115, 129, 155, 159
primordialism, 12, 25–26, 32–36, 39–40, 43, 44, 47, 73, 222, 227, 229
print media, 33–34, 35, 158, 178
proselytization, 36, 85, 139–141, 153, 155, 182–183, 184, 194

race, 25, 34, 136–138, 140, 148, 179
  Malay race, 145, 148, 172
  racism, 171
radicalism, 3, 43, 86, 116, 138, 187
Reformasi, 191–192
religion, 1–7, 8–15, 16, 25, 26–28, 29–32, 33–39, 41–48, 49–52, 54, 55, 57, 60, 73, 83, 84–85, 88, 89, 101, 108, 111–112, 115, 120–121, 123–124, 126–127, 129, 132, 141, 147, 151–153, 154–156, 164–165, 168–169, 171–172, 174, 175, 176–178, 179–180, 184, 186, 191–193, 195, 200–203, 209, 212–213, 214, 215, 216, 218, 219–223, 225–231
  comparative religion, 24
  freedom of religion, 143, 163, 166
  indigenous religions, 24
  institutionalized religion, 46
  minority religion, 157, 161
  national religion, 159
  religious belief, 2, 24, 45, 47, 215
  religious communication, 45
  religious community, 29, 48, 52, 192, 228
  religious creed, 4–5, 116
  religious discourse, 4, 16, 18, 126, 135, 169, 198, 226
  religious doctrine, 57, 155
  religious expression, 44, 114, 218
  religious identity, 8, 9–10, 12, 15, 18, 23, 29, 31, 36, 39, 44–45, 48, 52, 63, 102, 111, 121, 138, 139, 170, 173, 185, 187, 196, 204, 207–208, 212, 215, 216, 219, 221, 224, 225–226, 228–230
  religious imagination, 20
  religious institutions, 39, 50, 126
  religious intolerance, 1
  religious knowledge, 24, 114
  religious law, 49, 66, 109
  religious leaders, 45, 123, 124–125, 143, 146, 163, 169, 179
  religious metaphors, 2, 15, 126, 206, 223
  religious mobilization, 2
  religious narratives, 13, 15, 51, 59, 84, 127, 165, 174, 203, 206, 220
  religious practice, 49, 133
  religious rights, 29, 167, 190, 191
  religious tradition, 37, 51, 52
  sociology of religion, 12
religion and conflict, 19
  inter-religious conflict, 2, 219
  religion and violence, 12, 19
  religious contestations, 11
  religious violence, 16, 19–20, 22, 23, 176, 202, 206, 208
religious extremism, 3
religious faith, 71
religious moderation, 116, 219
Renaissance, the, 23–24
resistance movements, 56, 58, 117
rights, 17, 18, 29, 44, 48, 54, 71–73, 136, 138, 142, 145–148, 156, 157, 160, 163–169, 173, 174, 191, 193, 210, 212, 214, 223, 224, 227
  constitutional rights, 50, 152, 156, 169
  denizen rights, 9–11, 29, 166
  land rights, 77, 205–207
  political rights, 41, 212
  religious rights, 29, 167, 190, 191

science, 221
  scientific rationality, 24–25
  scientific understanding, 21
sectarianism, 1, 28
  sectarian conflict, 3, 10
  sectarian violence, 15, 176
secularism, 4, 20, 23–24, 26, 33, 56, 81, 86, 145, 178, 185, 191–192, 214, 221–222
  secular nationalism, 5, 39, 126, 177, 178, 220
  secular nation-state, 36
  secular state, 27, 30–31, 138, 184
  secularization, 3, 5, 27, 38, 39, 221
self-determination, 7, 10, 13, 16, 30, 44, 45, 55, 60, 63, 70–71, 80, 85, 96, 119, 127, 228, 229, 230
self-rule, 60, 81
self-government, 45, 71, 82
separation of church and state, 24, 27, 30
separatism, 41, 93–96, 103–104, 113–114, 124, 132, 195–196, 199
  separatist groups, 229
  separatist insurgency, 61, 126
  separatist movements, 66, 115–118, 125
  separatists, 75–76, 106, 109, 120–121
shari'a, 31, 82, 112, 123, 151, 154, 159, 167, 184–187, 192–194
social movement theory, 12–13, 51, 58–59
  social movements, 51, 52, 53–54
social order, 11, 49
society, 5, 7, 9, 19, 23, 25, 28, 30–31, 33, 35, 45, 62, 71, 82, 96, 112, 138, 158, 190, 199–200, 215, 222–224, 227–228
  civil society, 67, 142, 146, 150, 153, 162, 168, 171–172, 174, 214, 215
  Indonesian society, 175, 181, 183, 191–193, 208, 210
  Malaysian society, 140, 142, 144, 146, 148, 155
  modern society, 5, 38–39, 51, 221
  Muslim society, 80
South Asia, 3, 111, 140, 166
sovereignty, 33, 76, 77, 78, 80, 145, 199
  sovereign state, 40–41, 66
space, 1, 44, 57, 145, 169, 201
  cultural space, 170
  ideological space, 6
  physical space, 6
  political space, 216
  public space, 69, 129–130, 164
  religious space, 143
  sacred space, 167
  social space, 201
Sri Lanka, 28, 42
state building, ix, 7, 26, 223, 229
statehood, 6, 8–9, 26, 33, 37, 40–41, 47, 186, 191, 218, 222
Sulawesi, 15, 17, 176, 182, 187, 193–196, 197–198, 200–205, 209–210, 223
Sulu, 16, 62–63, 66, 72, 75–77, 78–79, 85, 91–92, 93, 95–96, 97
symbolism, 1, 20–21, 22, 43, 55, 59, 102, 109, 128, 130, 223
symbols, 5, 11, 18, 39, 43, 45, 46, 47, 52, 56, 101, 110, 126, 130, 133, 160, 179, 216, 218, 220

technology, 33, 93, 221
territory, 26, 28–29, 32, 45, 46–48, 62, 64, 66, 77, 88, 102, 106, 127, 179, 196–197, 226
  territorial integrity, 80, 186
  territorial state, 6–7, 8, 9, 28, 33, 40–41, 43, 45–46, 48–49, 60, 63, 66, 72–73, 104, 152, 222, 226, 228
terrorism, 2, 3, 19, 176
Thai Rak Thai (Party), 119–120
Thailand, 1, 6, 15–16, 31, 43, 46, 88, 99, 135, 138, 153, 179, 205, 221–222, 224, 226, 229, 230–231
theology, 11, 19, 37, 124, 173, 176, 183, 202, 210, 212, 214
trade, 71, 91, 140, 182

ulama, 67, 84, 118, 138, 173, 179–180, 189, 207, 211, 213
ummah, 46, 112, 173, 215
UMNO, 137–138, 142–144, 150, 151, 152, 155, 157, 160, 166, 168, 170–172
United States, 30, 64, 66, 76, 92

violence, 1, 2, 4, 9, 12, 15, 25–26, 48, 64, 68, 78, 79, 82, 93–95, 100, 103–105, 109, 111–112, 114, 117–118, 119, 122, 125–127, 130, 132–133, 153, 158, 173, 176–177, 182, 194–195, 196–203, 208, 210, 211, 212, 216, 218–219, 223
  political violence, 15, 42, 55, 97–98
  religious violence, 16, 17, 19–23, 48, 123, 124, 205–206, 208

Index

warfare, 64, 71, 94, 219
West, the, 26–27
    Western civilization, 23–25, 35, 38
    Western colonialism, 34, 107–108
    Western culture, 31–32
    Western imperialism, 85
    Western society, 30, 38, 76, 220–222
    Western world, 54
worship, 4, 6, 47, 79, 87, 128, 151, 154, 156, 159, 164–165, 170, 194, 213

Yala, 99, 106–107, 123, 128